On Jazz

Few musical genres inspire the passionate devotion of jazz. Its mystique goes far beyond its melodies and rhythms, with its key players and singers discussed by aficionados with a respect that borders on reverence. The creative, extemporising variations the musicians bring to their complex art are as much a source of fascination as their own lives, loves and personalities. Jazz is a culture of rich variety. Many books on the subject offer little more than theory, dry facts or (at the other end of the spectrum) gossip, and so in their different ways relinquish the 'essence' of what jazz really amounts to. This book is different. One of the most influential and respected modern writers on the subject here describes, through vivid personal reminiscence and zesty anecdote, his life in jazz as a player, broadcaster and observer. These recollections form the prism through which both the music and its practitioners are viewed in sparkling new definition. Alyn Shipton recalls his many friendships with legendary musicians, while offering fresh discoveries about such luminaries as Fats Waller, Louis Armstrong, Count Basie, Duke Ellington, Charlie Parker, Abbey Lincoln and Geri Allen. Shipton takes the reader with him on the road, into the exciting and intimate embrace of dancehalls, theatres and clubs, down the stairs into basements electric with anticipation, behind the scenes and right up close to the stage, so that the atmospheric world the book conjures is now unforgettably spotlighted as never before.

Alyn Shipton is a writer, publisher, broadcaster and jazz double bassist. He has broadcast about jazz since 1989, and currently hosts BBC Radio 3's long-running and much loved programme Jazz Record Requests. His biographies of Dizzy Gillespie (1999) and singer-songwriter Harry Nilsson (2013) both won Association for Recorded Sound Collections (ARSC) Awards for Excellence; and Nilsson also gained an American Society of Composers, Authors and Publishers (ASCAP) Foundation Deems Taylor/ Virgil Thompson Award. His *New History of Jazz* (2001) was the Jazz Journalists' Association (JJA) book of the year and named 'the most outstanding single-volume history of jazz' by the Jazz Institute of Chicago. His most recent work, *The Art of Jazz: A Visual History* (2020), was described as 'indispensible' by *Publishers Weekly*. He co-leads the Buck Clayton Legacy Band, and is a research fellow of the Royal Academy of Music in London.

'This is the back story of the gods who create the magic.
I loved it.'

– Sonny Rollins

'This immensely readable and compelling book describes unique
encounters with the leading figures of jazz – including extensive
interviews with Sonny Rollins and Oscar Peterson – from the
perspective of one of the world's leading jazz authorities.
Respected by musicians, fans and academics for his encyclopaedic knowledge, Alyn Shipton is familiar to wider audiences
through his prolific writing, broadcasting, bass playing and
bandleading. He now offers the reader fascinating insights from
his life in jazz, and vividly narrates many great stories which
appear in print here for the first time.'

– Catherine Tackley, Professor of Music, University of Liverpool, and
author of Benny Goodman's Famous 1938 Carnegie Hall Jazz
Concert and co-author of Black British Jazz

'Alyn's approach offers profound new insights for musicians,
record collectors and aficionados of jazz history. His inclusion
of the many personal encounters and anecdotes with swing and
bebop greats really brings the music to life in a novel way.
Providing insights into the humour and irreverence of the jazz
community, it conveys the deep passions, cultural contradic-
tions and creative geniuses that forged our music.

'I've really enjoyed the convivial chat with Roy Haynes,
Harry Dial's off the cuff remarks and apocryphal stories about
Bud Powell. It's not hard to be re-seduced by the music – as every
page is filled with unmined gemstones, from an artform you
thought you knew. All too often, jazz tomes seem unnecessarily
lofty, or purely academic. However, this is both a very personal
semi-autobiographical journey through jazz, and it describes the
social context and cultural milieu that these great innovators
emerged from.'

– Soweto Kinch

'The book is a treasure trove of fascinating information for anyone who has a passion for the incredible gift to the world that is American Jazz! As a musician who has immersed herself in a lifelong exploration of early jazz and blues, and been blessed to know and perform with many of its great legends, I was delighted to discover in these pages such an enormous wealth of "inside" information. Alyn Shipton's passionate dedication and insatiable curiosity to learn everything he can about the genre and its history leads him to connect in a very personal way with so many great musicians, and elicit from them the most wonderful personal accounts of their careers, life stories and creative evolutions. As a musician himself, he establishes a great rapport with so many seminal artists; and because he's a musician, he asks all the right questions, which lead to compelling narratives rich with intimate details and previously unknown revelations. I learned so much in these pages of things I wasn't aware, about many artists I knew (Dr John Danny and Blue Lu Barker, and Ray Brown – to name but a few). A must-read for any serious jazz lover!'

– *Maria Muldaur*

On Jazz

A Personal Journey

Alyn Shipton

CAMBRIDGE
UNIVERSITY PRESS

University Printing House, Cambridge CB2 8BS, United Kingdom

One Liberty Plaza, 20th Floor, New York, NY 10006, USA

477 Williamstown Road, Port Melbourne, VIC 3207, Australia

314–321, 3rd Floor, Plot 3, Splendor Forum, Jasola District Centre, New Delhi – 110025, India

103 Penang Road, #05–06/07, Visioncrest Commercial, Singapore 238467

Cambridge University Press is part of the University of Cambridge.

It furthers the University's mission by disseminating knowledge in the pursuit of education, learning, and research at the highest international levels of excellence.

www.cambridge.org
Information on this title: www.cambridge.org/9781108834230
DOI: 10.1017/9781108992473

© Alyn Shipton 2022

First published 2022

Printed in the United Kingdom by TJ Books Limited, Padstow Cornwall

A catalogue record for this publication is available from the British Library.

Library of Congress Cataloging-in-Publication Data
NAMES: Shipton, Alyn, author.
TITLE: On jazz : a personal journey / Alyn Shipton.
DESCRIPTION: [1.] | Cambridge, United Kingdom ; New York, NY : Cambridge University Press, 2021. | Includes bibliographical references and index.
IDENTIFIERS: LCCN 2021026025 (print) | LCCN 2021026026 (ebook) | ISBN 9781108834230 (hardback) | ISBN 9781108994712 (paperback) | ISBN 9781108992473 (ebook)
SUBJECTS: LCSH: Jazz – Anecdotes. | Jazz musicians – Anecdotes. | Shipton, Alyn – Anecdotes. | BISAC: MUSIC / General
CLASSIFICATION: LCC ML3506.S4704 2021 (print) | LCC ML3506 (ebook) | DDC 781.65–dc23
LC record available at https://lccn.loc.gov/2021026025
LC ebook record available at https://lccn.loc.gov/2021026026

ISBN 978-1-108-83423-0 Hardback

For my mentors Danny Barker and Buck Clayton
In Memoriam

CONTENTS

The plate section can be found between pp 148 and 149

PREFACE

This book draws together oral history, personal experience and jazz criticism in an attempt to discover more about the circumstances and settings in which jazz was and has continued to be created. Although it starts with New Orleans jazz and moves forward to the free jazz innovations of Ornette Coleman from the 1950s and beyond, *On Jazz* is not intended to be a jazz history in its own right. It is, as the subtitle says, a 'personal journey', inviting the reader to share my own voyage of discovery into the music. The chronological span of most chapters, except the last, might seem to finish somewhere around the end of the previous century. Yet in almost every area the music has continued to flourish and develop in the two decades since the millennium, and my intention is that this is reflected throughout the book. *On Jazz* is not an autobiography, although it is set in an autobiographical framework. My hope is that readers will see that being a working musician, as well as a publisher, writer and broadcaster, has helped to open plenty of doors into understanding jazz a little better.

I have used a method of approaching oral history that I outlined in detail at the 'New Jazz Histories' symposium at Salford University in 2008, which has been central to my work since the 1980s, in trying to gather numerous first-hand perspectives from those who were part of the music's development. These would often be, as I said at Salford, the views of 'a sideman or singer, rather than a bandleader, with a wide range of playing experience, work in several locations, and first-hand experience of the industry. The majority of my subjects would be African American. I would encourage them to talk about their entire lifetime experience, from their background and home circumstances to their adult life, but there would be a major focus on their musical work.'¹ The crucial point is that the memories interlock and interact so as to build up various levels of perspective on a period, band or event. Good examples in this book might be the collective recollections of Oscar Peterson, Ray Brown and Ed Thigpen on the time they played together in the Peterson Trio, the views of Louie Bellson, Jimmy Woode and Clark Terry on the pre-1956 Ellington band, or the experiences of Jewel Brown and Carmen Bradford in singing for the bandleaders Louis Armstrong and Count Basie.

I realize that aiming to represent the Black experience in America raises complex questions, given that I am a white European writer. As the Dutch cultural theorist Mineke Schipper (paraphrasing Larry Neal's essay 'The Black Musician in White America') says: 'How can a white person who is no part of "our" identity explain the significance of blues, whereas we ourselves are the physical manifestations of blues? Whites ... do not participate in the Black Experience and hence cannot evaluate it.'² All I can say in response is that from the 1970s onwards I have been made to feel welcome by several generations of African American musicians. In New Orleans and New York, and on tour in Europe, as well as making radio programmes in America and Britain, my experience has been one of unfailing generosity and friendship. I have edited books with Danny Barker and Doc Cheatham, and worked closely on many more, with authors as varied as Buddy Collette, Oscar Peterson, Sammy Price and Marshal Royal, and the prevailing impression from my work with all these distinguished musicians is that together we have helped Black voices to be heard, telling of lives that have really mattered in creating a marvellous art-form.

I hope that this book catches more such memories and experiences, to enrich all of our listening to and enthusiasm for jazz even further.

1 GETTING STARTED

I began listening to music before I could walk. Our family gramophone was the old-fashioned kind that played a stack of 78 rpm records. The first ran for around three and a half minutes, then another dropped onto the turntable, and so on. Five discs gave my mother some uninterrupted time for housework, while I sat listening to the music. Then I was quite happy to do the same thing all over again. And again.

When my father came home from his final wartime RAF posting in Hong Kong, he brought back a box of records. My parents were married in 1952, and this mix of music that had travelled halfway around the world with him started off our family collection. There was swing by Earl Hines and Fats Waller together with classical sounds from Walter Gieseking and Benno Moiseiwitsch. I was born in 1953, and apparently it wasn't too long before Fats Waller's records started making a big impression on me – mainly songs such as 'Your Feet's Too Big' and 'Twenty Four Robbers' rather than the instrumentals such as 'Honeysuckle Rose'. In due course, I sang along to my favourites, and somewhere around the age of five, started picking out the melodies with one finger on the piano.

Before I left primary school, my interest in jazz really took off. My way home took me past a second-hand shop, and one day, when I was about eleven, a box of 78s appeared on a table outside the door, so I started checking through them. I was thrilled to find some Fats Waller songs I had never heard, but there were other jazz discs by exotic names such as Leroy Carr and Scrapper Blackwell, Muggsy Spanier and Artie Shaw. Soon I was spending all my pocket money on my own jazz collection, and I'd rush home to put these 'new' 78s on the drop-down gramophone. The shopkeeper, Colin Bridgstock, was a jazz aficionado. He had once been the manager for Bruce Turner's Jump Band, and so he knew many of the brightest and best musicians on the London scene. He started tipping me off when any really interesting records came his way. We'd sometimes listen to the choicest finds in the shop on a little portable gramophone, which sat on a slightly wobbly table between his stock of dusty sofas and old chests of drawers. Once I had started at grammar school on the other side of town, I didn't get to Colin's shop so often, but unusual discs still came my way from time to time.

I owe him a lot for stimulating my interest in a wide range of jazz just as the Beatles were making their start on the national scene. Later Colin moved to the village of Selborne, formerly home to the naturalist Gilbert White, and from there he organized gigs in the North Hampshire area. This picturesque village was a rather unlikely tourist destination, but its little museum dedicated to White, and to the local resident Captain Oates, who perished on Captain Scott's ill-fated Antarctic expedition, brought in a number of visitors, as did the challenging walks across the steep hill, known as the Hanger, behind the village.

When I reached my late teens and began to play the double bass seriously, Colin brought in such well-known musicians as Bruce Turner and Bobby Wellins to appear at one or other of the local pubs around Selborne. Usually there'd be a local rhythm section and although still very green behind the gills, I was sometimes asked to play, usually when Toni Goffe, the ex-Bruce Turner bassist (and accomplished artist) who also lived in the area, could not make it. I treasure the memory of a couple of sessions I did with Bobby Wellins and the drummer Dave Wickins, along with local guitarist Colin Higenbottam.

I had a lot to learn about harmony and how to play more contemporary styles of jazz. But Bobby was very patient with me – an early lesson in the generosity of musicians who were keen to nurture a genuine interest in the music. I was also helped by a local legend, the valve-trombonist Hugh Stockbridge. Balding, bearded and immensely physically fit, often cycling the several miles between his Surrey village home in Tilford and Farnham railway station before and after commuting to London, Hugh was a psychologist for the Ministry of Defence by day, and a demon organizer of jazz gigs by night. I began playing in pubs with Hugh in my early teens and meeting a range of musicians from extremely diverse backgrounds. The trumpeter Geoff Burgon (later famous as a film and television composer, and at the time still an occasional member of the Royal Opera House orchestra) often roared down from London in his open-top Bristol to play with us, whereas on some other gigs the ex-Squadronaires and Ted Heath trumpeter Archie Craig would dash in before last orders, grab a pint, and show us how his sparkling upper register was undiminished with time.

Hugh had played jazz as an undergraduate in wartime Cambridge and later at Harvard. Consequently, he knew a wide circle of keen and knowledgeable fellow musicians of all ages, but more importantly for those of us who played regularly with him, he had also developed a knack of persuading local landlords in nearby villages that a jazz band was just what their pub needed. We played quite lengthy residencies in such unlikely settings as the rather upmarket Frensham Ponds Hotel, the excellent French restaurant at the Chequers in Well, and at the Four Horseshoes pub in Long Sutton (on the doorstep of RAF Odiham, with its ready-made audience of off-duty helicopter crews, and also under-age public schoolboys sneaking out from Lord Wandsworth's College next door). Hugh was also responsible for introducing me to my wife Siobhan Fraser, as she was the student organizer of the concerts at Farnham Art School. He persuaded her that her fellow aspiring painters and sculptors really needed us to play for them. She agreed, but told us on no account should we go to the pub before the gig, and we had to be ready at 8 o'clock sharp to start playing. When we rolled in from the Queen's Head at 8.25 for our first concert, she was not best pleased, but somehow we overcame that inauspicious first meeting, and she and I were married three years later in 1977.

Although I'd grown up on a diet of Fats Waller and other swing players, once I discovered Spanier, and then went on to listen to Sidney Bechet and George Lewis, I found traditional jazz the most compelling style to listen to. I loved George Brunis' jiving vocal chorus on Spanier's record of 'Dinah', and the shout of 'Oh, play that thing!' on the same band's 'Dippermouth Blues' as they roared into the thrilling final section.

Having trained as a cellist, I continued to play the instrument for many years. (My last public appearance on the cello was at the Henley Festival, the night of the Live Aid concert in July 1985.) Yet I always knew that the bass would eventually be my main focus. At the age of twelve I was rather too short to play the school's ¾-size double bass, so I stuck to the cello so far as my weekly music lessons were concerned. But I nagged my parents for a bass and in due course we found a slightly smaller instrument in a music shop in Aldershot, run by an ex-regimental bandmaster. 'That's a "gig" bass,' he said sniffily. 'Not a "real" instrument but the kind of thing our lads use when they're playing in the dance band.' It was a light toffee colour and the neck had clearly had some rather desperate repairs. It eventually snapped off a few years later, but an older bassist I'd got to know, called Dick Webb, had the neck of an old bass in his garage, along with the remains of a vintage Talbot 105. He'd intended to make this neck into the bowsprit of a sailing dinghy, but in the end he decided it might be better off being used for music again, so a local repairer grafted it into place, making a much better instrument than I had before! (When I eventually sold this bass to Jack Pamplin at Thwaites, one of London's old-established double bass dealers, he threw away the body and put the neck, which he dated to about 1850, on a deserving old English instrument.)

I started practising the bass until I felt fairly confident about it, though I usually had a crop of blisters on my right hand from my efforts to play jazz. During my mid-teens, once a week over a period of several months, after his long days working in London, my long-suffering father would drive me the ten miles or so to Sandhurst to play with a traditional band led by the Louis Armstrong-inspired trumpeter Denny Ilett. The venue was the Rose and Crown, not far from the gates of the Royal Military Academy, and I celebrated my fourteenth birthday on one such evening with my very first pint of beer in a pub. Playing 'Hotter Than That', 'Struttin' With Some Barbecue' and a host of other Armstrong-related tunes with really proficient older players was a great experience at that age.

Maybe the most difficult gig I did with Denny was a 'riverboat shuffle' on the Thames from Reading, with a band led by the taxi-driver, Alsatian owner and clarinettist Jane Gwynn. Denny dashed on to the boat at the last minute, opened the trumpet case and suddenly realized he had left his mouthpiece on the table at home. The remaining five of us did our best for the next couple of hours, but without Denny's formidable power the band was a shadow of its normal self, though the trombonist John Heighes, who was famously listed at the time in the *Guinness Book of World Records* for the longest period spent hanging upside down from a tree, did his utmost to make up for the lack of a trumpet.

When I was sixteen or so I went to hear Ken Colyer's Jazzmen at the local club in Camberley. I felt straight away that this was the music I wanted to play. The band, with Geoff Cole (trombone), Tony Pyke (clarinet), Johnny Bastable (banjo), Ken Ames (bass) and Malc Murphy (drums), was Ken's last full-time professional group before the onset of stomach cancer forced him to disband in early 1971. I bought all their records, and with some friends from school, with whom I formed a teenage band, we learned some of their repertoire. Most of us also played in the school orchestra or the West Surrey branch of the County Youth Orchestra, so we mixed our jazz diet with plenty of classical playing experience. (It wasn't until I got to university that I realized that my school, thanks to its visionary music master Alan Fluck, had been rather exceptional. Not everyone had had the likes of Malcolm Arnold, Richard Rodney Bennett, Thea Musgrave and Alan Rawsthorne – and particularly memorably in my case, John Dankworth – writing for and rehearsing with their orchestra.)

As 1971 went on, Ken Colyer's cancer went into remission, and rumour had it that he might be available for solo appearances. My parents had long been supporters of the local repertory theatre, and I hatched the idea of asking Ken if he would be prepared to play in a band that I planned to put together specially to accompany him on a Sunday night (between the theatre's regular weeknight shows) to raise some money for building a new auditorium. I was seventeen and really had no idea what I was doing, but to my astonishment he agreed, and I found myself both promoting the concert and leading the band, made up of local and West London New Orleans jazz enthusiasts.

Ken wrote to me a few weeks before the concert, and didn't seem in the least bit worried about whether our style of band would fit his lead trumpet (Figure 1). This was taken as read because I'd asked him in the first place. He was more concerned that we would find a suitable repertoire of 'rags, marches, blues and stomps'. I don't have my full reply, but on the back of the envelope of his letter I have the set-list that we worked out, including 'Royal Garden Blues', 'High Society', 'Walking with the King', 'Goin' Home', 'If Ever I Cease to Love', 'Bogalousa Strut' and a pair of the well-known popular songs that Ken liked to pop into a jazz set, namely 'Somewhere Over the Rainbow' and 'Alexander's Ragtime Band'.

Despite the band being a pick-up group for the occasion and never having worked as a unit before, the concert went down very well,

(a)

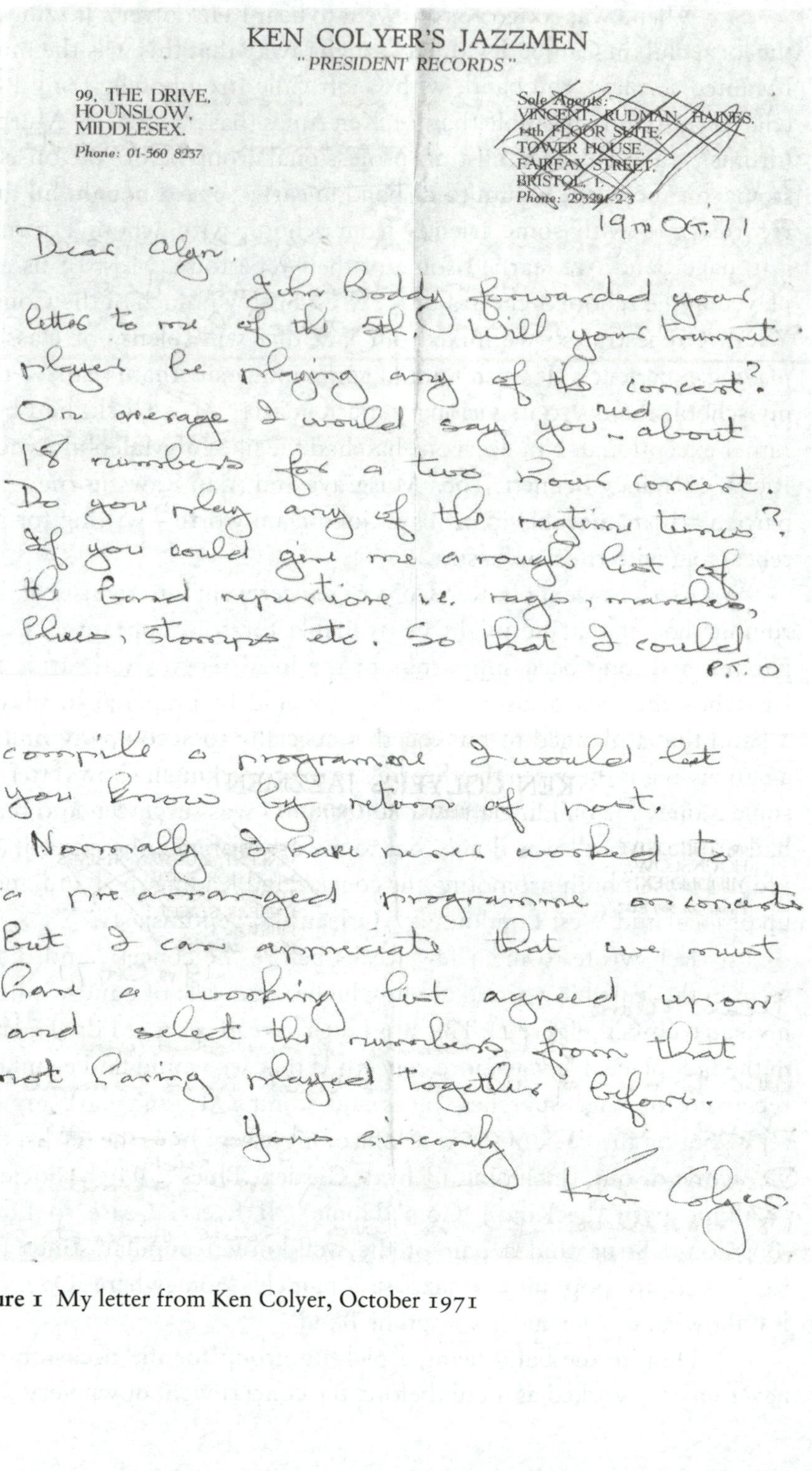

KEN COLYER'S JAZZMEN
"PRESIDENT RECORDS"

99, THE DRIVE,
HOUNSLOW,
MIDDLESEX.
Phone: 01-560 8237

Sole Agents:
VINCENT RUDMAN HAINES,
14th FLOOR SUITE,
TOWER HOUSE,
FAIRFAX STREET,
BRISTOL, I.
Phone: 293281/2/3

19th Oct. 71

Dear Algar,

John Boddy forwarded your letter to me of the 5th. Will your trumpet player be playing any of the concert? On average I would say you need about 18 numbers for a two hour concert. Do you play any of the ragtime tunes? If you could give me a rough list of the band repertoire i.e. rags, marches, blues, stomps etc. So that I could

P.T.O

(b)

compile a programme I would let you know by return of post. Normally I have never worked to a pre-arranged programme on concerts But I can appreciate that we must have a working list agreed upon and select the numbers from that not having played together before.

Yours sincerely

Ken Colyer

Figure 1 My letter from Ken Colyer, October 1971

and a few years later Ken asked me to play with his Jazzmen, which he put together (when his health allowed) for occasional gigs. I played with him on and off from 1978 to 1986, although from 1981 onwards I was working as a publisher between London and New York, so could only ever manage occasional dates with him. When he called to ask if I could do one gig in 1985, I told him I'd be away in New York at the time, and before he slammed the phone down, he shouted, 'I don't know why you bother to fucking come back!'

Such outbursts aside, and despite his gruff exterior, I liked Ken and got along with him pretty well. In the early 1980s, I sometimes picked him up at his house in Hounslow to drive him to gigs, and we would talk about all manner of things. He was particularly keen on the saxophonist Lester Young and got me listening to his records. He also had a passion for Rudyard Kipling. During his early years at sea in the merchant navy, Ken had learned many of Kipling's poems by heart and on our journeys back from the gig, after several gin and tonics, he would recite his favourites at length. He had a scheme to record them to his own guitar accompaniment, but this was thwarted because Kipling remained in copyright until 1986 and his literary estate was controlled by the National Trust. They refused outright to allow Ken to record what they feared would be 'skiffle' versions of the great man's poetry. This was a source of sadness to him.

So too was the rejection of his autobiography, *When Dreams Are in the Dust*, by Macmillan Publishers (for whom I was working by the early 1980s as music books editor). To satisfy the editorial board, I'd arranged to have the manuscript reviewed by John Chilton and George Melly, who read segments of it during their annual residency at Ronnie Scott's. Part of their report said, 'This is undoubtedly the definitive book on the art of peeling potatoes in the merchant navy, but as a book about jazz it leaves rather a lot to be desired.' Ken was unaware that I had made the decision not to publish it, but then a drummer who joined us for one gig rather innocently informed him that I was the head of Macmillan's music publishing. 'I thought he was the fucking tea-boy,' said Ken. He proceeded not to talk to me for six months, addressing me on stage via the banjoist Bill Stotesbury, 'Tell the bassist we're gonna play . . .' Yet he continued to book me for the band, although he got Bill to telephone so that he did not have to speak to me himself.

Then, one day, the hostility was all forgotten, as we got involved in an earnest discussion at Amersham Jazz Club on how to deal with rust in central heating radiators. Back in Ken's conversational circle again, I used to enjoy his perorations on what he had seen on television lately, not least because he always referred to any male actor in any film he happened to have watched as 'that Robert Mitchum'. All of us in the band also enjoyed comparing notes on the regulars who followed us, not only turning up for our Wednesday nights at London's 100 Club but also unexpectedly appearing at provincial gigs in places including Malmesbury, Swindon, Leicester and Maidstone. Particularly noticeable (as well as a regular posse of enthusiastic dancers) were Omar and Gus, both great characters whose vocal enthusiasm for the band was matched by their prodigious intake of real ale. I later discovered that, by day, Gus was a very talented motor engineer with a passion for old Rovers that was even greater than his love of jazz.

To anyone in Britain growing up when I did, Ken Colyer had a more than totemic importance in terms of New Orleans jazz. He had been to the city as a seaman in 1952–3 and played during that visit with many living legends, such as members of the George Lewis band. He also recorded there with the bassist Albert Glenny (who had allegedly played with the founding father of jazz, Buddy Bolden). From the 1950s to the start of the 1970s, Ken's Jazzmen, based in London, were seen by many as the epitome of the revival style in Europe. Yet Colyer had a far wider range of musical interests and influences. According to his fellow trumpeter Sonny Morris, whom he joined in the Crane River Jazz Band in 1949, Colyer had travelled to New York the previous year and fallen under the spell of the Chicagoan musicians in the circle of Eddie Condon. 'He was very young and fresh-faced,' recalled Sonny. 'He came back so enthusiastic about Wild Bill Davison, that I think he actually combed his hair to try and look like Wild Bill. This was somebody who made a big impression on him, not just musically but in his enthusiasm and his single-mindedness (not narrow-mindedness). He knew what he wanted to do.'[1]

When the Crane River Band started, Sonny Morris had never played the trumpet, only the bugle in the Boys' Brigade, but his friend, the banjoist Ben Marshall, persuaded him to take it up and planned that they would form a band when Sonny finished his National Service, along with another friend, the pianist Ralph Dollimore. They originally intended it to be a dance band but soon fell under the spell of New Orleans revivalism. Dollimore, who eventually went on to become musical director at the London Palladium, left shortly afterwards, following which the band quickly drew in a nucleus of traditional jazz players. Sonny remembered: 'Ken Colyer came along, with his brother Bill, knocked on Ben's door, and said they'd like to join the band. Ben said, "We've already got a trumpet player," even though I couldn't really play it at that stage, but Ken just said, "That's all right. Let's have two." And that was basically the beginning of it. We contacted the Davies brothers, John R. T. and Julian, and they came and joined in. Cy Laurie was approached to come and join us, but he couldn't make it, so he sent Monty Sunshine. We never had a piano player at that stage; we got Pat Hawes a little later. He came home on leave from the RAF and played a couple of gigs at the Camberwell School of Art, and as soon as he left the Service, he joined us.'[2]

Although Colyer had been inspired by Condon's Chicagoan circle in New York, he was very clear that the Crane River Band should follow the New Orleans revival model of Bunk Johnson and George Lewis. He spent time playing all Bunk's HMV records to the others so that they could learn both the tunes and the style. 'We had "The Saints", "Snag It", "Just a Closer Walk", "Franklin Street Blues", "One Sweet Letter From You". That was it. I was sold. I thought it was magic,' said Sonny. 'Enthusiasm is what got us from a local pub to playing at the Royal Festival Hall. One thing was that the band was always together. If we weren't playing, we were drinking and socializing. Fortunately, we lived within close proximity of each other and we'd go to pubs and have a good talk. It was always talk about jazz. Ken was always talking about it: Mutt Carey, Kid Ory, Jim Robinson, all those guys.'

Years later, Ken was still talking about the trumpeter Mutt Carey, who had recorded with Kid Ory from the 1920s to the 1940s. Carey had clearly made a big impression on him. Sonny Morris agreed: 'He was very strongly influenced by the Ory band, I think, and Mutt was a more powerful influence on him [as a player] than Bunk Johnson. He loved their Creole numbers too, like "Creole Song" and "Blanche Touquatoux".'

The Crane River Band broke up in 1952 and Colyer went back to sea, eventually making his way to New Orleans. Deported the following March for overstaying his seaman's 'ticket' or temporary visa, on his return to London he joined a co-operative band, assembled by Chris Barber and Monty Sunshine, becoming its titular leader. This was a fully professional group. With his American recordings under his belt, and soon afterwards a 10-inch LP by the British line-up, Colyer assumed his leading role in the UK revivalist movement, playing his take on the music he heard in New Orleans at the time. 'We weren't trying to sound like the 1920s,' recalled Barber. 'We were trying to sound like 1953, because it was 1953.'[3]

The band with Barber, Sunshine et al. broke up in 1954, with five of the six musicians going on to form Chris Barber's Jazz Band. Colyer started afresh with a new group. In due course, this settled into a regular line-up that – particularly for the next five years – became the byword for authentic New Orleans revival jazz in London, with clarinettist Ian Wheeler and trombonist Mac Duncan, plus the drummer Colin Bowden. The band took up residence at what became known as the Ken Colyer Club at Studio 51 in Great Newport Street in London, a venue immortalized in Michael Winner's otherwise eminently forgettable film *West 11*. Except, as Winner told me, what you see in the film is Colyer's band playing in a perfect replica of the club that had been constructed at Elstree Studios, since the limited access to 'the 51' would have made it impossible to escape in a fire and thus too much of a risk, what with all the lights and equipment needed for film-making.[4] Colin Bowden explained that in the venue itself, even the musicians were worried about working there, week in, week out. 'It was a very small, windowless basement, about the length of a church hall, but not quite the width, with the stage taking up all of one end. There was no liquor licence, but it sold soft drinks and sandwiches, and it was run by two ladies, Pat and Vi were their names, who had a huge Alsatian dog, and you daren't go down the steps if the dog was out. You'd get a couple of hundred people, maybe even more, crammed in there. Sometimes they'd have to pass our drinks over the heads of the crowd, because we couldn't get out. Fire regulations didn't seem to exist. I always said to myself, if there's a fire here, that's it. No way out. But the atmosphere was wonderful.'[5]

I never got to Studio 51 to hear the Colyer band while the club was still in operation, but in 2016 I was contacted by BBC television to contribute to a programme about one of the very few female singers who ever worked with Ken. Her name was Rosina Scudder and she often sang at the 51. She had a remarkable voice, preserved on a few recordings, and Ken liked her a lot as she sounded like the New Orleans singer Lizzie Miles.[6] Standing just over three feet tall, Rosina overcame considerable odds to pursue a professional singing career in the social climate of the 1950s and 1960s. She sang with Colyer's Jazzmen by standing on a box or beer crate in front of the band. By the time we filmed the episode, in September 2016, the site of Studio 51 had been redeveloped into an apartment block named 'The Colyer'. So to capture something of the atmosphere of Studio 51 for our film, we shot it at the Troubadour on Old Brompton Road, one of the last surviving similar basement music clubs in London. As well as playing a part in the careers of Elton John and Charlie Watts, not to mention hosting Bob Dylan in 1962, the Troubadour was the home of a modern jazz club on Sundays in the 1960s, at exactly the period when Colyer's band was playing traditional jazz at Studio 51. So authentic did the film look that some old Colyer regulars asked how on earth we'd filmed in Ken's former club after it had been demolished! For my part I was glad to have had the opportunity to pay tribute to Rosina, who was a remarkable blues and jazz singer.[7]

Back in the 1950s, once the personnel of his regular band with Wheeler and Duncan had settled, and with the later addition of the pianist Ray Foxley, Colyer recorded some orchestrated ragtime in the manner of Bunk Johnson's 'Last Testament' session. 'I think that's one of the best recordings he ever made,' recalled Bowden. 'Nothing was deliberately set out. It was just the way each one of us thought about ragtime. You couldn't "rave up" rags, you had to lay back and play with that lovely lilting feel. And if you listen to a lot of ragtime records, Ken was the only one that caught that lovely lilt to it. Wheeler played a clarinet line that danced in and out of Ken's trumpet lead. It just worked, that front line was a perfect ragtime concept.'[8]

Years later, when I was in Colyer's band, we all enjoyed recapturing some of the feel of those 1950s ragtime recordings, especially when both Ray Foxley and Colin Bowden were reunited in the rhythm section. There was a similar atmosphere with Ray Smith on piano, with whom I later played in the London Ragtime Orchestra, which he co-led. But there were other aspects of New Orleans music that we explored together, too. On the last session I played with Colyer, in December 1986 (which was also recorded and later released on both CD and DVD),[9] both Ray Foxley and Colin Bowden were in the band, and clarinettist George Berry played tenor saxophone on some tunes. Back in the 1950s, traditional jazz fans in Britain had been scathing about the saxophone. When Bruce Turner joined Humphrey Lyttelton's band on alto sax, a banner was unfurled on the balcony of Birmingham Town Hall reading 'Go home, dirty bopper', and it was assumed by his fans that Colyer's band, with just a clarinet and no saxophone in sight, was a 'purist' revival band. In fact, maybe because of his interest in Lester Young, Colyer was a great enthusiast for the saxophone, even occasionally picking up the tenor himself. With George Berry's playing on that session from 1986, for the traditional tune 'Sing On' and a couple of other pieces that were not recorded, we somehow recaptured a hint of the New Orleans dance hall atmosphere, typical of players such as Emmanuel Paul.

Ken had the reputation of being a curmudgeon, I suspect because he was fed up with answering the same half dozen questions from fans over and over again, when he could have been enjoying a drink at the bar. What I recall most is his impish sense of humour, his open-mindedness, and willingness to experiment occasionally and to expand his repertoire. The British critic Richard Cook once reported that when Acker Bilk (in Ken's second 1950s line-up) asked him if they could do a number drawn from Armstrong's 1920s Hot Five repertoire, Colyer replied he 'wouldn't try anything that modern'.[10] Ken always had a fine line in irony, something lost on Acker, and it seems on Richard too. In fact, Ken knew all the Hot Five and Hot Seven numbers inside out. And like all of us, he loved those records. We played a lot of Louis Armstrong and King Oliver material, as well as pieces from contemporaneous bands such as the New Orleans Wanderers. You never knew on a gig when Ken might call something associated with Louis including 'Mahogany Hall Stomp', 'Dippermouth Blues', or 'Struttin' with Some Barbecue' (all of which he recorded). Of the Hot Five or Seven pieces, the most frequent ones we played in my time were 'Come Back Sweet Papa', 'Muskrat Ramble', 'Willie the Weeper', 'Wild Man Blues', 'Weary Blues' and 'Savoy Blues'.

Ken didn't read music and had no formal knowledge of keys, but he had a huge number of tunes and lyrics in his head. Chris Barber once told me that the repertoire of their first band included Gerry Mulligan's 'Bernie's Tune' (in traditional style) alongside quite obscure 1920s numbers such as 'Too Busy'. Every gig with Ken was about listening intently and following his lead. Even when we ventured into ragtime territory, weaving through the various segments of a composition by Scott Joplin or Arthur Marshall, we were all playing by ear all the time.

Another aspect of Colyer's fascination with New Orleans jazz was his formation in the mid-1950s of the Omega Brass Band, the very first attempt on the European side of the Atlantic to put together an ensemble along the lines of the Onward and Eureka brass bands of the Crescent City. Sonny Morris (by then leading his own band) rejoined Colyer to play trumpet alongside him in this group. 'Ken had this idea, and he was a great innovator in British jazz. He wanted to do it and he knew that I was interested in it. I liked brass band music, so it was a short step to get interested in New Orleans brass band music. He got me into it, and also trumpeter Bob Wallis. He said he was going to make this recording, and pay for everything, which he did. And he paid for all the refreshments on the day we made the recording, too. And we did a few parades as well.'[11]

Some of the literature surrounding the Omega Brass Band links it with left-wing protest movements, particularly because in 1959–60 the band headed the CND (Campaign for Nuclear Disarmament) annual Easter weekend march into London from the UK Atomic Weapons research station at Aldermaston in Hampshire.[12] Colyer and his musicians did not march the whole distance, but led the final mile or two to Trafalgar Square. Cultural commentators such as George McKay see the band's music as 'an accessible form of musical expression in keeping with the democratic sympathies of many activists and cultural workers of the time.'[13] But political identification was far from the minds of the participating musicians, who had first established the band as a one-off idea to play for the Soho Fair in 1955.

'It wasn't a political thing at all,' observed Morris. 'It was a reason to go out and play.'[14] As Morris pointed out, it wasn't easy to get a band of this kind together, because all the musicians worked professionally, virtually full time, in other bands. Colyer's own group provided five of the players, with their banjoist Johnny Bastable switching to play the bass drum, but the others were drawn from Morris' band and similar revivalist groups around London. The brass band played a few concerts, including one at the Adelphi Theatre, but 'we didn't do a lot with the Omega as a going concern', recalled Morris. Far from being passionate about radical politics, Colyer's motivation was predominantly musical. In the mid-1950s, the era before people such as Harold Dejan and Danny Barker worked hard to reinvigorate the New Orleans brass band genre in the city itself, Colyer was genuinely worried that this form of the music would die out. He believed passionately that recording the Omega was his own opportunity to get this style back in the public eye.

When the historian, violinist and record producer Bill Russell recorded Bunk Johnson's Brass Band and put this type of music on disc for the first time, in May 1945, he had just the same concern.[15] Although Colyer had seen and heard several of the city's working brass bands playing live on his 1952–3 visit to New Orleans, Russell's earlier recordings were very much the model for the Omega, just as Bunk Johnson's 1940s jazz band discs had influenced the Crane River Band and then Colyer's own six-piece group. The CND paid somewhat more than expenses to have this professional brass band playing for them, and in this respect, regarding protest marches, nothing had changed by 1971.

Although I was still at school that year, I had briefly taken up the sousaphone as well as the bass, and some of my London jazz-playing friends invited me to join a New Orleans-style band (including a number of ex-Omega members) to lead a procession of striking postal workers that was to march from Hyde Park to Parliament, via Oxford Street. We had no real interest in the cause, in fact several players moaned about their letters not being delivered, but we were to be paid by the Musicians' Union, in support of 'our postal colleagues'. The fee easily covered my train fare from my home in Farnham to London and left me a surplus on my week's pocket money. So I took a day off sick from school and joined the march. Playing a sousaphone in a brass band at the head of a demonstration in central London is not much of a hiding place, and unfortunately, that evening my headmaster saw a televised report on the parade, in which I was clearly visible. My protests, that such a gig was really so unusual that I had to do it, did not go down well.

I kept the sousaphone for a few years, and with bass drummer Mike Brown we eventually formed the Excelsior Brass Band in London to play this marching band music ourselves. Before that, as a student, I not only organized a few New Orleans-style street parades for Oxford Rag Weeks or to advertise some of the May Ball events, but also at the 1973 'Mayfly' festival in Oxpens park (where the Oxford ice rink was later built) I somehow inveigled myself into playing somewhat more avant-garde fare with Mike Westbrook's Brass Band. We had a glorious early summer afternoon playing Mike's very individual take on the traditional repertoire for the undergraduates and townsfolk who'd gathered in the park, with plenty of dancing and singing. Then on the spur of the moment I organized an impromptu concert that evening at my college, St Edmund Hall, where, advertised by little more than word of mouth, Mike, Lol Coxhill, Paul Rutherford and Phil Minton played to a packed audience of almost 100 students.

This started a sporadic friendship with Lol, with whom I shared a train and ferry journey to Denmark later that year. He managed to cut his head rather badly as we boarded the train to Esbjerg and the only antiseptic he had in his bag was Listerine. Several other passengers were dissuaded from joining us in the compartment when they saw the dried blood on his bald pate surrounded by a rather sinister looking orange-coloured stain. He was en route to play in an avant-garde theatre production in Århus, whilst I was heading on a little further to Aalborg to stay with the classical bassist Per Folke.

I'd met Per in the Jeunesses Musicales World Youth Orchestra in Britain for which I had a short summer job as a roadie, and discovering we shared a mutual interest in jazz, he asked if I'd like to come over and deputize for him on bass in a stage show on the nights he had other gigs. I joined the little five-piece jazz band in the orchestra pit of the local theatre, and though at first I had some trouble understanding the cues in Danish, I was well looked after by the other players, and my three or four gigs there helped pay for the holiday. (At the closing night party, a riotous celebration for cast, crew and musicians, I was introduced to Aalborg schnapps, resulting in the only time in my life I have been rendered completely immobile by alcohol.)

Among the later gigs I played with Lol was a 'riverboat shuffle' on a vintage steam launch from Marlowe bringing a posse of well-heeled passengers to the Henley Royal Regatta. The boat became trapped when the lock above Henley seized up and failed to open. The passengers were soon whisked off in a hastily provided coach, but the organizer – who looked and sounded rather like the former prime minister Edward Heath – turned to us and said, 'Sorry chaps, no room for you musicians.' So Lol, Dave Holdsworth, George Ricci, Robin Jones and I talked to some rather drunken students in a holiday narrowboat tied up below the lock, and asked if they would turn round and take us to Henley, where our transport was waiting, while the lock was fixed. They agreed and we set off, the steersman occasionally bumping the banks as he tried to see the way through his alcoholic haze. We finally arrived and found ourselves veering unsteadily between the buoys of the regatta course in midstream, whilst a flotilla of angry, blazer-wearing men in small boats with megaphones tried frantically to get us out of the path of the next sculling race. We were finally dumped, with our instruments, in a field a short distance from the town. Lol had a gig in London that night, but despite the high drama of our escape from the lock, I don't think he quite made it.

I mentioned that I had sent the manuscript of Ken Colyer's book to George Melly and John Chilton. By then I had known both of them for a considerable time. While I was still at school I started to visit the jazz bookshop that John Chilton and his wife Teresa ran in Great Ormond Street in London. In my sixth form years, my sister was a junior exhibitioner at the Royal Academy of Music, so I would often travel up to London with her on a Saturday and while she was having her lessons, I would spend time either at Dobell's record shop or at John's bookshop. I bought quite a few shabby volumes there, including such things as *Call Him George*, the biography of George Lewis by Jay Allison Stuart (actually the novelist Dorothy Tait, who managed Lewis' tours in the late 1950s and early 1960s) and *My Life in Jazz* by Max Kaminsky. Once John recognized my genuine interest, he encouraged me enormously by continuing to suggest good books on jazz, so in due course I invited him, and the regular pianist at his weekly sessions at New Merlin's Cave in Clerkenwell, Collin Bates, to play a concert at the same Farnham venue where Ken Colyer had appeared earlier with my scratch band. They came, and on a similar basis subsequently visited the Oxford University Jazz Club with another more famous guest.

I organized most of the club's concerts during 1973. At that point George Melly (who sang regularly at John's London sessions) had become something of a cult figure among students, on the back of his recently released and mildly risqué album *Nuts*. Apparently, quite exceptionally for a jazz album, it sold 12,000 copies in a few months. At the time, according to George, 'my audiences are getting younger, and even my 17-year-old son not only comes along himself, but brings his friends'.[16] The Oxford club needed money, and I reckoned that if John, Collin and George came down as guests to play with me, drummer Andy Crisp, clarinettist Tony Blincow and trombonist Mike Wills, we might make enough on the door to cover their fees, pay off the club's debts and fund the coming season's concerts. And so it proved.

George was kind enough to do a long promotional interview with me for the university magazine *Isis* the week before he came down, and in the process we spent an enjoyable afternoon at his house in Gloucester Crescent, just north-east of Regent's Park, discussing jazz and also surrealism. He still owned Magritte's canvas *Le Viol* at that time, which was carefully hung in his sitting room, together with several other works by other distinguished painters who had exhibited at E. L. T. Mesens' gallery when George had worked there some years before. He turned out to be a one-man vade mecum to the London art scene, and when I later thought of doing a PhD at the Courtauld Institute on the painter John Minton, George kindly introduced me to several of Minton's friends and associates, including Henrietta Moraes, to whom Minton had bequeathed his house (sadly her spiral into drug addiction meant that by the 1970s she no longer owned it, though at the time she lived not far from George, in Hanover Terrace).

I never got round to doing that PhD, as I'd also applied to join Macmillan Publishers' graduate trainee scheme and to my surprise was one of four candidates they selected out of several hundred applications. So instead of art history, in the autumn of 1975 I found myself working first as an educational, and later an academic, editor. But I kept my involvement in visual arts going, and every time I saw George, he provided plenty of ideas about different painters and sculptors whose work he thought might interest me.

The unexpected side effect of George coming to sing for our unruly and far from sober crowd of students at the Roebuck pub in Oxford was that he decided to turn professional again and to go on the road with John Chilton's Feetwarmers. The trigger was when we all went to find something to eat before the gig, having set up the bandstand in the late afternoon. George, John and Collin walked down with the rest of us to the High, where a man known to most of Oxford as Joyce used to sell hamburgers and kebabs from a converted minivan with a sort of glass conservatory on top, which included a minuscule serving hatch. That day Joyce was wearing a ballerina's tutu and had been making himself up using the mustard for his cheeks and tomato ketchup for his lips. He was, as George noted, 'carrying on like a pantomime dame'.[17] When our three guests returned to the pub before the gig, George was saying, 'we just don't see things like this in London, we have to get out and about more. We should go back on the road.' And as John Chilton confirmed in his autobiography, it was this gig in Oxford that prompted their decision.[18]

I remained on good terms with John for the rest of his life. He was very much my mentor as a jazz researcher, and I was glad in the years that followed to have been his editor at three successive publishing houses, bringing out his books on Sidney Bechet, Henry Allen and Roy

Eldridge, as well as commissioning his *Who's Who of British Jazz* and a new edition of his earlier general reference book, the *Who's Who of Jazz*.

In my final year at school, I first played bass with one of London's leading New Orleans revival bands, led by the trombonist Mike Casimir. By my second year at Oxford, in 1973–4, I was going to London once a week (or more) to play with Mike's band. Lugging a bass through Oxford's streets as I went to and from the railway station did make me wonder why I had chosen this instrument over, say, the clarinet (which my sister played), but in due course I left a bass in Mike's Holland Park flat, which made the journeys far easier. I used the tranquil time on the train to write my weekly essays for tutorials. However, on one occasion when I needed to bring that bass back to my lodgings in Jericho, next to the Oxford Canal, I found myself at one o'clock in the morning trapped on the towpath between a hostile swan, who thought I was attacking its nest, and a very drunk tramp, who decided I should give him all my money. In the end I decided the tramp was the least threatening option and he subsided with a groan into the undergrowth as I thrust the bass in his general direction whilst making a run for it towards my digs.

Mike's New Iberia Stompers played for a while at the Target, a huge pub on the A40 at Northolt, but then we moved to the Southampton Arms in Mornington Crescent, which – as well as a regular crowd of jazz fans – had a ready-made late evening audience of postal workers, after their shift ended at the nearby Mount Pleasant sorting office. One post-man, who became quite a regular, sidled up to us at the bar one night to tell our trumpeter Tony O'Sullivan that he was OK but not a patch on Eddie Calvert (whose former hit 'Cherry Pink and Apple Blossom White' was perhaps one of the slushiest trumpet solos ever recorded!). Mike had excellent connections in New Orleans and from time to time visiting musicians from America sat in with us at the Southampton Arms, including trumpeters Alvin Alcorn and Kid Thomas.

Playing these regular gigs with Mike did a lot to prepare me for my inaugural trip to the Crescent City in 1976. So too did the fact that one of my Oxford contemporaries was the clarinettist Tom Sancton, a PhD student and Rhodes Scholar, who had grown up in New Orleans and learned from such great players as George Lewis and Louis Cottrell.[19] Tom and I briefly had a band together as students (also involving the drummer Trevor Richards, at Surrey University at the time, and who had already been in the USA studying drums with Zutty Singleton). Tom, Trevor and I were later reunited on a couple of occasions in a quartet, with pianist Ray Smith, at the Ascona Festival in Switzerland in the late 1980s. Through the organizational skills of Mike Casimir, with whom I continued to play on and off throughout the 1970s, I eventually made my first visit to New Orleans, paid for by a small legacy from my grandfather who had known how passionate I was about the music. And that is where my jazz journey really began.

2 NEW ORLEANS 1976

Landing in the dusk at New Orleans International Airport in 1976 was a perfect time of day to arrive in the city for my first visit. The plane door opened and a gust of warm air entered the cabin. Later, the heat and humidity of an April evening accompanied the blizzard of lights and hoardings along the highway, heading towards the French Quarter of the old city. It was the Monday night before that year's Jazz and Heritage Festival began, so I checked in quickly to the hotel before heading out to hear some music. Away from the bright lights of Bourbon Street, the quarter's old buildings with their filigree balconies and weathered bricks were dimly lit. These blocks, beyond the bustle of people and traffic, had a very distinctive atmosphere, not least the city's unique smell of flowers, spicy food and just a hint of drains.

In those days, some fifteen years after it opened, Preservation Hall on St Peter Street was already deliberately shabby. The musicians played in the former art gallery to an audience who were crammed in, sitting cross-legged on the floor or squeezed onto the benches round the walls. It wasn't so much the down-at-heel building that created a lasting impression but the Kid Thomas Band in full flow. I had heard individual New Orleans musicians – including Thomas himself – in Britain, and even played support (with Mike Casimir) to the Legends of Jazz, a group of some of the city's elderly players led by expatriate British drummer Barry Martyn, during their short visit to London. But the visceral shock of hearing a genuine New Orleans group on home ground, with its 79-year-old trumpeter roaring into 'Algiers Strut', has stayed with me ever since. The front line of Thomas, clarinettist Manuel Crusto, tenor saxophonist

Manuel Paul and trombonist Homer Eugene was strong and vigorous, but the rhythm section made an even greater impression. Drummer and singer Alonzo Stewart might not have been the finest technician or timekeeper in the city at the time, indeed he could be rather heavy-handed, but with banjoist Manuel Sayles, pianist Dave Williams and the bassist Joe Butler, the collective effect was combined power and subtlety.

One minute they created a wave of sound behind the trumpeter's stabbing, staccato phrases, the next, they'd dropped back to support a delicate chorus in the chalumeau register from Crusto. Despite an air of studied nonchalance, these were men listening intensely to one another and working together to build a cohesive whole far greater than the sum of its parts. To be sure, they were playing a limited repertoire. They had probably played those pieces dozens, if not hundreds, of times, but those first few moments of listening to them made me want to discover all that I could about New Orleans jazz and how it worked.

Within the fortnight or so that I stayed in the city, there was little time for sleeping. I wrote at the time that without leaving the centre of town you could hear live music from lunchtime until the small hours of the next morning.[1] A little further afield, the Jazz and Heritage Festival at the Fairgrounds broadened the palette. It offered a really wide stylistic range of jazz, going way beyond the city's own music. Passing the modern jazz tent, I couldn't believe my luck that Charles Mingus was there, playing a fascinating solo set (alternating between bass and piano) before reappearing to demonstrate his telepathic rhythmic empathy with drummer Dannie Richmond in a forceful quintet performance.[2] The flurry of energy from Elvin Jones in the following show was equally impressive. Despite his pugnacious image, Mingus offstage was delightful and charming, joking with me and my English friend, the trumpeter Teddy Fullick, in the interval, as he entrusted his lion's head bass to us beside the stage while he went off to find the restrooms, and then chatting with great good humour until the time came to head back up to the stand with his quintet.

Yet my abiding memory from the festival tents was hearing music from the early days of jazz come alive. Some of it went back to the very dawn of jazz history. For example, the pianist Eubie Blake, then aged 89 and a survivor from the ragtime era, played a solo set. Dapper, limber and charming, claiming to be rather older than he actually was and telling stories of his early days in the African American theatre, he dropped in after his show to my hotel, where he nimbly demonstrated some tap-dancing steps. Hearing Eubie play his own pieces, including 'Charleston Rag', 'I'm Just Wild About Harry' and 'Memories of You', I sensed that however up-to-date his right-hand phrasing might have been, his left hand never entirely escaped the rather rigid timing of the 1890s. He was a living connection to African American piano music in the era just before jazz.

The American stride and Jelly Roll Morton specialist Butch Thompson sat near me in the audience. He told me later that Blake referred to his own playing style as 'assembling tricks'; in other words, putting together phrases that are difficult to copy and which became Blake's trademarks. One of these is the almost boogie-woogie-style left-hand pattern in 'Charleston Rag' that Eubie referred to as his 'wobble bass', and another is what Butch terms his 'bongo drum' effect, an alternating percussive pattern between the left and right hands that linked melodic sections of a piece. 'When it came down to playing two-fisted piano,' says Thompson, 'Eubie was playing ragtime. It's not stride piano exactly, it's a transitional style . . . but in terms of the development of what became stride piano and the East Coast school, Eubie is a seminal figure.'[3]

The other pre-jazz echoes on show that April in New Orleans were an equally special treat from the world of blues. Pianist Little Brother Montgomery (originally from Kentwood, Louisiana) infused his solo concert at the Fairgrounds with a laid-back feeling – at moments he seemed so far behind the beat that the time appeared to be suspended, particularly in a daringly slow 'Vicksburg Blues'. Following him on stage came the Arkansas-born local resident, Roosevelt 'The Honeydripper' Sykes, complete with white fedora and a huge cigar. His hypnotic repetitive left-hand patterns conjured up the dancing feet of long-ago patrons in honky-tonk bars, along with the clarion call of his blues lyrics.

Yet fascinating as these early approaches to jazz timing were, the collective feeling of the New Orleans traditional jazz bands and their rhythm sections was the main attraction for me on this short visit. In particular I heard a thrilling Fairground set from Percy and Willie Humphrey, emotionally charged because their regular trombonist Jim Robinson had been taken seriously ill and Louis Nelson was deputizing for him.[4] That band's rhythm team of pianist Sing Miller, banjoist Narvin Kimball, bassist James Prevost and drummer Cié Frazier rose to the occasion magnificently. Over the time I was there I learned that in the best of these groups, following a tradition that goes back even further than the nineteenth-century percussion and dancing in Congo Square, almost everything hinges on the drummer and what they give to the rhythmic 'feel' of a band. In later styles of jazz, and in particular music from the 1940s onwards, the double bass has a pivotal role in the rhythm section, but in the kind of New Orleans bands I was experiencing, drummers were generally the dominant partners.

Many European bands that played revivalist jazz at that time adopted a straightforward four-four rhythm, the bass drum sounding on each beat of every bar. The Chris Barber band, in its many recordings from 1954 onwards, and even in its earlier discs with Ken Colyer as leader, is typical. Barber's influence was so pervasive that other British, Dutch, German and Scandinavian groups copied his rhythmic approach with considerable accuracy. But listening to the drummers in New Orleans, much of their swing came from a relaxed two to the bar, sounding the bass drum on beats one and three. Older players such as Cié Frazier or Louis Barbarin (with Papa French's band) often used such a bass drum pattern, leaving it to the double bass or banjo to lay down four beats, perhaps behind the latter part of a solo or to build excitement in the final chorus of a song. But my real education began a few days after I arrived, through sitting in with drummer Chester Jones at a party. A stocky ex-prizefighter who had become a community leader in his native Tremé area, Chester was a tough man but he also had a gift for getting on with people.

Being the only bass player there, I had a busy night. From the start Chester was immensely kind, showing me, with a nod, a wink and an occasional word, how to lock in with him, when to push up into four beats and when to remain in two. He had a really powerful bass drum sound, and everything was anchored on that. Like the players in the city's brass bands that I heard – particularly bass drummer Emil Knox – Chester liked to accent the final beat of the last two bars of a tune, which local players called the 'eighth beat' in a two-bar phrase. Followed by a thumping downbeat in the following bar, it was a brilliant way to create momentum and swing. Some of Chester's best playing on record (of which there is far too little) is on the *Sammy Rimington Quintet on Washington Avenue* album,[5] where that bass drum sound rings out on tracks such as 'If Ever I Cease To Love'.

Playing for an evening in the courtyard of the Olivier House Hotel with Chester and a variety of local pianists and banjo players was a great way to experience the New Orleans rhythm section 'feel' at first hand. And what a privilege to support such celebrity guests as the trumpeter Alvin Alcorn and the veteran trombonist Preston Jackson, who each dropped in to play a number or two in that informal setting. Next day I went along to hear Chester's friend and colleague Freddie Kohlman on drums with the Dukes of Dixieland at their rooftop club in the rather grand Hotel Monteleone. I'd already seen Freddie playing on Bourbon Street during some afternoon sessions – keeping flawless time on one such occasion while simultaneously drinking a soda and holding a conversation with someone who was off to the side of the bandstand.

His playing on stage with the Dukes was outstanding. His rhythmic complexity, his lightning fast stick-work and the sheer inventiveness around his timekeeping were all extraordinary, but above and beyond that, this one person embodied that elusive sense of swing that I so much wanted to understand. I little knew then that the following year I would be playing with him for several nights running in the UK, and that he would teach me more about rhythm section playing than anyone, before or since.

Freddie, born in 1918, grew up across the river from New Orleans, in Algiers, where his father ran a tavern. There was jazz in the family bar in his childhood, but as a teenager he made his mark on the city at large, playing with the likes of Papa Celestin and Sam Morgan. He was taught to play drums by Louis Cottrell Sr and when we later talked about the history of jazz drumming, he could demonstrate almost every early style to perfection. Before he was twenty he was in Chicago, playing with Albert Ammons and the New Orleans trumpeter Lee Collins, as well as working occasionally with Earl Hines. The Windy City was to become something of a second home for him, as the house drummer at the Jazz Ltd club for much of the 1950s and early 1960s. He backed many of the guest musicians who came through – I remember him telling me about working with Billie Holiday – and he also deputized briefly in Louis Armstrong's All Stars. From the mid-1960s he had been resident back in New Orleans, and with his ample girth tucked neatly in behind his kit, 'Fritz', as he was universally known among his peers, was an asset to any band.

During our week at the relatively newly opened Pizza Express jazz club in Soho, London, in November 1977, Freddie would talk me through my solos in a series of stage whispers. 'Play some melody on this chorus . . . now walk one . . . play through to the end of your solo . . . give the band a phrase to build on!' It was all fantastic advice, and pianist Richard Simmons and I learned a huge amount from him about how to swing a band and how to play together as a rhythm team.[6] I worked with Freddie many times after that and he was always generous and encouraging, especially in Ascona, Switzerland, when we were both with Bob Wilber's Bechet Legacy in 1987. As is so often the case, our friendship developed off the bandstand, with a shared love of fine food and cooking, as well as following an incident on his second visit to Britain when he lost his beret at Heathrow Airport and my wife promptly knitted him a replacement. He proudly wore the green woolly hat with 'I'm Freddie, Fly Me' emblazoned on the front for the rest of his stay. (Blaming the airline for his lost headgear, 'Fly me' was an ironic reference to the British Airways advertising slogan of the time!) When I dropped in unexpectedly to hear Freddie in the Hotel Monteleone in the mid-1980s, he rather charmingly introduced me to the other Dukes of Dixieland as 'a friend of the most swinging piano player in London', namely Richard Simmons.

During my first trip to New Orleans, this was all in the future. By 1976, I had learned quite a lot about how the double bass sounded in traditional jazz from records including such influential players as John Lindsay (with Jelly Roll Morton), Al Morgan (with the Jones-Collins Astoria Hot Eight) and Slow Drag Pavageau (with Bunk Johnson and George Lewis). And when he came to London with the Legends of Jazz in March 1974, I'd had the opportunity to see and hear the pioneer bassist Ed Garland, who had made his first records with Kid Ory at the start of the 1920s. But now that I was in New Orleans I could experience a wider range of traditional bassists, and so that is where my investigation into my own instrument continued. There were the slap players, Chester Zardis, Joe Butler and Chink Martin, who used the percussive snap of their gut strings against the fingerboard to add depth and drive to their playing. There were hard-swinging players who used more modern strings of nylon or metal and tended towards more of a four-four feel, most notably Placide Adams, Frank Fields, Jerry Green and Walter Payton Jr. And there were bassists who sat somewhere in between, such as James Prevost.

On record, prior to that visit, the sound that most fascinated me was the powerful rhythm section of the 1950s George Lewis band:

Alton Purnell on piano, Lawrence Marrero on banjo, Slow Drag on bass and Joe Watkins on drums. They were a far more cohesive and hard-swinging unit than the 1970s Kid Thomas band, and they had an extraordinary dynamic and emotional range. One minute they could power along 'Red Wing' or the 'Gettysburg March', whilst the next they'd drop back to provide the most minimal accompaniment to one of Lewis' delicate hymns or blues such as 'Just a Closer Walk With Thee' or 'Burgundy Street Blues'.[7] Yet there was always a sense of unreleased power, of something held in reserve to swing the band even harder and with more energy. Later I was fortunate enough to spend some years playing on and off with the band led by a student of George's, the English clarinettist Sammy Rimington, and he embodied this same sense of latent power in his playing.

As it turned out, although it was seven years after his death in 1969, the bass that Slow Drag had used in the Lewis band had been stored in a cupboard at Preservation Hall, so off I went to examine it. Despite the instrument missing a string and having a rather warped bridge, I worked out that he had produced his slap sound by pulling the string directly away from the fingerboard and then releasing it. The 'action' – the height of the string above the lower end of the fingerboard – was about half an inch, allowing his right hand to catch the string from behind and pull it outwards. This explained why he often bound the ends of his fingers with adhesive tape, as this method is particularly tough on the skin. I spent the next morning listening to his oral history tapes at the William Ransom Hogan Jazz Archive at Tulane University, and when interviewer Bill Russell asked Slow Drag to demonstrate his famous slap in the setting of a domestic living room, away from the bandstand, he seemed almost unable to do it.[8] His style depended on being in the right musical surroundings, alongside a drummer and a chordal instrument. At his finest, the rhythmic thrust of Slow Drag's percussive slap bass playing reminded me of Humphrey Lyttelton's famous description on BBC Radio of that other great New Orleans bassist Pops Foster 'chopping down trees' in the rhythm section.

At Preservation Hall a few nights later, I was able to see and hear double bassist Chink Martin, who had also first recorded (initially on tuba) in the 1920s, with the New Orleans Rhythm Kings. His slapping style in the 1970s was comparable to Slow Drag's and also involved taping up his fingers. Yet Chester Zardis, who had recorded with Bunk Johnson in 1942, used an even higher action and drew his strings partly across (rather than away from) the fingerboard, thereby retaining more of the tone of each note and creating slightly less of a percussive thud when the string was released. Like Pavageau and Martin, he used gut strings. His style was complex, because to get the slap sound precisely on the beat, a greater degree of anticipation was involved than for those bassists who employed a slightly lower action height.

I asked various Preservation Hall musicians about why different bass players of the same generation, performing very similar music, used such contrasting instruments. The banjoist Father Al Lewis told me that many of the local basses had been repaired and set up by his fellow banjo player Narvin Kimball.[9] He said that Kimball used a higher than usual action on his banjo so that, playing acoustically without amplification, it would project as loudly as possible, and he took the same approach to his bass building. Certainly, Zardis used an uncommonly high action. He seldom used tape to protect his fingers, preferring to soak them in salt water to heal blisters and harden the skin. When I asked him if he had any tips for building up callouses on the fingers, he said, 'piss on them'.[10] I never discovered if he put this advice into practice himself, and I failed to follow his recommendation. However, Zardis created a huge acoustic tone on the bass and sounded fantastic with drummer Louis Barbarin, banjoist Al Lewis and pianist Sweet Emma Barrett, urging along trumpeter Ernie Cagnoletti's band with great force and power.

Sweet Emma was one of the very few female instrumentalists working in New Orleans jazz in the mid-1970s. Known as the 'Bell Gal' from her red garters with small bells sewn on to them, which jingled as she stamped her feet to the music, and immediately identifiable from her matching red beanie hat, she had a distinctive rather nasal blues singing voice. She recorded with the Humphrey brothers for the Riverside label back in January 1961 in the 'Living Legends' series, and there was no doubt that by 1976 she was indeed such a legend. Emma worked for most of her life in her home town but after that Riverside disc she began travelling nationally and internationally with the Preservation Hall Jazz Band, until she suffered a stroke in 1967. This affected her left side, and from having been the stomping two-fisted player heard on her Riverside recording, by 1976 she just used her right hand for playing, and related mobility problems meant that she had to be carried to the stage in Preservation Hall. This at least made for a dramatic entry and exit.

Yet once seated at the piano, her right-hand flurries of notes and her plaintive voice had enough emotional power to give you shivers down the spine.

Sweet Emma was one of a trio of singer-pianists of the era who were regarded as the principal female instrumentalists involved in revivalist New Orleans jazz in the early 1970s. I missed hearing Billie Pierce, the wife of cornetist Dede Pierce, because she had died in 1974, but until then she had been a frequent travelling ambassador for Crescent City jazz. Fortunately, I did get to hear Billie's sister, Sadie Goodson, married to the trumpeter Kid Sheik Colar, whom she regularly accompanied on concerts. Sadie continued working well into the 1990s, living to the remarkable age of 101. She was affable and approachable, as was her husband, with whom I later played in the UK, whereas Sweet Emma, away from the bandstand, was a woman of few words.

Aside from that group of female singer-pianists who kept New Orleans jazz close to its folk and blues roots, I also heard, and later got to play alongside, a very different order of musician, Jeanette Kimball, who encompassed a far wider range of musical interests. She appears together with Chester Jones on the *Sammy Rimington Quintet* album mentioned earlier, but in 1981, the entrepreneur Colin Strickland brought her to Britain to play with Kid Thomas, in a rhythm section with Louis Barbarin, Emanuel Sayles and James Prevost.[11] Jeanette was a delight to hear and I got the chance to play a few pieces with her on that visit to the UK. Chatting with me and her daughter, she looked back with affection at several landmarks in New Orleans jazz history. She had a sophisticated harmonic ear and a tremendous, gentle sense of swing, developed over a lifetime of playing – from the 1920s, when she first worked in Papa Celestin's band, through to her reunion with him in the 1950s, and continuing with the group under Papa French's leadership. Fortunately, she was one of the most widely recorded musicians of her generation owing to her versatility, and it is still possible to appreciate her playing in a great variety of settings.

After my first New Orleans visit, I later had the opportunity in the 1980s to hear Chester Zardis again in Louis Nelson's touring group in Europe with pianist Butch Thompson, banjoist Danny Barker and drummer Stanley Stephens. Despite what I had learned from Chester Jones and Freddie Kohlman, in this particular rhythm team, with its delightful, but rather un-assertive, drummer, the core of the band's rhythm came from Barker and Zardis.[12] In 1976, however, it was not Zardis but three other bassists who gave me more to consider.

Firstly, Jerry Green played at the time with the trumpeter Alvin Alcorn and his trio, the third member being clarinettist Ralph Johnson. This was an object lesson in how to play in the most minimal setting with no chordal instrument and no drums. Jerry's light touch and adept harmonic knowledge made the band sound fuller than one might have expected from the three instruments. His harmonic and rhythmic role was no less important than Bob Whitlock's with the original Gerry Mulligan Quartet. I spent time chatting to Jerry in a yard party at Alvin Alcorn's house and, as so often was the case, he was warmly encouraging to me, as he was to anyone who seriously wanted to learn more about New Orleans and its music.

Secondly, Walter Payton Jr (father of the future trumpet star Nicholas Payton) had an outlook that went way beyond the city and the bands he played with there. He suggested I check out some of the international associations for bassists and – in those pre-internet days – gave me some magazines and articles to read that made me think hard in the longer term about the choice of strings and the sound I wanted to make. Walter and I had another thing in common, in that he played in the New Orleans Ragtime Orchestra, and I had just become a member of the nascent London Ragtime Orchestra. In later years the two bands were to do some back-to-back concerts in Europe, but it was very helpful to talk about how to tackle the orchestrated rags from the *Red Back Book*, the historical collection (mainly by Scott Joplin) that both bands used as part of their repertoire. Did we stay true to the scores, just playing root notes on the first and third beat of each bar, or did we subtly work in a little more jazz feeling? Walter's advice was really helpful in suggesting just where and how to add 'a little something' of our own to the written notes.

In the end it was Frank Fields, to whom I later lent a bass for a UK tour, and who was playing at the time with Papa French's band (which I heard on one 1976 session with Ellis Marsalis on piano and his 14-year-old son Wynton sitting in on trumpet) who steered me towards realizing that the instrument sounded better with modern steel strings and a chance to 'sing' throughout its registers, rather than relying on the percussive slapping sound that to some extent stifled its natural tone. Yet Green, Payton and Fields all instinctively knew how to work with the two-beat New Orleans style when playing in local rhythm sections and in effect demonstrated how the traditional style of bass playing would develop authentically in the latter part of the twentieth century.

In 1980 I had the opportunity to play with and learn from a musician who had been in the legendary Bunk Johnson band at the Stuyvesant Casino in New York in the 1940s. This was Don Ewell, Baltimore-born and a well-schooled pianist, who took Alton Purnell's place with Bunk. He also recorded some trios with Bunk and the drummer Alphonse Steele. After playing in the Johnson band, he worked in Chicago with the likes of Muggsy Spanier, and then joined Kid Ory for a while in California. He spent some years in Jack Teagarden's latter-day bands, which is how he came to meet the British trumpeter Pat Halcox, who (playing with Chris Barber) had shared a bill with Teagarden on one of their US tours.

Don came over to Britain to play a series of concerts with Pat (during his annual break from the Barber band) and I was lucky enough to be asked to play on them, together with the drummer Norman Emberson, saxophonist Bill Greenow and trombonist Jim Shepherd. Don played a completely individual mixture of rollicking stride piano and a gentler style, modelled on that of Jelly Roll Morton. He was a delight to play alongside, always inventive, with a touch that remained delicate and sensitive, even when he was stomping out a striding tribute to 'little Fatsy Watsy' as he called him. He also gave me plenty of advice about how to blend my bass lines with his striding left hand. We had a splendid opening gig at London's 100 Club and then moved on to the Bull's Head in Barnes, where the plan was to record an album to help raise funds for Don's daughter, who was suffering from cancer and needed some hefty medical bills paid. In the event, a persistent out-of-tune whistler in the audience, close to one of the microphones, made most of the session unusable, but two relatively unscathed tracks were eventually issued in 2015.[13]

We made plans to record again (hopefully whistler free) at a different venue later in the tour, but that was never to happen, because just a couple of days after the Bull's Head job we heard that Don had suffered a serious heart attack. He was staying with the tour organizer Dave Bennett and had been rapidly admitted to Dave's local hospital in Hampshire, which was not too far from the Macmillan Publishers' office where I worked. So, once Don was off the critical list, for the following ten days or so while he was kept in hospital, I dropped in during my lunch break or after office hours to see him. Although I have never been a particularly good chess player, it was Don's passion, so most afternoons we played a game, and he took pleasure in beating me regularly in as few moves as possible. Those visits gave us time to chat about many things, not least because he hated being in a ward full of geriatrics with comparable heart problems, who seemed to have no interest whatever in the outside world. On one of my evening visits I asked him how he was. He looked up ruefully and said, 'I've spent the best years of my life in here this afternoon!' He told me that our chance to discuss music and what was going on in the news offered him some escapism from the dullness of the ward.

I remember Don saying that he thought Bunk's 1940s Stuyvesant Casino band had been playing 'contemporary folk music' rather than some kind of ideological revival jazz and that he realized whilst making the trio records that Bunk was 'some kind of genius'. Certainly not many New Orleans trumpeters made forays into repertoire such as 'Where the River Shannon Flows' and 'When the Moon Comes Over the Mountain', part of a set of pieces that I've always listened to rather differently following that conversation. But Don also recalled his time with Teagarden, whom he greatly admired as both a singer and a trombonist, and he recounted his memories of his fellow musicians in Jack's band who were not really much known in Britain, such as trumpeter Don Goldie and clarinettist Henry Cuesta (who went on to spend over a decade with Lawrence Welk).

I drove Don to Heathrow Airport when he was well enough to travel home. He'd had a battle with alcoholism and been told not to drink after his heart operation, but after he'd checked in I caught sight of him downing a sizeable gin and tonic. He gave me a large wink before heading for the departure lounge. It was the last time I ever saw him, but it had been a privilege both to play alongside him and to get to know him a little, albeit in sad circumstances. Before his death in 1983 Don invited my friend Ray Smith from the Colyer band to study with him in Florida, and I always felt that Ray managed to keep some of Don's very individual style alive in the years we played together after that.

3 BEFORE KATRINA

Just across St Peter Street from Preservation Hall in New Orleans is Johnny White's bar.[1] On my 1976 visit, I'd often go there for a quick drink before heading over to hear whoever was playing at the Hall that night. During the Jazzfest week, there'd be a man already installed at the bar almost every evening, with a greying beard, long hair tied back, and wearing a beret. We got talking, and he obviously knew a lot about the city's music, urging me to check out a bar in Carrollton called the Maple Leaf where I might be lucky enough to hear one of the city's piano specialists such as James Booker. In the end I did go there and heard a band led by the British-born drummer Andrew Hall, with the blues-tinged saxophonist Ernest Poree, plus bassist Melvin Yancey. (I struck up a conversation with Yancey and a few years later he called and borrowed my bass for some concerts in England.)

Quite how I failed to recognize that the man in Johnny White's was Dr John (Mac Rebennack) I don't know. When Chris Barber brought him over to Britain for the 'Take Me Back To New Orleans' tour in 1980 (in which I was involved because Freddie Kohlman was also part of it, and I drove him to some of the gigs, as well as accompanying him on a VIP trip to the Premier drum factory in Leicester), I immediately recognized the man from the bar, and we had quite a laugh about it. Although Dr John lived in Los Angeles in the 1970s, he had come back to New Orleans for a few days at festival time, during a hiatus from touring and following what had been a somewhat chaotic time for his band. He went on from this visit to work on *The Night Tripper* and *MalcolM RebbenacK* records that came out the following year.

I might have recognized him from the cover photo on the latter, but the man in the bar certainly didn't resemble the elaborately costumed figure on previous albums such as *Remedies* or *Zu Zu Man*. Whenever I spoke to him, conscious of his home town's long musical traditions, Mac was emphatic about the importance of drummers in a New Orleans rhythm section, and on the concerts during the Chris Barber UK tour it was tremendous hearing his forceful piano knitting together with Freddie Kohlman's drums.[2] On the initial German leg of that Barber/Dr John package, on which Freddie only arrived during the second week owing to other commitments, it was none other than Chester Jones who was drafted in in his place on drums.[3]

I caught up with Dr John numerous times in the years that followed, but we had a long conversation when Mac made his 2004 album *N'awlinz: Dis Dat or D'Udda*,[4] which now stands as a pre-Katrina snapshot of a huge range of New Orleans music, a scene that was irrevocably altered by the 2005 hurricane and its aftermath. So representative is it, that it works as the road map for this chapter. We began by talking about another drummer whom Dr John and I both admired (and with whom I had been lucky enough to work on a concert with singer Lillian Boutté's band). This was Smokey Johnson, who had previously played with Dave Bartholomew, Fats Domino and Snooks Eaglin. By the time of Mac's recording, Smokey had suffered a stroke, which prevented him playing kit drums, but he added percussion to several tracks, his rhythmic empathy seeming to nudge great performances out of his fellow drummers on the record. Asked about this, Dr John said: 'He's the one to tell everyone if they're playing their shit funky, or if it's not funky … On the album he mainly plays tambourine, but also on some of the brass band pieces he plays bass drum. That's incredible to have him on bass drum and Earl Palmer on snare! You just can't get more funky than that. On the tracks where the other drummers, Herman Ernest III and Earl Palmer are playing, I said to Smokey, "You tell 'em what you think!" And I said to them "Listen he *will* tell you!" because Smokey don't mince his words. A good example of that is on the piece "Shango Tango" that Willie Tee (Wilson Turbington) and I wrote. It's a short piece but it didn't sound right, so I said to Smokey, "Tell Herman how to play it." Well he sang something, and it was so exactly right, it fit right away. Herman got it and played more or less what Smokey had sung, but Smokey says, "No, man. You're not doing this part!" And he sang some more. His shit is complex, but it's worth taking time to get it right, so the rhythm just jumps out at you.'[5]

On the concert with Lillian Boutté, Smokey and I were joined in the rhythm section by the veteran Texas-born pianist Sammy Price. His boogie-inflected playing instantly clicked with Smokey's New Orleans beat. Two bars into the first number, a grin spread over Sammy's normally inscrutable face and he just muttered 'Heavy!' at me. From him, that was a supreme compliment. For me, it was an evening to treasure.

N'awlinz: Dis Dat or D'Udda does not only focus on the drums. Central to it is the New Orleans keyboard tradition of which Dr John himself was such a vibrant exponent. One player, represented on the disc by his best-known composition, was the man working across the street with Kid Thomas in Preservation Hall in 1976, at the very time I was having my first conversations with Mac about the city's pianists, namely Dave 'Fat Man' Williams. His song 'I Ate Up the Apple Tree' became a Bourbon Street standard and is sung on the record by Randy Newman. 'I loved Dave Williams' piano playing,' Mac told me. 'And I loved his songs, especially this one. Dave was a special guy in New Orleans, full of heart, and he used to play at a Spiritual church in my neighbourhood. Plus, of course, he used to work round town with his own quartet. This song was so well known I used to sing it as a lullaby for my kids, but to be sure I got all the verses for the album, I got hold of Dave's record to learn the song properly.[6] You know the funniest thing? When we came to record it, Randy already knew the song. He'd never seen or heard Dave Williams play, but he knew his best-known song inside out.'[7]

Another musician who features on the record is one of New Orleans' better-kept secrets: Eddie Bo. He was a fine keyboard player, vocalist and songwriter, who added a spoken vocal to trumpeter Dave Bartholomew's song 'The Monkey'. 'I've known Dave since my childhood,' said Mac. 'And I consider him the best blues trumpet player there is. There may be better jazz players in New Orleans, but there's nobody better when it comes to heart. When I asked him if he'd do the record, he said he never played on nobody else's session unless he was the producer, but in the end I won him round. He came in, made one take, and nailed it ... Eddie's story is more complex. There was a time when he was recording for Apollo, way back, when he really had a bit of the game. That song he wrote, called "I'm Wise", became "Okey Dokey", and then Little Richard recorded it as "Slippin' and Slidin'", and it was a hit. That's just one example of how Eddie, so many times in his career, has been real close to breaking through, but somehow he's never managed to promote himself beyond the regional level. The same thing happened when he wrote "My Dearest Darling". Etta James had the hit with it, and Eddie didn't get the promotion he needed, although he wrote the song. But he's a great player and still playing as well as ever. He's featured on "St. James Infirmary" on my album. I wanted to be the singer on it, doing some goofy stuff, but I wanted him to sing on it as well, and he does. It typifies his approach because what he does is 100% Eddie Bo. That kind of attitude is always uplifting, and it was the same years ago when some of the first sessions I ever played on were with him.'[8]

Bo's vocal on the track is dramatically different from Mac's, and he immediately soars into a higher register, singing about 'A cold, cold night last winter, when there were twelve black horses on Britannia Street', creating an instant, almost theatrical impression of a funeral parade. Hearing Eddie with his own band, on tour in Europe, he frequently demonstrated this knack of suddenly creating a new and vivid verbal image that jumped outside the traditional lyrics of a song.

'I get these lyrics from the street,' he told me after one of his concerts. 'In the street, in the pool halls, just hanging around with different people. I listen for things that could be useful and cause

Figure 2 Eddie Bo's visiting card

people's minds to catch an image. Such as "Hook and Sling". I was working with my dad, earning some extra dust. He was a foreman on the river, and one of the other workers said to me, "You don't look like a pianist. You look like one of these people who just hooks and slings." We was loading bales of cotton. And I said to myself, "Hook and Sling" – that's a good title![9] The guy just laughed, but in a few weeks I had put that down. It's like "Slippin' and Slidin'". When I first recorded it, I called it "I'm Wise". Little Richard re-recorded it on Specialty, and he called it "Slippin' and Slidin'". I wrote it, but it looks like everybody gets credit for it. I'm the correct writer. I have to say this, because when my royalties are sent to me, I only get about 25% of something that I wrote. That's just part of the business.'[10] He went on to tell me he had written at least 160 songs, but those are just the ones that are documented. He was sure there were more, but some had been written so fast that not all of them were properly preserved.

Eddie had a distinctive, almost scholarly, appearance in later years, with a neat grey beard and distinctive Taqiyah headgear. Softly and elegantly spoken, he was – like so many New Orleans musicians – part of a family musical dynasty, the Bocages. Indeed his stage name is a corruption of Edwin Bocage. Among his many musical cousins was Peter Bocage, who played both violin and trumpet, a pioneer recording artist in the 1920s with Armand J. Piron, as well as a member of the 1960s Eureka Brass Band. Eddie's piano-playing mother got him started on the instrument and helped school him in the style of Professor Longhair (Roy Byrd), who was also the major influence on Dr John. After army service, Eddie attended the Grunewald School of Music in New Orleans, and he told me that he had a synaesthetic sense of harmony, experiencing chords as colours. This was something he tried to carry into his own writing.[11]

When we began talking about the musicians who influenced him as a pianist, Eddie had some very specific thoughts. Firstly he named his slightly younger contemporary Ellis Marsalis, with whom he studied the work of Art Tatum, both from transcription and playing along with the records. But his second major influence was a less well-known figure, Edward Frank. He said, 'We studied together, Ed and myself. There was a thing where we'd go from club to club, and then all the musicians would gather at one of the clubs and it'd be a jam session. They don't have it any more, but you might have had twenty pianists, ten trumpets, so many saxophones, and you'd take turns playing. It gave each of us a concept, a "one-ness", because our minds could hear what everybody was doing.' He went on to explain that, in a rather different way from the famous cutting contests of the stride piano players in New York, who were trying to master and outdo each other in a very specific style, these New Orleans sessions were about developing and presenting a completely individual musical personality. 'It helped me get to where I am now, and those harmonic "colours" gave me a different approach. Ed and I would get together, drink a few beers and we would study. And studying with him was phenomenal because he would take you to other levels. We learned from each other and it was a great, great union. I was so sad when he passed.'[12]

What Eddie had not mentioned is that Ed Frank's left arm was paralysed and he played entirely with his right hand, though generally creating a fuller sense of jazz piano than many a two-handed player. I had met Ed both in New Orleans, at a party in the Seventh Ward, where I marvelled at his playing with the veteran trumpeter Emery Thompson, and in Europe, where he toured frequently with Lillian Boutté. So I mentioned to Eddie how brilliantly I thought he had conquered his disability.

'I'm glad you know of him,' he replied. 'A lot of people didn't know about Edward Frank, but he was one of the best pianists around. He wasn't spoken of as much as he should have been, but when you said "piano" and "Edward Frank" all the musicians knew that you were in for a treat.' A good example of Ed Frank's playing (which also includes guest appearances from Dr John) can be heard on Lillian Boutté's 1993 album *The Jazz Book*.[13] I was grateful to Eddie Bo for reminding me about Ed, yet the part of our conversation that I most vividly remember from the time I spent with Eddie was his encyclopaedic knowledge of the classical piano records of Vladimir Horowitz.

Another of the pianists whose work was represented on the 2004 Dr John record was the blues singer and composer Cousin Joe. 'He was my favourite guy of all blues writers,' said Mac. 'He was also one of my all-time friends. He cut a lot of discs a long, long time ago, which remain some of the greatest records, and later on, he'd bring things to me and say, "I want you to record this", or "Can you try playing that?" I never did get around to doing all of them, although it was through me that Art Blakey cut a version of "One Way Ticket", a new version of which is on the album. Back then I used to perform [Joe's song] "Such-a-Much" myself pretty often. That song has about 40 different names, but what you hear on the disc is quite close to what Joe himself used to sing.'

I'd heard Cousin Joe singing 'Such-a-Much' at first hand when I invited him to come to Ascona for the annual New Orleans Jazz Festival in 1988. On his first night there, he was being interviewed by the blues and jazz scholar Paul Oliver, who asked him a simple opening question, and after a very terse answer, Joe went straight into his solo act for the next hour, leaving Paul sitting, not quite sure what to do with himself, alongside the piano. After launching into the Beach Boys' 'Cotton Fields Back Home', with a passing reference to growing up on the Whitney Plantation, Joe sang a verse or two from most of his own best-known songs, 'Such-a-Much' amongst them.

When I spoke to him on the telephone prior to his visit, Joe had been anxious about playing at a jazz festival because, he said, 'I only play piano in but two keys, B flat and E flat, will that be OK?' I assured him that he'd be fine, but this solo performance proved that his fears about hypersensitive European critics were completely groundless. Here was a jazz and blues piano player and singer in his prime. Before the gig he had been so physically stiff, after the long flight the day before, that I'd had to help him get his shoes on, and laced them up for him, but on stage the energy flowed and all signs of age or stiffness disappeared, a phenomenon I have seen many times since with performers from all walks of jazz and blues. Afterwards he was reunited for the first time since the legendary 1940s King Jazz recordings with guitarist Danny Barker and pianist Sammy Price and it was interesting being a fly on the wall for their conversations, not least because Danny was a staunch Democrat and Sammy was a Republican. The presidential campaign between George Bush Sr and Michael Dukakis was under way, and I learned something of how this looked from an African American perspective, although Cousin Joe himself was cynical rather than committed.

Another of his own songs that Joe sang on that first night in Ascona was 'Hen Laying Rooster', and this appears on Dr John's record, with B. B. King as the guest vocalist. 'It caused me quite a few problems to get it in a suitable state to perform on the record,' mused Mac. 'Years ago, Joe gave me the lyrics, but I'd never heard the music. He told me to check this song out, and then not long after that he died. When I got hold of the tune, I had to add some extra lyrics to make everything fit properly, because the lyrics he gave me didn't quite work. Then his widow moved, and I had to track her down to make sure she got the money, but finally I got all that straight and we went in to record it. Originally I was going to have Wolfman [Washington] sing on it, but then B. B. came and sang on it instead and that blew Wolf's verse out. But the great thing about this one is the incredible viola solo by Gatemouth Brown. The way he recorded it was originally a long, long solo – if you heard the whole thing before we dubbed the vocal shit you'd be amazed – but it was awfully long, and I just had to cut it down for the record.'

Listening back many years later, it's a shame the full solo isn't there instead of the very tightly edited excerpt on the track, because Gatemouth was another of the relatively unsung performers who – after moving back to his birth state of Louisiana in the 1970s – worked the New Orleans clubs and the international touring circuit for many years (including a lengthy tour of the USSR in 1979). And, at the time of writing, guitarist Wolfman Washington is still a stalwart of the touring circuit, as well as having played regularly for many years at the Maple Leaf, to which Dr John directed me back in 1976.

Moving away from keyboard players, my conversation with Mac Rebennack turned to a track on his album called 'Chickee Le Pas', a song he wrote along the lines of the traditional song 'My Indian Red' which he had recorded on his *Goin' Back to New Orleans* disc in 1992.[14] A mixture of English, Creole patois, and the secret language of the marching Mardi Gras Indian societies, 'Chickee Le Pas' is a beguiling vocal cocktail. 'I wanted,' he told me, 'to get the Mardi Gras Indians themselves involved and it meant a lot to me to get members of the Golden Eagles, the Mighty Cloud Hunters and the Mandingo Warriors in there. But it's Danny Barker who takes a lot of the credit for getting those songs recorded and preserved.'

Back in 1976, I'd first encountered the Mardi Gras Indians with their fabulous feathered costumes and their marching traditions. But it was when the British drummer Trevor Richards (who had moved full-time to New Orleans after our student days playing together in England) suggested that I should meet guitarist, banjoist, singer and raconteur Danny Barker, that I was to learn far more about them. Trevor told me that Danny had been writing an autobiography for years, but apart from a few sections used by the sociologist Jack V. Buerkle in the book *Bourbon Street Black*,[15] with which Danny was not particularly happy, nobody had ever shown any interest in publishing it.

On my next visit to New Orleans, Trevor introduced me to Danny, a charming storyteller and one of the most quick-witted and alert people I have ever met. I visited his tiny clapboard house on Sere Street, and was amazed at the amount of paper and memorabilia crammed into every nook and cranny. Although he had performed music as a child in the area of the former Storyville red light district, Danny had begun his professional career in New Orleans in the late 1920s, playing with the trumpeter Lee Collins. In 1930 he had moved to New York, working with all manner of jazz luminaries from Red Allen to Jelly Roll Morton, and eventually playing in the big bands of Lucky Millinder, Benny Carter and Cab Calloway. In one way or another, he documented every stage of his life and work, and he had also – uniquely among his generation so far as I am aware – gathered information in letters, interviews, questionnaires and photographs from his contemporaries and colleagues. This qualified him for a role at the New Orleans Jazz Museum, which he'd left owing to illness shortly before I met him. He was also an indefatigable educator, establishing the Fairview Brass Band to keep the city's marching traditions alive with a new generation of players.

In 1981, when I took on the role of Music Publisher at Macmillan in London, the idea intrigued me of trying to help Danny get his book out. At the same time, Barry Martyn, another British drummer living in New Orleans, and whom I had met years before with his Legends of Jazz, offered me the manuscript of Barney Bigard's autobiography, which he had been editing. I suggested to the company that it might be possible to produce a small series of jazz lives, and in the end that is what came about, thanks largely to Sheldon Meyer, Editorial Vice-President at Oxford University Press in New York, a huge enthusiast for the music, and already a seasoned publisher of books about jazz, who agreed to underwrite the venture by committing to publish quite sizeable American editions of each book, while the Macmillan version sold in Britain and throughout the rest of the world. We ended up launching a series that also included work by Buck Clayton, Bob Wilber, Art Rollini, and Bill Coleman. When I finally secured a contract for Danny to publish his book, he kindly asked if I would work on it closely with him as his editor.

I have related the full story of how Danny's book *A Life in Jazz* came about in the introduction to the second edition, published by the Historic New Orleans Collection in 2016, which has dozens of additional photographs and several sections of new text, which Danny and I worked on after the original version came out in 1986. That initial edition of the book had involved bringing together three different types of source material: firstly there were some sections that he had written and polished over several decades that just needed minor tweaks, secondly other part-written sections needed to be expanded into fuller chapters, and finally we used taped interviews to fill any gaps in his life story. One aspect of our work that may be a little unusual in terms of oral history books is that we read the whole thing aloud to each other at every stage, so that Danny felt it properly captured his authorial voice. What I did not say in the new edition or in the introduction to our second book, *Buddy Bolden and the Last Days of Storyville*, is that over the last decade of his life, and largely because of the time we spent reading to one another, Danny and I became great friends. We regularly exchanged letters, and during my visits to him in New Orleans while we were working on the original book or planning its sequel (which came out after Danny's death), not only did we sit on the porch of his Sere Street house, listening to music and talking late into the night, evening after evening, but he also took delight in driving me round the city in his large, green, and rather shabby Lincoln, to see places he felt I ought to know about if I had a serious interest in jazz history. We saw Louis Armstrong's birthplace, houses where Buddy Bolden and Don Albert had lived, venues where Sidney Bechet had played, the areas where Danny had grown up and gone to school, and the sites of some of the city's legendary dance halls, clubs and cabarets. In addition he took me to meet and hear musicians, and to find out more about the music and traditions of the city.

The marching societies of Mardi Gras Indians embody one such tradition, and I was pleased that in the new edition of *A Life in Jazz*, my editor Molly Reid and I were able to discover more about the pioneering 'King Zulu' recordings that Danny made, which were the first ever documented recordings of their traditional songs, 'Chocko Mo Feendo Hey', 'Tootie Ma Is A Big Fine Thing', and 'Corinne Died on the Battlefield', together with 'My Indian Red', which Dr John revisited in 1992.

Danny had, in the mountains of paperwork in his little house, mislaid any documentary material relating to the making of these discs, which he produced himself, but Molly diligently researched the background, so that we were able to date them more precisely than earlier discographies, to 1953. While working on the new edition, I looked further into the history of Mardi Gras Indians, and this was prompted by mentions of the trombonist Earl Humphrey, brother of Percy and Willie Humphrey. Earl appears in some of Danny Barker's collection of old photographs of New Orleans musicians from the 1920s, but he happens to be a soloist on the first ever recording to use a title drawn from the secret language of the Indians. As Al Kennedy puts it in his study of this local subculture: 'The tradition honours the American Indians who fed, sheltered and protected the African survivors of the middle passage and their African American descendants who escaped from slavery in Colonial and Ante-Bellum Louisiana ... the enslaved and the American Indians often worked together, fought together, and struggled together to survive.'[16] As Kennedy reports, according to Mardi Gras Indian Big Chief Robbe: 'If a runaway slave made it to the Indians, no slave master was going to look for him there.'

As I mentioned, to this day the Mardi Gras Indians use a secret language, adapted from Creole French, and in March 1927, Louis Dumaine's Jazzola Eight acknowledged it in the title of 'To-wa-bac-a-wa', on which Earl Humphrey plays. The tune is basically the old standard 'My Bucket's Got A Hole In It'. The title derives from the Creole term 'Touez pas quais' – 'Kill anyone who blocks your way ...' The title, now attached to a different tune, lives on, as Big Chief Donald Harrison (father of the bebop saxophonist of the same name) demonstrated on the 1992 album *Indian Blues*.[17]

When I was talking to Danny after the original appearance of *A Life in Jazz*, we got onto the subject of the Mardi Gras Indian societies back in the 1930s, that have little more than a passing mention in the first edition. They'd been violent, prone to gang warfare and based in the Uptown area of the city. Here's what he told me about their principal leader: 'The man who brought about a change was Brother Tillman, who was the chief of the Indians uptown. I think he was a cousin of the sousaphone player Wilbert Tillman, from the Young Tuxedo Brass Band. He had a big reputation, because the police called him in and said, "If you're going to amass, then you've gotta be licensed. You've gotta have identification, and if any of your Indians get into trouble, then you report it to the police." And Brother Tillman did what they asked, and so now they don't fight any more, and carnival day itself is beautiful.'[18]

The Creole society from which Danny and his Barbarin cousins hailed was Downtown – in the French Quarter of the original city of New Orleans – but it was Uptown that spawned the most famous Mardi

Gras Indian societies. It's no accident that Clarke Peters played a Mardi Gras Indian chief in the HBO TV series named after the area known as *Tremé* – it is their heartland. As Al Kennedy says: 'The intersection of Orleans and Claiborne Avenues was a central location for the New Orleans African American community's Mardi Gras activities and the Mardi Gras Indians gathered there.'[19] Trombone Shorty – one of the city's younger stars – commemorates this in his 2005 record *Orleans and Claiborne*.

As Danny suggested, Brother Tillman, who helped bring in registration and permits for parades, and who helped keep the casualty departments of the local hospitals clear during Mardi Gras, was the dominant figure in the Indian societies in the 1930s and 1940s. Prior to his work, the NOPD tried to prevent parades. As Donald Harrison told Al Kennedy: 'The police didn't want us on the streets . . . we had to go to the backstreets, but we persisted. They put us in jail. They would beat us up. They would shoot us. And they would kill us. This is the truth, but every year we say: "We're going out there anyhow. We know what we got to run into."'[20] There was a strong racist element in the NOPD's attitude, and Big Chiefs Tillman, Harrison and Robbe have all in various sources described marching as a tradition of resistance, akin to the Civil Rights movement. But Kennedy also talks of how under Tillman's guidance the members 'learned techniques of singing and sewing', and there's a parallel here to Muhal Richard Abrams' work with the AACM (the Association for the Advancement of Creative Musicians), using engagement in the arts to quell the social unrest of the 1960s race riots in Chicago. Al Kennedy discusses the ritual roles of the Indians: the spy boy who precedes the parade, flag boy who carries the colours, almost like a regimental standard-bearer strutting before the Big Chief, and finally there's the Wild Man, who runs hither and yon clearing the road. Some societies have a trail chief protecting the rear. It's not a male-only business, because Big Queen accompanies the Big Chief along with her acolytes, and 'Tootie Ma' in Danny's song is a female marcher, if also, as he would have said, a 'do-wrong' character.

When rival tribes meet, it is the spy boys who encounter each other first and there's a ritual choreography for this to work well – if it's ignored, things tend to work badly and end in confusion. No physical contact is the current rule. And the lyrics are usually improvised on the spot, embodying a mixture of tradition and a role akin to a hip-hop MC. It was Danny Barker who first recorded the way these terms were codified into the traditional song 'My Indian Red', which focuses on the big chief, and the fact 'we don't bow down, on nobody's ground'.

> *Here comes the spy boy,*
> *The flag boy*
> *But watch that crazy wild man*
> *The wildest in the low lands,*
> *And we love our queen,*
> *Queen of New Orleans,*
> *Oh how we love to hear you call us Indian*
> *Red.*[21]

Big Chief Donald Harrison was to the 1970s, 1980s and early 1990s what Brother Tillman had been in the 1930s and 1940s. Al Kennedy and the other notable historian to have written on this subject, the photographer Michael P. Smith, both of whom were researching after Barker's death, found Harrison to be a fount of knowledge similar to my experience with Danny. And it's notable that on the previously mentioned album *Indian Blues*[22] made with Dr John and his son Donald Harrison, Big Chief Harrison references exactly the same characters of the march as Danny had done forty years earlier. These Spy Boys, Wild Men, Flag Men, Chiefs and Big Queens amount collectively to what Michael P. Smith calls an astonishing store of cultural memory.[23]

Al Kennedy and Michael Smith have both proposed the theory that the long-established tradition of having a 'second line' marching alongside a New Orleans Brass Band funeral or celebratory parade owes its existence to the Mardi Gras Indians, and that these additional marchers originally took on a protective role. Looking back at the early 1900s, when he was still living in the city, Jelly Roll Morton recalled the way the second line eased the transition between neighbourhoods, crossing the 'dividing line', saying: 'They'd have a second line behind 'em, well, maybe a couple of blocks long, with broomsticks, baseball bats and all forms of ammunition, we'd call it, to combat some of their foe when they come to the – to the dividing line. And of course they'd start. The band would get started. They'd hear the drums.'[24] Morton goes on to explain how the original second lines protected the marchers. 'You see, whenever a parade would get to another district the enemy would be waiting at the dividing line. If the parade crossed that line, it meant a fight, a terrible fight.'[25]

By the late 1930s and publication of Ramsey and Smith's *Jazzmen*, Brother Tillman had done his community relations work, and the book mentions the second line 'dancing along' behind the musicians and the Indians, but as Michael Smith points out, 'In days past second lines were more often functional: they allowed safe passage (safety in numbers) to and from the city, or provided a means to cross town through unfriendly territory, allowing visits between friendly urban villages separated by a hostile population.'[26]

The Mardi Gras Indians tradition was just one element of New Orleans and its music that I worked on with Danny Barker. Many other aspects of the city's musical life are covered in the two books we did together.

4 TWO WOMEN OF NEW ORLEANS

While I was putting the finishing touches to our second book, *Buddy Bolden and the Last Days of Storyville,* for press in 1997, it was after Danny's death. So I spent a lot of time with his widow, Blue Lu Barker, thanks to his daughter Sylvia, who opened the family house and her father's memorabilia to me, just as Danny himself had done. Lu had been present for many of our earlier meetings, although she was often bedridden, so she left most of the conversations to Danny. Talking to her again, I realized that very little of her own story had been told. So I asked her to look back at her life, as a singer who achieved national fame with records for both the Decca and the Capitol labels as well as the more specialist Apollo imprint.[1]

She was born Louise Dupont, on 13 November 1913 in New Orleans. 'When I was a little girl,' she recalled, 'our favourite game was "concert". One day we were playing this, and I was singing a blues. There was a lady there, standing up listening, and she was giving a real concert that Sunday. She said, "I'm going to ask your Mamma, could you sing in my concert?" I said that would be all right, so she went and asked my mother. She agreed, so I went that Sunday and sang – just me and the piano player. From then on, I started singing in other people's concerts, and in yards, and things like that. But then when I got to about eleven, my mother told me I couldn't sing those blues songs no more. Because people would think I knew what I was talking about!

'So I went from singing to dancing, when we moved from around here to the Tremé.[2] Soon someone asked, "D'you wanna be in a concert?" I said, "I'm not allowed to sing, but I can dance!" So I was a dancer, and was until I went to New York, where I started singing again. I had a partner, Odette De L'Isle. We danced together, doing tap dancing, and I did the "Georgia Grind", shaking down to the floor! The people would throw money. You might get $3.50 for a concert, plus what they threw at you. And if they liked what you was doing, they threw more money! When the curtain fell, they'd go pick up the money, and then it'd be a big argument, because us girls would say, "They didn't give us all our money. They've cheated us!" After that I never went back to dancing, but when I'm on the stage, I move. I'm not flat footed, and in between the songs I'd be out there moving.'

She went to New York in September 1930, having married Danny, on 8 January that year, aged just sixteen, following three long years of courtship. (Some of his affectionate letters to her from that time are included in the 2016 edition of *A Life in Jazz*.) Her train journey from New Orleans to New York took two days and a night, and she was chaperoned by the clarinettist Lorenzo Tio, then 36 years old, and making the move back to Manhattan (where he had worked in the 1920s with Armand J. Piron) to settle there permanently. Blue Lu had no idea how long the journey would take, but starting just an hour or two away from New Orleans, every so often she would ask Tio if there was far to go. Each time he said 'Not far yet. Nearly there.' So – with no idea where she was, or when they would arrive – twenty hours away from New York City she ate the last of the food her mother had given her. All journey long, she clutched a parcel close to her, which was wrapped in newspaper and tied tight with thread. She still clutched it when they changed in Washington DC from the segregated carriage from the South onto the train to New York on which African Americans and white passengers were allowed to mix – something she had never seen before in her life. She was met at Penn Station in Manhattan by Danny and his uncle Paul Barbarin (the drummer with Luis Russell).

'What's in the parcel?' asked Paul.

'I don't know, but it must be mighty important,' said Tio.

It was her favourite doll. Although she was a bride, she was still practically a child.[3]

Danny, who had gone north a few months ahead of Lu, was playing gigs with whomsoever would hire him when he first arrived in New York. He soon encouraged Lu to sing to his accompaniment, which they would do when he was not working with another band, up to the time he permanently joined Lucky Millinder's Orchestra in 1937. 'Some fella said to Danny that I ought to go make an audition, and maybe make some records,' she recalled. 'So [the following year] I was called to go to work. I found my way to the studio, which was the Decca studio. Cozy Cole was there, and Erskine Butterfield, because it was his date. He was trying out a Hammond organ, and they were trying out me. They asked if I knew "A-Tisket A-Tasket", because during that time Ella [Fitzgerald] had put out a record of it. I knew the song, because I'd known it since I was a little child – we used to play the game of A-Tisket A-Tasket. When it came time for me to sing, although I'd sung with a piano, or a guitar, I'd never sung with no horns, but the A and R man gave me a sign when to come in. Nevertheless it took us from nine to twelve to make one side. But a week later, and at that time they used to say that record companies often used to steal talent from one session to another, Decca called me and they gave me a contract! And that's how I came to make "Don't You Feel My Leg" in 1938.'[4]

This song, with its risqué lyric, is the reason (according to most musicians I spoke to) that Lu acquired her nickname of 'Blue' Lu – having much more to do with the innuendo of this (and her other songs) than the blues. She always, rather coyly, denied this, but the message of the penultimate line of the chorus was unequivocal:

> If you feel my leg, you'll want to feel my thigh, and if you feel my thigh, you'll wanna move up high ...

That session from 11 August 1938 was made just after Danny had left Lucky Millinder and he was working on and off with Benny Carter's band, which was mainly active in and around New York. So, being in the city, he was able both to play on and to organize Blue Lu's first sessions for the label. Indeed Carter himself played the trumpet on the first recordings.[5] He was a good friend of Danny's, and in 1938 they were living just a block away from each other.

'Danny'd get all the musicianers,' Lu said. 'All I had to do was turn up and sing. A lot of people would bring tunes to the company, and if I liked them I'd do them, but if I didn't like a song I didn't have to do it. He got all the good musicianers, and in the studio I never drank nothing. I couldn't drink and sing, because I was always scared I'd forget the words. By that time I was doing a bit of singing in clubs, on 52nd Street, where I would always be the extra "added attraction". And we'd get extra jobs, a lotta house parties, things like that, just me and Danny. After a while we had a trio, but if they wanted a seven-piece, then he would find it, and do the job. There were a lot of singers there and everybody was trying to make it. On our jobs, those people in New York didn't go for blues, so I sang popular songs and standards. But for the records I had to sing blues. They could get somebody else to sing those other songs, but I sang blues for the Race Records.

'On those discs Sammy Price played the piano, and there was [Wellman] Braud on bass, and on some of them we had Henry Allen, that's Red Allen, on trumpet.' When we talked, Blue Lu was not too happy about the issue in 1980 of the compilation LP *Red Allen and the Blues Singers* on the Jazz Archives label, where four of her tracks are included alongside Frankie 'Half Pint' Jaxon, Lee Brown and Johnny Temple. She felt the company had unfairly made Allen the star whereas back in the 1930s, she was emphatic that *she* had been the star. She saw this as an example of putting a male jazz musician on the LP cover, rather than (in her case) the singer who was originally identified with the music. 'I didn't say nothing to the company,' she said, 'but I hope his son got the money!'

She knew Allen well, because when she and Danny first came to New York, they stayed for a year or two in a three-bedroom apartment on 136th Street with both Paul Barbarin and Henry Allen and their wives. 'We were friends with all of them until they died,' said Lu. 'And with Little Henry Allen, Red Allen's son. I christened him. And he always sent me a card on Mother's day, Valentine's Day, Christmas Day. Paul Barbarin's wife was a good New Orleans cook, a Creole cook. Allen's wife was a good cook too, and they took it in turns to teach me how to cook. One would prepare the meal on the first day, one on the second, and on the third I'd cook and one of them would sit down and tell me what to do. So we always ate at home. And in that apartment I met people like Al Morgan and Pops Foster, when they came up from New Orleans to New York.

'But I was just a little girl to them. They would come and talk to Red Allen and Paul, and I'd just sit and listen in this big high chair in the living room. But I could never get in the conversation, because they didn't even know I was there! But one day the four of them were together talking and one of them said, "They've got a new dance out called the Cody."

'So I suddenly said, "I know how to do the Cody."

'Pops said, "How old are you?"

'I said, "Sixteen."

'He said "What d'you know about the Cody?"'

'I said, "I know how to dance it."'

'So he said, "Get up and show us!" Well it wasn't nothing but three steps and a dip, so I got up and showed them. They asked where I'd learned, and I said in New Orleans. But you danced that with a partner, and I told them how they used to sneak me into the dance halls back home. They'd dress me up and I had plenty of hair, so when I got to the ticket man, they'd start pushing the queue and I'd be pushed away from the ticket man so he didn't get a good look at me being under age. I was there so that other men didn't dance with somebody's girlfriend too long. They'd have to dance with me, so I knew all about the dances. And that was the first time those musicians in New York talked to me, because before that, they just hadn't noticed me. But I had to be careful not to talk to other musicianers once Danny had said, "Meet my wife". Because if he thought I was too friendly with any of them, he wouldn't call them no more. He'd get jealous. But it wasn't like that with the Barbarins and the Allens.'

This is a good illustration of how the New Orleans musicians lived and stayed together in 1930s New York. When I worked with the Arkansas-born trombonist Snub Mosley, on a UK tour in 1980, he told me how when he had been in Luis Russell's band, supporting Louis Armstrong in 1936, he had felt squeezed out socially by the tight New Orleans 'clique' in the group. This was mainly Allen, Barbarin, Russell, and Pops Foster, who, when they were on the road, ate together, roomed together and generally hung out together, at – as he saw it – the expense of the other musicians. (As an aside I should mention that for my first session with Snub, a pub gig in Hampshire, playing to a local audience, he turned up wearing a formal tuxedo and a fur bow tie. He played trombone beautifully, sang his hit song – which he co-wrote with Mary Lou Williams – 'Pretty Eyed Baby' and treated us to 'Moonlight in Vermont' played on his own invention, the slide saxophone, which was rather like a glorified Swanee whistle with a soprano sax mouthpiece!)

The comedienne Moms Mabley lived in the next-door house to the Barkers, Barbarins and Allens. There was a pulley line for drying washing that ran from Lu's window to directly outside Moms' apartment. 'I had flannelette underwear and cotton undergarments my mother had made,' recalled Lu. 'When I unpacked my trunk, Henry's and Paul's wives told me to put them away, because they weren't the kind of thing "show people" would hang on their line and it would embarrass them with Moms. I should get something more like they wore. They were small, and I was fat! But they still made me send my trousseau back home that my mother had made for me.'

For Blue Lu's first two recording sessions, Danny Barker didn't just pick the band members, he contributed several of the tunes. 'Danny wrote "That Made Him Mad",' recalled Blue Lu. 'Him and I wrote "Don't You Make Me High" together. The title we put on it was "Don't You Feel My Leg", but in those days that was vulgar, so Decca made it "Don't You Make Me High". We made an audition with that song in the Cotton Club, and everybody liked it. Bojangles' wife she was laughing, and so was everyone, and they thought we had the job, see. But then he [Bojangles] came from the back and got mad, saying how could we sing that kind of stuff in front of his wife? She clammed up and said nothing. I think he was afraid he'd have competition if they hired me. But Cab Calloway needed a banjo and guitar player, he'd heard the audition, and he hired Danny. That's how Danny came to join Cab's band. And then Danny went away and we didn't have much chance to work together. But we had our daughter Sylvia by then [who was born in 1935],[6] so I didn't do much work, I just stayed at home with Sylvia.'

Although Danny was often away with Calloway, he only missed one of Blue Lu's Decca sessions, on which Ulysses Livingstone played guitar, and where Sammy Price's place was temporarily taken by Lil Armstrong. When he left Cab in 1946, Danny started doing regular gigs with Blue Lu again, and their trio re-formed. They also returned to the studios that year for Apollo and re-made several of their earlier songs, with some of Danny's former Calloway colleagues such as trumpeter Shad Collins and saxophonist Teddy McRae in the backing band.

Things were, as Blue Lu put it, 'not so hot' at that point as the big bands were breaking up and bebop was taking hold in jazz clubs. So, keeping on their New York apartment, which by this time was in a brownstone in the Bronx, they went first back to New Orleans, and then in late 1948 to Los Angeles, California. 'We were there about eight months,' recalled Blue Lu. 'Then we came back to New Orleans, and then we took our band bus and went back to New York. But I made some records for Capitol in Los Angeles. One of them was "Here's a Little Girl". Another girl singer made a record of it, but Capitol sent it to me and told me to copy it. Well I copied it, but I raised the tempo. And within three weeks I was overriding her sales. Her company said they were going to put someone from Capitol in jail. We read that in the paper, and that they were going to sue Capitol for taking the tune. People were calling me up telling me I might go to jail too, but I didn't know nothing about it. They give me the record date today, I make my record tomorrow, and forget about it. But it sold so well I was in *Billboard*. And in those days if you made *Billboard*, you were *some-body*! I didn't really like California, because the show people were not so friendly as they were in New York. All I really did in California was make records. When we came back to New Orleans, Capitol came down and recorded me here. Danny found the musicianers. Paul Barbarin was here. He played on them and we did quite a bit of work in and around New Orleans – that's when we had the band bus – but in the end we were glad to get back to our home in New York. We worked again there and I remember once we were back, I used to have to wash the band shirts! We had rehearsals, we had the trio, and Herbie Nichols played piano for us at one time.'[7]

Blue Lu and Danny moved back to New Orleans for good in 1965, and she resumed her singing career at the city's first jazz festival. This took place at the Municipal Auditorium in 1968, a couple of years before George Wein began producing the annual Jazz and Heritage Festival at the Fairgrounds. 'After Wein took it on, I played the jazz festival every year from 1974 until 1986,' she told me. In her later years she was practically bedridden, but even in 1974 she was having problems with her legs. Yet she recalled that – in common with Cousin Joe – she often needed to be helped up on to the stage, but once there she forgot all about the pain, walked to the mike, started singing and even danced a few steps. 'Then when I got off, they gotta help me get off the stage again! That's what happens with show business, you forget all those pains, until after it is over. Danny was the same. Often he was sick, but he'd go play a job, be fine, and then be sick again when it was over.'

In those years, although she often worked with Danny, she also sang with Papa French and with clarinettist Louis Cottrell. She also recalled that during a flying visit to New Orleans when Danny's father was taken ill, in 1954 or 1955, before Larry Borenstein's art gallery on St Peter's Street became Preservation Hall, she and Danny had played a party there for an exhibition opening with another all-star collection of local players including George Lewis and Slow Drag Pavageau. The band was set up in what is now the entrance carriageway alongside the hall, and the exhibition was in what is now the performance space, which in those days opened directly onto the sidewalk. The art show featured newly designed clothing as well as paintings. While Lu sang, people put money into a kitty for the band, as they subsequently would do when the Hall began. Borenstein distributed the takings among the musicians, and completely forgot to pay her. He was mortified and, dashing back into the exhibition, came out carrying a new skirt from one of the displays, which he gave her in lieu of money. She still had it and proudly showed me, over forty years later.

This snapshot into Blue Lu's life shows a much more sporadic career than that of her husband, not least because she was mother to Sylvia and had to take care of her from the 1930s to the 1950s. But she achieved a level of national fame that very few women in jazz managed in the 1930s and 1940s and her records have remained in print and available. Unlike Sweet Emma Barrett, the Goodson sisters and Jeanette Kimball, she travelled away from New Orleans and this helped her career greatly.

Blue Lu mentioned that she had sung at every edition of the New Orleans Jazz and Heritage Festival from 1974 to 1986, and there's no doubt that this event acts as an international showcase for local talent. Another singer for whom this was the case is Topsy Chapman, who covers almost every style from gospel via traditional jazz to contemporary music. She travelled to Europe in the 1980s with the revue *One Mo' Time*, and subsequently she became a firm favourite at many international events, but the festival in her home town holds a special place in her affections, because it led to her international career. The year I talked to her there, 2002, she had been at the Fairgrounds in a semi-staged revue very similar to *One Mo' Time*.

'It's getting bigger and bigger every year,' she said.[8] 'And we have people coming here from places you'd never believe or even imagine, including lots of little small towns that we haven't heard of in the United States, they come from everywhere. That *One Mo' Time* show actually got me started doing the traditional-type music. But before that show, where they found me was in the gospel tent here. But everything stems from the gospel stuff anyway, the gospel and blues kind of thing, from back in the '20s. Actually I'm still singing in the gospel tent as well, this year, along with my family. And I still do the jazz things too.

'I started singing gospel in the house where I grew up. You could not sing any other music except gospel – my father wouldn't allow it. Of course, when we went to school, he allowed us to do projects there because our teachers had us doing things that covered other kinds of music. I used to do Mary Wells stuff and my brother used to do Sam Cooke's material, that we would always get trophies for. And I played piano for myself, doing songs like "Please Mr. Postman", back in the '60s. When I came to New Orleans, at maybe 17 or 18 years old, my brothers and their wives were already here and we formed a gospel group together, which was after I left Kentwood, Louisiana, where I grew up. We were called the Chapman singers and we used to go and perform at the Jazz Festival. We used to sing in local churches before we did the festival, but somebody saw us and asked if we'd like to be part of it. We said yes, and that's how it began. We had no idea the festival would be so big like this, today.

'I was the leader of the group. Vernel Bagneris [who devised and starred in *One Mo' Time*] said he passed the tent where I was singing and said to himself, "That's the voice I'm lookin' for." The festival in those days, when it started was like a family. A small family – like a man and a woman getting married and maybe having one child. And then later on this man finds himself with his children, their children, like five or six different generations of kids and he's still alive watching it! That's what it looks like today: a huge family of people, because actually we are all family. Even the tourists who come in seem like family because we've been knowing each other for so many years! And the ones who've not been here before, they make themselves known, and then the next year they're also like family, so it just grows and grows.'

I had first met Topsy at the first night party for the London production of *One Mo' Time* at the Cambridge Theatre in London in 1981, not long after Vernel Bagneris had spotted her talent in the gospel tent. That show featured her alongside Vernel and Sylvia Kuumba Williams, plus a band (led by the Swedish pianist Lars Edegran) that included Walter Payton Jr, the veteran swing trumpeter Bill Dillard, and the young drummer Herlin Riley, who would go on to be a cornerstone of Wynton Marsalis' many bands from the 1980s to the 2010s. It so happened that on the first night, the Preservation Hall Jazz Band had been playing at the Royal Festival Hall in London, and so they turned up for the party too, and we had a very convivial evening as those of us in Mike Casimir's band (which had been hired to play for the party) had the chance to jam with Percy and Willie Humphrey, pianist Sing Miller, and members of the *One Mo' Time* cast. It is the only occasion I recall Percy Humphrey standing up to sing a blues in front of the band.

A year later, in September 1982, also with Mike Casimir's band, I was playing with the New Orleans trombonist Louis Nelson at the Empress of Russia pub in Clerkenwell in London. Again the Preservation Hall Band was in town, but this time it was just clarinettist Willie Humphrey who trekked across the city to see his old friend. Although his show at the Festival Hall was over, ours had yet to begin, because we were in what was normally one of London's oldest Irish folk clubs and the deal was that the jazz would start after a set of Irish traditional music. Willie Humphrey and Louis Nelson sat in the front row watching the performance intently. I was just behind them when I saw Willie jab Nelson excitedly in the ribs, during a beautiful rendition of 'Kathleen Mavourneen, the grey dawn is breaking.'

'See,' he said, 'they don't just play jazz in British pubs!' I realized his entire experience of the UK was being carted from jazz club to jazz club, and he had never experienced the full range of music that could be heard in the back rooms or upstairs halls of public houses across the country. It was a good reciprocal wake-up call for a European jazz critic to realize that, just as a visiting American musician like Willie Humphrey may never get to grips with the UK music scene, it's hard to do more than scratch the surface of what a place like New Orleans has to offer.

5 FINDING FATS

My experiences in New Orleans led me to start exploring the swing era, aiming to play somewhat more mainstream jazz, and trying to back that up by finding out as much as I could from the generation that created the music. After starting work with Danny Barker on his autobiography, he began putting me in touch with other musicians who were either already working on memoirs, or planning to do so. They were almost all swing players, whom he had known during his time with Lucky Millinder, Benny Carter, or Cab Calloway, plus others he met later, in the 1950s, before moving back to New Orleans.

There were some failures. I was unable to broker a co-publication deal for saxophonist Eddie Barefield's memoirs, which made his book financially unviable, and a letter I wrote in early 1989 to Roy Eldridge about his fledgling manuscript was returned unopened, as he died before it could be delivered. Trevor Richards brought me some fascinating segments of the New Orleans drummer Ray Bauduc's life story, covering his career with Bob Crosby, and written in slanting capitals on yellow legal pads. Sadly it was not completed before Ray's death in 1988. The fact that Trevor left a set of Ray's cymbals under my stairs for six months, between visits to the UK, didn't quite make up for never seeing a finished book!

The successes far outweighed the failures, as I tried to follow up the suggestion of the British critic, author and record producer Albert McCarthy, in his book *Big Band Jazz,* that it was important to capture as many full-length musicians' memoirs in print as possible, before it was too late. I was glad to be able to publish (albeit posthumously) the memoirs of Bill Coleman, after his widow sent me the original English text for his book *Trumpet Story*, which had been somewhat attenuated in the French edition that came out during his lifetime. It was a privilege to work on pianist Art Hodes' memoirs, and we corresponded for quite a while after meeting in England. And it was equally fulfilling to produce the UK edition of the wonderful swing saxophonist Bud Freeman's autobiography *Crazeology*. I'd got to know him when he briefly lived in Britain, as an habitué of John Kendall's second-hand record shop in the basement of Dobell's on Charing Cross Road. I played a gig or two with him in London, and sitting next to him once on a plane to Holland en route to a festival, Bud revealed an ability to recite Shakespeare's sonnets every bit as accomplished as Ken Colyer's recall of Kipling. I always had the feeling on stage that every number he played was about to mutate into his set-piece 'The Eel', but Bud was always great company and the hours we spent chatting and listening to records in Kendall's basement (in between Bud nipping out to put a bet on his preferred tip from that day's *Racing Post*) were truly memorable. He had a knack of bringing characters from the Austin High School Gang and the swing era circles of Benny Goodman and Eddie Condon vividly to life.

It was also through Danny Barker that I first made contact with trumpeter Buck Clayton, whose remarkable career took him from pioneering days leading an African American band in Shanghai, via the Count Basie Orchestra, numerous records with Billie Holiday and his own 1950s Jam Sessions, to becoming a much-loved teacher and arranger, as well as directing his latter-day Swing Band in weekly Greenwich Village sessions. When I first contacted Buck and his co-writer Nancy Miller Elliott in New York, they felt their book was done, but although it was very atmospherically written, the manuscript stopped in the early 1970s when Buck's lip troubles forced him to abandon playing the trumpet, only to be followed by a serious illness. The book ended as he left the ICU after a life and death struggle, facing an uncertain future. I suggested to Buck that he should bring the story up to date, explaining to readers how he had reinvented himself once he could no longer play, and ending on the very positive note of his successful later career as an arranger and bandleader.

Buck, with Nancy's enthusiastic help, duly did so, and as the final chapters took shape, we became good friends in the process. During and after our work on the book, Buck would always meet me on my regular visits to New York, either just to get together for a drink and a chat, or to go and hear some music. Together we heard some fine sessions with the likes of Ruby Braff, John Bunch, Tal Farlow, Milt Hinton and Sweets Edison, and we had some great interval and post-gig conversations with other friends he invited along, including Jack Lesberg, Bennie Powell and Joe Newman.

When we just met for a drink, Buck loved the bar at the Grand Hyatt, at Grand Central Station on East 42nd Street, as from a seat just inside its huge two storey windows, one could look down on all of Manhattan's busy sidewalk life bustling past. He'd love to point out passers by and we'd try to guess who they were, what they did and where they were going – a game the Basie band had enjoyed when it was on the road in Buck's younger days. In London on one occasion, just after his book came out, Buck also introduced me to another Basie band pastime, namely 'rug-spotting'. Playing theatres and dances and egged on by Lester Young who was one of the founders of the game, the band awarded one another points for identifying those in the audience who were wearing wigs or toupées. At the very smart London restaurant where we'd gone to celebrate publication, Buck appeared to be having trouble reading the menu. The waiter kept bending forward to help him and Buck later confessed that he hoped one of the ceiling fans would blow the man's toupée off onto the table.

Knowing about this game was an instant ice-breaker when I later interviewed Harry 'Sweets' Edison for the first time, and I asked him if he had been sent to jail for dislodging a diner's hairpiece at another table by throwing a bagel across a restaurant. It was, of course, true and Harry burst out laughing, and told me I was 'a very well-informed young man'. He then gave me a generous and thoughtful interview that ranged well beyond the music he was publicizing at the time.

In the late 1980s, as I mentioned, Buck was leading his Swing Band, which played quite regularly at the Village Vanguard, and was a vehicle for his latter-day arrangements.[1] It was a sizeable group, with four reeds, three trumpets and two trombones, plus rhythm, and he successfully brought the whole band to Europe during the last year of his life in 1991.[2] By then, it was very much a contemporary swing orchestra of the 1990s, but whenever I heard it, I hankered for the cleaner, harder-swinging sound of the smaller groups that Buck had brought to Europe in the 1950s and 1960s, with the likes of Emmett Berry, Earle Warren,

Buddy Tate, and Dicky Wells, plus Buck's childhood friend Sir Charles Thompson on piano.[3] When Buck died in December 1991, Nancy Miller Elliott contacted me, and in due course she handed over a box of his sheet music, with a message from Buck saying 'You kept my memory alive with the book, maybe you can do the same with my music?'

The box was bursting with lead sheets, band parts and full scores. But as everything seemed to have been written for a slightly different line-up, it wasn't going to be easy to put it into some kind of order, let alone create a band to play it. In due course I worked with the brilliant German saxophonist Matthias Seuffert (a specialist in older styles of jazz, who was temporarily living in the UK) to select the most suitable pieces from the amorphous collection of repertoire, and he re-arranged them from Buck's original manuscripts into a consistent set of parts for an eight- or nine-piece band, with the intention of achieving a sound as close as we could get to Clayton's touring group of the 1960s. We launched the project at the 2004 Ascona Festival in Switzerland, with the great French trumpeter Patrick Artero taking on Buck's role, but after a few isolated concerts, it took us until 2011 to settle into a regular line-up, with Menno Daams from Amsterdam joining us in place of Patrick, who by then was working with Claude Bolling's big band.[4] Since its first national UK tour in 2011, the band has played all over Britain and Europe – including a memorable session in Breda, Holland, with our special guests trumpeter Randy Sandke and trombonist Dan Barrett, who had been members of Buck's own Swing Band. Another highlight, in 2017, was bringing Buck's music to Tomasz Stańko's *Jazzowa Jesień w Bielsku-Białej* festival in Poland. In 2019 we played in Limoges, where Buck – a frequent visitor to the city from 1949 onwards – had been honorary president of the local Hot Club. For the occasion, Menno produced a new full band arrangement of 'Mes Amis de Limoges', which we premiered there (Figure 3). Years before, Buck had sketched out a lead sheet, dedicated to the club and to his great friend, its long-term president Jean-Marie Masse. We were gratified that the current president of the Hot Club, Alain Charbonnier, who had been a good friend of Buck's, later wrote: 'The musicians all played their roles perfectly, whether in the blowing ensembles, in the rhythm section, or in their solos.'[5]

Many of the conversations I had with Buck in New York turned sooner or later to Count Basie, and he was always keen to remind me

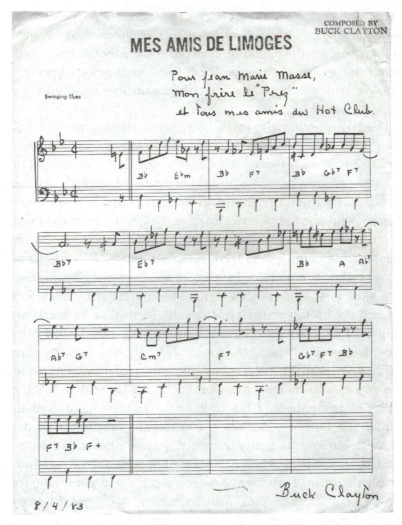

Figure 3 Lead sheet for 'Mes Amis de Limoges', courtesy Fonds Paulette and Jean-Marie Masse, Bibliothèque francophone multimedia de Limoges

that Basie had at one point had a few informal lessons from Fats Waller. It turns out that one thing Buck and I had in common, despite the forty-two-year difference in our ages, was that both our fathers had introduced us to Waller's music. 'My father had a little liking for jazz,' recalled Buck, 'and his favourite jazzman was Fats Waller. "Jus' listen to old Fats play this," or "Just listen to ol' Fats play that."'[6] We laughed a lot about how we'd listened to some of the same records from the start of Waller's career, often with almost the same paternal commentary, and somehow or other Buck convinced me that I ought to write a book about Fats myself. I loved the way Waller's little six-piece group, the Rhythm, just oozed propulsive swing. I already knew a little about him from reading the biographies by Charles Fox, Joel Vance, Ed Kirkeby and Waller's son Maurice, but I resolved both to attempt to talk to as many of the surviving musicians I could find who had worked with him and to try to get to grips with what made his music swing so infectiously.

I had already met guitarist Al Casey, who had the longest continuous career of any of the original members of the Waller recording group. By 1986, when I began the book, he had played in Britain several times. I'd been lucky enough to work with him on numerous concerts during a couple of those visits. His relaxed four-to-the-bar comping, played on an amplified instrument rather than the acoustic guitar he'd used on Fats' records, was a great first-hand introduction to learning some of the skills of swing era playing. He made everything seem effortless, and it was easy to lock on to his flawless timing and work with him as a team, marking the stylistic move away from the drums as taking the dominant rhythm section role, and passing the baton to guitar and bass. As time went on, I got to know Al better, and whenever we talked about Fats, he was always keen to emphasize the wonderful opportunity that Fats had given him, by bringing him into the group as a teenager. When – much later – we eventually sat down in Al's Manhattan apartment for a formal interview, this is where he began.

'I was originally from Kentucky, and there I had three uncles and an aunt that had a singing group called the Southern Singers. They'd done pretty well, they even came to New York, and they knew Fats because they'd worked with him in Cincinnati on a radio programme, called *Dream River*, every midnight.[7] When they came to New York, they got known here, working with Fats on WAEF, and others of those old AM stations. Then my grandmother decided to bring me to New York, so I came here. The group took me to Fats' house – he was living on Edgecombe Avenue – and they told him I played a little guitar. He said, "Come again, bring your guitar, and we'll play a little bit." I got here in 1930, and that would have been back in '33 or '34. And it was like an audition. I didn't really know what I was doing, but he said, "Okay – you're on my next record date at Victor!" So I did the date, and, thank God, it caught on. I was still in school,[8] but I recorded with him on all the record dates. Then I got that feeling about wanting to go on the road – that happens to you in music, you know – and he said "No! You show me a diploma, and then you've got a job on the road." But in the meantime, I was still recording with him.'

Over many conversations, I realized that because Al Casey was still a student when he joined Waller's band, he did not know too much of the background to its formation. Al was also a diplomat, and although on our UK tours we talked long into the night on journeys back from gigs across the country, he tended to keep his stronger opinions to himself, although he did once tell me that the only way to cope with being billeted in the soulless new town development of Basingstoke for a fortnight during one of his UK tours was to drink vodka in the daytime.

The thing that really clinched our friendship, however, was when my wife and I promoted an extra concert in our local village hall during one of his tours. We were worried that ticket sales would not cover the fees for the musicians, so we organized a raffle, and Al agreed to draw the winning tickets. The proceeds of the raffle far exceeded our expectations, until we realized that one of our enthusiastic volunteers had sold the stubs as well as the tickets, so we actually had nothing left for him to pick out of the hat. I had to let Al in on the secret. He found it extremely amusing and with a completely straight face, drew out blank pieces of paper, and appearing to peer closely at each one, announced the 'winning' numbers. He feigned surprise when more than one person appeared to have a successful ticket – but it meant we dispatched the prizes in double quick time and nobody seemed any the wiser. After this, as we travelled about, Al opened up on many subjects in a way that he hadn't before, including confiding in me about his crush on Lena Horne, which had been reciprocated, but he seldom volunteered more memories of his Waller experiences.

Consequently, to explore more of the background to Waller's recording group, I made contact through Buck Clayton (who had worked for a while at the American Federation of Musicians Local 802 branch in New York, and as a result had a huge circle of acquaintances) with drummer Harry Dial. He, like Al, had played on Fats' very first session by the Rhythm, in 1934. It was a chill October day in 1986 when I set off from midtown on the M4 bus to meet him. I was heading to 160th Street, and the large apartment block at 555 Edgecombe Avenue. In 1939, Harry had been one of the first African Americans to move into 555, an imposing building constructed in 1914–16, which had originally been restricted to white residents. The neighbouring park is named after the block's designer, the former British army officer Roger Morris. Once the colour bar had been broken, 555 attracted prestigious tenants, and swiftly became home to a number of celebrated Black artists and musicians, including such luminaries as bandleaders Count Basie and Andy Kirk. It had – at the time of my visit – quite recently become generally known as the 'Paul Robeson Residence' after another famous occupant.

Harry was immediately, and unreservedly, charming and helpful. He said he was happy to do anything for 'a jazz friend'. He began by filling in his own backstory, explaining how he had begun his career as a musician: 'When I started out I was one of those trick drummers, throwing up the sticks and catching them behind me, or bouncing them off the floor, and all that stuff. I had more rhythm than the other drummers that were doing that. But I left all of that in St Louis, where I was raised and started playing. After that I began to study music, and understand what rhythm really means, and that's what I put into practice when I came here to New York, via Camden, New Jersey, in 1934, after playing in the Walkathon with Ira Coffey[9] ... I've always been noted as a swinging drummer, and after I learned and understood what rhythm is, I played for the support of the guys I was playing with. I didn't play for myself.'

A walkathon was a kind of dance event crossed with an endurance test where couples paid to walk in rhythm around a dance hall to the accompaniment of a band, and gradually fell by the wayside until only one pair was left, who collected a cash prize. It was a popular way of trying to earn a little windfall during the Depression years. With its particular version of this novelty, Coffey's band toured all over the United States but when it reached Camden, en route to Georgia, the lure of nearby New York was too strong for some of his best musicians. Dial, along with the trombonist Clyde Bernhardt and trumpeter Joe Thomas, quit the group and headed for Manhattan. Dial was already an experienced musician, having worked with various bands in St Louis and Chicago, as well as playing for a while with Fate Marable on the river steamer *Capitol* that plied the Mississippi between St Louis and New Orleans. He'd been invited to join Sam Wooding's group that took big band jazz to Europe between 1925 and 1927, but turned down the offer so as to stay in America. In 1933 he had been a member of Louis Armstrong's touring band, and had also recorded with Louis.[10]

This reputation helped him to get work almost immediately after he arrived in New York. Although the American Federation of Musicians rule was that a player had to wait six months before transferring to a new Local of the union, and was thereby restricted in the amount of work it was possible to take on, Ed Smalls, the owner of Harlem's famous Smalls' Paradise club, wangled a fast-track application for Dial as he was able to sight-read the drum parts to accompany the venue's floor show. This was a musical called *Emperor Jones*, loosely based on Eugene O'Neill's play about the former Pullman porter who rules a Caribbean island, and it cashed in on the success of the recently released film of the story starring Paul Robeson. Smalls' apparent favouritism went down badly with Ferman Tapp, the bandleader, who did not like Dial, and nicknamed him 'Teacher's Pet'. But I realized, in just a few moments' conversation, that Harry had high musical standards and was quite prepared to tell his fellow musicians when he felt they weren't up to the mark. He told me: 'A couple of the guys in the band didn't like me, 'cos I was telling them how rotten they were, and the band was, so they decided they wanted to get me out. They couldn't play nothing, but they finally succeeded, and gave me my notice. So Mr Smalls found out about it, when I had the notice, that I was being let out in a week. He called Ferman Tapp the leader, and he said, "Look, all the trouble we had getting a drummer to play this show and you gonna let this man go?"

'He said to me, "You wanna work here?"

'I said, "Where else am I gonna work? I'd sooner work here than any place else."

'So he issued an ultimatum: "You keep this man on the job or you take them all out of here!" That guy wouldn't do that, but I got to make two more weeks!'

When the fortnight was up, Harry went on to take two further regular jobs that saw him better off than he had been in *Emperor Jones*, despite some fairly antisocial hours: 'When I left there I went to work up at the Cotton Club in the relief band. And from that relief spot, I got to play at an after-hours session at a place called the Log Cabin up on 133rd Street, in a band with Dicky Wells. I was getting $35 a week for the Cotton Club, and then three dollars a night down at the Log Cabin. In the Cotton Club I used the drums that were already there – except the snare drum. I left my set in the Log Cabin, 'cos I was there from the time I got there 'til the next morning.'

There had, however, been another reason why Ed Smalls had originally interceded on Dial's behalf at his Paradise club, which was that Fats Waller, who frequently visited the venue, had taken a liking to the young drummer, particularly because of his sense of rhythm. Through Waller, Dial was introduced to the circle of Harlem 'stride' pianists including James P. Johnson, the song composers J. C. Johnson and Alex Hill, as well as the lyricist Andy Razaf. Occasionally Smalls beckoned Dial off the bandstand during a show to go and socialize with Waller's party, which was also a surprise in that Dial was teetotal, compared to the hard-drinking Fats and his colleagues. The upshot was that when Waller first landed his contract to make a monthly small group recording date for Victor, he asked Dial to join the band as his drummer. As soon as the deal was signed, Waller's friend Bud Allen toured the various clubs where the chosen musicians were working, and arranged with them that the day before the first session, the band would have its one and only rehearsal at Waller's Edgecombe Avenue apartment, where he had auditioned Al Casey. In the room, along with Fats, Al and Harry, were Herman Autrey, trumpet; Ben Whittet, clarinet; and Billy Taylor, bass, and these were the musicians who made the first session on 16 May 1934.

In Harry Dial's opinion this band had the better of the two rhythm sections in which he played with Fats, as Billy Taylor was a more accomplished bassist (and, he believed, a nicer person) than Charlie Turner who replaced him in January 1935. Nonetheless, one of the sides Harry was to make with Turner, in March 1935, in which his propulsive brushwork urges on Al Casey's deft guitar solo to push the band forward into the final chorus, attracted some press attention. He told me: 'I used brushes most of the time with Fats, and one of the magazines, *Metronome* or *Down Beat* or something, I never did see it I was just told about it, said that "Oh Susannah", which we recorded, the last few minutes, was the greatest piece of rhythm that had ever been recorded.'

Much as that piece charges along, and there's clearly a particular empathy between Casey, Waller and Dial – Al Casey talked of Fats' 'clean stride' left hand which left space for guitar chords, and Dial told me 'Fats and I, we felt one another's music' – there's a far better example of Dial working for 'the support of the guys I was playing with' on an earlier session (with Taylor on bass). 'Believe It Beloved' from 7 November 1934 shows Dial making more use of the full drum kit, compared to 'Oh Susannah'. He opens positively on brushes, drops back behind the vocal, and then his cymbal work behind Bill Coleman's solo prefigures the use of the hi-hat and involves an early jazz technique that Freddie Kohlman showed me, of using one stick under the ride cymbal to 'choke' it, or to create a counter rhythm to the other stick, which is used above it. And this is important because in 1934 record companies were still cautious about recording drums at all, let alone full kits. Many 1920s records give us precious little idea of how bands actually sounded because the drummer either played minimal percussion, or was sited well away from the main recording microphone. Zutty Singleton's clip-clopping effects with some of Louis Armstrong's late 1920s records such as 'West End Blues' are a case in point. Gene Krupa had been one of the first to use a full kit in 1927 with the McKenzie/Condon Chicagoans, but according to Harry, in 1934 the Victor engineers in New York were very cautious about Gene doing the same with Benny Goodman (although this would all change the following year).

Harry recalled that from the very outset with Fats he used a full kit: 'The cymbals were there, I put 'em up, but I barely played on them. I was using a bass drum, and not only was I using a bass drum, but Oberstein[11] set me on a platform, and Gene Krupa said – if he told me once he told me a dozen times – "I'm gonna have you make a record of one piece with Benny Goodman, because I don't believe it can be done." But I did it, without padding my bass drum or anything. So that I could be picked up sufficiently enough, Oberstein put me on a platform about *that* high, and set me right in the centre of the band. That was the way we recorded. The reason I was in touch with Krupa was that I was the copyist for Edgar Sampson, and sometimes I'd meet Krupa at rehearsal with the music I had copied for him. Sampson was the arranger for Benny. And of course news gets around amongst musicians. [Before that] they always put the drummer way over in the corner – in another city I used to call it. But I was right in the centre of that little group.'

Dial was in the centre of the group in another respect. He was directly responsible for bringing in two key musicians to the Rhythm, one of whom worked with Fats right through to the end, whereas the other only appeared on two recording dates, but created some of the finest moments in the entire Waller recorded output. The first was reed player Gene Sedric, and the second, the trumpeter Bill Coleman. Harry believed that the rhythm section played better with the right front-line instrumentalists, so maybe it is no accident that Dial's backings for Coleman were some of his finest work for Fats. He remembered: 'Bill was one of the smoothest and most fluent trumpet players I ever heard in my life. He was simply marvellous and when I brought him into the band on this session, Fats and Oberstein went crazy about him. And he fit in that group perfectly. Fats used to call me and tell me to get the group together. Billy Taylor lived round here, just a couple of blocks away on 159th Street. Billy was about to join Ellington and I went by Fats' house to tell him. At that time Herman Autrey was playing with Charlie Turner, and they were in the Apollo Theatre. This record date was on a Thursday and it was the last day that Charlie's band was in the Apollo, so I went by, and told Fats . . . I said that Herman would be at the theatre, because Charlie wouldn't let him off, and said it should be set back from the Thursday.[12] Fats said, "I'm not putting anything back, so get me a trumpet player. I want him there at one o'clock."

'Now Coleman was playing with Teddy Hill at a club that had just changed its name to the Ubangi club.[13] So I went by and engaged Coleman to make the record date the next day. And Herman Autrey, I know, always talked about "I didn't try", but I don't think he ever wanted to know the truth, I guess. The reason I know he felt that way was later we were playing the Colonnade Hall down in Washington, and he came to me on the bandstand in the intermission and stuck his finger in my face. I felt like spitting in his face when he did that but I didn't. He said, "We gonna get you out of this band." And they worked on it and worked on it. Kept feeding Fats that I couldn't do this and I couldn't do that. I hired Herman for most sessions because that's what Fats wanted me to do, but I didn't like his playing. It was very, very stiff. He just wasn't a good trumpet player as far as I was concerned. You won't find but a few like Bill Coleman.'

There was another reason, as well as the music itself, why Dial recalled the Coleman sessions with affection, which was that the second one, from January 1935, was rather more lucrative than usual. He said: 'We went to Camden where they put Fats on the organ. Victor owned a church down there, that they bought with an organ in it, and they were afraid to dismantle the organ, for fear they would not be able to put it back together again! So even on their symphony recordings, when they used an organ, they sent them down there to Camden. We always liked to go because that was a $100 deal, but the sessions here in New York on 23rd St were just $20! The studio was on 23rd Street, but that's all I remember about the one in the city, except in those days they didn't have no tape, it was done on wax.'

Bill Coleman himself remembered the sessions well. A decade before meeting Harry Dial, I had been introduced to Bill backstage at the 1976 Breda Jazz Festival in Holland (where I was playing with, of all people, Kid Thomas). Coleman was a tall, elegant, grey-suited figure, specializing by then on flugelhorn, and it had been wonderful to hear him in person, though the concert had been on a rather odd outdoor bandstand suspended from a kind of pyramid that rose high above the city's cathedral square. After he clambered back to earth, I asked Bill about those dates with Waller, and a big grin crept across his face as he recalled how 'beautiful' the experience had been. But, after making those two very productive sessions with the Rhythm, Coleman was no longer available. He left New York to move briefly to Cincinnati, before returning to Europe where he had already made a successful impression during a short visit in 1933.

Consequently, Harry had another idea about the ideal trumpeter for Fats, in preference to Autrey (who was the man who eventually came back into the band). Dial said: 'If it had been what I wanted to do, Joe Thomas would have been there a long time ago. He was also from St Louis, and we came to New York on the same day after the Walkathon. But I couldn't have got him in, because he had joined Fletcher Henderson. And they were out on the road, so that's why I couldn't have him.'[14]

Harry was very forthright regarding his opinions on the merits of various musicians, especially when we came to talk about the reed players who worked in the Rhythm: 'Ben Whittet, that's his name, was on the first records, but he was kind of cornball. Oberstein knew that and he complained about his playing. So Fats got Mezz Mezzrow. But he was as bad as Ben Whittet! One day when I went down to Fats' house to get my money for the recording, he asked me if I knew a clarinet player. Well, I was surprised because Fats knew everyone, but even though Gene Sedric hadn't been back in the country too long after working with Sam Wooding, when I asked Fats if he knew about him, he said no. I told him what a good musician he was. And Fats said, "Bring him over to the next session." And everybody liked him.

'Fats used to say, "That guy can play a second part to any theme."[15] 'Cos we didn't have no arrangements, nor nothing. When we went in the studio we had no idea what we were gonna make. We'd make four tunes, and all that Oberstein had for us was piano parts. He gave everybody piano parts. A lotta people don't believe that, 'specially when you consider a number like "Serenade for a Wealthy Widow"[16] – but there was no arrangement, we didn't even have a lead sheet. And Al, the bass player and Fats, they'd got to transpose.[17] He'd run through first on piano because he would vocalize on everything. It was phenomenal how he'd sit down and having never heard of a composition, go over it, and then sing it like he'd been singing it for six months. Sometimes they wanted a second instrumental version – Oberstein wanted that. He'd want an instrumental version of the same thing because he figured the band was good enough. I know it happened twice, maybe three different times that happened, we made a vocal and then an instrumental of the same thing.'

That idea of giving the impression that something incredibly hard to do – sight-reading a song, whilst simultaneously transposing it down a tone, and making it sound completely familiar – was actually the easiest thing in the world, was something Waller did in common with the other New York stride pianists of his era.

Butch Thompson, who was lucky enough to hear and play alongside Fats' contemporary Willie 'The Lion' Smith, in the 1960s, recalls: 'Willie had the derby on his head and a cigar, and he kept up a constant patter fairly often while he was playing. It's a kind of bravado that stride pianists seemed to have, and a lot of them had it. Eubie Blake did it too, talking, carrying on a conversation, or talking to himself. Eubie often said, "Talk to me! Talk to me!" while he was playing. Willie "The Lion" would do the same, and Fats does it all over the place on his recordings. And it's part of the music, it's a show, to prove that it's really nothing to sit down and play all this difficult piano. It's so easy that you can cross your legs, turn to the audience and talk to somebody about the latest gossip, and keep both hands going like crazy. The Lion was deceptive that way, you just didn't realize how much he was doing, unless you really tried to listen through all that bravado.'[18]

When they met, the Lion had travelled up to Minnesota to play with the band in which Butch was the clarinettist,[19] and Thompson recalls that much of the Lion's piano style went right over his head, particularly the quasi-classical rhapsodic phrases, or what Smith's generation called 'beautification', imported into pieces such as 'Morning Air' and 'Echo of Spring'. But it was a different matter when it came to the romping New York style of stride. 'We were absolutely thrilled when he took a chorus with the band and would start digging in to play all that stride, which he was a master of. And a lot of the time it was even more effective because he would contrast it with some highly beautified filigrees that would go on for a few bars, and then suddenly he would start stomping out some incredible barrelhouse stride piano that would just kill everybody.'[20]

This same effect, of course, is at least part of the secret of the marvellous swing qualities of the records by Fats Waller and His Rhythm. If we explore one of the sessions (apart from the tracks using the organ) that Harry Dial was most proud of, and which I'd rate amongst Waller's very best, with Bill Coleman on trumpet, we can hear Fats transferring much of this modus operandi (both in terms of verbal comments and piano technique) to disc. The Camden date from 5 January 1935[21] begins with 'I'm A Hundred Percent For You', which opens with a sensitive piano and trumpet introduction in which Fats and Coleman trade phrases. The vocal follows, after which there's a piano chorus, and then a sublime solo from Coleman, in which Fats and the rhythm section provide solid hard-swinging support. With the pianist's left hand, plus Turner, Dial and Casey firmly on the beat, Fats adds a slightly delayed right-hand spread chord on the second and fourth beats of each bar, which serves to make the solid punch of the downbeat even stronger. As Sedric comes in, and exchanges musical phrases with Coleman, Fats starts his verbal patter:

'Oh beat that rhythm on out there, beat it on out! Yeah!'

And then: 'Ha-ha-ha! Oh stop it Joe! Oh Joe, you tickling now, cut it out! Don't drop your curls, don't drop your curls, no, no! Ha-ha-ha!'

And finally we're led back into the final vocal chorus. The reference to 'Stop it Joe', a well-known vaudeville blues originally recorded by Viola McCoy in 1924,[22] is a coded message to listeners in the know. Her lyrics went:

> I don't mind dancin' til the band gets
> through
> You've got to stop that wiggling, too,
> I mean
> Stop that wigglin' with me!

This is a clear reference to what Danny Barker euphemistically called 'belly rubbing' in the dance hall. Fats is Signifying, suggesting a comparable *frisson* of sexual excitement in the battle between clarinet and trumpet, and a metaphorical suggestion that if there's too much agitation, one of the dancers' carefully coiffed and curled hair would 'drop'. Such messages would go right past most listeners, but for those in the African American community, used to hearing those well-known blues lyrics in various contexts from recordings to vaudeville shows, it reveals Fats putting on what Butch Thompson called 'a show' – adding knowing quips to a part of the performance where his dazzling piano is driving the whole band on.

'Baby Brown', which was recorded next, opens with a full-blooded piano chorus from Fats with the rhythm section, and is followed by the vocal, in which Fats is 'shadowed' by Sedric's clarinet. Again it is Coleman's entry that provides the drama, because here, instead of roaring into an open-horn chorus as Autrey might have done, Coleman produces a restrained muted solo that deftly weaves its melodic line across the four-square rhythm of piano, bass, guitar and drums. But just as Waller apparently did on his *Rhythm Club* broadcasts the previous year, he feels compelled to provide a running commentary. 'Kick me on out there now / Yeah!' And as Sedric's clarinet enters for the bridge, Fats exhorts him: 'Toot that thing, Boy!' Behind Sedric's tenor solo Dial adds cymbal effects to his earlier brushwork, building the rhythmic tension into the final chorus, on which Fats abandons the lyrics, scat-singing through the bridge and shouting 'Oh, Mercy!' in the final segment, before a mournful half-spoken 'Baby Brown' closes the disc. Again, we're hearing the 'show' on record. Both these tracks were also done as instrumentals, and on the vocal-free take of 'Baby Brown' the tension behind Coleman's muted solo comes not from Waller's asides and forceful piano, but from the interplay between Casey and Dial, adding subtle cross-rhythms. This time round, there's no cymbal work behind the tenor and Dial restricts himself to brushes all the way through. It's a fine performance, but it lacks the drive and personality of the vocal version, and clearly the band is less enthused.

On 'Because of Once Upon a Time', Waller more or less plays a full stride chorus behind Coleman's trumpet solo. His right-hand figures constantly create countermelodies and rhythmic variations behind the open horn, which launches his virtuoso solo piano segment on the bridge of the song. There's a similar trumpet/piano balance on the final track of the session, 'You Fit Into the Picture', where Coleman plays the melody off the sheet music as Fats produces some rollicking stride behind him. Then in the vocal, Coleman adds a muted trumpet commentary behind the words, much as Buck Clayton was to do a few years later for Billie Holiday. Then we get a strong stride piano solo, and the band plays as an ensemble to lead into the closing vocal. It is a perfect example of the recording formula that Waller would use throughout the eight-year career of this little band.

It was only a matter of time before promoters began asking for Fats Waller and His Rhythm to play his 'show' for them in person. Dial recalled: 'We made one session a month, for a year, before we ever went on the road. The first tour that we made was with the small band, the six pieces, which was up in New England here. When we went on tour, Sedric was working out on Long Island with Broadway Jones, and they were making $50 a week. We were still in the Depression years, and that was a good salary. He didn't want to lay off for a while and go with Fats, so we took Emmett Matthews. We had Emmett on saxophone and Charlie Turner on bass. We played in the Arcadia Ballroom and they were the two different people we had in. Fats was like Louis Armstrong – he was a show by himself. That first tour we made was all one-nighters. The first thing we heard when we got back was that he was going to enlarge the band. And that's where it fell to pieces compared to the small group, because Fats wouldn't take no time with anything.'

It is significant that Dial stressed that Fats was 'a show by himself', as this chimes exactly with the persona he put out on record or radio. Yet most big bands of the time had a 'straw boss', in other words, a musician who rehearsed the others, took charge of the arrangements, and made sure the band was ready to support its star leader. Luis Russell did this job for Louis Armstrong, and Walter 'Foots' Thomas similarly worked to support Cab Calloway. Cab was like Waller in that, according to his bassist Milt Hinton, 'Cab wasn't interested in rehearsing the band. He was an artist.'[23] But whereas the Calloway and Armstrong orchestras had skilled musicians working to ensure that the band sounded good, and a road management team that would make the travel arrangements, Waller's backroom organization on both counts was slack, and in some cases non-existent. By the 1940s, the Waller big band was making some decent recordings, but there's little to suggest it achieved such panache early on, and nor did it often carry a supporting cast of singers and dancers as Calloway did, although Al Casey recalled it backing other acts at the Apollo in New York and one or two comparable theatres. It travelled in much less comfort and style than the groups of those other leaders. Dial said: 'Travelling with Louis you got to sleep on the train, you got a berth and all that. Travelling with Fats you got to sleep on the bus, it was terrible, awful. I was gone with the big band maybe four or five weeks at a time. It never was an extended tour like Duke or Cab.'

Fats may have been nonchalant about some elements of tour organization, but one musician at least was grateful to him. Al Casey recalled, 'Because I was still in school, there was a guy name of John Smith, and Fats took him on the road. But one summer, during the holidays, he took me on the road. Not to play, but just to get the experience, so I became the band boy. He had two other guys helping, and I joined in, just to be on the road. Two years or so after that, I graduated, and I had a job. I worked for Fats all the time. Every spring he got the big band together, seventeen or eighteen pieces, and we went on the road to play dances and theatres. So that was a kick for me too, playing in the big band and the small band. The musicians were all older than I, and they all took care of me on the road.'

In terms of overall organization, things do not seem to have improved as time went on, as other musicians had memories of subsequent tours with Fats that were quite chaotic. The saxophonist Franz Jackson was in a late version of the big band, and felt that Fats' management hadn't worked out how to keep them working every night on a national tour in 1940. Trumpeter Franc Williams recalled this as the worst tour he ever undertook, and in photographs taken at the time, Franc snipped out the image of Waller's manager Ed Kirkeby from any shots in which he appeared! Also discipline was lax and the band was drinking too much, following their leader's example of what Franz called 'dissipating'. He told me: 'We worked our way out to Los Angeles, but we had to deadhead our way back. Deadheading means there are no jobs. Once you hit the mountains there are no places to play. We didn't work anywhere coming back, we just came straight back on the bus over several days.[24] They stopped to let Fats off in Chicago, so he could take the train back to New York. I remember telling him where the Union Station was. And then I thought I'd quit the band there too, so I shouted, "Let me out!" and I pulled my bag and all off the bus. My mother was in Chicago so I thought I'd go stay with her for a while. I thought I'd straighten myself out, 'cos I was drinking a fifth a day, of whiskey.'[25] Jackson stopped drinking for a while, and did indeed straighten himself out, such that by good fortune he was in the right place at the right time to join Earl Hines' new line-up as he reorganized his big band. Ironically, it was back in Los Angeles where Franz made his first recordings with Hines, when the band travelled there in late 1940. He spent a year in Earl's band, which was better organized than Waller's and during that time recorded in New York, London (Ontario) and Hollywood as well as in its home city of Chicago.

In 1981 Franz made a solo tour of the British Isles, and for one of his concerts (on which I played) we managed to reunite him and Al Casey for the first time since their days together with Waller. It was a very successful reunion, and both men played wonderfully, though I remember it for quite different reasons. I met Franz at King's Cross station in London to drive him to the concert at Farnham Maltings in Surrey. In the car he regaled me with stories of the fine Scottish breakfast he had in Edinburgh. He'd then had a four-course lunch on the train, and an hour or two later, afternoon tea with scones, jam and Cornish clotted cream. Not long before the gig, we got to my house where my wife was about to feed the rest of the band. 'Oh great!' cried Franz, 'Chili con carne, my favourite!'

I said, 'Franz, you've eaten quite a lot already, haven't you?' He gave me a charming smile and said, 'Young man, as we used to say during the Depression, when it rains porridge, hold your bowl out!' He was delighted when, after the concert, my wife gave him a recipe book, and on the subsequent occasions we worked together, he held forth on the delights of the various dishes he had conjured up with its help.

By the time Franz Jackson was in the Waller band, Harry Dial had been out of it for four years, his place taken successively by Arnold Bolden, Yank Porter (whom Harry had replaced in the Armstrong band) and Slick Jones, the drummer whom Charlie Turner and Herman Autrey had all along wanted to get into the group. Yet the fundamentals of the 1940 small group and the big band were more or less the same as when Dial was the regular drummer back in 1934–5. He remembered that they never had a regular band bus, there being a different vehicle and driver for every tour, sometimes for different days on the same tour. He also remembered Waller's capriciousness about playing away from New York. 'One time we were on our way someplace, a one-nighter. Guess we were halfway there. So Fats told the driver, "Turn this jalopy around! Let's head back to New York!"' The band all looked glum, thinking about the money they would lose, and so Fats made his way round the bus and paid them all off, explaining that the manager of the venue had said something he didn't like last time they were there.

Although the big band seldom travelled with its own show as Cab Calloway did, often when it played a theatre engagement it became the pit band, and accompanied the other acts on the bill. For this Fats hired a relief pianist, who in the early years was another Harlem stride master, Hank Duncan. He had been in Charlie Turner's band with Herman Autrey, and there was great mutual respect between Hank and Fats. 'Hank was from my home in Kentucky,' recalled Al Casey. 'He idolized Fats. He played exactly like him. He tried to sing, but he couldn't sound like Fats! But he played piano exactly the same way and that's why Fats hired him. Sometimes Fats would take off from the band for a while and you wouldn't know the difference unless you were looking at the stage. He was some pianist.'

At one point each night on theatre shows there'd be a 'cutting contest' between the two pianists, when, accompanied by the band, they would play alternate choruses, each trying to outdo the other with the stride players' tricks of the trade. Harry said, 'Fats would shout "I've gotta get him! I've gotta get him!" as they battled.'[26] On one-nighters where just the band and Fats appeared, both pianists played throughout the evening. 'I preferred the small group,' reflected Harry. 'The big band was always rather loud and often out of tune.'

Then he added with typical candour: 'But all the coloured bands were that way: Count Basie, Cab Calloway, every one of them was out of tune. Ellington had good players but it was years and years before his band got in tune. I don't know how they did it. They all had different types of instruments, all them different kinds of tones and one thing and another. They'd tune the horns up a lot of times but then they'd overblow them or something. Some would blow a few notes and then say, "That's close enough for jazz!" That was the attitude they had. But I came up under Fate Marable, and he was a master musician and a hell of a piano player ... Henry Kimball was on bass on the riverboat with Fate, but when I first went there it was George Foster – Pops Foster – before Kimball ... but Henry was a nice musician. See, Pops had never learned to read music, but he had the rhythm! And in those days it wasn't too hard, because we weren't being given compositions like "Tenderly" or "Body and Soul". You had four or five chord changes and that's it. But Fate's band was always in tune.'

In these remarks, Harry ties his own sense of rhythm right back to some of those New Orleans players discussed in Chapter Two. After starting out as a 'trick' drummer, his formative experience as a serious musician was of plying up and down the Mississippi, working each night in a rhythm section led by the man whose band was known as 'the floating conservatory' and which was generally seen as the launching pad for a number of New Orleans and St Louis players of talent and ability. Marable's drummers included Baby Dodds, Zutty Singleton, and a man whom Harry reminded me about, Floyd Campbell, who later led his own band in St Louis. Harry himself replaced Zutty Singleton, who – by a quirk of fate – would play on Fats Waller's final band recordings for the film *Stormy Weather* in January 1943.

Quite coincidentally, as I was leaving Harry's apartment after the interview, he introduced me to a neighbour whom we just happened to pass in the lobby, who also lived in 555. This turned out to be the veteran bandleader Andy Kirk, and in due course, although Andy was very frail at the time, I ended up working with him and his co-author Amy Lee to bring out Kirk's autobiography *Twenty Years on Wheels*. This is a fascinating memoir of one of the key territory bands, and I owe Harry Dial a lot for making the introduction.

Harry's memories of Fats Waller in RCA's Camden studio chimed with those of another musician whom I first met when Sammy Rimington brought him to Britain in 1977. Trumpeter Jabbo Smith had been a serious rival to Louis Armstrong in the 1920s, and records with his Rhythm Aces such as his 'Jazz Battle' stand as some of the most innovative playing of the late 1920s. In a somewhat scatter-shot career, Jabbo drifted in and out of the limelight, a high point being a set of beautiful big band records under his own name in 1938, including 'More Rain More Rest' and 'Absolutely', which are just as original as his small group work from a decade before. By the time of his London visit, as a consequence of several years of playing at most sporadically, and at other times not at all, Jabbo's lip was not in the best of shape, and it was sometimes quite heart-rending hearing his brilliant ideas being not quite able to escape the bell of his horn. But as a singer he was as fine as ever, and he had not yet suffered the first of a series of strokes that curtailed his trumpeting career in the early 1980s. Indeed, in 1977 he was yet to spend some months singing and playing in the cast of the *One Mo' Time* revue in various parts of the United States.

Even before his Rhythm Aces records, Jabbo had recorded with Waller and James P. Johnson (as part of the pit band of the revue *Keep Shufflin'*) under the name of the Louisiana Sugar Babes. In the mid-1980s I met up with Jabbo again in New York, where he was appearing as a singer at the Village Vanguard with Don Cherry's inter-generational group Collaboration, and we talked about the Camden recordings. He particularly recalled the problems of time-lag as they recorded with the organ, compared to the instant attack of James P.'s piano, around which he and reed player Garvin Bushell were grouped. But his main memories of Waller were of a man 'full of fun, both on and off the stage'. At the end of the New York run of *Keep Shufflin'* he had travelled with the production as it made its way to Chicago, where he quickly found work at the Sunset Café, and went on to make his first series of great recordings. He told me that he had Fats and the revue to thank for launching what became his first period of fame. He was a most engaging conversationalist, often able to take a sideways or elliptic view of his life and events, and he also had some of the most distinctive handwriting of any musician I have met. I treasure a photograph he signed for me as a memory of this most remarkable man, who offered yet another window into the life of Fats.

6 SWING ERA LEGENDS

Moving on from the subject of my Waller biography,[1] I was interested to find out from Al Casey about his playing with other stride pianists. 'I played with Willie "The Lion" and James P. Johnson. On the records with James P. we had Frankie Newton, who was a bit older than I, but a fine trumpeter, and a bit of a character. And then we had Mezz Mezzrow. He was a fine writer and said some nice things about me in some things he wrote in Europe, which helped me in later years. And of course, there was the reefer thing. He had a name for that here in New York, where what made you high, made you feel good, was called a "Mezz". It wasn't for me, but that's what he was known for. He played a little clarinet, and he was a nice cat. The sessions with James P. were produced by Hugues Panassié, who was a real jazz aficionado. He knew what people liked, what they wanted, especially in France, when he came over here [to New York] and recorded. The records worked well here, too. He was an awfully smart fellow.'

We then digressed as Al regretted the fact he had not made more of the reputation that Panassié had helped to build for him in France, as he had been unable to travel to Europe with Fats Waller on his 1938 and 1939 visits.[2] This was in part due to the long-term British Musicians' Union dispute that prevented all but a select few American musicians from playing in the United Kingdom. But Al said that one benefit of Fats' absence in Europe was that the other members of his band were offered freelance work. And this continued after Waller's premature death, aged just 39, in 1943.

'It wasn't hard to get a gig, because they knew us. People would call: "Would you like to make a record with Art Tatum?" "But of course!" And I did record with him a couple of times.[3] It was hard to play with him, very hard. I tried but it wasn't too good. There was only one guitar player that could work with him, and that was Tiny Grimes. He had a four-string guitar, but he could play all the little fast stuff that Tatum played, and fit. They were wonderful together, in that trio they had. I couldn't do that. I played differently.'

Another musician who experienced playing with Art Tatum was the bassist Truck Parham. He had been playing in Roy Eldridge's band at Chicago's Three Deuces, and Tatum came in during 1935 on a long contract to take over the gig. After a somewhat unsuccessful career as a boxer, Parham had originally been a tuba player, working with Zack Whyte and the Chocolate Beau Brummels. He had not long taken up the bass when Tatum arrived, having started out in Zutty Singleton's trio and then joining Eldridge. Although he had had some informal lessons with Walter Page, he was by no means certain he was up to playing with such a piano virtuoso. He said, 'I told Art I didn't know much about the bass. But he said, "You're good at the sound, I heard you with Roy. And I liked what I heard."

'So I said, "OK."'

'And he said, "To tell what I'm playing on the piano, just watch my left hand." And that's what I did. I played with Tatum for two years, just watching that hand of his! While I was there, all the guys from the Chicago Symphony would come down at night after their concerts. They'd hang out. And one of the bassists,[4] I guess he was the number one bass player, came up to me and said, "You've got a good sound, man." But I guess he knew that I wasn't formally trained and that I was fingering all wrong, and technical stuff like that.

'He gave me his card and said, "Call me up". He lived in Oak Park, and he started teaching me. He taught me for about two years, because he wanted me to play legitimate bass. I said, "I don't want to play in a symphony or nothing, I just want to play bass well enough to make a living."

'He knew jazz was my thing, and he said, "Well, whatever you want to do, man." Finally, I felt I had all that I could get from him. But years later he wrote me to say he had left Chicago and gone to Los Angeles to work for the Red Network. And when I went out there with Earl Hines, he had let many people know, "This is my best student, and he's coming out here with Earl Hines!" And he had me over to his house.'[5]

Before leaving the subject of Tatum, another musician I talked to compared his month and a half working with Tatum to a similar period accompanying Charlie Parker, during both of which (whilst in his early twenties) he became somewhat star-struck. This was bassist Jimmy Woode, best known for his work with Ellington and then a long sojourn in Europe, but in the early 1950s he was a busy musician in and around Boston. He recalled: 'I had the good fortune and pleasure and honour to have worked with Art Tatum for fifty-four days. It didn't faze me out and I was not nervous, I was certainly excited, but I was so busy listening to Mr Charles Parker or Mr Art Tatum that I would forget where I was. I was so knocked out, and enjoying what they were doing so much, that I wasn't taking care of business the way I should.'[6]

Al Casey, having talked about Tatum's work with Tiny Grimes, moved on to other guitarists, and in particular the two that had the biggest impact on him. Towards the end of 1946, Al was leading his own trio on 52nd Street, and Django Reinhardt was brought down to the club to meet him. The manouche guitarist had arrived from France at the beginning of November to undertake his first American tour, which included some concerts with Duke Ellington. But, as ever, Django was somewhat unpredictable. Before he came to hear Al, he had astonished the agent who booked him, according to jazz columnist Len Lyons:

> Said the agent, as soon as Reinhardt was cleared through customs, 'Let's go to my office.' 'Where's Dizzy Gillespie playing?' asked Reinhardt ... 'In Baltimore,' said the booker. 'Now, in my office I have some newspapermen, and ... ' 'Never mind,' Reinhardt interrupted. Then he immediately bought a plane ticket to Baltimore, and flew there to hear Dizzy Gillespie, the American trumpeter he holds in high esteem.[7]

Reinhardt returned from Baltimore and, after meeting up with Ellington, made his American debut with Duke at the Lincoln Auditorium, Syracuse, New York, on 30 November 1946.[8] Al saw him on one of the later concerts with Ellington at Carnegie Hall, but barely managed to hear Django again in person, even though, billed as 'the World's Greatest Jazz Guitarist', Reinhardt began a residency at the Café Society Uptown at 128 East 58th Street, on 16 December 1946.[9] The hours there coincided almost exactly with those of Al's own gig.

'But just before that he came down to hear me on the street. He didn't sit in with me, but I'd listened to all his records and things. He was a genius,' remembered Al. 'I steal a lot and I stole from him, but I tried to put it my way. The other one was Charlie Christian. I just loved the way he played. He played so different than everybody else. He played guitar like a horn player, swinging over the changes, and I liked that too. With Fats it had been rhythm guitar and chord work behind him, but when you go out on your own and you want to work, you have to try to play like the ones that are playing now. So I had to learn, or try to play, single string, and then mix it up, single string and chords too. And it seems to work, so far! I still love playing chords, specially background chords, because my first love is just playing with a band and playing rhythm. That's big band work, but in a small band you have to learn how to do both. But thinking of rhythm, Freddie Green was the greatest section man I ever heard in my life, playing with the bass and drums. He had a sound of his own, the way he made his chords, which seemed to fit particularly well with the bass. To me he was the greatest. He was a good friend of mine. You might meet him on the road sometime, if you were working the same town. So then we'd hang out and have a taste. And we'd meet here [in New York]. Maybe we'd meet at the union, and hang out. You could see everybody here, when you weren't on the road. Everybody seemed to be working all the time!'

One of the other musicians with whom Al worked on 52nd Street, after Waller's death, was Billie Holiday, who sang with his trio at the Onyx Club, first opposite the Dizzy Gillespie / Oscar Pettiford Quintet in December 1943 and then again – after a short break – in January 1944. They were back on the Street at the Downbeat club later in the year. Casey's little group included the pianist Sam Clanton and bassist Al Matthews, and they would later record with another singer, Alberta Hunter, but it was his work with Billie that Al mainly remembered.[10]

'I'd already worked on recordings in Teddy Wilson's band behind Billie Holiday,' he recalled. 'That was quite an experience working behind her. Then with her and the Trio it was mainly on the Street, but we went on the road too, places like Baltimore and Washington. Sam Clanton was quite a guy. He played and sounded like Teddy, because he loved Teddy Wilson, and that helped. He was a very young fellow, who passed too early. There are lots of stories about Billie, 'being this" or "being that" but I thought she was a real artist, and in the studio she did the right thing all the time.'

Al was only 17 when he first met Billie, at a time when she was a virtual unknown, singing at Pods and Jerry's in Harlem. 'I looked up to her and always did. Later, as popular as she was and the name that she had, I *had* to look up to her. Before I joined her the first time in the studio, she and Teddy had already been recording before, so it made me feel this was really quite something.'

Another musician who worked with Billie and who – apart from one altercation she had with a band member – equally remembered her on stage as 'doing the right thing all the time' was trumpeter Doc Cheatham. After a period away from music after leaving Cab Calloway, he had come back to regular playing with Eddie Heywood's sextet, and in the spring of 1944 they accompanied Billie, both at the Café Society and for a couple of record dates at Commodore. His fondness for smoking a pipe with very pungent tobacco between sets came in handy for Billie, as she asked him to sit outside her dressing room to mask the smell of pot drifting under the door. Smoking marijuana was something of which club owner Barney Josephson vehemently disapproved. Doc related his memories of working with her in his autobiography, for which, as with Danny Barker, I was his editor and co-author, and although he felt he was 'not her favourite trumpet player, and she would have preferred Buck Clayton or Roy Eldridge, she treated me very nicely all the same'.[11]

Not long after Doc's book came out, I dropped in to his regular Sunday brunch session at Sweet Basil in Manhattan, and the band launched into 'Embraceable You'. During Chuck Folds' piano solo, Doc hopped across to my table, and, reminding me that he had recorded this song with her, came up with a string of memories of Billie. The music itself had prompted his thoughts and it was a shame we never got the chance to jot these ideas down, or find a way to include them in the paperback edition of the book. Yet this was a valuable idea for future interviews, and in the years that followed, I often used specific pieces of music to unlock memories from players I talked to.

That is exactly what happened when I met another of Billie's accompanists, pianist Mal Waldron, when he was paying a brief visit to Britain in 1995 to make a record with saxophonist George Haslam. We had agreed to meet in a noisy pub in the small Oxfordshire town of Abingdon to talk about his long career in Europe and his work with avant-garde players such as Archie Shepp and Steve Lacy. While we were in mid-conversation, amazingly a Billie Holiday record came on the sound system, prompting Mal to recall his work as her accompanist, on records that are notable for his restraint, allowing her to shine.

'I don't think I had any special gift for drawing out Billie or any other singer. I'm just a very ego-less person, and so I can provide a carpet for them to walk on, and not resent it! Support has always been my thing, rather than being out in front. That's why I chose the piano, because when I first got into jazz I started out with saxophone, but that was so "out front" there was nothing between you and the audience but air! So I decided I wasn't an extrovert, I was an introvert. And so I got behind the piano ... and I worked with Billie in 1957. I was working as the house pianist at Prestige, playing with people like John Coltrane, and I was doing gigs with Billie Holiday too. I didn't see her final years as a tragic moment in her life. She was very happy at that time, she told jokes and liked to listen to other musicians' jokes, and she saw something humorous in everything. Even in tragedy she saw humour! And I felt that was a quality that was very necessary for her to exist in this world. Her voice was not like it was before, but she adapted to what she had to work with, and she did miraculous things with that. Most of the discs we made were live recordings, except for the orchestral things we did with Ray Ellis, so that shows you exactly how she sounded on a gig. I like to think of myself as her carpet-maker!'[12]

Returning to Al Casey, he mentioned that he worked in Teddy Wilson's band on several recordings with Billie, but I remembered that he had also briefly left Fats Waller to join Wilson's short-lived big band in 1939–40. 'That's a story in itself,' he laughed. 'I asked Fats if I could leave and go with Teddy when he first got the band together. It was a different kind of band, with almost no solos, and that's what I wanted to do. And Fats said, "Yes, go right ahead. And if anything happens, come right back." I'll never forget that as long as I live. The band only lasted a year and I went back to Fats. But it was a great experience and it was what I wanted to do. He had good men. They had J. C. Heard and Al Hall in the rhythm section, and that was something with Teddy on piano. In the band he had Ben Webster and a lot of guys that had been stars in their own right. He even had a couple of guys from out of town – Jake Wiley on trombone and Karl George on trumpet. They were both from Detroit, and they were both super. Karl played alongside Doc Cheatham, who was one of the greatest section men in the world, and he could play his own solos too. So he and Karl got along just like that. We opened the Golden Gate, and that was a night I'll never forget! They had about seven bands there, white and coloured. It was a beautiful spot. But it didn't last. It was too close to the Savoy, if I can put it like that, and whatever happened to close it down – well, use your judgement!'

There is not much literature on the Golden Gate Ballroom, although for a while it was a major Harlem attraction, comparable – as Al suggested – to the Savoy. The seven or so bands he talked of were spaced out over its life, but there were three major attractions to start with, when its opening in December 1939 drew admiring press reviews, including from syndicated columnist Al Moses, who reported: 'Andy Kirk, Teddy Wilson and Claude Hopkins put on a show at the spankin' new Golden Gate that made "continuous dancing" a thing of pleasure and rare rhythm, rather than the usual torture routine. The very newest Harlem dance craze, "Hep Hep" was beautifully executed Friday night by a couple known as Virgal (*sic*) Boone and Jessica Hawkins.'[13] It was reputedly New York's largest dance venue, with a capacity of 5,000, and was quickly dubbed the 'million dollar ballroom'.[14] Both the Kirk and Wilson bands broadcast twice a week from the Golden Gate over the MBS network and New York's local WOR station on Wednesday and Saturday nights from 11.30 pm.[15] But by May, the venue had closed. 'Teddy Wilson,' ran the reports, 'served walking papers on half his bandsmen at the close of a long engagement at the Golden Gate Ballroom. He is now rebuilding a seven-piece sweet combo.'[16] It was at that point that Al Casey returned to Fats Waller.

During its short life, the Golden Gate Ballroom garnered a lot of press attention, largely due to its African American press agent Allan McMillan, who kept the papers well fed with stories about grand balls, dance competitions and visiting bands, such as Les Hite's. Such a high profile did not go down well with its long-established competing venues, who were generally a little less adept at publicity. But whereas Al Casey was diplomatic about its fate, his fellow bandsman Doc Cheatham was matter of fact: 'In the end the Savoy people bought out the Golden Gate and closed it.'[17] Fortunately Columbia managed to record eight sides by the Wilson big band, in December 1939 and January 1940, so an audio snapshot of the band in action does exist, notably on J. C. Heard's drum feature 'Wham (Re Bop Boom Bam)' and the atmospheric 'Moon Ray' that catches all the ensemble skill that Al Casey so admired, as well as a vocal from Jean Eldridge.[18]

Doc Cheatham recalled that the Golden Gate had two bandstands, similar to the Savoy, from which the resident bands would alternate during the evening. 'Teddy Wilson's band was so great,' he told me. 'It wasn't a hard-swinging band like some of those Savoy bands, exactly, but it had such great musicians in it and it was really beautiful to play with.' Despite Al Casey's recollection of Doc's lead playing, which had been a great feature of his previous work with Cab Calloway, he had suffered something of a nervous breakdown after leaving Cab, and became physically very weak. With the help of his jazz friends, including Ben Webster, who was instrumental in getting Teddy Wilson to recruit him, he slowly recovered. But part of the Wilson band's unusual and rather mellow sound was down to the arrangements he made to accommodate Doc, who said, 'In my condition I couldn't play lead . . . so what Teddy did out of the kindness of his heart, he wrote out a whole set of special parts for me, doubling up what the lead player would play, an octave lower. That gave the band a special sound, a different sound, by doing that.'[19]

Working on Doc Cheatham's book was a very different experience from the Barker volumes. Unlike Danny, Doc was not a prolific and natural writer or storyteller. But he was anxious to get his story told, and when he was in Switzerland at the Ascona Festival in 1988 with Lars Edegran's group from New Orleans, we were introduced by Bill Greenow, the band's British saxophone player. Doc knew about Danny Barker's *A Life in Jazz* which had come out a couple of years before, and he knew that he had things to add to that account of the first-hand experience of working with Cab Calloway, because he had preceded Danny in the band by some years. So, as we talked, I became more and more fascinated by his musical experiences, and by the end of a long summer afternoon sitting in the shade on the banks of Lago Maggiore, involving several glasses of iced water, we had agreed to work together. Just as Doc's reminiscences were prompted by the Billie Holiday song I mentioned earlier, he might remember some pertinent fact wherever he was and whatever he was doing. So over the seven years it took us to finish the book, I got a steady stream of letters on hotel notepaper, or from his home in New York, or from his daughter's house in Florida, updating the story. Some were in Doc's hand, others he must have dictated to his wife Nellie.

The underlying narrative was based on transcriptions of a series of cassettes he had started to work on with another author who had died before finishing the project, together with a number of taped interviews with me, largely done after several of his Sweet Basil gigs, plus a major conversation recorded in London for the BBC, which became a three-part series on his life and music.[20] As with several of Danny's observations about his early days in New Orleans and life on the road, I was shocked by Doc's matter of fact acceptance of the segregated racial climate in pre-war America, but his description of growing up in the relatively tolerant atmosphere of Nashville helped me to understand different aspects from those that Danny had taught me about the life of African American musicians during the swing era. In Doc's case, his own impromptu drawings and sketches (Figure 4), as well as some highly evocative photographs, enriched his descriptions.

His father's barber's shop served whites only, and although the Cheathams were an African American family, with Native American ancestry on both sides, they lived in a white neighbourhood, the house having been bought by white friends and sold to Doc's father. Doc recalled: 'Everyone was allowed in the department stores, but if you were Black, you couldn't go in there and try anything on. If you wanted a hat, shoes, gloves, clothes, you had to pay for it, and if it didn't fit, well, that was too bad. We could go in any restaurant, in the front, and order some food and take it out. We couldn't sit down. And we couldn't sit in the front of the white theatre. We had to go out in the alley and walk up into what we called the "buzzard's roost" . . . The whites could come to our theatre when they wanted, and to our dances, when big names came there. But these were the laws of the land, so naturally everybody abided by them.'[21]

Growing up on the edge of the Meharry medical school campus, where every student seemed to be nicknamed 'Doc', as he eventually was himself, Cheatham learned soprano saxophone and cornet while he was still a schoolboy, and in his teens, as well as playing in the pit band at the Bijou Theatre, occasionally backing the likes of Bessie Smith, Ida Cox or Ethel Waters, he played a lot of local gigs with a one-legged pianist named Dan Stafford. At 19, he took a vacation to Atlantic City and was hired to play with Charlie Johnson's band, until they discovered he could not read music and immediately fired him. So a female pianist, in another band with which he sat in, taught him to read the charts. Before long he was on the road with John 'Bearcat' Williams (and his

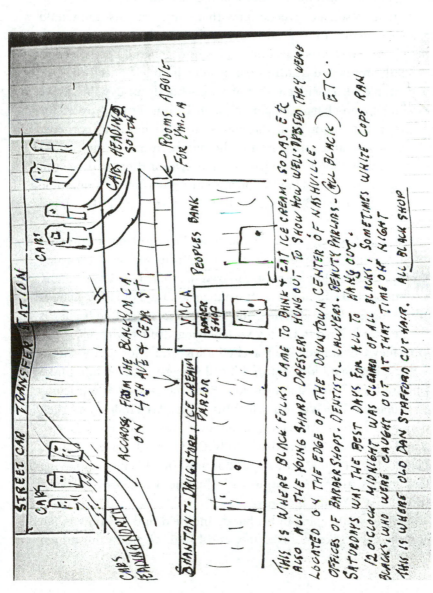

Figure 4 Doc Cheatham's drawing of the African American neighbourhood in Nashville, showing the barber shop where pianist Dan Stafford worked by day

wife, Mary Lou Williams, on piano) before joining Marion Hardy's band. In one of those connections that is all too common in this era of jazz, the bassist was Charlie Turner, who would later work with Fats Waller, and whom Harry Dial compared unfavourably to Billy Taylor. Cheatham travelled with Hardy to Chicago, where the band broke up. Doc stayed, and the city became his passport to a musical career, starting with Al Wynn's orchestra and including subbing for Louis Armstrong, about which there is more in the next chapter.

In many cases, a conversation with a swing era musician would turn into a discussion of a racial issue, as did my meeting with Truck Parham, which led to the subject of what is now generally presumed to be the racially motivated death of bandleader Jimmie Lunceford. Our route to the topic began with another of my boyhood enthusiasms, as we were winding up our chat about playing with Tatum. Truck worked for many years in the 1950s with the pianist Red Richards in cornetist Muggsy Spanier's band – a musician who had been one of my earliest heroes from my boyhood 78 collection. The two of them had been in Muggsy's band for one of my favourite later recordings, 'Lonesome Road' (from the 1954 Brunswick LP *Hot Horn*). Had that band been fun?

'Oh yeah! Muggs! One of the most beautiful musicians and a great trumpet player, man. I learned a lot from Muggsy. I learned a lot of tunes that I didn't know. It amazed me that there are so many Dixieland tunes, and you can never learn them all. But I did learn a lot of them from Muggsy. I stayed in the band a long time, when Red Richards came in the band. Barrett Deems was playing drums with us, "The Deem-on" they called him! We travelled a lot. Did a lot of TV shows in New York, and that kind of stuff. I loved Muggsy, but he didn't take care of himself. He was a chain smoker. But I met a load of musicians through Muggsy – Pee Wee Russell, Miff Mole, Art Hodes, and then I ended up playing with Art a lot. I made some bass-piano records with Hodes, and trios with [clarinettist] Volly De Faut – I played with so many people, I can't think of them all! But most of all I enjoyed playing with Earl Hines and even more with Jimmie Lunceford. I loved Lunceford. He was such a nice guy.

'People would come in his band, and he'd find out how much schooling they got. Like he asked me, and I said, "I didn't finish high school".

'He said, "Don't worry about it, I'll fix that." He was a real educator. Now I was with him from late '41 through '47. And I was with him when he died.[22] He had me in libraries, and every town we'd go to, he'd arrange to have me sit in different classes at various schools. If he'd have been living now, I'd still have been with him. He was just a great guy.

'He asked me to join him. He'd heard me with Earl Hines, at the Apollo Theatre and I joined him from there. Of course, Sy Oliver, who I worked with in Zack Whyte's band, had joined Lunceford before me. I remember when he joined. He'd just written "For Dancers Only", and he'd sat up all night in his room with his trumpet, writing out all the parts. That's how he arranged, by using his trumpet. By the time I got to Lunceford, he had gone on to other big bands, but we never forgot each other, because it was Sy who named me "Truck" because I used to drive the truck for Zack. I used to hear from him a lot. He'd drop me a card or if I was coming to New York I'd call him up. Sy Oliver was a great guy, from Zanesville, Ohio, and from what he told me, he never had formal musical training. He was one of those gifted guys who just knew how to arrange, and became a great arranger who made a lot of tunes for a lot of bands! When I came in the Lunceford band, Willie Smith, Joe Thomas, Trummy Young, all those guys, they took me under their wing. I had a great rapport with them all. I loved that band. And when Jimmie died it was just like losing a father.

'We were in Seaside, Oregon, preparing to play that evening, as we'd got into town from Portland early. And the band was set up. It was a sort of big resort place with all the college kids coming to hear us. And we were outside because the weather was so nice. Some of the guys were shooting dice and some were playing cards. And Lunceford said he was going down to the record store to sell some records. And he set off. He was gone about an hour, when a little kid came up to the table where I was and said, "One of your bass drummers is sick down at the record store."

'Now Omer Simeon wasn't doing anything, so he said to us, "I'll go down and see who it is." He went down there and it was Lunceford. He was on the floor, frothing at the mouth. Simeon stayed 'til the ambulance came. But before that, we'd been in the restaurant at the place where we were playing, to eat.[23] We lined up at the table and they didn't want to feed us. It was the first time I ever heard Lunceford curse. He said, "God dammit, call the manager. We're playing in this damn place! What do you mean we can't eat in here?"

'So he went to see the manager and when he came back out, they said, "Okay, we'll feed you." Me, I'd been through a similar thing to that once with Roy Eldridge, going to New York, and I didn't eat. Because when you say you don't want to feed me, I won't eat. But they had some beef and everyone was offered beef sandwiches. Now, Lunceford was sitting next to me. When he finished, he took a B C Powder, like he had pain or gas or something. But when he went off to autograph those records, that was the last we ever saw of him.

'It was payroll night, but the place we were playing kept all the money. The guy that booked us in New York found out about it, he called, and made them give the money back to our road manager. They said they were "protecting" the money to see nobody would take it! It was pay night, as I said, and we finally got paid. Then we were all there asking each other what next? But the road manager said we had to play three more dates on the tour, so we did. And we ended up in Seattle. That was the last date.'

Truck was utterly convinced that Lunceford had been poisoned for insisting that his musicians were fed, in a venue, the Bungalow Ballroom, which catered for a white clientèle. Indeed, the band (which played its first set unaware that Lunceford had died on the way to hospital) watched a large group of African Americans who wanted to hear them being turned away by the management.[24]

Lunceford was, assuming Truck's conviction was correct, a high-profile victim of the racial climate of the age. But his was one of many African American lives needlessly lost. When I first published Danny Barker's book, many readers homed in on his description of a New Orleans dance venue, the 'Animule Hall', which, as *Chicago Tribune* journalist Howard Reich observed, was 'the historic night-spot Jelly Roll Morton immortalised in the recording "Animule Dance".'[25] But in the first edition Danny did not tell the story of what happened to the venue's bandleader Long-Head Bob. When we revisited the book after publication, he recounted a conversation with Chester Zardis who told him that Bob had gone to play a gig out in the Bayous. Two of the band came home late that night, but two of them did not, including Bob. Next day his wife became anxious and asked to be taken to the venue.

'So they get in a car and they head back down there and they find the proprietor of the joint where they played. And she asks, "Do y'all know what time Bob left? Or where he's at? Did you see him?"

'He says, "He went back by the canal," and gestures over his shoulder. "Back there ... "

'Sure enough, Bob and the other musician who didn't come back are lying there in the canal, dead, and starting to swell up, because they had been in the water ... a couple of days. So they had to call the undertaker and the sheriff, who started asking questions. But nobody knew what happened, or if they knew they weren't saying. Nobody remembered seeing nothing ... as time went on, nobody done nothing about it.'[26]

Throughout my exploration of early jazz and the swing era, accounts such as this were a sober reminder of the realities of African American life in all too many parts of the United States. Elsewhere in Danny Barker's recollections and those of Little Brother Montgomery, there is an account of the similarly gruesome death of a pair of Black gamblers shot dead in a juke joint in Mississippi, where the two musicians had been due to play. Clarinettist Joe Darensbourg's memoirs contain the story of 'Crackshot', the Black bartender in Baton Rouge with a .45 bullet lodged in his skull from a failed attempt to kill him. And trumpeter Evan Thomas was less lucky. He was murdered on the bandstand at a dance in Rayne, Louisiana, in 1932, the shock of which event triggered his fellow trumpeter Bunk Johnson's retirement from music for a decade.[27]

7 LOUIS ARMSTRONG

Many of the musicians I have already mentioned spent some part of their career in big bands. And thanks to my one-time BBC Radio colleague Humphrey Carpenter, in the late 1980s I had the opportunity to experience working regularly in a large swing orchestra that specialized in the repertoire of the 1920s–1940s. Humphrey was the founder of Vile Bodies, which played twice weekly at the Ritz Hotel in London for the best part of a decade. He was also its bassist, but when he needed to devote himself full-time to writing his biography of Benjamin Britten (which eventually appeared in 1992), he asked me to take his place in the band for what ended up being a couple of years. There were Ellington and Basie transcriptions, plus pieces from the repertoire of Charlie Barnet, as well as Humphrey's own passion, British dance bands of the 1930s, such as those of Lew Stone and Bert Ambrose. Indeed, when I was researching several entries on British jazz and dance musicians for the *Dictionary of National Biography* in the early 2000s, he was writing his biography of Dennis Potter, who had shared a love of this era. I more often than not found the books and magazine issues I was looking for piled up in Humphrey's regular corner in the Upper Reading Room of the Bodleian Library in Oxford!

Vile Bodies gave me an opportunity to play alongside some of the best British musicians in the older styles of big band music. Trumpeter Tommy McQuater, for example, had worked with Ambrose and the Squadronaires, and his section-mate Duncan Campbell had played with Ted Heath's orchestra. The peerless Gordon Campbell was a regular guest on trombone, and in the reed section, alongside our fine regular saxophonist Jim Tomlinson, would be such first-rate players as Alan Barnes, Don Rendell and Olaf Vas. I still remember the dancers spontaneously moving forward and crowding round the bandstand one night as Don took an extended solo on 'Honeysuckle Rose', the audience eventually breaking into applause after his many choruses, much as must have happened in the swing era. On drums was Tony Augarde, a very astute jazz critic, whose day job was Editor of the *Oxford Dictionary of Quotations*. The lead trumpeter Ian Smith and I formed several subsequent bands together and he has played in the Buck Clayton Legacy Band since its foundation.

By coincidence, my very first oral history interview was with a veteran of the Duncan Campbell and Tommy McQuater generation. As an undergraduate, I wrote for the Oxford University magazine *Isis*, mainly for the arts page, and as well as covering concerts – not to mention promoting George Melly – I also reviewed art exhibitions. The Oxford Playhouse regularly had such shows in its upstairs bar, and in early 1973 I went along to preview a collection of paintings by Billy Scott-Coomber. The idea was to combine the review and an interview feature with this Anglo-Irish painter who had been a student of Sir William Orpen in the 1920s. A chance remark of his led me to realize that I already knew his name, because he was credited as the vocalist and guitarist on the labels of some of my 78s of Jack Payne's band. Our conversation immediately moved away from painting, and, for a fascinating hour, he vividly brought the world of 1930s London swing orchestras to life. He had also travelled abroad in that era with Payne. 'I was playing l'Empire in Paris,' he said, 'and after the show I remember going to a little bar in Pigalle, with a friend who said I had to hear the Quintet of the Hot Club of France. They were a knockout … I was so impressed that when I came back I helped to arrange Stephane Grappelli and Django Reinhardt's first visit to England.'[1] Billy told me that shortly after that it was being overwhelmed by the sheer technical skill and boundless technique of Segovia, whom he heard at the Queen's Hall in London, which made him give up the guitar. Although he sang with and directed Payne's band throughout World War Two, he then became a BBC Radio producer, which he combined with reviving his career as a painter. But I realized that February morning in Oxford, as he described playing at the BBC's Savoy Hill studio, and the smartest London hotel ballrooms, that his generation had plenty of stories to tell, and few of them had been told.

So in the wake of that early encounter, this chapter, and the two that follow – in the same way as the previous ones – aim to draw on the experience of the musicians who helped create this type of music, and look at three particular big bands: those of Louis Armstrong, Count Basie and Duke Ellington.

Louis, having started in New Orleans, went on to front small recording groups and then led a sizeable swing big band, until he scaled down to his six-piece All Stars in the late 1940s. As a big band player, he made a huge impression on the young Buck Clayton, who heard him at Frank Sebastian's new Cotton Club, not long after Buck first arrived in California in his early twenties. When Clayton asked Louis how to play a glissando on the trumpet, Armstrong took him to the men's room, and sat on the toilet, smoking a reefer, and explained the half valve technique.[2] Clayton also recalled how Louis told him that had Buck come from New Orleans, he would not have shown him. Such was the rivalry between trumpeters from his home town, Armstrong confided, that had he been back there, 'I'd put a handkerchief over my valves so nobody could see how I did it!'[3] I remember Buck chuckling at the memory, and also saying how much he loved and admired Armstrong.

Doc Cheatham also benefitted from Armstrong's generosity when, having quite recently arrived in Chicago in the 1920s, Doc was asked by Louis to substitute for him at the Vendome Theatre, with Erskine Tate's band. The audience were disappointed not to hear Armstrong stand up to take a solo on his current hit 'Poor Little Rich Girl', and Doc initially wished a hole in the floor would open and swallow him up. But, he told me, 'I knew my horn and I played fine, playing Louis' part. I played it like I played it because nobody in the world could play it like Louis.'[4] It was obviously a success, because Louis hired him a few more times to come and take his place. Doc believed that there was 'an unwritten law' that Louis wouldn't employ other New Orleans musicians to stand in for him, so he called on the young man from Nashville instead. Nonetheless Doc counted himself fortunate to have heard many other Crescent City players at first hand in 1920s Chicago.

'I was very lucky, when I went up to the South Side for the first time and heard the New Orleans musicians. I hung out and slept in alleys. I didn't have any money, but once in a while I'd get a little job that didn't pay much. So I slept outdoors. I even slept at the back of the Sunset where Louis was playing. That's what I wanted to do, and

I learned a lot from Louis, and Freddie Keppard, and Joe Oliver, but I thought Louis was just about the greatest of all of them, so I paid more attention to his playing than anybody else's. I liked Freddie Keppard, but he didn't have the soul that Louis had. No one did. None of them had the soul that Louis had.'⁵

Doc generally heard Armstrong in the context of a larger band in which he was a solo attraction. Many jazz enthusiasts know Armstrong's 1920s work from his small group recordings with the Hot Five and Hot Seven, but from the time of his brief New York stint with Fletcher Henderson in 1924–5 he frequently played in larger aggregations, and from the late 1920s his main recorded output was fronting just such groups. In particular there was the band organized to accompany him by Luis Russell, and already mentioned in connection with Paul Barbarin, Pops Foster and Henry Allen.

Danny Barker recalled the Armstrong small group records causing a sensation among musicians as each one came out. He also wrote in *A Life in Jazz* how Louis' singing voice on his big band records influenced a generation of vocalists. When Danny worked at Jimmy Ryan's in the 1940s with Lee Blair (originally from Savannah, Georgia), who had been the guitar and banjo player in the Luis Russell band, Lee mused as to why he, rather than Barker, with his home town and family connections, had been chosen to work with Louis Armstrong. Barker told him, 'You have a bigger name, having worked with Jelly Roll [Morton], great banjo solos on "Shoe Shiner's Drag", and you have a great reputation known in the four corners of the jazz world.'⁶ The two laughed and drank one another's health.

One of Blair's successors with the Armstrong big band was another veteran of Jelly Roll Morton, namely Lawrence Lucie. He played guitar on the 1939 Bluebird sessions that are the high water mark of Morton's late work. Born in Virginia, he was the only non-New Orleans member of Jelly's rhythm section alongside Zutty Singleton, Wellman Braud and Morton himself. 'I met Jelly Roll Morton at the Rhythm Club on 132nd Street and 7th Avenue,' he recalled. 'That's where all the musicians used to go and stay on and talk, and have fun. That's where I met Jelly, and we got to be such friends I used to meet him almost every day and we'd talk about music. I'd talk to him about history that I didn't know about – New Orleans and things like that. He knew, and he would give his opinions. So, one day we were at the Rhythm Club and Jelly was playing, and I had my guitar, so I sat down and played with him. He said, "I like the way you play, because I used to play guitar! I'm gonna do a session. I'd like to have you on my session."

'I said, "Okay!" So that's how I got on that session, just by being a friend and sitting down and playing with him at the Rhythm Club.'[7]

Shortly before that 1939 studio date, Danny Barker took a well-known photograph of Jelly holding forth to his fellow musicians outside that selfsame club, waving a slice of watermelon to emphasise his narrative. Seeing this atmospheric shot, it's easy to imagine Lucie being charmed by the loquacious and charismatic Morton. On one of my visits to New Orleans, I dropped in on the historian and jazz antiquarian Bill Russell, who showed me Morton's original handwritten arrangements for the Bluebird sessions on which Lucie played. Some of these charts were subsequently published (by Karl Knudsen, of Storyville Records) in Russell's book *Oh Mister Jelly! A Jelly Roll Morton Scrapbook*.[8] I remember poring over the band parts with Bill, and seeing how the tenorist Happy Cauldwell had pencilled in his name on his, as well as marking notes on fingering and breathing. Listening to Albert Nicholas and Sidney Bechet on the record of 'High Society', and comparing this to the score, it was clear that they pretty much ignored their sheet music, but (like Cauldwell) the other seasoned big band players in the line-up, trumpeter Sidney DeParis and trombonist Claude Jones, made good use of theirs.[9] In the photographs of the session, everyone has a music stand in front of them, and Lucie is clearly reading his part, though he rather downplayed this when we met.

'I had met the other musicians at the Rhythm Club before, but not to talk to,' he recalled. 'Everybody came to the Club, as all the musicians used to socialize there. But I hadn't played with any of them before, only heard about them and read about them. On this particular session, everybody seemed to be knowing every song he was going to play, and I think he only wrote out a couple of things for me. I was the youngest one on the session, of course, and everyone knew the songs that we played. I'd played several of the New Orleans songs before, but not with Jelly. Before then I had played in a dancing school with June Clark. When you play in a dancing school you play *all* the songs, hundreds and hundreds of songs. You'd spend the whole day learning new songs, the ones that you don't know, so you can play them later that day. So from playing in this dancing school I knew a lot of the songs, but I didn't learn them with Jelly. They were standard songs.'

By the time Lawrence recorded with Morton in 1939, he was something of a big band veteran, having played for Benny Carter, Fletcher Henderson and Lucky Millinder, as well as briefly deputizing for Fred Guy in the Duke Ellington Orchestra. But the following year, at the age of 32, he began a long stay with Louis Armstrong's big band, directed by Luis Russell. One permanent souvenir of his time with Armstrong, of which Lawrence was particularly proud, was his appearance in a movie.

'We did a movie – *Jam Session*. We made that in Hollywood of course, and I was suggested to do the part with "I'll Be Glad When You're Dead You Rascal You". I did the arrangement on that song . . . so the producer suggested that I act with Velma Middleton. That's how I happened to get onto that, because he thought I was the suitable one to be Velma Middleton's boyfriend, so that Louis could sing "I'll Be Glad When You're Dead" at me, as though Velma was *his* girlfriend! That was an act we put on. I got paid double for that.'

Lawrence slightly mis-remembered this event, because although he appeared with the band at the time on a radio version of Sam Theard's song 'I'll Be Glad When You're Dead', the song in the movie is Fields and McHugh's 'I Can't Give You Anything But Love'.[10] Dressed immaculately in white tuxedos, and with the leader sporting a derby hat, Armstrong's is the only African American band in this 1944 film, and its performance kicks off a sequence by six swing orchestras (including Charlie Barnet's band, and Glen Gray with the Casa Loma). The plot is a somewhat flimsy cinematic vehicle for dancer Ann Miller, posing as a scriptwriter's assistant in order to get a job in movies. Armstrong's band stands out as the only one to play its natural act – relaxed, swinging and humorous – in what was billed as 'Columbia's jiving jamboree'. In addition to the slightly comic rendition of the vocal, Louis' central trumpet solo is scintillating, with a virtuoso break in the middle, and there are brief solos from altoist Carl Frye, clarinettist Prince Robinson and tenorist Joe Garland. Despite really effective playing from Barnet's group and the light and gently swinging sound of the Casa Loma, their on-screen personae are stiff and rather serious, whereas Armstrong, as ever, appears to be having fun.

Lawrence believed this was simply because it was a great band. 'It was wonderful, and it was like most of his other bands – an all-star band. We broke it up everywhere we went! It went over so big, so well. We had a lot of good music and a lot of very good musicians. The tunes were all written out and arranged but when you heard the band you heard something special.' On Armstrong's recorded version of 'Hey Lawdy Mama', from 10 March 1941 with a septet drawn from the bigger line-up, you can hear Lawrence himself taking a guitar solo that showed that he, too, was something special. At that point Johnny Williams (like Lawrence a veteran of the Lucky Millinder band) was the bassist, but in 1945, the year after Lawrence himself left, the bass chair was taken over by 22-year-old Arvell Shaw, who would go on to work with Armstrong for much of the rest of the trumpeter's life.

I knew both Johnny and Arvell a little. I first met John Williams Jr (as he signed himself in my address book) when he borrowed my bass at the outdoor jazz festival in Lugano in 1979. Mostly that week, the weather was perfect, but on a couple of evenings, winds whipped up across the lake, and rain gusted almost horizontally across the main square where the audience, huddled under flapping umbrellas and plastic hoods, loyally stayed to listen. Johnny's amplified 'stick' bass gave him an electric shock during one such thunderstorm as water blew unexpectedly onto the platform, and he felt my conventional wooden instrument might be somewhat safer! I was due to follow the Harlem Blues and Jazz Band (in which he played) onto the otherwise relatively sheltered stage, as a member of Rudi Baillieu's band from Belgium, accompanying the New Orleans pianist Sing Miller. So we were already standing in the wings to keep dry. Consequently, Johnny and I did a quick substitution with my instrument and, after sharing a drink at the end of the concert, kept in touch over the years that followed. We had a very joyful reunion when he toured Britain a few years later with Bob Greene's package show the 'World of Jelly Roll'.

Johnny introduced me at that time to Tommy Benford, their drummer, who had actually played and recorded with Morton, somewhat earlier than Lawrence Lucie. Tommy had wonderful memories not only of Jelly Roll, but also of playing and recording with New Orleans clarinettist George Lewis – 'a little skinny fellow' as he recalled. Also in Bob Greene's band was the very distinguished clarinettist Herbie Hall, brother of Edmond Hall who had played with Louis Armstrong. I'd worked with Herbie on his UK tour in 1981, spending a few nights in residence at Dean Street's Pizza Express in Soho, and then travelling into East Anglia for a sequence of concerts in, among other places, Cambridge and Thetford. We made a record during our time at the Pizza Express, featuring Herbie's sensitive and swinging clarinet playing, which finally saw the light of day in 2015.[11] On guitar and banjo with Bob Greene was Marty Grosz (son of the painter George Grosz), with whom I'd made a Radio 3 broadcast during an exhibition of his father's paintings at the Royal Academy. And Bob himself I knew from Manhattan dinners with the writer James Lincoln Collier (whom I had published at Macmillan) together with the cornetist and *New Yorker* cartoonist Lee Lorenz. So that night with Bob's band, at the Hexagon in Reading, the dressing room witnessed a series of happy reunions. The only musician whom I hadn't previously met was the World of Jelly Roll's cornetist Ed Polcer, but we were to enjoy playing together a few years later in Ascona with the band led by the Italian swing guitarist Lino Patruno.

From the mid-1990s, Arvell Shaw was also a regular visitor to the Ascona Festival in Switzerland, and in 2002 he was due to be there with Lars Edegran's band from New Orleans with Duke Heitger, trumpet, Evan Christopher, clarinet and Freddie Lonzo, trombone. For this band, the festival concerts were to be preceded by a short tour of northeastern Italy, playing in small towns and villages in the Friuli area, bordered by Udine and Venice. Arvell decided he didn't want to do a string of one-nighters, so I took his place for the road tour, and then when he joined the band in Ascona, I spent plenty of time with him during the festival. My friend from schooldays, Norman Emberson (a student of Cié Frazier and Freddie Kohlman), played drums on the tour, as Ernie Elly, from New Orleans, took a similar view to Arvell, and joined the band when it reached the festival in Switzerland.

It was a privilege to be asked to play the Italian concerts in place of Arvell, the invitation coming because I had known Lars Edegran and his British-born wife Kathy for a very long time, and they knew I'd met Arvell in New York the previous year, a month or so after 9/11. I visited him in his apartment, perilously close to Ground Zero, and in which he'd been a virtual prisoner during the weeks after the tragedy. He was glad to have some company in those difficult times, and we spent most of a day together recording his life story.

A little before he joined Louis Armstrong for the first time, Arvell had worked with another titan of New Orleans jazz. He recalled: 'The first time I met Sidney Bechet, I was still in the Navy, during the Second World War, because I was stationed at the Quonset Point Naval Air Station right outside of Providence, Rhode Island, which is only an hour from Boston. And I used to spend my liberty, of an evening, going to Boston. They had a jazz club in Boston called the Savoy, where there was a very famous bandleader called Sabby Lewis. He introduced guys like Paul Gonsalves and Big Nick Nicholas on tenor. He featured hot tenor players. And they always had two bands at the Savoy. They'd bring in stars like Pete Brown, who was a great alto player of those days, and Sidney Bechet would come there quite often. I would go in and sit in with him. Sidney seemed to take a liking to my playing, so I'd go in every night that I had liberty, and pretty soon he said, "You're here almost every night, why don't you just take the job when you can?" So I worked with him during that time at that jazz club, the Savoy, and this was in about 1944.

'Bechet was a strong leader, very strong. In fact trumpet players hated to work with him because he would take over the part of the trumpet, and that would leave the trumpeter nothing to play. So no trumpet player would work with him. He didn't mind. There was just one trumpet player he didn't want to work with, and that's Louis Armstrong. Now, Buck Clayton knew Sidney for years, and he wasn't going to start competing for the trumpet role, so what Buck started doing was playing the clarinet part! And Sidney took the lead like a trumpet player! [When we played the 1958 World's Fair in Brussels] Buck said, "I'm not goin' to bust my chops trying to outplay Sidney Bechet." Bechet could play as loud as any trumpet, and with that vibrato, you couldn't drown him out ... To me, Bechet is of equal stature in the history of jazz as anybody: Duke Ellington, Louis Armstrong ... Bechet deserves that kind of place in the history of jazz.'[12]

In Buck's autobiography he is very diplomatic about Bechet, saying that it was a pleasure to work with the soprano saxophonist and 'he and I got along just great'.[13] But in his home it was rather a different story – he had a coffee mug with Bechet's picture on it, on which Buck had drawn a pair of devil's horns emerging from Sidney's forehead!

Arvell moved on in our conversation from Bechet to Louis Armstrong, whose big band he joined not long after his Navy service and those gigs in Boston. And the drummer in the Armstrong big band at the time was a figure not normally associated with this style of jazz, but with bebop – Roy Haynes. 'Roy was a swing drummer,' Arvell assured me. 'He could really swing. Kenny Clarke was also in Louis' big band at one time and so was Dexter Gordon. A lot of what they call "modern jazz" came out of that big band. Being the age I was, I would have just naturally gone into that, but I just loved playing with Louis. I loved the feel, I loved Louis' sound, and I just could not get that same feeling with bebop or modern jazz. So I stayed with the big band and in fact when he disbanded it, he only kept me and Velma Middleton.'

Arvell went on to talk about his time in the All Stars and working with the various musicians who were in the sextet, including pianist Earl Hines. I was never lucky enough to hear the Armstrong All Stars in person. When Louis played his final residency in the UK at Batley Variety Club for two weeks in 1968, some older boys from my school decided to go, and asked me if I'd like to come. But my mother put her foot down and said that if I thought I was going to travel the length of the country, aged just 15, in a VW Dormobile driven by a 17-year-old who had just passed his driving test, I was very much mistaken. So I never got to hear Louis on his last visit to Britain with the All Stars. (It was virtually his last time in the UK as well, apart from a single charity event at which he appeared solo in 1970.) My friends, of course, got to Batley unscathed and had a wonderful time.

I did see a rather odd latter-day version of the band, long after Armstrong's death, at a mid-1980s concert at the Hexagon Theatre in Reading led by the British trumpeter Keith Smith. Dubbed the 'Wonderful World of Louis Armstrong', the group included five original All Stars members: clarinettist Peanuts Hucko, trombonist Big Chief Russell Moore, pianist Dick Cary, plus Arvell Shaw and Barrett Deems. The idea was that the show would begin in a blackout. So the band crept out on to the stage in the dark, but someone had forgotten to lock the wheels of the Steinway. As Russell Moore headed through the gloom towards his stool, he missed, and slipped backwards, knocking the piano. It shot to the back of the stage, so that as the lights came up the pianist was holding his hands over an absent keyboard like a mime artist and the trombonist was flat on his back. The lights quickly dimmed again, as the stagehands brought the musicians and their instruments back together into approximately the right positions. This time round, as the lights came back up and the band went into the opening bars of 'Sleepy Time Down South', there was a nostalgic moment of chills down the spine.

Thinking of the original band and Velma Middleton, I wondered what it would have been like to share the stage with Armstrong as a fellow vocalist. Velma herself died in Sierra Leone after suffering a stroke on tour with Louis in 1961, but I was lucky enough to meet and talk to her successor, Jewel Brown. Knowing that I was British, she began by recalling her debut in London. 'I believe it was the Royal Festival Hall. We played there.[14] I never shall forget the London fog got in my throat, and it seemed that nothing would come out during the first half! The second half we were able to do a little better. And I do remember the Queen was there. We were all a bit in awe, and then Louis said, "And now we dedicate this number to Ol' Liz!" Then in the lights we caught the shining of her teeth, laughing, and everybody started to smile and laugh about it.

'I came in because Velma died in Africa, and she'd been a big part of Louis' life, and they loved each other dearly, in the way of friendship. Her death was a tremendous heartbreak to him. They were very reluctant to put another singer with Louis. And I believe he played for a little more than a year without a singer.[15] Then they decided to take some of the stress from Louis and add a girl to the show. When I was working in Dallas, they decided to interview me, and test me out for a couple of weeks. After which they decided that I was the one. They had about 500 singers wanting the job, and how I got over that I don't know! But I became the one. Those years were all quite good, very educational. There's not enough you can say about those years, I treasure them to this day. Everybody that Louis would hire had a bit of stardom in their own right. That's the way he wanted it. When I joined I had had quite a few achievements of my own, not internationally, but in and around America, and I guess that's what merited my being able to be included.'[16]

Jewel went on to talk about her travels around the world with the All Stars, and in particular her fondness for Europe. She laughed at the memory of looking out of the dressing room window in 1960s Budapest for the first time, and seeing what looked like a sea of bicycles outside the concert venue as thousands of listeners had turned up on two wheels to hear the band: 'The thing I liked about being with Louis in Europe in particular is that the people were so appreciative of authentic music, and it brought out the best in me as a performer because they were so involved in and appreciative of our music.'

In all, Jewel spent just over six years with the All Stars – just under half the length of Velma Middleton's stay. In the first of the Macmillan jazz autobiographies that I published, the band's clarinettist, Barney Bigard, was withering about the way Armstrong and his manager Joe Glaser treated Velma at the end of her life. He gives a chilling description of the effects of her stroke, as she lost her feeling and the ability to speak, and appeared 'glassy-eyed'. She was taken to what he calls a 'funny little hospital' and then basically abandoned there as the band finished its African tour and set off for France. 'I'll never forgive Joe Glaser and Louis for that,' he wrote, 'because they said it would take too many people to lift her onto the plane.'[17] Although Velma was overweight and suffered from numerous minor health problems, the callous way she was abandoned by Louis' management resonated with Bigard's experiences of how many other African American musicians were sometimes treated.

However, since Bigard's death, his comments should be qualified. A letter has emerged from Louis to Joe Glaser, pleading with him, and saying, 'What she needs now is to be taken from that small hospital from Freetown, Africa, and brought to America, USA, put into hospital right away where they may save her life.' This was not to be, but Glaser did arrange for her body to be repatriated so that her family could hold a funeral, and Velma's remains would be buried on American soil. Louis' wife, Lucille Armstrong, recalled 'Joe Glaser ... pulled all kinds of strings to get her over here.'[18]

8 COUNT BASIE

The risk and uncertainty of a swing musician's life also came up quite early on in a conversation with Buck Clayton's old friend and colleague, the Texas-born tenor saxophonist Buddy Tate. We'd met in New York (memorably when he was recording the album *Swing Summit*[1] with Sweets Edison and Frank Wess for Candid in 1990) but, along with my BBC producer Derek Drescher, I was taken to his house in Massapequa on Long Island to visit him on the occasion of his 80th birthday in 1993, where Nancy Miller Elliott (Buck's co-author) and I sat down to talk to him about his life's work.

We began with the very early days of his career, before he joined T. Holder's band in 1930, when he'd played for a travelling circus. I was interested in how this band might have sounded, and he told me it was typical tent and medicine show fare, with the popular hits of the day dovetailed into the special music needed for the clowns, jugglers and tumblers. But I most remember him saying that as long as the circus could afford to keep the lion, the musicians were going to get paid and get fed. Rumour had it that the moment the circus shot the lion, there was not going to be any money or food for the musicians!

Buddy subsequently joined Count Basie's first (but short-lived) orchestra which was set up in 1935 after the Count took over Bennie Moten's band, following Moten's sudden death from a failed tonsillectomy operation. There was no lion to indicate the financial health of the band, but its chronic lack of funds was apparent from quite early on. 'It started out being a big band,' laughed Buddy, 'but they slipped off one by one. It's hard to leave, to say "Sorry man I can't make it." So they'd slip off. I remember one night I caught Rush [the singer Jimmy Rushing] – he was slippin' off. He said, "Man, I'm goin' to the drugstore." I said "There ain't no drugstores open this time of night. I know what you're doing!" So that time he didn't go, but later he slipped off and left Basie.'[2]

Tate would later rejoin Basie in his mature band, replacing Herschel Evans, but by the time he came back into the Basie fold, he had already met his sparring partner, the band's other saxophonist, Lester Young. The revue *Tan Town Topics* had originally been written by Fats Waller, Harvey Brooks and Andy Razaf for Connie's Inn in Harlem in 1926, but like so many revues of the time a version went on tour before it returned to Broadway in 1929. We know, for example, that it was in various parts of Indiana and then Chicago in 1927,[3] and it was during part of that tour in Oklahoma that Buddy heard his teenaged future colleague: 'I had heard Lester early in years. In *Tan Town Revue*. Heard him in Tulsa. And when *he* came to hear him, Basie said, "If you are playing the way you played the last time I heard you, it will be your engagement." I sure did know him well. People called him fey. He sure hated that. Broke his heart.'

Some who did not know him better may have perceived Young, with his private language, his habit of creating nicknames for colleagues, and his ethereal tenor sound as 'fey', but those who worked with him knew he was a tough, resolute musician. Trumpeter Clark Terry, who joined Basie in 1948, recalled the Count using a variation on 'the dozens', a semi-ritualistic African American game, and a form of Signifying, involving ever more fanciful insults about family members, and mainly focused on the protagonists' mothers, to goad his tenorists into battling one another on stage. Traditionally, the dozens is played between two battling wordsmiths trading what the social theorist John Dollard termed a 'pattern of interactive insult'.[4] But Basie did not assume the role of one of the sparring partners – he used the verbal tools of the game to spark a *musical* battle of mental acuity and instrumental proficiency between his star saxophonists.

'It goes back to Count Basie's days with Herschel Evans and Lester Young,' Clark said. 'Before their particular era, the tenors used to sit together. But Basie started them being like enemies, sitting on opposite ends of the reed section. Then he'd go and speak to one of them, like he'd go to Herschel and say "Man, Red said somethin' horrible 'bout your mother."

'"He did?"

'"Yeah."

'Then Basie'd say to the other one, "He says your sister was a prostitute."

'"What?"

'Then he'd say, "Both of you guys go out and play some ... " And they'd go out there as if their instruments were axes or knives and they were trying to annihilate one another! So this became known as the "Tenor Battle". Basie used to do that consistently and it became very, very popular.'[5]

As an aside it is worth noting that the blind British-born pianist George Shearing became proficient at the dozens when he was working in New York with Sarah Vaughan, and when his quintet later toured in support of Basie's band, he would often take on his fellow bandleader in the dressing room in a bout of verbal sparring. 'He'd turn to me and say, "Don't start!"' remembered Shearing. 'I'd say "No I won't, how is she?"'[6] And then they'd be off, trading maternal insults, until Basie called a halt.

From the late 1930s onwards, the Basie or Ellington orchestras were the ones most jazz musicians aspired to join, but there were other bands that were very significant training grounds. One name that comes up over and over again is that of Lionel Hampton, whose orchestra launched many a career. Indeed, Buck Clayton himself worked with Hampton in Los Angeles some time before Hampton joined Goodman or Buck joined Basie. Clayton was quick to point out that 'I never did work with Lionel Hampton's band, not five minutes of any day in history,' but he was compelled to use Hampton as his drummer when Buck's own group played Frank Sebastian's New Cotton Club in Culver City, because Hampton was the house drummer. Consequently, Buck knew all the members of Lionel's resident band and in 1935 (shortly after his return from Shanghai) he coaxed Herschel Evans into leaving Hampton and joining his own line-up in Los Angeles (the last group Clayton led before heading for Kansas City and joining Count Basie).

It's certainly the case that many members of the post-war Basie band started out with Hampton, such as trombonist Al Grey, who told me: 'Lionel didn't give them credit, but he had everyone. If you look down the list, do your studies or your homework, you're gonna find that Lionel had them all. You name them, and they'd come through Lionel first. He was more of a jump band, a happy band: "Hey bop-a-rebop".

But I learned so much from Lionel, creatively, [how] to have a personality.'⁷ A significant friendship with Quincy Jones was also formed in Hampton's early 1950s brass section that later led to arrangements being written to feature Al Grey during his stint with Basie: 'We played together in Lionel Hampton's band, when Q had just started out. And this was when we didn't even have enough money to get a room for the night. Quincy and I used to room together, quite a lot of times, because we didn't have that three dollars. Quincy had quite good ideas about how to write.'

One aspect of Hampton's band that was passed on to the musicians who worked with him was his instinctive sense of movement on stage. Al recalled: 'When I first left Benny Carter and went with Jimmie Lunceford, you had to sit up straight and everything. And fall out with your tails, clothes and shirt right. It was very stiff. People looked up and there you were. You never did clap your hands or smile. It wasn't done. Jimmie Lunceford directed the band with his baton, and everything. You was just like Paul Whiteman's band, that's the way it was represented. But when I went with Lionel Hampton, he'd come over to me and say, "Hey! Clap your hands, Gates!" I didn't know what he meant at first. And then he'd demonstrate – clapping your hands, because, in those days, they had routines of clapping your hands. That was an education in itself to get that down with all the different routines that he had. Like when we played the Apollo, the curtain would go up and "Bam!" But with Jimmie Lunceford's band it'd be: "Look straight ahead, don't move!"'

A musician who had similar experiences of the Lunceford band, and whom I got to know well, was the clarinettist and saxophone player Benny Waters. I first played on one of his UK tours in March and April 1980, including a memorable concert at the Bulls Head in Barnes, at which Freddie Kohlman (who happened to be passing through London en route to Frankfurt) dropped by and, with the enthusiastic encouragement of our drummer Robin Jones, sat in for the second set along with the tour's regular rhythm section of me and the marvellous pianist Fred Hunt. Spurred on by Freddie's playing, Benny pulled out all the stops, playing an energetic opening to each number on alto. Then, after Fred's solo, he'd come back to show his virtuosity on clarinet, before throwing the challenge to me. He would conclude with some absolutely searing choruses on tenor that also involved exchanging eight-bar phrases with Freddie. It was a truly memorable evening, the more so for me as the cornetist Ruby Braff was in the audience. We asked him to sit in, but he said he was enjoying it too much, just listening to the torrent of energy coming from Benny, who was then aged a mere 78. (I played with him again from time to time as he moved into his eighties and his energy level on stage was always phenomenal.)

Driving back after that gig, Benny told me how he'd joined Lunceford in the summer of 1942, replacing the alto saxophonist Ted Buckner. Lunceford's meticulous approach to the music meant that Benny had to learn some of Ted's solos note-for-note from the band's records, so that the audience 'would recognize them'. He then hummed the alto solo from 'Margie', which he could still remember in every detail. It was another of those moments where a musical cue had set up a conversation, because hearing Freddie Kohlman earlier in the evening had reminded him of Jimmy Crawford, Lunceford's drummer, whom Benny always admiringly said was 'something else' when it came to jazz rhythm playing.

Another member of the 1950s Basie trombone section was New Orleans-born Bennie Powell, and he also came through the Hampton orchestra. 'I went back to Tulsa [after playing in Chicago], and as fate would have it, Lionel Hampton's band had just played Oklahoma City previous to this. There was a trombone player who was with Lionel's band named Chips Alcott, who had left them in Oklahoma City. So here they were in Tulsa, not really looking for a trombone player, maybe, because the normal pattern would be to just play a couple of days without. Now I didn't know how they heard about me or I heard about them, but we did hook up. I found out later that Betty Carter was pretty much responsible for me joining Hamp's band. At this time, she was sort of Hamp's adviser on bebop, because she was very much into the bebop idiom. Hamp came to her and said, "What do you think of him?" And she gave me the thumbs up.

'I don't know if that's totally why I went with Lionel's band, but it sure helped me, when I joined them in 1948. In the line-up was Jerome Richardson, Jimmy Cleveland, a guy named Fox (from Indianapolis), and Al Bartee – one of a couple of drummers. Hamp would wear out drummers, or rather, they would just physically wear *themselves* out. But Hamp was really very innovative and there were a lot of things that he did that he didn't get credit for, as they were sort of wiped away by his showmanship.'[8]

Both Bennie Powell and Al Grey subsequently joined what became known as the 'New Testament' Basie band, in other words, the big band he re-formed in 1952 after being compelled a couple of years or so earlier to scale down to an Octet at the end of the swing era. But his 'Old Testament' band was vitally important to many of his later players including Al Grey, who told me he was first inspired to play jazz by going to hear that original Basie orchestra in the 1930s. 'I never had seen a performer to perform like Jimmy Rushing. "Mister Five by Five". You'd see this big man just belting it out, and everybody's jumping. And it's where I learned a couple of licks from Dicky Wells. Later on in life, Dicky Wells became a dear, dear, friend. I took one of the licks from him that everyone used to use, 'cos I was one of those guys who'd get some licks from a myriad of different trombone players ... And then "Ding Ding", that's Vic Dickenson, who was called that because he always used that word – "D'you wanna do one, Ding?" – we worked a lot together. Norman Granz accepted Vic and me after J. J. [Johnson] and Bill [Harris], and we worked together as the trombone players with Jazz at the Philharmonic.'

Another member of the trombone section in the 'Old Testament' band, who had previously been with the Count (and several other future Basie musicians) in the Bennie Moten Orchestra, and who joined Basie in August 1937, was Eddie Durham, also a pioneer of the electric guitar. On his very first session he contributed arrangements for the band, including Jimmy Rushing's 'Good Morning Blues' and the band number 'Topsy', which featured Buck Clayton, baritone saxophonist Jack Washington and Herschel Evans. I never had the chance to interview Eddie, but I met him several times, both when he was a member of the Harlem Blues and Jazz Band alongside Al Casey, but also when, quite by chance, we found each other sitting side-by-side at Carnegie Hall in June 1982 for a double bill concert by the Stan Getz Quartet and the re-formed Benny Goodman Quartet (with Panama Francis on drums). Although he mainly played trombone with the Harlem group, Eddie loved to talk about his pioneering work on guitar, and that night (knowing I was a friend of Al Casey's) he kindly introduced me to Tiny Grimes who was also in the audience. We had a good discussion after the show about the merits of the four-string guitar versus the conventional six-string model.

The last time I saw Eddie, he was playing in the Harlem band for a jump-jive contest at a midtown Manhattan hotel. It was a particularly good edition of the line-up with a stellar rhythm section including Al Casey, alongside pianist Sammy Benskin, bassist Peck Morrison and drummer Johnny Blowers. During the interval Eddie told me that playing for all the lindy-hoppers reminded him of his days working in the early 1940s with the all-female big band the International Sweethearts of Rhythm, whose stage act was quite choreographed. His successor as musical director in that band was the former territory bandleader Jesse Stone, who was brought in by its leader Anna Mae Winburn to develop the band's stagecraft still further when it first appeared at the Savoy Ballroom in New York. There'd been some competition between Durham and Stone back in the early 1930s when Thamon Hayes' Kansas City Rockets (with Stone on piano) had won a battle of bands against the Bennie Moten band with Durham and Basie in its ranks,[9] and a little of that old competitive spirit was still there when I talked to Stone in his Florida home. Jesse remembered, 'Eddie was *only* an arranger for the band. He didn't write songs for them or coach the players as I did. Previously he had even played for a while in my band. He was one of the many musicians who came through, when I was working in the Midwest.'[10]

Before returning to Basie, it is worth spending a moment considering the International Sweethearts of Rhythm. Its singer, Evelyn McGhee, met and married Jesse Stone while he was touring with the band, but she had a sharp recall of the experience of working with an all-girl African American band in the 1940s, although her arrival in its ranks seemed to her like a fairytale. 'I was discovered, in Anderson, South Carolina,' she said. 'I was eighteen years old, just coming out of the Depression years, and the International Sweethearts took me on. They were originally a school band from Piney Woods, Mississippi, who raised money by putting together an all girls band to help support the school. They came to Anderson this particular night, and played at the community centre. That's where we Blacks went for entertainment. We had no other place to go to have fun in Anderson. I was asked to sing with the band by the mortician there, whose name was Mr Peake. He went to the manager and said, "Please let Evelyn sing!" So I did two songs, including "Stardust", and they were so impressed with me that they asked if I would like to continue to sing with the band. Actually I was ready to sing with anybody's band! So Mr Peake drove me, and the road manager Rae Lee Jones, up to my mother's house, to ask her if I would be allowed to leave home to join the band. I didn't think she'd let me go but I prayed a little. At first my mother said "No way!" But I started begging, and she allowed me to leave that very night. I didn't even have a suitcase. I put my stuff in a cardboard box and I was off with a bunch of strangers! I didn't know anybody.

'At that time I think I was one of the oldest ones. Some were as young as 14, most were 16, or 17. We travelled all over the United States, though not so much at the very beginning, because then we played mainly in the Southern states: Georgia, Alabama, Mississippi and Tennessee. At that time, the band's arranger was one of the teachers from the school, Edna Williams, and she played trumpet. She wrote some arrangements for me, because I didn't have any music – in fact I didn't have anything. Travelling in the South we often stayed in people's homes, private homes, because we couldn't stay in white hotels. They had a bus though, and that was a sleeper, with beds and a portable toilet. On the road, the girls could sleep in the bunk beds. It was huge, but sometimes it was too cold to stay on the bus, and that's when Miss Jones would go and see if people would allow us to stay in different homes.

'I was with the band six years. As soon as I joined, Miss Jones put me in front of the band, and I was supposed to direct as well as sing, because Nina Cruz, who had been doing that, was sent back to Piney Woods when I came in. But I didn't have any idea how to use the baton! I was a singer and had been all my life. But I had to learn quickly. I didn't have to "know music" to stand in front of the band and swing the baton. I imagine I was not using it correctly, but I did have it in my hand, though I was mostly singing.

'We ended up, the year that I joined, in the New York World's Fair. It was 1939, and we were on a stage outdoors. I can see it now. They set the band up with a mike and everything, and I sang "Trees" as one of my songs. I don't think I've sung it since. That first day I sang two songs, and it was broadcast. And I was the star. It was the first time I ever felt "Oh! I've made it!" A lot of people said I sounded like Billie Holiday but that upset me because I don't think anybody sounds like Billie. She didn't have a great voice, but she had charisma and style, emotion. We're both Southerners, and I had style, but I guess they heard something in my delivery that was a little like her.'[11]

When I spoke to Jesse and Evelyn Stone in 1997, he was 96 and she was in her mid-seventies, but they were still busily working on a new album, as well as playing a weekly gig. In the years between the

International Sweethearts of Rhythm and the end of the twentieth century, he'd had the more illustrious career, helping to set up Louis Jordan's Tympany Five, and later writing 'Shake, Rattle and Roll' for Big Joe Turner, which became an important song for many other singers as well as Joe. By the 1990s, they were part of a flourishing community of musicians in the Orlando area, which also included Panama Francis and Nat Adderley. Their comfortable surroundings, helped by the continuing royalties from Jesse's songs (including standards such as 'Idaho'), were quite a contrast from the privations of the early days of the Sweethearts, or of Jesse's original territory band in the 1920s.

Going back to Basie, that battle of music in which the Moten band had taken on Thamon Hayes' group with Jesse was not an isolated event, as I discovered from a musician who was in the 'Old Testament' band and who stayed right through until just before the formation of the transitional Octet, namely trumpeter Harry 'Sweets' Edison. 'I was the last one to join the original band,' he told me. 'We had three trumpets, three trombones, four saxophones and four rhythm. Buck and all the rest of the guys had left Kansas City with Count Basie. I took a youngster's place named Bobby Moore. Wonderful guy. He was only about 18 years old, and he had a little difficulty mentally ... But he was a fantastic trumpet player. He was with them in Baltimore when I was still with Lucky Millinder and we had a battle of the bands. That was quite an event, because we did give Basie a wonderful go for it that night. At that time, they used to have bands playing against each other, like two prizefighters, so it was very popular in those days. Bands would have a battle of music against each other. It was great. It was wonderful. After that I continued with Basie until 1950. He had many, many tenor players in the Basie band. He was trying to find another Lester Young, after he left, which was an impossible task because there was only one Lester Young. No one has ever captured that sound that Lester had. He was an originator not an imitator. Paul Gonsalves was in the band for a while. He took Lester Young's place. Because Lester went to the army. And later on Paul Gonsalves went with Dizzy, and then he went to Ellington, and stayed with Ellington the rest of his career.'[12]

The trumpeter Clark Terry, who stayed on in Basie's scaled down Octet had joined the big band only just before Sweets left. He recalled: 'Basie ran into some financial difficulty, and he was compelled to work with a small unit, which was the first small band Basie had had since the Kansas City days. So he kept Gus Johnson [on drums], and we had found this bass player in Kentucky a short while before the band broke up. His name was Jimmy Lewis. So he had Jimmy, Gus and himself, that was the rhythm section, eventually Freddie Green just re-hired himself. I just looked up one day and Freddie was there. Basie said, "Where are you goin'?"

'He said "I'm goin' on the bandstand, where d'you think I'm goin'? I give you half my life an' you goin' to leave me? It'll never happen!"

'So he just came back and all Basie could do was laugh. We had Buddy DeFranco on clarinet, shortly after that we got [tenorist] Charlie Rouse. Then he left and we got Wardell Gray. When Rouse was there we had Serge Chaloff, Rouse, Buddy DeFranco and me. And that was during the period when the two of them were very ill, Serge Chaloff and Rouse.[13] I used to have to play and hold one on each side . . . maybe that's why my shoulders are in bad shape now!'

The octet with Charlie Rouse recorded in May 1950 for Columbia, in a session that produced such tracks as 'Bluebeard Blues' and 'The Golden Bullet'. I wondered how it was that for this one session Buddy Rich replaced Gus Johnson as the band's drummer. Clark laughed as he recalled: 'On that date Buddy Rich came down just to say hello to Basie. They were very close. We played the first take and Buddy was sitting there. Then all of a sudden he says to Gus, "Hey, take the day off! Go home, take the money, I'll just do the date." So he played the date. And Gus was happy to take the money and run!'

'The Golden Bullet' is a simple twelve bar blues, and after a chorus of rhythm section introduction, in which Jimmy Lewis' playing leaves the Walter Page arpeggio style behind and points the way to the more melodically mobile and fluent bassists such as Eddie Jones who would subsequently work with the band, there are three choruses of four-bar exchanges by baritone, clarinet, trumpet and tenor. The simple head arrangement does not appear until after Rich's drum chorus, but with DeFranco taking the melodic line that would normally be that of the lead trumpet, above the pitch of Terry's horn, and with tenor and baritone spaced below them, the overall effect is that of a much fuller band than an octet. The Basie 'sound' remained intact in the octet in a way that it had not done in his previous small group Kansas City Six and Seven recordings.

In due course, Basie set his sights on re-forming his big band. In trombonist Grover Mitchell's view, it was essential for the rhythm section to acquire a similarly distinctive personality to that of the 1930s band. He said, as regards that 'Old Testament' group, 'Jo Jones invented modern drumming. He didn't play with that old stomp-stomp-stomp four-beat bass drum. He was really as slick as a greased snake. But he went though a few emotional and mental problems and we went through a few drummers, but then we got to Sonny Payne and all of a sudden we had that excitement back, plus that ability to play in the rhythm section. Gus Johnson was good, a good drummer for this band, but he wasn't a soloist. He had great time and he played good fills and everything, but he didn't play solos at all, so Sonny Payne actually replaced Gus Johnson.'[14]

Sonny's successor, Butch Miles, described exactly why Payne was right for the band: 'Sonny Payne was first of all a fine drummer, an excellent drummer, but second of all he was a magnificent showman. He really put on a performance on stage, which just gave an audience a wonderful time. *He* was having a wonderful time as well as performing right off the edge. He would chew up the scenery as you'd say about actors sometimes, sticks would be flying in the air, he'd be bouncing them off the drums, catching them behind his back. Maybe the band would be screaming, then they'd stop short for a two-bar break, a pickup for an instrumentalist to go into a solo and he'd throw both sticks up in the air and catch them just as they came in on the down beat. Now a few times he might miss them, which was part of the fun too, but Sonny was a very, very extrovert individual and a little of that rubbed off on me.'[15]

In addition to building his 1950s rhythm section, in which bassist Eddie Jones replaced Jimmy Lewis, a key part of Basie's strategy was to have a new 'book' of arrangements to consolidate a markedly different style from the old band. This involved recruiting a coterie of writers, or hiring sidemen who could also arrange. The Octet's 'Bluebeard Blues' for example was a collaboration between Basie and Neal Hefti, who would go on to be one of the key arrangers for the 1950s band, culminating in the 'Atomic' Basie album, recorded in October 1957. The drummer Louie Bellson, who had a brief stint in the band, recalled: 'Those arrangements played themselves. That "Atomic" album with Basie, which is all Neal Hefti, you can't beat that. It's laid out perfectly. The guys enjoyed playing them, and it fit the rhythm section perfectly. And the same thing with Ernie Wilkins.'[16]

Although Hefti had started out as a trumpeter and had played with Charlie Barnet and Woody Herman, by the time he worked with

Basie he was focusing on arranging. In contrast, the arranger and saxophonist Ernie Wilkins became a regular member of the reed section in Basie's new band, which created a closer relationship with his colleagues. Trumpeter Joe Wilder recalled: 'Ernie Wilkins was writing – a guy who, as a player, was a fine player and his arrangements reflected that. It was a good band, they had a wonderful book, and you looked forward to going to work at night.'[17] It had been Joe's section-mate Clark Terry, who stayed on in the Basie big band after the Octet period (before moving to Ellington), who recruited Wilkins. He told me: 'For some strange reason Basie and Duke, when they would need new personnel, they would always come to me and ask me who they should hire. Or who I would recommend. I'd say: "I got just the guy for you!" Holy (that's what we used to call Basie in those days) was taking a shower – no it was a steam bath – so he was in the steam thing, and he had a phone there. So while he was in the bath I called long distance to St Louis. Ernie was in St Louis working with a guy called George Borders, making about five dollars a night. And I'm whispering so Basie can't hear over the sound of the steam, "Hey Ernie, can you get a hold of an alto saxophone and come to New York and join Count Basie's band?" So it took me about ten minutes to convince him that I was not pulling a practical joke, which I was kind of noted for in those days. I told him to get Jimmy, his brother, who was a trombone player, and I said come on to New York, I don't want Basie to know you're from out of town. I'll make a reservation for you at the hotel on 47th Street where I'm staying. So I hand the phone to Basie and say, "Base, this is your new alto player and your new trombone player! Ernie Wilkins and Jimmy Wilkins, and sometimes if you are a little short on arrangements, Ernie might be able to help you out in that department."

'Now Ernie had never played alto before in his entire life. Never. So I had stuck my neck out for him. But he was a competent enough saxophone player to be able to handle any woodwind, and I knew he wanted to get out of St Louis and I knew he wanted that job. So he *had* to play alto. His mother borrowed an alto from some kid who played the alto in a church choir, not even a professional. So it was an old, battered, un-lacquered saxophone, of the kind we used to refer to as grey ghosts! So he showed up with this and all the cats ribbed him about his grey ghost, but eventually he managed to get a proper one. But he did have a beautiful sound on it and he was a good reader, I knew that. So, as I suspected, he sat there and played things, just as if he was an old pro at it. Eventually he started writing a chart or two and Basie liked the way he wrote and everything is history from that point on. He wrote all those things that made Joe Williams popular.'

Back in the 1930s, it was really only Jimmy Rushing who was noted for singing or in some respects 'blues shouting' with the Basie band. But the changing times meant that the 1950s New Testament band was associated with several vocalists in addition to Joe Williams, such as the trio of Lambert, Hendricks and Ross. Bennie Powell was convinced of the importance of singers to the band in more ways than one. He said: 'The thing that saved Basie was vocalists. We started doing tours with Billy Eckstine, and then Sarah Vaughan. They all worked at Birdland, and then we'd do tours. I remember one tour we did was the "Birdland Tour of 1956" and I think that was Billy Eckstine and Sarah Vaughan with Count Basie's band, and maybe a couple more people. Billy, as I said, sort of rescued Basie. I think Billy gave Basie some of his arrangements when Basie organized his big band again, and then Billy was very popular during that time, so the combination of the two of them did them both very much good.'

As Bennie said, the singers who worked with him greatly helped Basie's band in terms of its popular appeal, not least Tony Bennett, who cut two records with the band in 1958 and 1959. The 1958 album, *In Person!*, was made for Bennett's label Columbia, and was supposed to be the live recording of a November concert at the Latin Casino in Philadelphia. In the event, the producer, Al Ham, discarded the tapes, because the evening had been captured in mono, and so he took the band and Bennett back to the studios to record the repertoire again in stereo during the week after Christmas, dubbing in fake applause. In a reciprocal deal, Basie's label, Roulette, recorded the band with Bennett a few days later, for the far more successful *Basie Swings, Bennett Sings*. Both albums have Bennett's British-born accompanist and musical director Ralph Sharon on piano, although Basie himself joins his band for two tracks on the latter album. The 1990s reissue of *In Person!* removed the fake applause, and is a fine example of remastering, but it did not resurrect the original concert tapes. This is a shame, because in terms of touring and a sequence of live performances, Bennett told me: 'I was the first white singer to sing with a Black band, and it was a shock. It wasn't supposed to happen.'[18]

It seems that singing with the Basie band was also a rare treat for the vocalists themselves. 'His piano playing was always wonderful ...

those introductions and his timing and phrasing,' recalled the band's last singer, Carmen Bradford, who worked with the orchestra up until Basie's death in 1984. 'It was just perfection, absolute perfection, I just never heard a night when it wasn't just wonderful. And very simple – simplicity y'know – just very simple and swingin', swingin', swingin'.'[19] Carmen – the daughter of the well-known trumpeter Bobby Bradford – was 23 when she got the job with Basie, and at first those characteristic introductions weren't quite so straightforward for her, as I discovered when she remembered how she had come to join the band.

'You know, when you're 23 you have no fear. At that age you don't mind hearing the word "no". I was a student in Austin, Texas, and my boyfriend of the time had the job of opening the show for the Basie band when they came to Austin. He asked me if I'd like to do a couple of tunes, and I said "Why not?" At the time I was singing in a band called Minor Miracle, doing nothing but Chaka Khan and Aretha Franklin tunes, wearing cowboy boots on stage, with a sweatshirt and Levi's. By this time, Basie was already riding on his little motorized cart, and in that particular theatre, he couldn't make it downstairs to his dressing room, so he just sat backstage. So I just walked up to him and said "My name is Carmen Bradford. I'm opening the show for you tonight, and I just wanted you to know you'd make billions of dollars if you'd hire me! I know you have a male vocalist already, but there's nothing like having a pretty girl in your band."

'And he said, "Oh, really?"

'So I said, "Yes, will you listen to me sing?"

'So he said "Sure sweetie I'll listen to you when you go out." So I went on and sang "A Foggy Day in London Town" and "Lost in the Stars".

'I came offstage and said, "Well, what did you think?"

'And he said, "It was very nice."

'So I said, "Are you going to hire me?"

'And he said, "Yeah, I think I will!"

'So I said, "Really? When?"

'He replied, "Don't worry. We'll call you." And he just pushed me away with his hand. And that seemed to be that. I went back to school, and my room-mate said, "He's not going to call." Three, four, five months went by. And it was my birthday. I was putting the candles on my cake and I said, "Please let Count Basie call me tomorrow!"

'Tomorrow came and I was leaving to jump in my saxophonist's car to go to my weekly rock and roll gig, when my room-mate came running out shouting, "Hey there's some old man on the phone, maybe you should come back in?" I thought it was probably my grandfather, and I'd already more or less forgotten about the wish, so I went back in and said, "Hello?"

'A voice said, "This is Bill Basie. Do you still want to work with me?" I thought it was my cousin Otis, who was a practical joker, and so I said it was a cruel trick to play. I hung up, and went back out to the car. A second time, my room-mate came rushing out after me and said, "That old man's on the phone again." So I go back in, and a voice says, "This is Bill Basie, and if you hang up on me again, I'm gonna give the job to some other little girl! D'you wanna work with me or not?" I said I was sorry, and that's how I started.'

It took three weeks after she met up with the band in Boston to get her arrangements sorted out, the first ones being by Eric Dixon and Dennis Wilson, but she remembers the first time she went out to sing with the band as being terrifying. She recalled that those Basie introductions were so similar that she mistook the beginning of one song for another, but he gave her a cautionary look and she pulled herself together, realizing that this was very different from playing in an informal setting in Texas. 'Suddenly you have eighteen musicians behind you, and there's some structure involved,' she recalled. 'It took me a few weeks to realize that the arrangements were created to caress everything that you sing. But once I'd really learned to listen, to work out where the horn shouts came and how they fitted with the vocals, I got a lot more comfortable!'

Few of the other musicians I spoke to joined Basie in quite such a dramatic fashion. Before he joined Basie, Bennie Powell had left the Lionel Hampton band in Canada, where he liked the much more liberal racial climate, but after a few months he was deported for not having the right papers to allow him to settle. 'I think when I first came back to New York I might have had a couple of months not working steadily. But in the meantime I was really looking for various jobs. There was Charlie Ventura. Then I wanted to go with Illinois Jacquet's band – Henry Coker had just left him. And I had maybe one other band pending. So while I was playing at the Apollo Theatre, Charlie Fowlkes happened to be in that band, and he said that Basie's band was organizing again. He told me there were going to be rehearsals – at

NOLA studios I believe. He told me when it was, and I came there. I made a rehearsal. Then I found out when the next rehearsal was going to be, so I came back. This went on for a little while, until finally we had a job, and I think the first job I played with Basie was at Symphony Hall, October 31st 1951, in Boston. I was very much aware that Basie was an adult, and I was a little greenhorn kid from New Orleans, so I'd approach him first of all very timidly. Because this was Count Basie!

'Anyway after about three or four weeks of playing, in order to find out whether I'd got the job or not, I sort of conveniently was standing next to him, and I said, "Mr Basie, how are the trombones sounding to you, tonight?"

'He said, "Well, they sound okay, kid." And that was one of his closing remarks, so I couldn't take it any further. Next time I spoke to him I asked him if he was satisfied with the trombone section, but I don't think I ever got the nerve to ask him, "Am I hired?" So this went on, and I don't think the whole twelve years I was there, he ever said, "Bennie, you're hired". But as I kept on asking in those early days he said, "Well, you're here, aren't you, kid?" And that's as close as I ever got to a "Yes" from Basie. But I found out later that it was part of his persona. But I loved him, he was a great man!

'When I got there, the other trombonists were Matthew Gee and Jimmy Wilkins, the brother of Ernie Wilkins. Henry Coker joined later. He was a fine trombonist. I learned a lot from him as well as from Quentin Jackson, who was a phenomenal man.'

Bennie's mention of those names in the trombone section prompted another question. I'd always been struck by the incredible precision in the section work of the 'New Testament' Basie band. Where did that come from? A broad grin from Bennie: 'Marshal Royal, Marshal Royal and Marshal Royal! He was responsible for that. Marshal was such a stickler for precision, but Marshal was not just a saxophone man. When I first joined the band I thought he was the biggest bully in the world, and I started having all these conversations with myself, where I'd say "If he says this to me, I'm going to say *that* to him . . . " Because as I said, I was just a greenhorn kid, not understanding and stuff. But Marshal was responsible for all of that because Basie didn't really have any hand in it. But what Basie was brilliant at was if somebody brought in an arrangement, Basie could instinctively feel what was right. So if you brought him an arrangement with letters A, B, C and D, he might run it down the first time and then ask you to play

D where A was, and as a matter of fact I was there when Neal Hefti brought in the arrangement of "Li'l Darling". It was marked at a much faster tempo, but Basie decided to slow it down, and it became one of Basie's big hits.'

When my BBC colleague Charles Fox talked to Basie, the band-leader was quick to attribute his talent for tempi to his original mentor. 'Bennie Moten was good about tempos. A great tempo town. Bennie knew where to put a lot of things. And Bennie taught me quite a few things, you know.' But Basie took this mastery of how to play an arrangement further. He'd settled on an immediately identifiable style for the 'Old Testament' band, and he quickly achieved an equally distinctive aural fingerprint for the 'New Testament' band. Trombonist Grover Mitchell (who later led the posthumous Basie band for a few years) believed that the band's aural identity was so strong that it imposed its personality on the work of whoever wrote for it, whether Neal Hefti and Ernie Wilkins, or Benny Carter and Quincy Jones. He said: 'Basie was always telling them, don't try to write like we play. You write what you write and we'll play it the way we play it. That's still the secret. That's the thing he did. Sam Nestico came into the band and the first thing he did was try to imitate something that went on in the past. But it never worked. The thing is "You be who you are, we'll take care of that".'[20]

Basie's skill was not just down to choosing a tempo and know-ing how to configure an arrangement. He also knew how to make the best of the soloists in his ranks – such as Al Grey who had joined him directly from Dizzy Gillespie's band: 'In Dizzy's band, if you had a chorus, you had all the choruses you wanted,' Al recalled. 'Whereas in Count Basie's band, that would be it. You had two choruses, and if you ever went further than two choruses he'd put that finger up! You automatically knew that you had really done something for Basie. That was a signal that everybody knew – when that finger went up, "Uh Oh!" and that's when you'd tried to play everything that you ever thought you knew. Because Basie was satisfied with what you had played. He'd say, "You had two choruses. What else you gonna play?" He figured that you'd be repetitious and playing something over and over again. That was his belief, if it was too long. On the recording called *Dance Along with Basie*, Thad Jones did this arrangement of "Makin' Whoopee". So I go in the studio – I'd just joined the band – and I played so much bebop in the number I thought I had done good. When it was over they come out to hear the playback and Basie called me off to the side. He said, "Don't try to play all you know in one number." I didn't know what to say. I really wanted to cuss him out, but I'd just joined the band. So then he started humming it, and said, "I think it'd be a little better for you to stick around the melody." So I said, "Okay Chief". And I went back in and I stuck around the melody quite a bit, except Thad had a few phrases that let me stretch a couple of changes. I couldn't understand why they wanted to hear that melody – but it's my greatest number, from then to today, right now!'

Al arrived in Basie's band at the same time as the tenor saxophonist Billy Mitchell, who had also been with Dizzy. 'I had got Billy Mitchell the job, in Basie's band, after Dizzy broke up his orchestra. Frank Wess moved over to the alto, and Billy Mitchell came in on tenor, and Lockjaw [Davis] played the other tenor.'

Al Grey was in the band when I heard the Basie orchestra in concert in a double bill with Ella Fitzgerald at the Royal Festival Hall in London on 30 April 1977. There were two houses that sold out almost immediately, but I was lucky enough to get last-minute seats for the 6.15 matinee. The only ones left were on the stage itself, just a metre or two behind Freddie Green, and it was wonderful to experience this maestro of rhythm guitar in action, so close that it was almost like being part of the band. Butch Miles was on drums with the Basie band for that concert, but he did not back Ella, as her own trio did that. Despite the fact they played many a similar concert double bill with her, Butch seldom got to back Ella himself. He recalled: 'Ella was one of the sweetest people in the world, just a darling and I just enjoyed being around her. I didn't really get the chance to play for her, because Bobby Durham was her drummer, and she had her own trio. The only time I would get to play for her was when she would come out, possibly as a surprise guest artist, and do a tune or two. Then we did an album many years ago called *A Classy Pair*, Basie, and the band and Ella, but without her rhythm section. There was another one, called *Ella and Basie* I think, which was recorded live in Montreux in '77 or '78,[21] where we did the switch. Her rhythm section came out and played the concert with the Basie band and I went backstage where there was a monitor and watched it on television like everybody else. But there was at least that one *Classy Pair* album with Ella and the band. Many times what happens in a situation like that when you're touring is that an artist of Ella's stature doesn't just come out to do a couple of dates with the band, we'd do possibly a week if we were playing at a music fair somewhere, but oftentimes they'd be performing somewhere before we'd get together and often stayed on after we'd got together, so it made it possible for them to carry their rhythm section full time.'[22]

Ella's pianist on that London concert was Tommy Flanagan. I spoke to him about it in New York some years later, asking about the final number or two when the brass and woodwind joined Ella, with him, Keter Betts and Bobby Durham plus Freddie Green. He said, 'You had to transform in an instant from being a trio into a rhythm section. It was a lot of fun, and I loved that band, so it was no problem for me! That London gig was on a tour of something like two or three weeks. On all of the concerts the Basie band did its own thing, then Ella did her set with the trio, and finally most of the band joined us. It never failed. It was wonderful. I remember the first gig we did after the tour ended. Ella came over to me and said, "Tommy, something's missing!"

'I said, "Yeah, fifteen men, that's what"'[23]

In the 1977 London concert, I remember Bobby Durham's crisp drumming contrasting with Butch's more flamboyant style. Equally memorable was witnessing Al Grey going out front of the Basie band to take a solo and hearing him from behind the band, clearly projecting over the roar of the full orchestra. Tenorist Jimmy Forrest was equally impressive on his solo outing.

I knew that by that point both Lockjaw Davis and Al Grey had left the band some time earlier, but before this UK tour Al had rejoined. Al told me: 'I was with the Basie band for almost twenty years of my life, though I left twice. The first time I got fired. We were playing Birdland in New York and a snowstorm came. My hotel was right across the street from Birdland, on 52nd Street, the Alvin Hotel. They didn't clear away the snow on the door sill and I went to come out. There was ice and I did a flip and broke my ankle. It was so cold and everything, but we were getting ready to go play for the President. I'd been going to the studio and doing some recordings, propping up my ankle, which was ok, but here we were, going to take the bus from New York to Washington, and the doctors advised me, "If you do that, you might not ever walk again." The manager came to me and said, "If you can't make it for the President, you can't make it for nobody. You're fired."

'So I was fired. After I got well and everything, I was working in the studios, and playing with Teresa Brewer at the Rainbow Room, in

New York. And I get a telegram from Japan, from Lockjaw Davis, that Basie wanted me back in the band. He was going to go out on tour with Frank Sinatra and Sinatra wanted me. So this is when I went back with Basie. Frank took a liking to me, and we recorded, and I have the only instrumental tune on the album *Live from the Sands* with Frank Sinatra. But when you play with Frank Sinatra, the band don't get no chance to play. In the first place we'd do three numbers, the opening number with Basie, which would most of the time be "All of Me", which would scare the people out of their seats. Then I'd do a tune and then it'd be Sonny Payne on "Ol' Man River". Then they'd bring on Frank Sinatra. So all those years, I had a spot, and then got to play the solos with Frank, like "I've Got You Under My Skin", which I would change every night. It wouldn't get stagnant with him because he was one of those types that wanted something different all the time.

'By the time I came to leave again in the '70s, I knew the book so well I didn't need to look at the music ever. That's the way it was. All the time we needed new music and sometimes Sam Nestico would bring in new things for me. I was happy that arrangers wanted to bring in tunes for me in that band. But in those twenty years, Basie and I, we had so much love for each other. He was like my father, because when I first went with the band I was pretty wild, from the bebop days of Dizzy Gillespie. Whereas Basie's band was more like Paul Whiteman's band in the United States. Marshal Royal was always scowling at me, sometimes unfairly, because I was an outstanding player in the band. But then so was he, when it came to play ballads. But travelling with Frank Sinatra you don't have no time to play no ballads. So you're grounded. I used to love to play ballads myself, like with Lionel Hampton or even today [1999] because I had a record that just came out with Tony Bennett – all strings, Wynton Marsalis and me.'[24]

Sometimes the reasons for particular pieces of music being written or commissioned were not straightforward, often arising out of life on the road. In his first few months after originally joining the band, Al Grey was whisked off on a tour of Europe. Unlike their regular hotels in the United States, not all the places the 1950s Basie band stayed in Europe had bedrooms with bathrooms attached. As the new boy in the band, Al always found himself at the back of the queue. Finally, he was in line for a room with a bath, when Marshal Royal pulled rank and took the room for himself. Al told me he was ready to explode but before he lost his temper, he just happened to see Basie sitting in a corner of the lobby, so he went over to him and explained his plight. 'Basie cooled me down. He said, "You know Marshal. He's the straw boss, and so he has the privilege to do that. But that's all right. I have a suite, so you can come over and be in the suite with me." Well that cooled me down, and then he said, "We'll write some arrangements for you when we get back to the United States." And sure enough when we got back, Thad Jones wrote a tune called "H.R.H." – "Her Royal Highness" – and that changed the scene because Thad wrote this for me, Al Grey, to play the lead part along with the Basie saxes, sticking out like a sore thumb! On the record I played so high, I wondered if I could ever play like that again.'

9 DUKE ELLINGTON

Whereas Al Grey left Basie to pursue a freelance career, co-leading small groups with various saxophonists including Al Cohn and Billy Mitchell, and even rejoining Lionel Hampton in his latter-day Golden Men of Jazz, his section-mate Bennie Powell is one of the select few musicians who worked with both Basie and Ellington. 'I loved that,' he smiled. 'I didn't get the chance to know Duke as well as I got the chance to know Basie, because I was with Basie for a longer period of time. But Duke has always been one of my favourites. He was always larger than life to me, as was Basie. And then the ultimate thing was when I got the chance to record with them both, because we did an album called *Battle Royal*, with both Count Basie's and Duke Ellington's bands.

'A very funny thing happened with that, because much later on I had been going through kidney failure. At one point I had to have an MRI scan. So when the guy was putting me in the machine, which is rather like a tunnel you have to go into . . . they put you on a kind of tray and slide you into the tunnel . . . it can be very claustrophobic. So the attendant who was preparing me asked what I did and I said I was a jazz musician. I had earphones so we could talk to one another and he could ask if I was comfortable and so forth, and he said, "I'm going to play some music to take your mind off it." I should say this machine makes a terrible noise, so that for a while when he first put me under I couldn't hear anything, but then he put the record on, and I think the chances would be about a million to one, because what he played was this very record, *Battle Royal*! He asked, "Do you know any of these guys?"

'I said, "Yes, I know all of those guys and I'm fortunate enough to be on that record!" It was really great for me because I was under quite a bit of stress with this machine, because although it's not painful, you're strapped to this table with your arms strapped to your side and you gotta lie there for a half hour, so this was just perfect because I was listening to this and then reminiscing about the album, so I consider that a blessing for me!'[1]

Bennie told me he loved the end of the 'Battle Royal' track itself, with drum exchanges between Sonny Payne and Sam Woodyard punctuated by huge stacked chords from the bands. 'When I listen to it now I still get chills, because it was just so exciting. Because here I am playing with both Duke Ellington and Count Basie. There are these chords, these giant chords, and I'm playing my horn, but I felt like I was levitating or something! It was quite an experience. I sat right between Duke and Count Basie, and I thought I was in jazz heaven. But the diplomacy between these two guys was just phenomenal. I think when we played "Take the A Train", Duke would say to Basie, "Mr Basie, this number just demands your presence." Which meant he had to play a solo on it. Then Basie would say, "I wouldn't dare in your presence!" So it went on like this, both of these guys – they were like double Henry Kissinger or something – diplomatic to the nth degree. And all with a sense of humour. I think it was one of the greatest moments of my life.'

So how had Bennie ended up playing with Ellington, albeit briefly? 'A lot of times during that period of his career, Duke would write music and just have a band come into the studio to record it. A lot of it was not released. I don't know if he just wanted to hear it. So this would occur when the band had a couple of days off. Chuck Connors lived in Boston, I think, and he was the other trombone player. So when they were doing these kind of dates, if he didn't want to come back, I was the one that they called. Also I got the chance to play a few one-nighters with the band, and that was magical too. Because I've always been a respectful young man, and when I was in the company of Lawrence Brown and Johnny Hodges and all of those guys, I was as quiet as a mouse. I was just in awe of those guys.'

Bennie's respectful recollections of Ellington from those sporadic dates between 1966 and 1969 were distinctly different from Clark Terry's, who, having left Basie in 1951, stayed full time with Duke until 1959. 'Being in a big band for so many years you figure out lots of things to do to break the monotony,' he said. 'We would play job after job after job. So much so that you didn't even have to get the book out, you'd know all the parts. So then I decided that I was going to learn how to play left-handed. I practised and many nights I'd try to play the whole job left-handed, and it reached the point where I could do it pretty good. Then I tried to do it with both, taking fours with myself, and I found it a little difficult because playing left-handed you had to have something to hold on to, in order to steady the horn. So on all my instruments I had a second ring – a finger ring – put on the bell side, so I could hold it with my fourth finger and work the valves with the other three. So it worked out beautifully. Afterwards I decided I'd learn to play upside down. And I kind of mastered that.

'Now when I was with Ellington we were doing a club in Chicago – Frank Holzfeind's club, the Blue Note. Now every Sunday all the Chicago people would have brunches and parties in the early afternoon, and some of these would happen before we got to the Blue Note for the matinee. So one Sunday I was a little late making it to the Blue Note for Sunday matinee after I'd gone to a brunch where I'd had a little champagne and was feeling kind of nice. Now Duke had a knack for waiting to see somebody come late, and he'd also spot when someone might be a little bit inebriated. If you had a combination of both, he'd really sock it to you.

'I came in and the band was already on the bandstand, and I was rushing to be ready for them to hit. And I hear Duke say, for the first tune: "Right now we'd like to present Clark Terry in a little specialty of his, called 'Perdido'." Now usually we used to play it in a kind of medium tempo, but this particular day, he revved it up. And he always had a knack when someone was late of announcing you as "the late . . . " person. So "Ladies and Gentlemen, the late Clark Terry!" And he was all set to have fun watching me stumble all over myself. But instead – I wasn't as inebriated as he thought – so I went out and played the whole thing left-handed AND upside down. And he just wigged out. He didn't speak to me for a week!'[2]

Given the time he spent in both bands, I wondered whether Clark felt Ellington's arrangements were tougher than Basie's? 'You had to get used to the sound with Duke. Because you'd be playing minor seconds and dissonances, and you'd think you were making a wrong note, but he'd say "Just play 'em in tune!" So this led to a completely different approach to playing. Listening and fitting in your part. Strayhorn's parts were somewhat the same, but he had a very simple way of making it swing. It was different arithmetic, the little rhythmic patterns. Some that you wouldn't hear other bands play like "bippity-bip, bip-bop baah!" instead of "Deedle doo, doo dah". He'd put the emphasis in other places. But harmonically he was just like Ellington. The two of them were so beautiful together, they used to complement each other. Strays was actually Duke's alter ego. When we were doing this movie, *Anatomy of a Murder*, Duke was writing in the hotel, and he had music all over the floor, and he called up Billy Strayhorn and said, "Hey Strays, I'm in the middle of something here." Now Strayhorn knew he was doing the soundtrack, but Duke says, "In this area here I wanna go up, 'Bing, Bing, Bing, Bing . . . ' but I could mix it up, 'Bing Bong, Bing, Bang!' Now what would you do?" and he played it to him over the phone on the piano. Strays says, "Well Edward, I think you're more qualified to answer that question yourself. However, if I had to make a decision, I'd come down, going, 'Bling Blang, Bling Blang.'" And Duke says, "Okay!" And then he went "Bing, Bing, Bing, Bing . . . " just like he was gonna do in the first place! They were funny that way.'

How about Ellington's other trumpeters? 'Ray Nance had a very individual approach. Shorty Baker was very, very different, Cat of course was boisterous, almost, and blatant and strong, but dependable and accurate. I had my approach and Willie Cook had his, so we all went our separate ways, except that when we zeroed in on precision in respect of time, that was the beautiful part about it, everybody's time was impeccable. It was very precise and this is what made the band really sparkle the way that it did. Ellington himself said it was one of the most precise-hitting sections he ever had. There was so much individuality in there, what might be seen as lackadaisicalness and individual approaches, which created an unusual atmosphere in the band. You had five guys as different as possible, but the overall idea was to be precise and punch it! Yet nobody tried to match anybody else's sound. We just did it with our own individual sound, but tried to hear it as one.'

I was interested to know if the brass section precision was helped by the rhythm section, and Clark agreed immediately. 'Sam Woodyard was the swingingest cat that came through that band. A lot of excellent drummers came through there that were beautiful and very close and good buddies of mine, such as Louie Bellson and Butch Ballard. All great drummers, you know. But Sam had the knack of just being able to sit right there and swing. Sam was a marvellous drummer, a great, great guy. One time I played in a little club in Paris called Le Petit

Journal, and Sam was pretty sick in those days, but he suddenly ambled into the club. So I said, "Ladies and Gentlemen, Sam Woodyard!" Out of courtesy I asked "You wanna come up and play a number with us, Sam?"

'"Yeah, OK." So he kind of crawled up on the bandstand, and I said, "What d'you wanna play?"

'He said, "Stomp it off. Anything." So I played the opening phrase of "Perdido", and "Bing, boing, bing" he lifted the roof off the house with his first beat!'

Another member of the 1950s Ellington band had similarly positive memories of Woodyard, who came into the Ducal fold in July 1955. Bassist Jimmy Woode had not long joined the orchestra himself, having replaced Junior Raglin, who took sick in Boston in early March that year, while the band was playing a lengthy engagement at George Wein's Storyville Club. Ellington was using the time that the entourage was in Boston, and not constantly travelling, to rehearse his orchestral suite 'Night Creature', which would be premiered on the 16th of that same month at Carnegie Hall in New York.[3] As Raglin failed to recover – he subsequently died in Boston that November – Woode found himself the new permanent bassist with Ellington. Once he knew this was going to happen, he quickly replaced Raglin's five-string instrument, which he had briefly used at the Storyville club, with his own more conventional four-string bass. He took the job despite the fact he had just left Ella Fitzgerald's trio, having promised his wife to give up touring!

'We were on salary [with Duke],' he recalled, 'and from your salary you had to pay your room rent, your hotel rent, as well. So you would double up. Clark Terry and I were room-mates, to save money. But when Sam came in the band, Sam had many problems, and he would not speak to anyone other than Clark, Paul Gonsalves, Ray Nance and myself. He was very uptight and tense, but he and I were good friends, so Clark suggested that I room with Sam and perhaps I could help him. Which I think I did. And that proximity between Sam and I helped out in the rhythm section as well. We didn't even have to talk about how we were going to set up the rhythm. Ellington was occasionally at the piano, but mainly he was busy in front of the band, conducting, or leading, or cajoling or talking to the people. So basically 80% of the rhythm section was Sam and I. And it was lovely, lovely . . . I can feel it now.'[4]

I first got to know Jimmy when I invited him to take part in a weekend symposium on Ellington at Ascona in 1989, along with the distinguished scholars Mark Tucker and John Hasse. After the formal presentations were over, he stayed on for the remaining week of the jazz festival, and was hugely encouraging to me. I learned a lot about big band bass playing from him. We even played a concert of bass duets together, which was great fun for us, but might have been less exciting for the audience! We remained in contact during the years that followed (Figure 5). On a visit to Britain, he kindly recorded a long interview with me after playing in Symphony Hall Birmingham in November 1992 with Lionel Hampton's Golden Men of Jazz (also featuring Sweets Edison and Al Grey), which I was presenting for BBC Radio. We sat

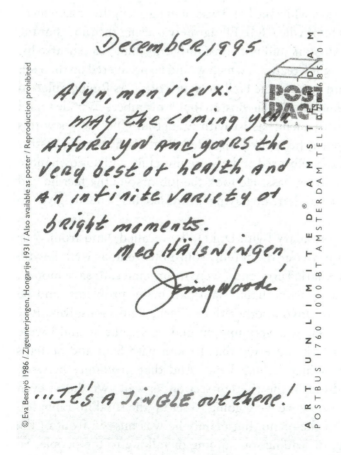

Figure 5 One of my annual Christmas postcards from Jimmy Woode

up most of the night talking, with the help of a bottle of fine amontillado sherry.

He said then that there is no better example of the rhythmic bond between Woode and Woodyard than the 1956 Newport Jazz Festival performance of 'Diminuendo and Crescendo in Blue', with its 27-chorus central tenor saxophone solo from Paul Gonsalves. The recording of this event is part of jazz folklore, the exhilarating saxophone solo so well known that it exemplifies the paradox proposed by Mark Katz of being 'music of the moment made timeless ... the spontaneous turned inevitable.'[5] The original album (which was assembled by Columbia's George Avakian from the live festival recording together with studio re-takes of the *Newport Suite*) carried the following producer's note: 'At about his seventh chorus, the tension which had been building both onstage and in the audience since Duke kicked off the piece, suddenly broke. A platinum-blonde girl in a black dress began dancing in one of the boxes (the last place you'd expect that in Newport) and a moment later somebody else started in another part of the audience. Large sections of the crowd had already been on their feet; now their cheering was doubled and re-doubled.'[6]

Avakian also speculates that the Ellington band might not have achieved its 'terrific beat' were it not for Count Basie's former drummer Jo Jones who 'egged on the band with nothing more than appreciation and a rolled up copy of the *Christian Science Monitor* ... The band picked up on Jo who was shouting encouragement and swatting the edge of the stage with the newspaper.'[7] This powerful description overlooks the fact that Avakian had only recently re-signed Duke to Columbia, and he needed to create a myth or two to help sell a band that in his view had not been at its commercial zenith for some time. Concentrated listening to the Woode/Woodyard rhythm team, before, during and after Newport,[8] immediately debunks the myth of them requiring external stimulus. Jimmy Woode himself was keen to refute Avakian's claim, albeit agreeing that in terms of *promotional* effect, 'that Newport performance was a turning point for the band.' He continued, 'Jo was there, on the side, slightly in front, because the stage was a little elevated, and he had a newspaper. But the band was into it. We really didn't need much egging on. Of course, it was inspiring to see him there, enjoying himself, having a ball. He was as knocked out as we were. It was so infectious to the public, to the whole scene. Ellington was trying to stop the band. George Wein was trying to get the band off, but the band refused to stop. It was just one of those rare moments in jazz history, that it happened. And now that I listen to it in retrospect, it was far too short! "Diminuendo and Crescendo in Blue" was an extension of a work that we were doing. The maestro called out this particular part, to be followed by that and followed by that, and it just happened. Which is the way it should happen in jazz. It should not be planned, just let it flow! That's what it's all about.'

Clark Terry was equally adamant that Jo Jones had nothing to do with the way the Ellington band sounded that night. He told me: 'I was there. I was playing lead on that tune, while Cat was playing the high notes. I was right there. Jo Jones standing in the back with a newspaper: "Come on! Come on! Come on!" He tells everybody he drove the band but he was just back there. We almost wanted to tell him, "Get the hell away from there!"'

The Ellington band's own ability to swing was not going to get in the way of Avakian's marketing strategy. On the back cover of the original LP was a snapshot of Jo Jones (his forename with a gratuitous 'e' added) labelled 'unsung hero'.[9] Similarly a photograph of the 'platinum-blonde' dancer (in reality Elaine Anderson, the wealthy wife of the clothing manufacturer Larry Anderson, who employed over 1,000 people at his factory on Fall River, MA) was captioned 'The girl who launched 7,000 cheers'.

George Avakian was a likeable polymath. He contributed to many of my BBC radio programmes over the years. I was a regular guest at his house in Riverdale, New York, and he was as forthcoming and knowledgeable about a wide range of subjects, from Armenian carpets to John Cage (for whom he helped to create recording opportunities, later discussed with me in a radio documentary),[10] as he was about jazz. But before I get to his Newport recollections, it is important to remember that George was recruited away from Decca by Columbia, to make pop music LPs, having previously produced some of the very first reissue 'albums' of 78s. In common with most pop music producers, he always saw his production career in terms of commercial success, and his version of events – such as 'rediscovering' Miles Davis at Newport 1955 and signing him to Columbia – usually put George centre stage. His first (very successful) Columbia vinyl venture was Frank Sinatra's *The Voice*, released on 15 September 1948 in the smaller 10-inch LP format.

'One of the great things I enjoyed about the period when almost everything we put out on pop LPs sold like crazy,' he told me, 'was that

I was able to put jazz on LP. I could take advantage of the long-playing feature of the LP with things like the *Buck Clayton Jam Sessions*, and the deliberate use of Erroll Garner, who was one of the few pianists who could sustain a long performance. And we went into the business of putting out counterparts on 45 rpm where we could get 6 or 7 minutes a side. So Erroll's first LP was a series of 6-to-7-minute tracks, which went both ways, 45 and 33.[11]

'The big thing is, we got such a strong sale out of jazz, such as no one had ever had before, that I could do a lot of things that might have been money-losing otherwise. There's no denying that Columbia's sales worldwide did wonders for a number of jazz artists. Well, Dave Brubeck's sales exploded because his performances took advantage of long-playing possibilities and made him a natural for LP. And when things happen like *Ellington at Newport*, with the incredible perform-ance of "Diminuendo and Crescendo in Blue", Ellington's career sud-denly jumped up. Joe Glaser was booking him and he would introduce me to people by saying, "Here's the man who brought Duke Ellington back. I couldn't sell him for years, and then all of a sudden, George put him on the map." And he said the same thing about Louis Armstrong, because *Satch Plays Fats* and before that *Plays W C Handy*, and along the way "Mack the Knife", made Louis a huge pop star, actually. Louis was marvellous to work with in the studio, and the great thing about the recent[12] edition on CD of *Armstrong Plays W C Handy* was that – without realizing it at the time – I had let the tape machines run in such a way that, thinking I might get a few minutes for a disc jockey promo-tion record perhaps, of Louis in the studio, [they'd] run for a long time. When I listened to it again, while making the final edition of the CD, I realized this is something that shows what it's like to work with Louis Armstrong in a studio. It's all right there. Early rehearsals, the discus-sions of changes ... changes one way not so good, try it again ... and it makes a great story. There's about, I guess, 22 minutes of that at the end of the album. I never did it again or before.'[13]

From this it is clear that Avakian always had an eye for the story, an instinct for promotion, and a strong sense of his own role in the narrative. I'll come back to *Ellington at Newport*, but for a moment I'd like to ponder George's claim that he was 'the man who brought Ellington back'.

In the conventional narrative of Ellington's career, the band reached a high point in the so-called 'Blanton-Webster' edition of the line-up from 1940 to 1941 (with bassist Jimmie Blanton and tenorist Ben Webster) and then went into a period of slow decline, until the 1956 Newport Festival concert revived both its artistic and financial fortunes. This critical consensus was summarized succinctly by Michael Ross, who wrote: 'By the early 1950s the tightly knit Ellington organization had begun to unravel, with the departure of several key members. Ellington's fortunes dwindled with the decline of big band music, but rallied after his stunning performance at the Newport Jazz Festival in 1956.'[14]

To be sure, some long-term members of the band did depart in the spring of 1951 – notably altoist Johnny Hodges, trombonist Lawrence Brown and drummer Sonny Greer. But talking to drummer Louie Bellson who came into the line-up, there was no sense that he and the other replacements were joining a sinking ship. He, altoist Willie Smith and trombonist Juan Tizol (veteran of an earlier edition of Ellington's orchestra) had all been with Harry James. 'I stayed at Juan's house,' Louie recalled. 'That was during all the time I stayed with Harry James – a whole year. And I noticed that Juan would be talking to Duke almost every day. They were very dear friends. One day Duke said to him: "Why don't you come back to the band? And I understand that Willie Smith wouldn't mind coming with the band because Johnny Hodges is leaving. And I hear you've got a pretty good drummer there, so why don't you three guys come on and join the band and play every day of the week instead of two days a week (with Harry)?" So we went to Harry James, all three of us, and we said, "Harry, we have a chance to join Duke Ellington's band." And Harry looked at us and his exact words were, "Take me with you!" So off we went and in 1951 we joined Duke Ellington.'[15]

I wanted to know how Louie felt about replacing Sonny Greer, who had played with Duke since the beginning, in the 1920s. 'Sonny not only had a large set of drums, but he had timpani, vibraphone, he had chimes, he had everything imaginable,' laughed Louie, but then he turned serious. 'Sonny Greer was a great drummer and he fit that band perfectly, so it was an honour for me to come in there and try to step into his shoes. But Duke made it easy for me. He said, "Look, I don't expect you to play like Sonny Greer – I wanna hear *you*!' And there was no drum book anyway. I had to memorize everything. So we got along beautifully well. It was so easy to play in that band, there were so many stars in that band, yet collectively they could really get together and swing.'

The reason Louie had taken the job with Harry James, which paid well for just two gigs a week, was to learn more about composition on his days off. For the best part of a year, he studied with Buddy Baker, whom he had discovered through Baker's arrangements for Herb Jeffries and who, before later becoming music director at Walt Disney studios, was a music professor at L.A. City College. The James band was in Los Angeles at the time Baker held that post, whilst Harry worked on the movie *Young Man With a Horn*, and began making guest appearances on various television shows. These studies with Baker meant that when Bellson arrived in the Ellington orchestra, he was one of the few musicians apart from the leader and Billy Strayhorn who contributed to the band's book of charts in the 1950s. Louie said, 'Before we joined the band, Tizol said to me, "Bring some of your arrangements!"

'I said, "Juan, you gotta be crazy! *Me*, bring arrangements to Duke Ellington and Billy Strayhorn? No, no, no!"

'He said, "Take 'The Hawk Talks', 'Skin Deep', 'Ting-a-Ling' and a few other things with you." So reluctantly I put them in my suitcase. When we joined the band, Duke came to me and said, "Juan says you can write! Why don't you bring one of your arrangements in?"

'But I didn't do it. So he came to me a second time, and said, "Where's the arrangement?"

'I said, "Well, maestro, I feel very embarrassed giving you music and giving Billy Strayhorn music. You guys are, like, geniuses!"

'He said, "No!" And then for the third time he said, "Bring the music in!" So I brought in "The Hawk Talks" and "Skin Deep" and he recorded "The Hawk Talks" right off the bat.[16] I can't tell you how I felt – the great Duke Ellington recording some of my music? Max Roach said, "You must have felt like a king when Duke played your music!"

'I said, "Yes I did!"'

Listening to the rhythm team of bassist Wendell Marshall and Louie Bellson there's the same immediate empathy as would later emerge with Woode and Woodyard. And in common with that later partnership, they are the entire rhythm section for those parts of every concert where Duke was out front conducting, rather than 'stealing the show' at the keyboard, as he sometimes put it in his stage announcements. A perfect example of this Ellington line-up in action is the concert from Seattle, recorded live by RCA on 25 March 1952, in which both 'The Hawk Talks' and 'Skin Deep' get an outing. (So too does Clark

Terry's previously mentioned feature 'Perdido'.) And far from being in decline owing to 'the departure of several key members', this is a big band at the top of its game, with exactly those qualities of precision and swing mentioned by Clark and Louie. As the liner notes for the original release (in 1954) say, 'Duke's everlasting youth and freshness, his sound and musical conceptions lead the way, his band is still one of the greatest on the current jazz scene.'[17] It is worth noting that 'Skin Deep' remained in the repertoire after Bellson had left, and was indeed played by Sam Woodyard at Newport in 1956.

The critical consensus that the early 1950s was a fallow period for Ellington broadly follows the influential scholar Gunther Schuller's 1989 observation that these were 'years of mostly modest artistic achievement'.[18] For Schuller the absence of 'the band's veterans', Hodges, Brown and Greer, not to mention Cootie Williams who had left earlier, diminished the band's 'lustre and uniqueness'. And this line of thinking persists among twenty-first-century critics, such as Katherine Williams, who writes, 'the beginning of the 50s brought a slump in Ellington's career'.[19]

There is one dissenting voice, in particular, who has taken the trouble to assess the period in detail, and that is the British critic Eddie Lambert, who wrote: 'Some of the richness of orchestral texture had inevitably been lost, but the leaner sound fitted well with the fifties concept of jazz. Some subtlety had [also] been lost but the new men were inspired by the challenges and rewards of playing Ellington scores. This inspiration showed in the music. Not the least important factor was that Duke was delighted with his new band.'[20]

There was new repertoire too. At the Metropolitan Opera House in January 1951 Ellington first aired the 'Controversial Suite' and 'A Tone Parallel to Harlem'. This was virtually the last recorded outing for the 'old' band, but by the time Duke came into Columbia's studios in December 1951 to make the first 'official' recordings of these works, the new line-up was in place and this music seems to fit it far better. The first movement of the 'Controversial Suite', titled 'Before My Time', could hardly be by any other composer. It is a dazzling – and very witty – parody of older styles of jazz, incorporating phrases from many Dixieland standards including 'Tin Roof Blues' and 'Tiger Rag' and not only balances a traditional jazz front line of Russell Procope, Shorty Baker and Quentin Jackson against the full force of the orchestra, but has more contemporarily flavoured solos from Clark Terry and Ray

Nance, before Procope's soprano saxophone leads the band into the Tiger-ish finale. The new line-up plays the piece with an *élan* that was largely missing from the Metropolitan Opera event.

But the new band's tour de force from the December recordings is 'A Tone Parallel to Harlem', a full-scale Ellington suite (originally commissioned by the NBC Symphony Orchestra), depicting the uptown area in all its diversity, that runs just short of 14 minutes and which again refines and revitalizes a work originally given at the Opera House. Conflating a two-note motif that articulates the word 'Harlem' with a long melodic, and somewhat spiritual, theme, it displays all the orchestral colour and vividness of Ellington's programmatic writing. One cannot imagine Greer at this stage in his career producing comparable flair to the aggressive Latin-style drumming that Bellson conjures up at around the 5-minute mark, and the reed section work, defined by Willie Smith's precision, is exemplary. The original liner notes by none other than George Avakian (who produced the 1951 album for Columbia) describe the piece as 'a summing-up to date of his musical experience . . . a constantly invigorating pattern of sound'.[21]

The band kept this work in its repertoire and it appears on the *Seattle Concert* album in a version that shows just how effective Ellington's variety of timbre could be in the acoustics of a live setting. It is significant, too, that despite all the hype about Newport 1956 being an exceptional 'live' recording, the 1952 Seattle event is one of a series of Ellington discs that captured the band in concert, allowing us to chart its progress in public events, as well as in its multifarious studio sessions. (Seattle was, however, the only one to be issued near to the date of recording.) The AFRS recorded a transcription LP of the band on a 'One Night Stand' concert in November 1945. The series of Carnegie Hall concerts was not to be properly released until Prestige acquired the rights in the 1970s, so the music was not available to record buyers of the 1940s and 1950s, but today we can hear several examples of the band in that august concert hall, during what critic Jack Sohmer referred to in a *Jazz Times* review of the Newport concert as 'its ten year slump'.[22] An early version of 'Diminuendo and Crescendo in Blue' is in the 4 January 1946 Carnegie Hall concert along with a reworking of parts of 'Black, Brown and Beige', plus a new work of Duke's – the 'Tonal Group', namely 'Melloditty', 'Fugueaditty' and 'Jam-a-ditty' – not to mention Oscar Pettiford taking the Jimmie Blanton role in 'Pitter Panther Patter'. November the same year saw the 'Deep South Suite', and the following year the 'Liberian Suite' given in concert. A line-up very similar to that of the Seattle concert (save that Willie Smith is replaced by Hilton Jefferson) was at Carnegie Hall in November 1952, and as we know from Jimmy Woode, 'Night Creature', with symphony orchestra, was given there in 1955 (a recording of which was released on the Italian I Musica Jazz label). Although further recordings that are now available (such as the series of late 1940s *Date With The Duke* broadcasts issued on Fairmont) could not be bought at the time, they demonstrate that the band was regularly to be heard on the radio.

Even if the evidence of the band's extant concert recordings were not enough to question the prevailing view that it was in decline or suffering a slump, it is worth looking at what was being written about it during the years leading up to Newport. The year after the Seattle concert we find a review of Ellington playing in South Dakota as part of a lengthy tour taking the band from Iowa to California. It notes that 'Ellington, one of the few top bandmen who have not disbanded his aggregation, has over the past 25 years built up an international reputation as a top figure in the American Music picture.'[23] His persistence in keeping the big band going into the 1950s – a feat only rivalled by Basie, Woody Herman and Stan Kenton – is noted here and in many other write-ups of the period.

In the latter part of 1954, following some back-to-back concerts earlier in the year by Ellington and Dave Brubeck, Norman Granz toured the band along with three small combos, as part of a 'Modern Music' package. The press announced: 'Duke Ellington and His Merry Men provide the hot stuff, and the cool music comes from three quartets led by Stan Getz, Dave Brubeck, and Gerry Mulligan. The tour will hit 16 cities from Boston to Los Angeles in late October and early November. Dig that crazy itinerary.'[24]

Yet when the concerts came to be reviewed, it was Duke, rather than the younger white musicians, who garnered critical praise. Syndicated journalists Leo Lesser Jr and Henry Butler reported respectively: 'The Duke still wears the crown' and 'Duke and crew need no "Package".'[25] A common perception about this period was that Dave Brubeck had cornered the student market, but in January 1955 we find that students at Cornell University paid to bring the Ellington band to Ithaca themselves. The local press reported that the young entrepreneurs made a profit of $1000 on the concert at Bailey Hall on 7 January after expenses, including Ellington's band being paid $2000.[26] A few weeks later, prior to the engagement at Wein's Storyville Club mentioned by Jimmy Woode, the band played a Navy dance at Newport, Rhode Island, and as well as playing for dancing they included some more programmatic material. Questioned as to why this was played at a dance, Ellington was quoted as saying: 'audiences know more musically, they're matured'.[27]

In the months leading up to Newport 1956, Ellington was again on the road with Brubeck in a package called 'Modern Jazz '56'. When they played in Davenport, Iowa, the press reported on the 'wide appeal' of this two-band show.[28] Once tickets for Newport became available in early May 1956, Ellington topped the bill in the press release: 'Jazz Festival Tickets are now on sale … those scheduled will include Duke Ellington's Orchestra, the Gerry Mulligan Sextet, the Chico Hamilton Quintet, vocalists Jimmy Rushing and Anita O'Day and the George Shearing Quintet.'[29] And before the buzz of the band's Newport appearance could influence other press notices for events that fell very soon afterwards, we see the band billed at the Berkshire Music Barn the following weekend, 14 July, with a quote from Whitney Balliett: 'Ellington inescapably remains after almost 35 years as a professional, the richest figure in jazz as well as one of the most inventive original minds in American music.'[30]

This is not the language we would expect of the spent force that some critics have suggested Ellington had become before 7 July. And we see similarly strong epithets for the band as it headlines the Connecticut Jazz Festival on 28 July, again with no mention of its very recent Newport success, but 'Heading up an all-star roster of top-flight jazz artists will be Duke Ellington and his world famous orchestra.'[31] It is worth noting that following Columbia's recording at Newport, ABC Paramount were prompted to announce that they would record Lucky Thompson and Oscar Pettiford's band at the Connecticut event, three weeks later. (But no resulting record seems to have been issued alongside this stellar combination's earlier 1956 discs.)

The Newport recording itself is worth exploring in more detail. Location recordings of jazz were by no means new in 1956. The already noted partial listing of such Ellington events demonstrates that. But it is one thing to record in a concert hall, with good acoustics, and effective backstage accommodation for equipment and engineers, and quite another to set up in the places where jazz was more normally being played as the 1950s progressed. Even though recordings in this period were still in mono, some quite sophisticated mixing was in play, with lines coming in from several microphones. Using his parents' house in Hackensack, New Jersey, as a studio, Rudy Van Gelder was already setting the highest of standards. Bebop historian Thomas Owens notes that his 'skill at getting a proper mix of instruments directly onto the master tape (long before multi-channel recording existed) was exemplary and his clean, crisp and well-balanced drum kit sounds were especially noteworthy'.[32] Van Gelder's biggest challenge at the time was to replicate the aural image of the Jazz Messengers that he had created under carefully controlled studio conditions, and which was already familiar to record buyers, when Blue Note's co-owner and producer Alfred Lion decided to record the band live at New York's Café Bohemia in 1955. 'I used to insist if I was doing a remote,' Van Gelder told me, 'that I'd go in there with one of my machines and put it on one of the tables, right off the side of the stage ... Club owners were universally unhappy about that, because it was money they could not make from me sitting at that table ... But that's the way I did it. I sat there with a pair of headphones, and Alfred on one side of me, and the machine in front of me, and that was it.'[33]

There was considerable wisdom in this decision. Seated just beside or in front of the stage, Van Gelder missed nothing of what was going on. If he needed to tweak the equalization of his microphones, to accommodate a soloist who was veering off mike, he could react instantly. And the band was attuned to keeping an eye on Lion, who would indicate such lapses, and bring any errant player back into line as speedily as possible. What George Avakian had in mind was altogether more ambitious. He had already recorded Dave Brubeck in concert on various university and college campuses, but an outdoor festival is a different matter entirely. And having convinced Columbia to invest in producing a number of recordings at Newport, he found himself tackling all kinds of new problems on that first weekend of July 1956, from inclement weather to a stage set-up which he shared with Voice of America radio, as well as the festival's own public address system. Any of us who have played at outdoor festivals also know that there is practically no natural acoustic to rely on. The ambient sound on a stage open to the elements is relatively dead.

As author John Fass Morton has pointed out,[34] there was a local radio network trying to record the concert as well. On top of that, the recording equipment for VOA and Columbia could not be set up within sight of the stage, but had to be located in the crowded green room tent that abutted the stage from behind.

Although Ellington had briefly returned to Columbia in January 1956 to record backings for Rosemary Clooney, he had not been formally signed to the label since the end of 1952, spending the period in between making records for RCA, Capitol and Bethlehem, as well as making numerous discs for his own use, some of which emerged after his death as the 'Private Collection'. The ink was barely dry on the new agreement with Columbia when the band bus rolled up at Newport.

'I had just signed Duke,' recalled Avakian. 'I thought, "Let's do something spectacular. Let's record Duke and other Columbia artists at Newport", which was something nobody had ever done. There had never been a formal major label recording at a jazz festival. So I called Duke, who was out at some very obscure town in the Midwest somewhere like Iowa or Kansas, and I asked him if he had something that he could do as an exciting first performance there, so that we can record the premiere, and call it, say, 'The Newport Jazz Festival Suite'. He said, "Billy Strayhorn and I always have something – we'll put something together." And they did. He called the musicians together, just before they went up on stage for that set, telling them, "Look, we've all worked very hard on the suite, and George has stuck his neck out for us and we just have one shot to record it. But don't fret about any mistakes. Billy Strayhorn is gonna check as we play and see where any patches have to be made and we're going into the studio the day after tomorrow to fix up patches." Now that wasn't going to be easy, I knew, but it was the only way we were going to get away with it, because we knew, Duke and I, that there were going to be mistakes. And after that he said, "Let's relax and have a good time. Let's play something we haven't played in a long time. Let's play 'Diminuendo and Crescendo'."'[35]

Avakian was aiming to get more than one LP's worth of material from the concert, to complement the other material he was recording over the weekend. And indeed that is what eventually transpired, although the second Ellington album (which is shared with Buck Clayton's All Stars, who occupy the second side) is not nearly so well known. However, compared with Van Gelder's insistence on immediacy to the performance, Columbia's recording team were stationed at the far end of the backstage tent on the stage left side. Engineers Ad

Theroux and Buddy Graham had to communicate with Avakian, who was perched at the side of the stage itself, using their colleague Cal Lampley as a literal 'runner'. VOA's team was in the corner on the other side at the back of the same tent. As Phil Schaap says in his notes to the complete Columbia reissue from 1999, 'The Voice of America's [mike set-up] was more intertwined with the live sound. Columbia Records' miking was far more independent.'[36] In the fullest yet account of the concert, John Fass Morton surmises that Columbia mainly used four directional mikes on stage, plus a pair of 'flyers' suspended above the band, that also picked up the audience noise we hear in the original release.[37] VOA had a mike for solos and vocals on the central PA microphone stand, and my BBC colleagues suggest that the third central 'flyer' visible in the photographs is a standard 1950s Outside Broadcast microphone, which would – in the manner of classical recordings of the time – give a fairly faithful account of the entire proceedings.[38] This proved to be extremely useful.

Avakian takes up the story: 'We had to record on our own microphones, not through the house microphones. We couldn't split the feed on the microphones of that time. And I warned everybody as they went up on stage, "Be sure you blow into the mikes that have a white handkerchief, those are our mikes. The house mikes will pick you up anyway. And we've got to ask you to play into our mikes so we can get a recording." Gonsalves forgot. He blew the solo into the wrong microphone. I was in the wings, wondering "How can I catch his attention?" Well it was impossible. I rushed back to the engineers, and I heard that he was way off mike. It took a long time, with nothing available except the simple equalizers of the time, to pull his solo up to as high a level as possible without destroying the sound of the band.'[39]

In the photographs of the session not one single white handkerchief is visible, so this might be wishful reminiscence on George's part. Plenty has been written about the 'Newport Suite' being largely re-recorded in the studio on 9 July, effectively eliminating most of the 'live' version from the originally issued record. Having played a transcription of this suite with my own band on our Swiss tour in 2017,[40] and subsequently on UK concerts, I can vouch for the difficulty of making this music work well on limited rehearsal. However the originally issued album – in which the patchwork versions of the suite and 'Jeep's Blues', with only short excerpts from the live concert included, were set alongside the actual Gonsalves 'Diminuendo and

Crescendo' performance, albeit overdubbed with crowd noise to cover some of the oddities of the rebalancing – became Ellington's all-time best seller. When Phil Schaap tracked down the VOA tapes, Columbia was eventually able to issue a kind of stereo version, with Gonsalves clearly on mike, for Ellington's centenary.

In 1956, Columbia's publicity department made the most of the remarkable public reception at Newport for 'Diminuendo and Crescendo', and by extension the rest of Ellington's concert that followed. A cover story about Duke had already been booked for *Time* magazine, and the rapturous audience reaction to this event (amplified by the photos of Elaine Anderson's dancing, together with the voluble crowd noise overdubbed onto the LP) gave the label's publicists all they needed to 'rehabilitate' Ellington, who went on to make some of his best later period albums for Columbia between 1959 and 1961. But if there's a lesson in all this, it is firstly to take note of what the musicians themselves had to say (discounting Ellington's encomium of praise for Jo Jones at Newport in *Music Was My Mistress*, which, partially ghosted in 1972 by the British-born writer Stanley Dance, has little critical to say about anyone). And secondly it is worth listening afresh to periods of the music that have sometimes been written off by critics and academics who, without re-evaluating the evidence, have, in shaping their opinions, perhaps relied too much on what was a brilliantly effective piece of marketing by a powerful and ambitious record label and its executives.

10 DIZZY AND BIRD

One thing that I learned from musicians in Buck Clayton's circle was that whilst critics and writers drew distinctions between 'swing' and 'bebop' musicians, when the new jazz was being developed in the 1940s, there were plenty of players who crossed the boundaries with ease, playing swing sessions one day and bebop the next. They slid seamlessly from one genre to another, with no labelling attached. So we find – for example – trombonist Trummy Young (a veteran of Jimmie Lunceford's band, and later to be a mainstay of Louis Armstrong's All Stars) recording in Dizzy Gillespie's early sextet, and we find drummer Doc West (formerly with Roy Eldridge and with Erskine Tate's big band, and also a regular deputy for the ailing Chick Webb) sharing the stage at New York Town Hall with Dizzy Gillespie and Charlie Parker. As Arvell Shaw mentioned, Dexter Gordon, Roy Haynes and Kenny Clarke all spent time in Louis Armstrong's big band (as did Charles Mingus).

One of the most versatile musicians who slid between styles was the pianist Clyde Hart, a very accomplished swing player who did much to draw together the early elements of bebop before his premature death from tuberculosis in 1945 at the age of just 35. Those who knew him recalled Hart's prodigious talent. For example, Billy Taylor, the pianist and composer who presented *Jazz Alive* on National Public Radio for several years, was in his early thirties when he heard Hart for the first time. 'I was at a jam session in Harlem with a dozen other pianists,' he told me, 'and Art Tatum was playing. Art pulled off a particularly impressive break and we asked him how it was done. The only other player in the room who got the hang of it instantly was Clyde Hart, and Dizzy Gillespie knew and respected this aspect of Clyde's talents.'[1]

Another pianist who made a similar transition was Sir Charles Thompson, known to all and sundry as 'Chase', who, despite a six-year age difference, first encountered Buck Clayton as a teenager, and later became a member of Buck's touring group in the early 1960s. Thompson had grown up in Clayton's home town of Parsons, Kansas, and while Buck was off in Shanghai and then on the West Coast, Thompson was touring the Midwest in the territory bands of Lloyd Hunter and Nat Towles. But the band that brought him to national attention (as would be the case with Al Grey and Bennie Powell) was that of Lionel Hampton, which he joined in 1940, not long after Hampton had left Benny Goodman's small group. I went to visit Sir Charles in his home in the San Fernando Valley, before he emigrated to Japan for what would be his final years, and as he recalled, surrounded by ephemera from his two passions, music and golf, another musician in Hampton's band had already assumed the role he would later have with Basie.

'The band was organized here in Los Angeles,' Sir Charles said, 'and Lionel got the best musicians. He would get them from everywhere, all over the United States, including Marshal Royal, who was a genius musician, well trained in discipline. And he was what you call the straw boss, took care of the music. He was the first saxophone player, and we also had Dexter Gordon, a young guy who had just come along with me, and of course Illinois Jacquet. He, that's to say Illinois, and I were very close to each other musically at that time. Lionel also had a guitarist by the name of Irving Ashby, who played like Charlie Christian. It a was great band in terms of music and one of the most exciting times of my life, just wonderful.'[2]

Not many pianists of that era can also claim authorship, or at any rate co-authorship, of a jazz standard, but Sir Charles' most enduring composition followed on directly from his work with Hampton. 'After Illinois and I had left the band,' he remembered, 'we were both living around Los Angeles. I had worked in a place called Billy Berg's – a small club here.[3] And Illinois played all these jobs around town. He was well known from his exciting exhibitions with Jazz at the Philharmonic, promoted by Norman Granz. I was a part of a couple of those sessions, too. In due course we had a recording date, Illinois and me, and he had many people bringing arrangements, which didn't turn out so good. They were okay, but at the end of the date we had five more minutes left, and Illinois turned his head and said, "Hey, Chase, ain't you got one of them tunes?"

'I said, "Yes, I'll play an intro, I'll play this part, then the middle, you play a couple of choruses and then out." In five minutes we did one take and created "Robbin's Nest".⁴ I told him what to play in the main theme, we cooked up that middle together, and that was "Robbin's Nest". Unbelievable! And that very simple melody reflects something significant in my life: saying a lot with very little. This comes from the two people I most admire, Count Basie and Lester Young – simplicity was their thing.

'All those notes don't mean nothing … To start with, nobody except musicians paid any attention to Charlie Parker, who they called Bird. I think they called him that because he played so many notes – he was flying round in the sky like a bird. He could do it with a beat, but Parker didn't become *really* famous until he made those records with strings. That's what made Charlie Parker really popular in the world, those wonderful records that were made possible by Norman Granz, with violins and strings, and they really established Charlie Parker as a genius, 'cos they found out he could not only play all those notes, but he could play beautiful melodies, which showed the real "inner" Charlie Parker.'

Sir Charles was saying this from plenty of personal experience of working with Bird. His own first recording with Parker came quite early in the bebop movement, not long after the AFM ban on recordings had been lifted in 1945.⁵ How had that session with Parker, Dexter Gordon, Buck Clayton, and none other than Danny Barker, come about? 'In those days we were all friends. All of these musicians that I played with, we were just like kids together, because we all enjoyed playing. We didn't make much money, we just liked to sit down and play. We played mostly for free. We'd go down to this place in New York called Minton's, because we liked to play together. So when I got a chance to make my first recording date with Apollo, I naturally got my friends whom I liked to play with: Dexter Gordon and Charlie Parker.'

Buck Clayton's father had been the minister at the church in Parsons where the Thompson family worshipped, and it was Buck himself who urged the young Sir Charles to keep going with the piano and aim at turning professional. Clayton was completing his wartime service at Camp Kilmer in New Jersey at the time of the first Thompson recording with Parker, and – being a short distance from New York City – had already played several Sunday afternoon concerts with Bird, promoted by Monte Kaye and Mal Braveman. As he was only able to take a brief period of time off from the camp, he turned up for the Apollo record date in uniform. 'Buck started me off, and that was quite a coincidence that he was around at the time I made those dates,' said Sir Charles. 'I couldn't have asked for a better man to play the lead trumpet. He is my man, Buck Clayton. He was a wonderful man and he took me to Europe for the first time.'

Those who only know Sir Charles as a swing player, maybe from his European recordings with Buck, or from the Vic Dickenson Septets, or from the Coleman Hawkins Quintet with Sweets Edison that famously recorded for BBC Television, miss the fact that he worked quite regularly with Charlie Parker from the time of that Apollo recording with Buck, Dexter and Danny, through to the mid-1950s. And it was Jimmy Woode who reminded me of some of those gigs. 'It was 1953,' he said. 'Kenny Clarke, who had worked with my father and my uncle, had come back from Paris, and was spending some time in America. And I'd known Kenny since I was very young. "Klook" as we called him. With me Kenny was more of a father, uncle, brother and mother to me than my father, because I didn't spend much time with my father. But Kenny would never *ask* me to do something, he would *tell* me. So Kenny called me from New York, and said "Baby Boy" (he always called me "Baby Boy"), "we're opening at the Hi-Hat in Boston: Sir Charles Thompson on piano, and you on bass and a saxophone player. And we start at . . . " He would command me! The saxophone player happened to be Charlie Parker. And Charlie Parker checked into the hotel, the Hotel Bostonian, and we were there for three weeks, but although he'd checked in, he never slept there. He always stayed at my house. My wife was a great cook, and he just didn't leave. He stayed there for the whole three weeks. Then I continued on to Providence, Rhode Island; New Haven, Connecticut; all with Charlie Parker. I had some great times with him.'[6]

The quintet with Sir Charles and Jimmy (plus the long-term Bostonian fixture at Berklee School of Music, Herb Pomeroy on trumpet) recorded an airshot on 22 September 1953, and we hear what Sir Charles called the 'real inner Charlie Parker' on the ballad 'Don't Blame Me', played with the same melodic flair and lyricism as his 1949 discs with strings. But on the up-tempo bebop standards, including 'Now's The Time' and 'Cool Blues', we also hear how Sir Charles had assimilated the new style, his single-note lines owing plenty to Bud Powell, to be sure, but interacting brilliantly with Clarke's rhythmic punctuations. The call-and-response patterns between alto and piano on the set-closer 'Groovin' High' reveal Thompson as a much more versatile pianist than his later mainstream work tends to suggest.

Sir Charles mentioned that he had worked at Billy Berg's in Hollywood, after leaving Lionel Hampton, and it was to Billy Berg's that the Dizzy Gillespie Sextet with Charlie Parker headed at the end of 1945, opening there on 10 December. Sir Charles had actually been in Parker's working band on 52nd Street in New York during late October and early November that year, alongside Miles Davis, Dexter Gordon, bassist Leonard Gaskin and drummer Stan Levey. During October, Ray Brown arrived in Manhattan from Florida, where he had been playing with Snookum Russell's territory band, and was in due course invited to join Dizzy Gillespie's combo for the California trip. Ray told me that he'd played in Dizzy's band (originally with Bud Powell on piano and Max Roach on drums) for about three months before they set off, but it must have been less than that. Both Parker and Gillespie were busy elsewhere until quite shortly before the group left for the West. They did, however, rehearse as a quintet with Bud and Max on 21 October 1945.[7]

In April 1996, after a preliminary interview at the BBC in London, I spent a couple of days with Ray Brown in Munich, recording his life story for a radio series. We met often in the years that followed on both sides of the Atlantic, and on one of his visits to England, he was very encouraging to my daughter, who was a double bass student. He told me during our long conversation in Germany that on his very first evening in New York, he'd met Dizzy, because he had gone to 52nd Street to hear his friend Hank Jones. Dizzy just showed up at the club, and on the spot invited him to that October rehearsal. 'The bebop movement was just starting,' said Ray, 'and sometimes in your life you're just in the right place at the right time. We went to California, but a week before we left, Bud Powell and Max Roach both got in trouble. So they didn't make the trip. We took Al Haig and Stan Levey, and we went to California. Milt Jackson also joined the band before we left. I'd never seen Milt before, but we became close, because we were the two young guys in the band.'[8]

That friendship was to last until Jackson's death in 1999. It was a marvellous experience for me to see Ray and Milt back playing

Plate 1 Ken Colyer's Jazzmen in December 1986. (Left to right): George Berry, tenor saxophone; Alyn Shipton, bass; Ken Colyer, cornet; Colin Bowden, drums (obscured); Mike Pointon, trombone; Ray Foxley, piano (plus a young fan). John Griffith, banjo, is just out of shot to the left.

Plate 2 Street parade in New Orleans by the Young Tuxedo Brass Band in 1976, with second line dancers, Mardi Gras Indian feathers in the background and Kid Sheik Colar (trumpet) and Greg Stafford (bass drum) in the band.

Plate 3 Alyn Shipton and Danny Barker.

Plate 4 Freddie Kohlman and Alyn Shipton.

Plate 5 Sammy Price, piano; Lillian Boutté, vocal; Alyn Shipton, bass; Smokey Johnson, drums, Ascona, July 1988.

Plate 6 Blue Lu Barker.

Plate 8 Alyn Shipton giving Buck Clayton the first copy in the United States of his autobiography, 1986.

Plate 7 Jabbo Smith at the time he appeared in the musical play *One Mo' Time*.

Plate 9 Part of Al Casey's UK tour in April 1980, Teddy Layton, alto saxophone; Alyn Shipton, bass; Al Casey, guitar; Dave Evans, drums.

Plate 10 The Duke Ellington band backstage at Newport 1956: Sam Woodyard, Willie Cook, Paul Gonsalves, Jimmy Woode, Ray Nance, Clark Terry.

Plate 11 Jimmy Woode, Birmingham, November 1992.

Plate 12 Louie Bellson at the time of his interview with the author.

Plate 13 The Ellington band on stage at Newport in 1956, showing the microphone positions discussed in Chapter 9.

Plate 14 Sir Charles Thompson's band recording for Apollo, 4 September 1945. Jimmy Butts, bass; Dexter Gordon, tenor saxophone; Buck Clayton, trumpet; J. C. Heard, drums; Danny Barker, guitar; Charlie Parker, alto saxophone.

Plate 15 Alyn Shipton with Ray Brown.

Plate 16 Roy Haynes.

Plate 17 Carmen Bradford, London, 2000.

Plate 18 Sonny Rollins with Alyn Shipton.

Plate 19 Alyn Shipton and Henry Grimes, backstage at Cheltenham Jazz Festival, May 2010.

Plate 20 Oscar Peterson at Birmingham Symphony Hall, on one of his last UK visits.

Plate 21 Mike Gibbs on his 80th birthday tour in 2017.

Plate 22 Geri Allen at the time of her interview with the author, London Jazz Festival, 27 November 2010.

Plate 23 Ornette Coleman's appearance at the 2005 Cheltenham Jazz Festival, as discussed in Chapter 16.

together over half a century after their first meeting, in Oscar Peterson's Very Tall Reunion Band in November 1998 at the Blue Note in New York, where their camaraderie and chemistry were still very much alive. I was there to write the liner notes for the album that they recorded that night, and as Ray reminded me before the show, 'These are some of my very oldest chums!' Oscar was also on top form that night. Afterwards, he said of the session, 'It's a very free feeling up there. This band has no established library as I have with my quartet or Ray has with his trio, so the whole thing is much more spontaneous than the kind of setting you'd normally hear us in today … it isn't a sculptured performance, it's a very dedicated jam session.'[9]

Going back to 1945, the drummer who went to California with the Gillespie sextet, Stan Levey, was almost the same age as Ray. Drafted in at the last moment, and therefore also a new acquaintance of Brown's and Jackson's, he was already a long-term colleague of Dizzy's, having worked with his quartet in Philadelphia (Stan's home town) over the turn of the year between 1942 and 1943, aged just 16. There he had seen the start of Gillespie's own transition to the new music at first hand. 'Dizzy still played like Roy [Eldridge] in those days,' he recalled. 'He hadn't evolved into what he became. He was Roy with a left-hand turn, if you know what I mean. He'd started to run the changes differently. He had ideas about what he wanted from the rhythm section and he'd sit down at the piano and play it for you. I worked with Dizzy there, and then he went to New York. He called me and said, "Come on over", which was maybe a year later, in 1944, and at that time I met Charlie Parker on 52nd Street.[10] He looked as if he'd just got out of a trash compactor! He was a mess – it looked like he fell off a turnip truck. He'd just got to New York and was just starting to play around town. I used to hear people say, "Bird is coming!" but at first I had no idea this meant Charlie Parker. But for me, just getting to New York was great – every door of every club had marvellous music coming out of it, all night long. Coleman Hawkins, Art Tatum, Erroll Garner – just one after the other. I started working on the street immediately. Dizzy got me with Oscar Pettiford. We then went to Boston for ten days, and came back, and I got a steady job with Barney Bigard, which was the old-style music, but it was a steady job in New York.'[11]

And this collaboration is a perfect example of the easy crossing of boundaries, with Stan, a musician who would take a big part in defining bebop, quite happily working with Barney, a great

Ellingtonian and New Orleans pioneer, playing swing. They even recorded together in Barney's racially integrated band in December 1944, which finds Stan, on his very first studio date, working effortlessly in a rhythm section with former Ellington and Waller bassist Billy Taylor, guitarist Chuck Wayne, and pianist Cyril Haynes, backing Bigard, plus trumpeter Joe Thomas (Harry Dial's friend) and tenor saxophonist Georgie Auld.[12] In many interviews, including mine, Stan recalled his very first session in New York, organized by Leonard Feather, as being with Art Tatum, and this statement appears in many biographical notes about the drummer. In fact, the Tatum session (also including Bigard) actually took place on 5 January 1945, a week after the December recording, which Feather also co-ordinated. But maybe it was more memorable for Stan, not just owing to the stellar company of Art Tatum, but because it acquired a particular kind of long-lived notoriety by including the hymn to reefer smoking, 'Sweet Marijuana Brown'.

By the time I met him, Stan was no longer playing drums, but had launched a very successful second career as a jazz photographer. His work adorns many 1990s issues of records by his old colleagues and friends, and I was able to contact him through one of the companies for whom he supplied pictures. He lived just a short distance away from Sir Charles Thompson, and I actually visited both of them on the same day. Neither was aware that the other was living nearby, and so I was able to reintroduce them, which led to quite an emotional reunion.

Back in March 1945, Stan had begun working on 52nd Street with Dizzy, and he recalled that their band at the Three Deuces included Charlie Parker, Al Haig and Curley Russell. Their nightly gigs ran until July. This would later be followed by Stan's aforementioned Spotlite club residency in October with Parker, Miles Davis and Dexter Gordon, along with Sir Charles Thompson. And it's worth noting, in terms of switching from one style to another, that the band that played opposite Parker's sextet at the Spotlite was a trio led by the swing jazz clarinettist Buster Bailey.[13] After such an apprenticeship, when Max Roach dropped out of Dizzy's proposed tour to California, Stan was the logical candidate to replace him.

'When we got to Billy Berg's it was just one of those bands where you couldn't wait to get to work,' said Stan. 'You didn't care what you made – I think it was around eleven bucks a night – who cared? The music was the thing. I'd met Al Haig and played with him before we left. He used to hang around the clubs and he was a listener. We got to meet him because he was always there, then he got to sit in, and finally Dizzy hired him. He played a little like Bud Powell, but he was very "worked out" if you know what I mean. He had his solos down pat, which was not very spontaneous. But he was a good player and he could really play the music. When we got to the West, a lot of others couldn't play it, so they tended to put down what we were doing and say it was just B.S. But it certainly wasn't negative overall, like in the movie *Bird*.[14] I guess for films you have to fictionalize, and make it palatable to movie-goers, but I think that movie was too dark. Berg's was a nice club, taking up the whole corner of Vine Street and the next street down from Sunset,[15] so it was a big place, very nice with a mixed crowd, a Hollywood crowd – a lot of big actors came in while we were there. And the other musicians in L.A. who were interested – they sure were there!'

The local press gave the band a mixed reception. Ray Brown recalled a review that likened what the reporter felt was the band's outlandish playing to 'Men from Mars'. Less extreme was the syndicated report from jazz correspondents Larry Frankley and George Epstein that marked the end of the engagement on 3 February. 'Dizzy was not too well received by the public, although the professionals packed the supper club every night.'[16]

Ray Brown concurred with Stan and the journalists: 'All the musicians were in there every night, 'cos they *knew*. Art Tatum used to come in every night, even. I mean if you had heard Charlie Parker or Dizzy Gillespie play at that time, you would *know*. If you suddenly ran across whoever was best in your profession you would know immediately that they were exceptional. The *Bird* movie said we got fired, but we didn't get fired. The guy said, "If you guys want to fill out this engagement, you're gonna have to be more commercial." So Charlie Parker wrote out a couple of arrangements where we were singing – the whole band were singing – and later they added another guy, Lucky Thompson, who was a great saxophone player, but he didn't match up to those guys. But we finished out the engagement.'[17]

Fortunately the Armed Forces Radio Service (AFRS) recorded the band in Los Angeles (prior to Thompson's arrival) on 29 December 1945 and we can hear what the announcer 'Bubbles' Whitman called 'Professor Rebop – and his whole class of cats' playing exactly the kind of repertoire they were performing at the club, especially 'Dizzy Atmosphere' in which Milt Jackson's vibes take a prominent role alongside Bird and Diz. Freed from the constraints of 78 rpm playing time, the band stretches out and solos run to whatever length the players wish. Parker plays dazzlingly on these tracks, but his agile, fluent soloing conceals a man who was not well.

'Before he even got there his health was shot,' said Stan Levey. 'On the train ride out, he couldn't get his drugs. We stopped in the desert for the engine to take on water, and looking out of the window, Dizzy said, "What the hell's that out there?" I said, "I think it's your saxophone player." Charlie Parker was walking away across the desert. So I went out and got him. But when we finally got to California, he was a wreck. He never really recovered. See, he could function in New York. He got what he needed and he was OK. But once he got out of New York, forget it!

'Meanwhile, Milt Jackson was there to make up the numbers. He sounded like a pile of old milk bottles at that stage – his instrument was so old and beat up, he wasn't really the Milt Jackson that we know today. He was incomplete, but you could hear what was coming in the old recordings we made, and Dizzy knew all his potential. And Dizzy hired Lucky Thompson because he knew that Parker would be late, or miss dates, so he hired Lucky to be there, because the contract said two horns plus the rest of the band. And Bird was late and did miss! It didn't matter what state he was in when he walked through the door, because when he got that horn into his mouth it was an extension of his head. Whatever was in there just came out.

'When the time came to go back to New York, Parker was gone. Dizzy gave me his ticket with the idea I could find him somewhere in the jungle out there. I searched but I couldn't find him, so I left the ticket at the hotel and that was it. He probably cashed the ticket and got some stuff. I didn't see him until he came back to New York in '46 or '47, and he was all bloated from drinking – but actually he never stopped anything for long, he just had to keep going.'

Only a few weeks after Dizzy's quintet left Billy Berg's, the act that followed them, vocalist Harry 'The Hipster' Gibson, succeeded in having bebop banned on the local radio station KMPC, as 'a contributor to juvenile delinquency'.[18] It seems that his songs were actually a long way from bebop, including such blues as 'Caldonia' and vaudeville songs such as 'Who put the Benzedrine in Mrs. Murphy's Ovaltine?' but what identified his act with the new jazz was that he incited the crowd to shout 'Boo-bop-a-loo-bop a rooney!' which, the radio station

said, 'aroused degenerate influences'. The press reports of this farrago
did at least include a brief statement from Dizzy, in which he said that he
and his sextet (blamed as the 'originators' of bebop in L.A.) 'were just
trying to figure out a new style'. Charlie Parker was quoted as saying,
'We were looking for a way to emphasize the more beautiful notes in
swing music, instead of just stringing a lot of meaningless notes
together. We didn't even give it a name – it got that because when you
hum it you just naturally say "Bee-bop, bee-de-bop."'[19]

One of the musicians who had made a point of hearing Dizzy
and Bird while their sextet was still playing in the West was the 18-year-
old trumpeter Clora Bryant. She had already been in a band called the
Prairie View Co-Eds, rather similar to the International Sweethearts of
Rhythm mentioned in Chapter 8 (and which, in later years, she would
join herself). In 1945 she and her family had recently moved to Los
Angeles and she had enrolled at UCLA. By the time the Gillespie group
arrived, despite being under age, she had already heard bebop being
played in the city as her brother had taken her to stand outside the
Downbeat at 4201 South Central Avenue. 'Inside was the band with
Howard McGhee and Teddy Edwards, and J. D. King on tenor sax, too,
Dingbod Kesterson on bass, Vernon Biddle on piano and Roy Porter on
drums. I was like a baby as far as bebop was concerned at that time,' she
said, explaining that many of the listeners inside the club already seemed
to know about the 'new' music.[20] This was not least because the
Downbeat was the epicentre of the Central Avenue scene, and any
new or unusual kind of jazz was most likely to be heard there or in
one of the other nearby clubs. Teddy Edwards himself recalled some of
the main venues, most of which are long-gone, as he and I looked out of
the entrance to the Dunbar Hotel – now a landmark building – where
many eminent musicians stayed in the 1940s: 'There was music all up
and down here on Central Avenue. On the block with the Club Alabam,
on the same side of the street was the Dynamite Jazz Club, and the
Downbeat Room. The Downbeat was my favourite all time jazz club,
situated at 42nd and Central, and now it's a bank or something, but
when I look at it I have all these memories. Across the street was the Last
Word – Nat Cole played there. It was a nice place and we used to jam
there quite a bit. The Barrelhouse was around the corner and so was the
Plantation, where the big bands played, like Billy Eckstine's. Up the
street was a little club with a very nice man who played there, name of
Marvin Johnson and we used to go there and sit in, and he loved to have

us – Wardell Gray, Sonny Criss and myself. Some people were against our music, but he was for us.'[21]

Clora Bryant explained that although audiences had been primed by what Howard McGhee, Teddy Edwards and drummer Roy Porter were doing, she, and they, were 'ready for the next step'. And that came on the broadcasts by Dizzy and Bird from Billy Berg's, which she listened to avidly. And it was during this period, when, after the late set at Berg's, Parker was regularly to be found at all-night jam sessions, that she took her horn along to sit in with him. Trying to keep up with Parker, she played flurries of notes, but after a couple of numbers he took her aside and sagely advised her to 'stick to what you can do, and know what you can't'.[22] But Bird saw promise in her, and some years later, Gillespie became a mentor to her in New York.

Another musician who had a similar reaction to Clora's, that Dizzy and Bird were the 'next step', was drummer Roy Porter. Although by late 1945 he had already been playing bebop with Howard McGhee and Teddy Edwards, he had never heard Charlie Parker in person. When the Gillespie band opened at Billy Berg's, Porter's own band was at the Streets of Paris club (a few blocks away on Hollywood Boulevard). And it was there, as he recalled, that Charlie Parker 'just strolled in and came up on the stand'.[23] Alerted to my work at Macmillan by the British critic and writer Mark Gardner, Roy contacted me out of the blue not long after I had started publishing musicians' life stories (Figure 6). He knew he had played a significant part on getting modern jazz established in the West, but at the time, he didn't feel that his contribution had been properly recognized. Would I help? We corresponded for some time as I worked to find an American co-publisher, and eventually Louisiana State University Press came up with an offer. I was happy to help get this story told in print for the first time and I still remember the excitement of reading about Roy's first gig with Bird: 'The people there were spell-bound when Bird got through playing. They had never heard anything like that in their lives. I knew I hadn't. I had heard Charlie Parker before on various records, but to be on the same stand and playing with him was a gas.'

Looking back on it, Milt Jackson had nothing but praise for what the Parker–Gillespie sextet had achieved at Billy Berg's. 'I was in seventh heaven, three times tripled over, I was getting the best education, I was going to the greatest conservatory in the world every single night, for eight solid weeks, and I loved every second and every minute.'[24]

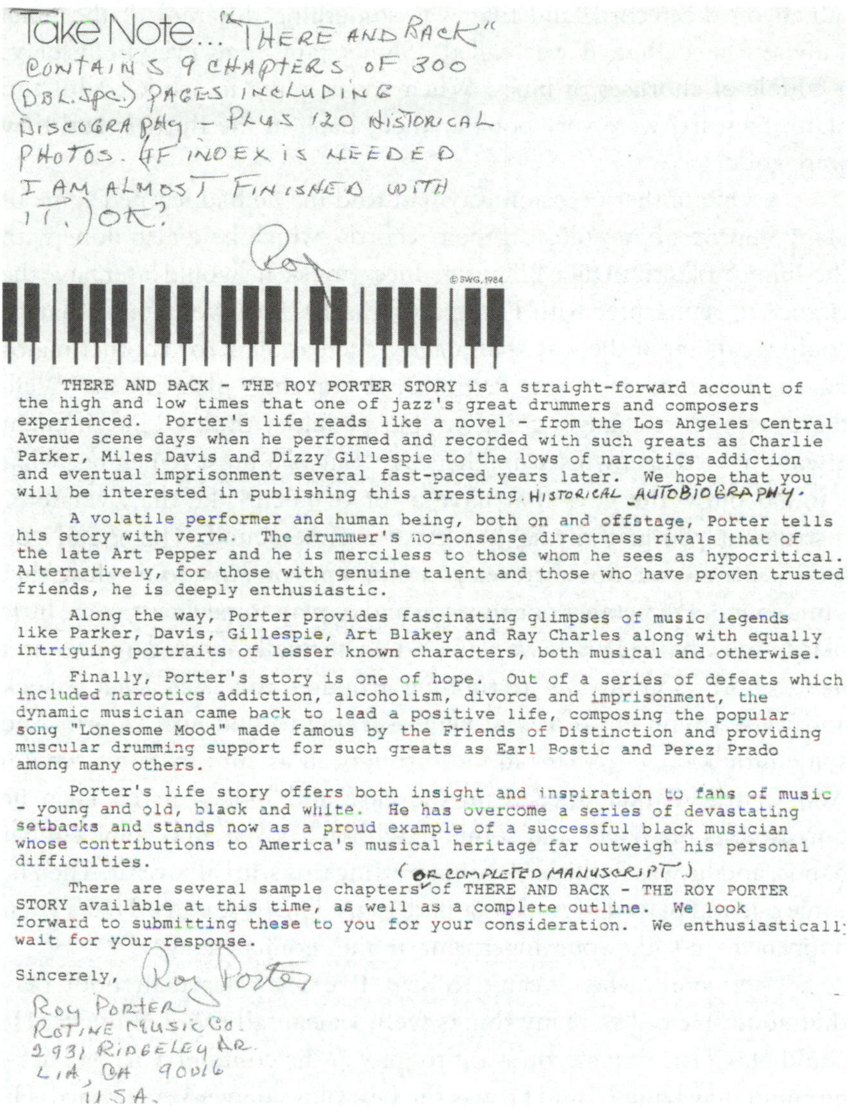

Take Note... "THERE AND BACK"
CONTAINS 9 CHAPTERS OF 300
(DBL. SPC.) PAGES INCLUDING
DISCOGRAPHY — PLUS 120 HISTORICAL
PHOTOS. (IF INDEX IS NEEDED
I AM ALMOST FINISHED WITH
IT.) OK?

© BWG, 1984

THERE AND BACK - THE ROY PORTER STORY is a straight-forward account of the high and low times that one of jazz's great drummers and composers experienced. Porter's life reads like a novel - from the Los Angeles Central Avenue scene days when he performed and recorded with such greats as Charlie Parker, Miles Davis and Dizzy Gillespie to the lows of narcotics addiction and eventual imprisonment several fast-paced years later. We hope that you will be interested in publishing this arresting *HISTORICAL AUTOBIOGRAPHY.*

A volatile performer and human being, both on and offstage, Porter tells his story with verve. The drummer's no-nonsense directness rivals that of the late Art Pepper and he is merciless to those whom he sees as hypocritical. Alternatively, for those with genuine talent and those who have proven trusted friends, he is deeply enthusiastic.

Along the way, Porter provides fascinating glimpses of music legends like Parker, Davis, Gillespie, Art Blakey and Ray Charles along with equally intriguing portraits of lesser known characters, both musical and otherwise.

Finally, Porter's story is one of hope. Out of a series of defeats which included narcotics addiction, alcoholism, divorce and imprisonment, the dynamic musician came back to lead a positive life, composing the popular song "Lonesome Mood" made famous by the Friends of Distinction and providing muscular drumming support for such greats as Earl Bostic and Perez Prado among many others.

Porter's life story offers both insight and inspiration to fans of music - young and old, black and white. He has overcome a series of devastating setbacks and stands now as a proud example of a successful black musician whose contributions to America's musical heritage far outweigh his personal difficulties. *(OR COMPLETED MANUSCRIPT.)*

There are several sample chapters of THERE AND BACK - THE ROY PORTER STORY available at this time, as well as a complete outline. We look forward to submitting these to you for your consideration. We enthusiastically wait for your response.

Sincerely, *Roy Porter*

Roy PORTER
ROTINE MUSIC CO.
2931 RIDGELEY DR.
L.A., CA 90016
U.S.A.

Figure 6 The letter I got from Roy Porter, with a post-it note stuck over the name of the previous publisher to whom he had submitted it unsuccessfully!

During my long conversation with Ray Brown, he happened to mention that Slim Gaillard's trio had been playing support to Dizzy and Bird at Berg's. Indeed, during the residency Gaillard cajoled some of the band into recording with him. Ray laughed at the memory, 'The thing I always remember about Slim Gaillard was that he made a record with Dizzy and Bird and Jack McVea and a few other people. Everybody talked on the record, and that was something different at the time. I always liked that, it was called "Slim's Jam" and everybody plays a couple of choruses of blues. When I was going to school, Slim and Slam (Stewart) were very popular then, back in the thirties, and they were good.'

On another occasion Ray had told me he had learned some of Slam Stewart's bass solos off their records, which he'd also done with the Jimmie Blanton/Duke Ellington duets (music he would later have the chance to reinterpret with Ellington himself). So I wondered what he could recall about the way that players such as Slam, or another major figure of the period, Oscar Pettiford, set up their instruments. 'Well, there are always changes going on, but people with that kind of talent always have their own set-up,' he said. 'But you must remember what I found out – the guys that have a lot of talent like that, whatever instrument you give them, they get the same sound. The sound you have is inside you. So whatever you pick up, you *have* to produce that same sound. I remember one time we had to play somewhere, some little place. And Charlie Parker was late. When he finally showed up he didn't have a horn. So now they're running around – this is at seven o'clock and we're supposed to play at eight – trying to find him a horn. And some little kid, a 14-year-old kid, brought in an alto from his school. And Charlie Parker opened up the case and looked at it. Then he borrowed some paper and some matchbook covers and some rubber bands, and he was in the back room putting this stuff all over it. Then he came out and played it. And he sounded just like *he* sounds. That's what happened – it's like your fingerprint, it ain't gonna change.

'Overall, when it came to Bird, I've never heard anybody play that good. He did so many things well, I mean all types of music. He could play fast. Fast as you want to play ... he could play it. Ballads – he could play ballads, and he was the best blues player I ever heard. He could just play anything.

'I never heard two guys play as well as Diz and Bird together. They just fit like a glove and a hand, and they sounded like one horn. If somebody could put one mouthpiece on two horns and play them at the same time, that's what they sounded like. Bird had small groups with Red Rodney and with Miles, but it was never like it was with Dizzy. And Dizzy had bands with other saxophone players, like Sonny Stitt, Dexter Gordon and James Moody, but nobody ever sounded like Bird did with him.'

11 THE MODERN JAZZ QUARTET

Back at the end of the 1990s, when I was working on my biography of Dizzy,[1] I covered this 1940s period of his and Parker's work in great detail, with much help from Ray and other colleagues of Gillespie's. But I also became curious about how one of the other most influential groups in jazz from the bebop era emerged from this very same setting – namely the Modern Jazz Quartet. When Dizzy came back from his 1945–6 trip to California, he led a small group for a time and then formed a big band. Ray and Milt Jackson stayed on with Dizzy after the West Coast sextet returned to New York, and became part of the line-up of this larger group.

'Whenever bandleaders find people in the band that have talent, they exploit it,' recalled Ray. 'And actually there were very few soloists in the big band who did the bulk of the soloing. Besides Dizzy, we didn't have a prominent trumpet soloist. There were some good players, but he did the bulk of the trumpet solos. And in the saxophone section we had James Moody. But most of the All Stars were in the rhythm section – John Lewis, Kenny Clarke, Milt Jackson and myself. We would spell the horns, after they'd played 'til their lips were hanging down. He'd tell the rhythm section to play two or three pieces and then the horns would play again.'[2]

Ray was keen to point out that when the rhythm section took its feature numbers during these breaks for the brass and reeds, it was not yet the Modern Jazz Quartet, and that probably any piano, bass and drums rhythm section, plus vibes, would have something of that aural character. It did, however, go out independently of Dizzy as a band in its own right from quite early in 1947, not long after both Ray and Milt Jackson won individual *Esquire* awards in January that year. For a quartet gig at Small's Paradise they were billed as 'The Atomics of Modern Music'.[3] So despite Ray's reservations, the beginnings were there of a special and distinctive sound, at least partially evident when Ray also recalled the extreme care that Kenny Clarke took with his drums, moistening the heads to suit the acoustics of each venue, and then positioning the drums and the bass so that certain frequencies would resonate. 'I don't generally find guys taking that much care about sound,' he said. 'People call the first records we made (under Milt Jackson's name) the beginning of the MJQ. It sort of was, but then again it wasn't, because it wasn't really the Modern Jazz Quartet at that point. It came together after I was gone, because when I told them I wasn't going to stay, they got Percy Heath, and then that became a permanent group.'

The change took place in what was still the Milt Jackson Quartet between August and September 1951, on two recording sessions for Dizzy Gillespie and Dave Usher's DeeGee label. On the first, from 24 August, which produced 'Milt Meets Sid' and 'D and E', the line-up is exactly as listed by Ray – Lewis, Jackson, Clarke and Brown. By the time of the band's return to the studio on 18 September, when it made a haunting version of 'Round About Midnight', Percy Heath had replaced Brown, whereas Clarke was temporarily replaced by Al Jones. Clarke finally left permanently in 1955 and Connie Kay took his place. Strangely enough, although I had no intention of discussing the MJQ when I met Percy Heath, it was Ray Brown's name that first came up when I spent time with him, because propped up in the corner of the room was a cello. Apparently, Percy had decided – following the example of Oscar Pettiford, Sam Jones and Ron Carter – to try using a cello for high-register soloing in the band he co-led with his brothers Jimmy and Tootie. When he'd talked to Ray Brown about it, Ray, who never had much time for the smaller instrument, packed up his own cello and sent it to Percy.

Some time before, I'd discussed this very instrument with Ray, as he disliked cello tuning pegs and had had it modified with a slightly wider-than-normal fingerboard and double-bass-style geared tuners. He'd passed it to Percy with a note saying, 'Watch out for three … ' Initially Heath couldn't figure out what he meant, until he realized that you couldn't use the orthodox Simandl bass fingering system on the cello, because the intervals were too small. Whereas double bassists using that method avoid using the third finger of the left hand in lower positions, it is essential for playing a cello, even if it is – as Percy's was – re-tuned in fourths. Recalling my own schooldays as a cellist, and the trouble I'd had trying *not* to use my third finger on the bass when I made the move to the larger instrument, I had a good laugh with Percy about Ray's cryptic message, and so before we turned to his work with Miles Davis and with his brothers we took a detour into MJQ territory.

'It was Milt's quartet to begin with,' remembered Percy. 'But it was renamed because John Lewis decided that he was going to write a different style of music for the instrumentation. And he wasn't interested in it being "Milt Jackson's Quartet" with his music, so we came up with the neutral name of the Modern Jazz Quartet, which happened to have the Milt Jackson Quartet's initials! But Milt was really the star, the established improvising person, it was beautiful.'[4]

Before the first recordings by the Milt Jackson Quartet, Dizzy had kept a small group going, having been forced in 1950 by financial problems to give up his big band. In this new sextet Jackson played both vibraphone and piano, a good example of which is the April 1951 recording of 'The Champ', where Dizzy plays piano behind Milt's vibes solo, and Milt returns the compliment as he slides over to the piano stool and backs up Dizzy's trumpet. But Jackson, who was nothing if not a perfectionist, already knew by then that he would never be a pianist at the very highest level.

I met Milt several times over the years, initially backstage after playing in the band that opened for him at the Reading Festival in England, on August Bank Holiday weekend, 1978. In those days, the National Jazz, Blues & Rock Festival, which had been founded by Chris Barber and Harold Pendleton, still had a jazz day – and after groups such as The Jam, Ultravox, Status Quo, Lindisfarne and Tom Robinson had headlined on Friday, Saturday and Sunday, the Monday was given over to jazz, with the Morrissey-Mullen Band, Cousin Joe, Chris Barber (with Alvin Alcorn and Tommy Tucker), and Milt Jackson. After a New Orleans-style parade around the campsite, the afternoon stage show opened with Sammy Rimington's quintet, in which I played. A couple of the other bands did 45-minute sets and then Milt took the platform for a mesmerizing session with the British rhythm section of Brian Lemon, Dave Green and John Marshall. Almost twenty years later, Milt was at the Brecon Festival in Wales, and following a storming concert with a quartet he co-led with Hank Jones, we met up for a lengthy chat. That seemed a good opportunity to ask why he'd not pursued his early career as a pianist. Pointing at the fourth and fifth fingers of his right hand, he told me, 'What hampered me from actually becoming a pianist was I couldn't separate these last two fingers. It was a handicap, and I thought if I can't do it right, then I won't. It took me a long time to realize, but I can't even today, really do it. For a while that led me to adopt the Lionel Hampton two-finger style, I give him the credit, because he did it first, but that's really why I gave it up. I just felt it stopped me from playing professionally as a pianist.'[5]

Yet playing alongside great pianists, not only John Lewis and Hank Jones, but such luminaries as Thelonious Monk, Al Haig and Bud Powell, gave Milt plenty of ideas that he absorbed into his solo vocabulary as a vibraphonist. 'Actually, it wasn't just pianists,' he said. 'It was every other instrumentalist that was known at the time that I got something from, because I listened to them all. If you listen carefully, you can find benefit from just about everybody that you listen to, so that is really what I did. I took these ideas into creating my own "voice" with piano, bass and drums. When you have a unique style, which most people, or at least most musicians, can all recognize, that's a major criterion of being a soloist. A lot of musicians become imitators, because they can't reach that point of originality.'

I was intrigued by what Stan Levey had said about Milt's early playing, and the fact his style was still coming together at the time he went to California with Dizzy. Yet even though Levey was dismissive about his original instrument, for Milt it was all part of developing his own sound. 'It began when I got my first set of vibes and discovered the vibrato which it made. I found I could match the vibrato of my voice as a singer. Going back a little further – I was a gospel singer from seven to sixteen. And I found that I could replicate the vibrato in my voice on the instrument by using the speed control which it has.[6] And I think that was also another thing that made me give up the piano. It comes from a philosophy of my father's, not to be a jack-of-all-trades. Concentrate on the one thing that you really like and be good at that one thing.' It helped that Milt had such natural musical attributes as perfect pitch and a photographic memory, the latter being a priceless asset as the MJQ began to perform the complex contrapuntal music written for it by John Lewis.

'What I like about jazz,' Lewis pondered when we talked, 'is that it's not actually necessary to produce a rhythmic beat, you can imply it. For example, "For Ellington", which was the title track of an MJQ album, I had in mind the three-four that gospel people use, and also something of the feeling that Ellington himself used in "Come Sunday".'[7] Thinking about this, I suggested to him that as a composer, as much as a player, he likes to create pictures in sound, such as his French-inspired pieces 'Vendôme', 'Versailles', 'Concorde' or perhaps most famous of all, his 1949 'Afternoon in Paris'. In reply, he recalled an early recording of that latter tune with Sonny Rollins and J. J. Johnson as 'a kind of jam session', but told me he came back to it many times afterwards, not least as the atmospheric title track of the album he made featuring the guitar of Sacha Distel in 1956, with Pierre Michelot and Connie Kay. He was equally keen to evoke a French atmosphere in his composition 'Django', written to commemorate the great manouche guitarist mentioned earlier by Al Casey. John first heard Reinhardt's playing on a jukebox in Rouen, during his army days in 1945, but then, like Al Casey, he heard Django in person during his post-war visit to the United States, when he came to work with Duke Ellington. 'I was playing on 52nd Street with Dizzy at the Famous Door, and Django would come and stay with us all night long. I still miss him. He was a continuously developing musician, he wasn't satisfied with remaining in one period of his work, he was always moving forward, and never stuck in one period or style.'

Talking about how the MJQ personnel came together in Dizzy's band, we got onto the subject of Ray Brown, and I discovered that his feature 'Two Bass Hit' was actually adapted from a piece that John had written for a service band when he was in the Armed Forces in World War Two. He then adapted it in the Gillespie big band for Ray, because John realized it would make an ideal feature for him. 'Ray Brown was a fantastic bassist – a revelation – when I first played with him. For me it was like something sent from heaven because he carried on the same tradition as Jimmie Blanton, who had totally changed bass playing. Working together in Dizzy's big band at the Spotlite in New York, we had a wonderful time. It was all new to us.

'Milt was most unusual at that time. He was one of the greatest vibraharp players that jazz has developed, and I wanted to make sure that everybody for whom we played knew this. So I made arrangements and composed things that would show this great talent. I guess I was maybe a bit surprised by the degree of our success once we had stopped being Dizzy's rhythm section and then moved on from the Milt Jackson Quartet to the Modern Jazz Quartet. I didn't maybe think about it at the time, but I was happy that we had a success, and that I was playing with good friends. I'd known Kenny Clarke in the army, as we were in the Special Service Company together in France. Then Milt and Ray were with us in Dizzy's band, and later I met Percy for the first time during one of a couple of visits to Philadelphia, where, of course, Dizzy had worked before he came to New York. Percy comes from a big loving family, and his parents were just huge jazz fans. It was always a joy to go visit Percy's home, so when he became our bass player, it still felt like he was one of the family.'

The tight-knit family spirit in the MJQ at its height spilled over into the music. 'It got,' recalled Jackson, 'so the people couldn't tell the part that was improvised and the part that wasn't. Because the group eventually got so tight-knit, it got so we could breathe together.' Ultimately, and perhaps like many a family, it was this very closeness that led to it breaking up – first in 1974, and then after reassembling for annual tours from 1981, separating for good in 1997, two years before Milt's death. He told me when I talked to him at the Very Tall Band reunion in 1998 that he was with the MJQ longer than he was married, and that it reached the point that he knew which shirts his fellow members would be wearing when they came down for breakfast. Yet it seems to me, even in their final reunions (one of which I presented on BBC Radio), that unlike the well-worn caricature of the lengthy marriage, they always seemed to have something new to say.

12 THE 'SWING DRUMMER'

Going back to my long conversation with Ray Brown, I was intrigued by what Dizzy had seen in the MJQ's original drummer, Kenny Clarke, which made him the first choice both for the small group and later for the original Gillespie big band. 'Kenny was the only guy Dizzy could find that played drums to fit in with the stuff he wanted to do with Charlie Parker,' said Ray. 'And he told him, "That's what I want the drums to do." So here's Kenny, in a band where he could do all his stuff and it was perfect. See, Max Roach hadn't really emerged at that time. And Max was mainly playing in small bands first of all. He had played big band with Benny Carter, but I think after he started working with Bird he changed his style. What he was doing didn't sit well with a big band. For me, he was basically a small band drummer.'[1]

Another of the drummers associated with bebop, Roy Haynes, as Arvell Shaw has mentioned, started his career in swing big bands, indeed playing alongside Arvell in Luis Russell's orchestra. He is a perfect example of a similar fluidity between styles to Sir Charles Thompson, moving with ease from swing to bebop environments and back again. I have interviewed Roy several times for BBC radio, but most memorably when we spent the best part of a day together at the beginning of May 1999. He had been scheduled to play that week at the Soho Pizza Express in London, but following the homophobic nail bomb attack in the nearby Admiral Duncan pub on the last day of April (killing three people and wounding dozens more), there was a police cordon around the area and all pubs and clubs were closed.

Roy was isolated behind the police lines in the apartment just adjacent to the Pizza Express, where American guests usually stayed. So as he could not come to BBC World Service headquarters, then still at Bush House in the Strand, for our interview, he suggested I met him at the flat. Waving our BBC passes at the constable on duty, together with my producer Oliver Jones (with whom I shared many great jazz adventures around the world), we crossed the blue and white police tape strung across the street and went to meet Roy. We had plenty of time, and he is a wonderful raconteur, so several hours passed quickly as we chatted through his life story. And, naturally, we began with Luis Russell.

'He and Louis Armstrong were really closely associated, and Louis used to use his bands,' recalled Roy. 'It seems like a dream now when I think back, that I joined Luis Russell in September 1945. Sid Catlett had been in the band, and he was quite a drummer, and before him, Paul Barbarin, whom I met when I went to New Orleans for the first time, which would have been 1945 or 1946. There was a younger drummer that was with Luis just before myself, and that was Percy Brice, and he's still around New York.'[2] Roy's route from playing swing, aged just 20, with the Russell band towards bebop took him by way of working with Lester Young, often seen as something of a transitional figure himself in the swing-to-bop era. But Lester is remembered by Roy as someone with a rather unorthodox approach to life itself. 'He definitely did have that. He had a personal language, and he was one of the most original people that I've ever met, in this business, or for that matter in any business! Lester had his own way of talking, his own way of dressing, his own way of playing. He was a very original person. I was with him for two years and it was quite enjoyable. Much earlier, like his brother Lee, he'd been a drummer, and one time I was listening to some other musicians talking about him. They were saying the reason why he left drumming was he'd have to be packing up his drums and everyone else would be leaving with all the girls. But I've always thought there was a reason other than that – we don't know how great Lester played drums! I'm sure whatever he played had a good feel and he could swing, but we don't know.'

What we do know is that on a piece such as 'Ding Dong' from April 1949, Young's rhythm section with Junior Mance on piano and Roy on drums is already moving a long way towards the kind of sound that Kenny Clarke and John Lewis had been getting with Dizzy, or the team of Max Roach and Al Haig were developing with Charlie Parker.

And before the end of the year, Roy had joined Parker's quintet himself. 'I was into the bebop thing, even before I joined Luis Russell's band,' explained Roy. 'Because I was from Boston, which is only a couple hundred miles from New York City, I would go visit New York and listen to Charlie Parker before I arrived in the city to live. So I was aware of it, you might even say it was in my blood at the time. But I'm sure it's also true that I was taking a slightly different approach from Kenny and Max. In fact when Kenny Clarke came back to New York after being in the army in Europe, and he first heard me playing, he told me I was doing something different from what the other drummers were playing.'

One session that teamed Roy together with a pianistic innovator of the era was the quintet led by Bud Powell that recorded for Blue Note with Sonny Rollins and Fats Navarro, plus bassist Tommy Potter, in August 1949, shortly before Roy joined Charlie Parker. Ray Brown recalled hearing Bud in the very early 1940s (while the bassist was still a teenager) in Pittsburgh, when Bud came through with Cootie Williams' band. 'I played hookey from school to see Bud at the theatre,' Ray told me. 'Everybody was talking about him. I remember on that show he was also playing behind a tap dancer called Ralph Brown, who wore a hat, and tapped and talked and sang a little bit, and was kind of smooth. While he was doing his tapping, Bud played "Cherokee" and he played so good that everybody was watching him and not the guy dancing. Ralph got mad and said "Whoa! Cool it down a bit back there, I'm the star here!" But Bud was really, really good.'[3]

Roy Haynes agreed. 'Bud and I were in our twenties then. I didn't particularly like the word "bop". I don't even like it now. It was just a new way of phrasing, maybe, but I consider myself a swing drummer, then and now. Maybe that's what has kept me out here so long! 'Cos I can swing, in the real meaning of the word "swing". I'm an old time swing drummer, with a modern touch.'

I have always rather liked the Club Kavakos sessions from Washington DC recorded off the air in April 1953 by the avid collector Bill Potts, and featuring the trio of Bud Powell, Charles Mingus and Roy. The record shows this group really taking off in a club setting, with plenty of 'swing' as Roy describes it, but also a complete commitment to bebop timing and harmony, so I asked him about the album. 'The recordings from there were sort of black market, bootleg things,' said Roy. 'If I'd known we were recording, I'd probably have acted different, but it was just a live performance, that was taped. Bud had just come out of a mental institution at that time, so it wasn't the easiest job, and Mingus wasn't the easiest guy to play with.' Yet the unfettered swing of the group and the excitement of the session make it one of the most dazzling Powell trio records, a track such as 'Salt Peanuts' moving a long way from the Dizzy Gillespie original into a flowing, inventive piano tour de force.

But again epitomizing the fluidity between genres, Roy's next job, for some years, was in the trio accompanying Sarah Vaughan. 'She was not just a singer,' he said. 'There's definitely a separation there. I played with quite a few singers, including Billie Holiday, Ella Fitzgerald, and Carmen McRae, and I recorded with Ray Charles. And when I was very young with Luis Russell's band, I had to accompany Nat King Cole. And I played with some blues singers. But Sarah Vaughan was a great musician, also. She had recorded with Dizzy Gillespie and Charlie Parker. She wasn't ever just "a singer". When you stop and think about that, that's why I was with Sarah Vaughan a lot longer than I was with other people. Five years – a long time – it was enjoyable, from 1953 to 1958.'

Our discussion went on to cover many other aspects of Roy's career, including his time deputizing for Elvin Jones in the John Coltrane quartet. 'With John Coltrane, I could express myself more so than any other time. Because the '60s was a time when a lot of things were changing – there were the Beatles, the style of dress, people were wearing long hair, and different things were happening. I felt I could really express myself on my instrument. We could play loud. We could play soft. I never wanted to be known as a loud drummer, but I wanted to be able to play soft and loud, and a lady came up to me at that time in Chicago, and she said, "Roy Haynes, I love your music because it reminds me of the four seasons, you have everything, summer, fall, winter, spring." So with Coltrane I could play the things that came to my mind and I wanted to play. Maybe some of the things I had wanted to play with Charlie Parker that I didn't play! With Coltrane I could let it all hang out. I always had it in me, I had a feeling, and I was a natural player. I wasn't one who woke up one day and decided I was going to go to school and study to learn to play drums, because drums were in me, ever since I can remember. John Coltrane could bring these things out. You could do things with John Coltrane that you couldn't do with some other artists. He had such a spiritual feeling, such a presence, in the way that *he* was doing what he was doing. He'd get somebody to play with him and they would sound different, so when I played with him it was different from Elvin. And that's a feather in my cap. At Newport we did the 18-minute version of "My Favorite Things", which people have said is much different than Coltrane's original version, which was made in the studio. You know, it's great!' Roy went on to discuss how, in the quartet, he liked working with bassist Jimmy Garrison, whose presence he said he 'felt' on the bandstand as much as heard. He thought the Coltrane quartet's 'After the Rain' was perhaps the summit of his achievement in that seminal group.

After we switched off the recording machine, we carried on chatting, looking back on his time with many musicians including Chick Corea, Kenny Garrett and Danilo Perez. Just before I left, he mentioned that during his time with Luis Russell, he'd admired a great trumpeter in the band who came from New Orleans, but could not remember his name. Without really thinking, I just said, 'What, some-one like Emery Thompson?' Roy stopped in his tracks – 'Yes, but how did *you* know that?' So I explained I had met and heard Emery (by then more generally known as Umar Sharif) in New Orleans, including on the gig I mentioned in Chapter 3 with Ed Frank. Roy and I were to talk again on several subsequent occasions, in which he was always a wonderful raconteur and convivial companion, but when he caught sight of me, he usually remembered that London conversation, and as we met would murmur 'Emery Thompson . . . '

Perhaps our most memorable chat after our Soho encounter was during an evening at Tanglewood in 2001, after a concert by his Birds of a Feather band, paying tribute to Charlie Parker. Once again, as he relaxed after the gig, Roy looked back with both affection and amazement at those formative years of bebop, and reflected on his new band of the time.

'It wasn't my idea to do the Birds of a Feather thing,' he said. 'The title came from my daughter after they did something on the internet. I think they ran some kind of rally or competition to find a title for it, and that's what came up. It was somebody else's idea to do a tribute to Charlie Parker, and because I was probably one of the few left that had worked with Charlie Parker who was still active and innovative, they chose Roy Haynes! A number of names for the band members were put forward but we ended up with Kenny Garrett, Dave Holland, Roy Hargrove and Dave Kikowski, which turned out to be very mellow!'[4]

13 JACKIE MCLEAN AND SONNY ROLLINS

It was listening to a Charlie Parker disc in his father's record store in Harlem that prompted another major figure in the bebop world to become a jazz musician. But Jackie McLean took that route because somebody else was in the shop besides the customer who asked to hear the record. He recalled, 'I was telling the man who was buying it who he was listening to, and I mentioned it was Bud Powell on piano. I sold him the record and he left. So this other guy who'd come in, who had paint splats all over his clothes and was wearing a sort of coverall, says, "That's my brother, Bud Powell."

'I said, "Really? No kidding. What instrument do you play? D'you play piano?"

'He says, "Oh no, I don't play any music."

'I looked in his face and said, "Yeah, right, you're Bud Powell's brother." I didn't believe him. And so he got angry about that. Not really mad, but he said, "Okay, I'll prove it to you." Now I forgot about it, and then three or four days later I was in there and he came back in. He said, "My brother is at the house. If you don't believe my brother is Bud Powell, you come and see him, now."

'So I closed up my dad's record shop, locked the door, took my horn and went up to the house. I didn't know what Bud looked like. So I was sitting on the couch. He came out and said, "You don't believe that I'm Bud Powell?"

'I said, "I don't know, I've never seen him!"

'He turned around, went to the piano and sat down. And the minute he sat at the piano, I knew immediately who I was looking at! So that was a fateful thing that happened to me, but it was the reason why I've done a lot of things in my life. And that includes starting a cultural programme in my home town of Hartford, Connecticut, to give young people a chance to be exposed to the arts in a way that might help to enhance their existence. They have to have our rich musical tradition opened up for them because in America now, they don't put enough emphasis on the richness of that culture, and the musicians that made great contributions – James Reese Europe, Don Redman, Fletcher Henderson, Duke Ellington and great performers like Louis Armstrong and Lester Young. All of us who came after 1945 are babies of "Pres" [Lester Young].

'See, when I was growing up in Harlem, the music was everywhere. It was coming out of the bars, out of the barber shops, out of the apartments, because that was the era of Louis Armstrong, Duke Ellington, Jimmie Lunceford, Earl Hines, and Billy Eckstine. Of course, I was hearing this stuff as a little boy, not realizing who was who. Billie Holiday was always very familiar to me because I heard her voice so much. My dad loved Louis Armstrong, so he played Louis constantly on his record player. So I heard him all the time. Then when I finally heard Lester Young on record, that was a real wake-up call for me. And that happened about a year and a half before I met Bud, which was in 1947, when I was coming up to 16.[1] I had been playing saxophone for over a year, and when I met him that day at the house, he asked me, "What have you got in that case?"

'I said, "It's my saxophone."

'He said, "D'you know how to play it?"

'I said, "Yeah, I know how to play 'Buzzy'."' That was a recording he was on, with Bird. That changed his whole attitude toward me. He said, "Oh yeah?" like I was just a kid. But then he said, "Get your horn out". And he sat down and played an introduction for me, and I knew when to come in, so I played the melody and then I went through my little things that I knew how to play. And he was quite amazed that I understood the form and stayed in the right key, because even though it was very elementary, it was on its way somewhere. He could hear that. It was great! It was like he gave me carte blanche. He invited me to the house again and said, "Come by any time!" So I would go to his house every week, and take my horn, and get a chance to play. Sometimes if he didn't play with me, or was away from home, I started [his brother] Richard playing. Bud didn't want Richie to be a musician so it was a big secret. Richie'd say, "Don't tell Bud that I'm learning how to play piano." So he and I had an alliance, behind Bud's back, because Richard was more my peer.'²

Jackie went on to say that Richie was an instinctive musician. Not long after they first met, Jackie took him to meet another local Harlem pianist called Bob Bunyan, who taught Richie the B flat blues. Before long he was dropping by to see Bob almost every day on his own, and within a matter of weeks, he called Jackie to meet him at his father's house. They played the blues together and then they played 'Celia' and a few other tunes, and Mr Powell Sr got out his tape recorder (quite a rarity in the 1940s) and recorded them. Jackie told me that he still (in 1999) had those tapes of Richie Powell's very first steps as a jazz musician.

By the time I first met Jackie, I had already published the biography of Bud Powell that I co-wrote with Alan Groves.³ Jackie came to play at the Cheltenham Jazz Festival in the UK in 1997, with a quartet including pianist Cedar Walton, bassist David Williams and drummer Victor Lewis, and I dropped in backstage to give him a copy of the book. We got into a long conversation about Bud then, and he also told me I was wearing 'a bebop tie' – apparently very much the type of neckwear that had been in vogue during the mid-1940s! He wrote to me about the book after the festival, and said that anything to keep Bud's name in the public eye meant a lot to him. So when I visited his home in 1999 for a further conversation, I wanted to know more about how he had become close to a man whose mental state meant he was not always a great communicator away from the keyboard.

The response was interesting, in that Jackie felt it had a lot to do with the way tight-knit African American families interacted closely in the Harlem environment. Not long after he started visiting Bud and Richie, his mother phoned Bud's mother to ask whether Jackie was coming round to their house too often. 'Mrs Powell said, "Oh no, we *love* having Jackie round here. Bud likes him. We love him to death. He's no problem." So my mother said, "OK."

'Mrs Powell liked me, and so if there was anything I could do for Bud, she'd encourage me to do it. So she might say, "I promised Bud that he could go down to Thelonious' house for two or three hours, but just for that time. But only if somebody could take him down and bring him back. D'you want to do that?" And I'd say, "Oh yeah Mrs Powell, sure I can do that." So I'd take Bud, get on the subway and go down to

Thelonious' house, who knew we were coming. We'd go in, and Bud could visit. He loved and adored Thelonious. I think he loved him more than anybody. Monk would play. Bud would watch. He'd sit on the floor and watch his feet. He was a very strange kind of guy.'

Jackie had been sure that owing to his close relationship with Bud, who constantly urged him to practise and develop his style, that for the 1949 Blue Note date mentioned earlier by Roy Haynes, he would be the saxophonist. 'I had learned all the stuff for the *Dance of the Infidels* album.[4] Bud had said, "I think you could be on this album, man, but you gotta learn this music." So I said, "Just show it to me, I'll come down every day." So I came down and he showed me "The Dance of the Infidels" and I played it and then he listened to me. He didn't say anything, and then later he said, "Tomorrow I'm going to have Sonny come over. But you work on that, man."'

The next time Jackie saw Bud, he was mortified to discover that Powell, together with Blue Note's Alfred Lion, had chosen Sonny Rollins to make the record instead of him, not least because Sonny had quickly absorbed and learned all the eleven pieces that would be recorded on 8 August. A year or so older than Jackie, and formerly a pupil at the same high school, Rollins had been, as Jackie put it, 'the king of the neighbourhood' at fourteen. Equally impressive at high school was Andy Kirk Jr, the son of the territory bandleader whom I mentioned in Chapter 5. The younger Kirk had absorbed many of the ideas that Bud Powell and Charlie Parker were developing, but Rollins overtook him. Shortly before the Powell Blue Note date, Jackie took the subway to Brooklyn to hear Sonny.

'I started walking towards the club. I heard this sax. I thought it was Bird, but as I got through the door I saw it was Sonny. What he was doing bowled me over. He had made a complete transformation, like a metamorphosis to a butterfly. Everyone on stage was mesmerized, including Miles.'

In the end, not being on the record worked to Jackie's advantage, when, almost a couple of years later, Bud – wanting to encourage his protégé, whom he now felt was ready to play at the top level – arranged for him to sit in with Miles Davis at Birdland. Despite some initial wariness from the tenor saxophonist Gene Ammons, who was playing with the band that night, it went well, and Miles invited the young altoist to his house to rehearse. A few days later McLean found himself in Miles' sextet alongside Davis and Sonny Rollins. 'Everybody idolized Sonny, he just destroyed other sax players,' recalled Jackie. 'But I was in a fortunate place being in Miles' band next to Sonny, even though they bruised me from night to night. They just mauled me. I was between the two of them. Miles would play, Sonny would stand at the side of the stage, so that behind Miles' great solo I would have to go and play ... When I finished Sonny would walk out, building some great image of stone in sound.'

A good example of Jackie squeezing in a solo between Sonny and Miles in this kind of setting is on his own piece 'Dig' (based on the chords of 'Sweet Georgia Brown') which the sextet recorded to occupy both sides of a 78 on 5 October 1951. In part one Jackie emerges after Sonny's forceful solo, and before Miles' rapidfire choruses, but he holds his own as an accomplished soloist much better than he implied when we spoke.

On and off, Jackie was to work with Miles for around three years. The shadow of heroin addiction fell over the band, but the group nonetheless made some fine recordings. In due course, all three of the front-line players weaned themselves off the drug, Jackie in particular becoming an ardent anti-narcotics campaigner.

In 2007 I was in New York, and got the opportunity to talk at length to Sonny Rollins.[5] It wasn't long before we were looking back at that same early 1950s period, although interestingly not initially at Miles or Bud, but at his August 1954 quintet with Kenny Dorham and the relatively little-known pianist Elmo Hope.

'Well, Elmo was sort of a legendary musician in New York,' Sonny recalled. 'He knew Bud Powell, I think he hung out with Monk and Bud, and a lot of people credit him with being one of the early pioneers in that style of music. He was a great, great player, and he's very much under-appreciated. There are echoes of Bud, they were both very similar and both around the same age, and people said one got something from the other. They're contemporaries, and actually it was hard to see where one leaves off and the other begins. Bud had his basic style, which was identifiable, but their basic styles were very much similar. When it comes to Kenny Dorham, he and I were very, very close. I heard him before I met him on some early records, including some with Sonny Stitt, and Bud Powell was also on some of those I think.[6] One was called "Good Kick", I remember that. I'd followed Kenny's career when he was with Billy Eckstine, and when I finally met Kenny, he'd moved up to our area of New York in Sugar Hill. He lived up there, a real nice guy and a scholar, so we always used to discuss the music and the different musicians and ways of playing, Then he got to work with Charlie Parker, and – as I said – we were very close. A lot of people lived up there. It was the preferred part of New York for the Black intelligentsia. Before the album we did practise a lot together.'

I started talking to Sonny about the Miles sextet with him and Jackie, but prompted by Jackie's early connection with Richie Powell, our conversation then took a leap forward to the Clifford Brown–Max Roach band in which Richie played. About this, Sonny was unequivocal, yet also remaining characteristically modest and even somewhat self-critical. 'Oh, that was a highlight of my career. As you know, I replaced Harold Land, who was the original saxophonist with the Clifford Brown–Max Roach orchestra. I had big shoes to fill, because they had a really tight-knit, singular-sounding group. They had made some terrific records and they had a group sound. So when Harold had to leave the band, I was in Chicago.[7] I knew Max a little bit from New York, and I'd met Brownie in New York, too. So they asked me to join the group, but it was a challenge, because not only was it tight-knit and everything arranged in advance, but it was very formidable task, and I did it with some concern that I'd be able to live up to the high standard of the band as a sideman. I'd been more prominent as a semi-leader, although I'd done stuff with Miles.

'As it turned out, I changed the character of the band, or so I've been told, and I believe it. I didn't do what Harold Land was doing. I played my own way – sort of "Sonny Rollins with that group". Some of my own compositions came in, and I put a different character on the band. And Brownie's wife told me that my coming in the band added something different in a positive sense. In other words it was a very positive relationship between Clifford and myself.'

I suggested to Sonny that not only is this noticeable in almost every note the band played, but also that there's a real sense that what each was doing complemented the other. 'Clifford, I thought, was not only a great musician, but just a phenomenal human being. Just a beautiful person,' Sonny responded. 'His musicianship was on such a high level that I said to myself, "I've really got to be on my Ps and Qs!"'

We then moved on to the tragic accident that robbed the world both of Brownie and of Bud Powell's brother Richie. And like Jackie McLean, Sonny had high praise for Richie: 'He was a great pianist and he was a great writer. He wrote some beautiful things, and I think he really was tremendous as a writer. Whereas he wasn't the soloist that Bud was – I mean to say, who was? – Richie had his own personality, and he was a fine arranger. He was arranging some really great stuff for that band, so it was a real shame that everything ended the way it did, because he had not only written some of what we recorded, but he was about to do further things just at the time he was killed. I think he probably was underrated because of being Bud's brother.'

Listening back to the band's records, all but one of the sides recorded by the quintet on the *At Basin Street* disc from January 1956 are Powell's arrangements. Among them, Richie's compositions, 'Gertrude's Bounce', 'Powell's Prances' and 'Time', are all tightly written and neatly arranged. They more than hold their own against the rest of the album, including Sonny's own works. 'Gertrude's Bounce' has a head that cleverly incorporates phrases that sound vaguely familiar, and includes a piano interlude that owes a lot to Richie's older brother. 'Powell's Prances' rockets along at breakneck speed before moving into solos played over a modal basis rather than chord changes, prefiguring Miles Davis' ventures into similar harmonic territory by a couple of years. Brown's solo is a masterly example of his trumpet attack, and Sonny picks up on his phrasing, almost for a moment as if the same improvising mind is at work on a different instrument, until Sonny moves on into lines that are distinctively his own. The piece that points most to Powell's originality as a writer is 'Time', exploring the idea of 'doing time' in jail, and built on a moodily introspective theme, with Brown and Rollins accompanied by the ethereal sound of Powell's celeste. Before the end of the opening melody, he has switched to piano, and the centre of the recording is a brief heart-rending, melancholic solo that nods in the direction of classical keyboard works, and is quite unlike the work of any other jazz pianist active at the time.

The last commercial recording by the Brown–Roach quintet was made in March 1956 under Sonny's name, for Prestige. In May he was to make the first of two further sessions for that label, just over a month before the road accident that killed Clifford Brown, Richie Powell and his wife. The first record, *Tenor Madness*, is particularly well known in the jazz world because on the title track, Sonny is joined by John Coltrane. 'I knew Coltrane,' he recalled. 'I'd played with him with Miles, so I knew of his prowess. And I think the musicians knew about it, too, but commercially he wasn't yet well known. A lot of people like that record, and my friend James Moody told me, "When I listen to that track, you sound like 'two sumo wrestlers'!" But it was great playing with John – not just on the record, but the times I played with him when I first met him with Miles. In fact Coltrane became one of my closest friends, Coltrane along with Monk. But Trane was a beautiful soul.' There's another Davis link too, in that the rhythm section for this album is that of Miles' band of the time with whom Coltrane was playing regularly, Red Garland, Paul Chambers and Philly Joe Jones. But when Sonny returned to the studio a month later, his own regular colleague Max Roach was on drums, along with pianist Tommy Flanagan and bassist Doug Watkins. The resulting album was *Saxophone Colossus*.

When I talked to Tommy Flanagan about it, he chuckled and said 'I think we got lucky with that one, it's held up so well, for so long. But I always find that saxophonists come so prepared that usually we can just do one take on a tune. And with Sonny I don't remember doing more than one take on any of those tunes. I thought he was just outstanding and marvellous, and he had such a beautiful sound, plus his concept of how to play the material, how to be within the idiom of the song itself, how to feel the time, and then how to give it a little extra in the rhythm and the time.'[8] My conversation with Tommy ranged far and wide, but there was no doubt that this album had a special place in his heart, along with his work with two other great saxophonists, Coleman Hawkins and John Coltrane.

For me, and I suspect a great many other owners of *Saxophone Colossus*, the piece that sticks in the mind, and which Sonny would often come to the front of the stage and play on his London concerts, is the calypso 'St Thomas'. He told me, 'That tune is a folk song from the Virgin Islands, where my mother was born. I recorded it and of course I made a little jazz arrangement that changed it around slightly. So whenever I'd meet people over the years they'd say, "Oh, you didn't invent 'St Thomas', it was a folk song." And I'd say, "Yes it was, but the record people put it on the album". That's what record people do, when they have a chance to get half of the publishing and so on and so forth, so it's listed as "St Thomas" by Sonny Rollins, but of course it originally was that Virgin Islands song. And let me say this – the Virgin Islands used to be possessed by Denmark, so St Thomas, St Croix and St John, they were Danish-owned. Now there was a Danish folk song called "Vive la compagnie" that I heard in a movie one time sung by Lawrence Melchior.[9] When I listened to that song, I thought, "It's basically the same as 'St Thomas'." And I suspect the native population were listening to that song, "Vive la compagnie" and turned it into "St Thomas".'

The *Saxophone Colossus* album was recorded just four days before Clifford Brown's fatal accident. Afterwards, Sonny Rollins and Max Roach continued to work together often, and there's perhaps no better example of their work later in 1956 than Sonny's final Prestige album, *Tour De Force*. With pianist Kenny Drew in place of Richie Powell, the quartet is completed by George Morrow, and two tracks also feature the singer Earl Coleman. But for me the high points of the album are the two exhilarating pieces that live up to their titles: 'B. Swift' and 'B. Quick'. Here both Max and Sonny take playing at speed to new levels of precision and excitement. 'They were fast, yes,' agrees Sonny. 'That was something Max and I used to do. We liked to play fast. And whenever we had a guy in one of these towns we played in that wanted to come and sit in with the band, we'd say "Sure! Come Up!" And then Max would hit the snare: "Brrrr ... " and we'd see if the guy could do it! But those tunes were fast, yeah!'

I'd already heard from Tommy Flanagan that with Sonny's combination of preparation and focus, albums like this would usually be a series of single takes. And to give some indication of the work rate of Sonny and Max at the time, *Tour De Force* was recorded in Rudy Van Gelder's New Jersey studio on 7 December 1956 after the two of them had convened earlier that same day in New York City to put the finishing touches to Thelonious Monk's *Brilliant Corners* album by recording 'Bemsha Swing'. Once again, when we started discussing that album it led Sonny to consider one of the less well-known musicians of the period, Ernie Henry.

'Nobody remembers Ernie Henry too much,' mused Sonny. 'Ernie was a great player. He was one of the guys that I looked up to when I was coming up. He lived in Brooklyn, and every now and then we'd go over to Brooklyn and sit in with those guys over there. There were a lot of musicians in Brooklyn. Max was in Brooklyn, too, but he wasn't really on this scene, what I'm talking about is the jam session scene. On my experience of meeting Max, he was always on a more elevated level, so he wasn't around all the clubs and places where Randy Weston and Ernie Henry and Cecil Payne and those guys would play. When it came to those *Brilliant Corners* sessions, I was fortunate because Monk liked me. He'd heard me, and saw something in me that he liked a lot. And I am honoured by it. It's great to know that he felt that way.'

As in any conversation, we veered all over the place as one idea followed another, including talking of Sonny's fondness for trying to find songs to connect with local audiences, hence his judicious choice of repertoire on his London concerts, including Noël Coward songs and even quotes from the opening music to the television show *East Enders*, and the BBC radio soap opera *The Archers*, which he had heard on many hotel stays in London. (We spontaneously started singing the theme tune to each other – one of the unexpected highlights of my journalistic life!)

Then we moved onto far more serious territory, his interest in connecting with the things that really matter in people's lives. Although we met in 2007, the 9/11 tragedy of six years before was still relatively fresh in our minds. At the time of the attack, Sonny had been in his New York apartment, only a few blocks from the World Trade Center, when the planes struck, and he became trapped in the building, without power or light, for twenty-four hours. Days later, at a concert in Boston, he poured into music all the emotions that he and his fellow New Yorkers had experienced, no longer divided by race, but united against a different threat. 'Being there at the time, and experiencing it, gave me an opportunity to revisit the consciousness-raising that had started with the *Freedom Suite*,' he said. 'I had to think about what I'd been through, and those who lived and died around me, and try to express it. W. E. B. DuBois remarked that it was the duty of the musician or artist to express social commentary in their work, and that you can use it to change and achieve better conditions. I agree with him, but I don't think that everybody should do it. Personally, I feel it strongly, but I'm reticent to suggest how other people should use their music.'

Sonny's mention of the *Freedom Suite* drew us back to consideration of that extended recording from February and March 1958 for Riverside of a 19½-minute theme and variations that addressed social and political issues, which are as relevant today as they were over sixty years ago. In his note on the cover Sonny says: 'America is deeply rooted in Negro culture: its colloquialisms, its humour, its music. How ironic that the Negro, who more than any other people can claim America's culture as his own, is being persecuted and repressed, that the Negro, who has exemplified the humanities in his very existence is being rewarded with inhumanity.'[10]

Before getting to the nub of his motivation for writing and recording the piece, we took a diversion to discuss bassist Oscar Pettiford, who joined Sonny and Max Roach in the trio on the disc. 'I knew him, of course,' recalled Sonny. 'He's on one of my all-time favourite records, "The Man I Love", with Coleman Hawkins. He took that great bass solo, where you can hear him breathing, so Oscar was somebody that I looked up to. He was one of the guys in the firmament of the music, Oscar Pettiford. Eventually I got to know him and he was very welcoming to young guys, like myself. He appreciated my work and I was really touched by that. He was very accepting of me when I first came on the scene.'[11]

'The record we made was "music with a message" and I think it was the first "music with a message" from our generation, in other words, from the modern jazz generation. The *Freedom Suite* was the very first one. Later on came all the other stuff as we moved into the sixties, with protest movements and all that.' I knew that he had encountered racial problems trying to rent an apartment, so presumably the motivation behind the piece had been personal?

'It was personal but it was indicative of a situation. It wasn't just my own little travails. There was a political situation which had to be addressed.'

When Sonny recorded *Freedom Suite* he was not yet 28, but as well as its political and social content, the piece shows remarkable musical maturity, with changes of time signature and tempo, and a melodic motif that is developed in several, very varied ways. 'I think it stands up as a piece of music, sure,' Sonny agreed. 'And it was written, but of course with Max and Oscar it became improvisational. We had a lot of space to extemporize on the music.'

Not wishing to abandon discussing his music in the 1950s, I'll come back later to some more of Sonny's work, not least because just a few weeks after our conversation in New York he reminded all his UK followers of his twenty-first-century brilliance, when he played one of the most dazzling concerts of the several I have heard him do at London's Barbican Hall. I wrote at the time that 'Rollins prompted and goaded his musicians with brisk phrases that darted across his instrument's full range, weaving in fragments of quotations from songs, including (as he is wont to do in London) portions of old British music-hall ditties. The first set closed with a riotous calypso, Rollins' own "Nice Lady", in which he produced umpteen choruses of stirring, positive improvisation. The torrents of invention, the repetitive jabbing phrases that crossed the underlying rhythm of the drums, and the bleak but imperious tone were all vintage Rollins.'[12]

But once our 2007 conversation had started to look at the way in which *Freedom Suite* addressed social and racial issues, it reminded me of a discussion I had with Abbey Lincoln about the way she and her then husband Max Roach had gone on soon afterwards to tackle similar issues, notably in the *We Insist! Freedom Now* album recorded in 1960, but then surfacing in many of the lyrics she has written since.

'It's the most important thing in the world to me,' she said. 'I'd like to know who I am, what I am, and where I am. I think I'm maybe like a maverick cow, because I always go the other way from the herd, and I've been like this since I was a child. Maybe life is like the *Titanic*? I don't want to go down with the ship just because everybody else is sinking. What's wrong with thought? A recent song of mine like "Learning How To Listen"[13] is like that, because I think I'm still learning and I want to learn. I started out singing songs about unrequited love, but I think that is really boring. There's a lot more to life than the relationship between a man and a woman. If you are privileged to be on the stage, and you have an audience where people come to witness you live, you have to have something to say to them!'[14]

I suggested to her that many of her songs on social themes are angry, a good example being the 1980 'Caged Bird' song that first appeared on her *Painted Lady* album with Archie Shepp, pianist Hilton Ruiz and trumpeter Roy Burrowes. She wanted her birds to 'fly away ... and sing' as they were created to do, rather than live in cages, tucking their heads under their wings to avoid seeing the men outside with guns. Abbey responded, 'I think that we as people, the whole species, we live in cages. We're not really free. Nobody is.' In 1998 on her *Wholly Earth* album she reprised 'Caged Bird', this time with singer Maggie Brown, the daughter of Oscar Brown Jr who had such a key role in writing lyrics for the *We Insist!* record back in 1960.

That *We Insist! Freedom Now* album was pivotal for her. She told Nat Hentoff at the time: 'I found out how wonderful it was to be a Black woman. And I learned from Max that I should always sound how I feel and that whatever I do, I should do it definitely. I got to know a number of other jazz musicians, and from hearing them talk, I gained insight into the kind of individuality that was mine and needed bringing out. And I decided that I would not again sing anything that wasn't meaningful to me.'¹⁵ As we know from Booker Little who wrote 'In The Red' on the album, he witnessed this change in Abbey. 'She isn't afraid any more ... she's not afraid of dissonances and of freeing herself musically.'¹⁶

But if Oscar Brown Jr had a key role in developing Abbey Lincoln's art, the other person who inspired her was Thelonious Monk. 'He told me I was a composer,' she recalled. 'Because I was writing all over everybody else's songs, following in the footsteps of Jon Hendricks and Oscar Brown Jr and I didn't ask the original writers or anything. I wrote lyrics to Thelonious' "Blue Monk" and it was a hit! I didn't do it for that reason, but I heard what he was saying and responded. I wrote to John Coltrane's "Africa", and he and Thelonious let me do that to their songs. But Thelonious said (on the release of my record *Straight Ahead*) "Abbey Lincoln is not only a great actress and singer, she's a great composer." Actually then I'd never written any musical composition in my life, but I believed him. I started to believe I could write and the first song was "People in Me". And I've been writing ever since, and I think I have about 75 songs for which I have written words and music.'¹⁷

Just as Coleman Hawkins was a significant figure for Sonny Rollins and Tommy Flanagan, his name came up again at this point with Abbey Lincoln, as he appears with her both on *We Insist!*, recorded in 1960, and on *Straight Ahead*, made in February the following year. 'I had a chance to record with Coleman Hawkins, and if it hadn't been for Max Roach I never would have,' she said wistfully. 'I hooked up with Hawkins and I remember when we were doing the *Freedom Now* suite and we were doing "Driva Man". Oscar Brown and Roach wrote the piece, and it was in 5/4 time. I had listened to Roach create the song on the piano and everything, so I knew it. I had no problem with the 5/4 and while we were doing it, Coleman Hawkins turned to me and said, "You *hear* that, huh?"

'I said, "Yeah!"

'Roach would play it by accenting the one – "Bam! Two-three-four-five. Bam! Two-three-four-five." He did that for Coleman Hawkins. So even these giants were human! But I met the great ones. Duke Ellington, who lived just two blocks up the street. I met him when I was about 24 or 25. Louis Armstrong, Billie Holiday, Sarah Vaughan – I knew them all. They set a great standard for the music, for our work. A very high standard. So I have always tried to live up to it. I started singing to save myself from all those people in the house when I was small. I'm one of twelve children, and I was the tenth child. So when I was five, I would sit at the piano and I would become free. Nobody would bother me, and I had serenity and peace. I would be just by myself, and my mother and father let me do this. If my mother had said, "Anna Marie,[18] get off that piano, you're getting on my nerves!" I never would have come near it again. But I didn't have to go through that.'

As we sat in her apartment, surrounded by Abbey's paintings, fabrics she had designed and some of her recordings, we seemed a world away from the passion and power she put into *Freedom Now* thirty-eight years before. But it was there, and she felt just as strongly about the issues as she had done in the 1960s, and that they still drove her work, not just as a singer, but her creativity as a writer and composer. 'I didn't know music was a career. It was before television and we didn't have a radio. We did have a Victrola, and when I was very small I tried to look inside and see who was playing, because I didn't understand what it was! When I did discover it could be a career, what was more important to me than anything in the world was the vindication of my ancestors. We fell from grace a long time ago – they lie on us, they steal and take our contributions, we're still seen as third-class people, but it's a lie. My ancestors brought the first world into being, and I know it. That's what I live for.'

Coming back to Sonny Rollins, and his motivation behind the *Freedom Suite*, I was intrigued that he had chosen the tenor, bass and drums trio format. Yet ironically, in one of his earliest recordings in this setting, as part of a piano-less quartet, he was accompanying Abbey Lincoln, in October 1957 on her Riverside album *That's Him*, backed by the other members of Max Roach's quintet. Paul Chambers played bass on most of the session, but for one track, 'Don't Explain', Wynton Kelly slipped across from the piano stool and played bass. Sonny's solo on the track is brief, but he is backed just by bass and drums, before Kenny Dorham and Abbey re-enter.

In our conversation, Sonny and I looked at his other ventures in this trio configuration that led up to the *Freedom Suite*, notably the first of them all, *Way Out West* from March 1957 with Ray Brown and Shelly Manne. As its name suggests, it was cut in Los Angeles, for Lester Koenig's Contemporary label, but Sonny was quick to point out that although many people now think of Shelly Manne as a West Coast drummer, he had already forged a great reputation in New York. 'Before he went out there, he made some records with Coleman Hawkins, who was my idol. So Shelly had established his pedigree. He was a great drummer. The two of them, him and Ray, clicked very well together on that. They really were excellent.'

Given their collective workload, it was fortuitous that the three of them were in the same place at the same time. Sonny was in L.A. with Max Roach's quintet, Ray was there with Oscar Peterson's trio and Shelly was fronting his own band, not to mention both Ray and Shelly fitting in some daytime studio work as well. Consequently, as Koenig reminds us in his liner note, the album was made after their normal evening gigs during a night-time session starting at 3 am, and before Ray had a further studio call the next afternoon. The cover photo of Sonny as a gunslinger, by William Claxton, and the choice of repertoire such as 'I'm an Old Cowhand' and 'Wagon Wheels' – the first starting with Manne's clip-clopping woodblock and rims, and the second similarly giving the impression of rather more horses in harness – show them coming close to Sonny's stated intention of achieving 'that loping along in the saddle feeling'. To me, there's nonetheless something tongue-in-cheek about parts of the record, despite the hard-swinging title track that prefigures the intensity of Sonny's later trio work, and a beautifully balanced and emotionally acute reading of 'There Is No Greater Love' spread across two takes that complement each other. Sonny disagreed with my tongue-in-cheek observation, seeing a deeper purpose in the two tracks that use hoof-beats. 'I don't discount any music in my lexicon,' he said. 'Anything is worthy of proper treatment, if you think of it that way.'

The Brown–Manne trio was a dry run for what would be Sonny's principal recording and concert format for a couple of years after the latter part of 1957. On 3 November that year he played both an afternoon and evening session at the Village Vanguard for Blue Note. The label's preferred engineer, Rudy Van Gelder, had previously pioneered location recording in other jazz clubs in Manhattan, as discussed in Chapter 9, but this was his first time at the wedge-shaped 7th Avenue club, and it was also the Village Vanguard's first ever live recording, starting a long series of fine sound documents of eminent musicians playing at this celebrated room.

'I don't know whose idea it was to do the record,' Sonny reflected. 'But it *was* the first jazz record recorded in that nightclub.

First, in the afternoon, I had Donald Bailey and Pete La Roca, who were very fine musicians, but the recording that seems to have endured more is the evening session with Elvin Jones and Wilbur Ware. Of course I liked playing with Elvin, and I'd played with Wilbur in Chicago. He was a very underrated player. He was just one of these natural musicians that just touched the bass and had a big sound. This just came naturally to him, so I gravitated more towards Elvin and Wilbur.'

Nevertheless, the afternoon session notched up another first as well, because it was the debut recording by 19-year-old Pete La Roca. Despite Sonny's preference for the sides with Jones and Ware, which were the majority of the originally issued tracks on Blue Note's *A Night at the Village Vanguard* LP apart from a vigorous version of 'A Night in Tunisia', La Roca later rejoined Sonny to tour Europe in his trio in 1959, along with bassist Henry Grimes. Pete had grown up in a musical family in New York, and his initial interests were classical percussion, playing timpani in the orchestra of Manhattan's High School for Music and Art, and later at Manhattan School of Music, but also playing timbales in various Latin bands (which is why he had adopted the surname La Roca, instead of his birth name of Sims). 'I loved working with the trio,' he told me. 'It was a great band and I'm glad it got recorded. Jazz was a tradition in our family, and I had an uncle who lived in a brownstone in Harlem, and who was very active in jazz. He used to rehearse in the meeting rooms above the Lafayette Theatre, and as a boy I'd watch rehearsals there. He had a great record collection, and I wore out some of his 78s. He picked up on my interest and I remember he took me to hear the legendary Baby Dodds – he was playing on a Saturday afternoon radiocast from the Carnegie Recital Hall. My uncle got himself and me in, and I remember afterwards I took an interest in the record Dodds had made just of himself talking and playing.'[19]

'I started playing jazz myself in the Brooklyn neighbourhood, and I remember in one of the places we played, Max Roach used to have his drums set up there – they had Diplomat heads as I recall, and he'd get through quite a few of them. Early on Max played there quite a bit. I think he knew that Sonny was looking for a drummer for that after-noon session at the Vanguard, and he put in a word for me. I hadn't ever worked with Sonny before the gig, but after that he called me for a couple of concerts, and some nights at the Half Note, and then a year or so later for the European tour. That was pretty much it for me and Sonny, but as I say, I really enjoyed working with the trio.'[20]

Not long after the Vanguard session, La Roca recorded again for Blue Note with Sonny Clarke in December 1957, and went on to make several other discs for the label, including the excellent quartet under his own name, *Basra*, with Joe Henderson, from 1965. By the beginning of the 1970s much of his musical work had dried up and Pete drove a cab for some years while qualifying as a lawyer, eventually, at the urging of pianist Hal Galper, making a part-time return to music in 1979, but continuing to work in the law. When I met him in the late 1990s, he was playing with some of the finest players in New York, including George Cables, JoAnne Brackeen and Dave Liebman, but he positively quivered with excitement as he recalled those early trio sessions with Rollins. The surviving documentary recordings of the 1959 European tour – perhaps more than the Vanguard album – show why Pete found this recollection so exhilarating.[21] A blistering 'St Thomas' from Stockholm, for example, combines calypso rhythm with straight-ahead swing in which Rollins unfurls idea after idea as La Roca goads and prompts him, over Grimes' hard-swinging bass lines (an aspect of Henry's playing that was less evident after his return from a 30-year hiatus from music in 2003).

In 2009 I had the opportunity to talk to Henry about his work (in front of an audience at the Cheltenham Jazz Festival in the UK), and I was surprised to discover the setting in which Sonny had first heard him: 'He auditioned me playing with Al Cohn and Zoot Sims, and with Lennie Tristano, so I felt I *had* to play with him in Europe! We started in Paris and that's how I ended up working with him a lot.'[22] I wondered if the openness of the trio setting had helped Sonny's ideas to flow, but he said, 'I think every musician in the trio was a supplier of ideas in that sense. I remember Kenny Clarke also was with us on some dates, in addition to Pete La Roca, and he was a great supplier of ideas.'[23]

Henry's lengthy absence from music is well known, but when it comes to a hiatus from playing, few are more famous than Rollins' own, when he returned from that 1959 trip to Europe and stayed away from professional music-making until January 1962, when he began recording with a new quartet featuring guitarist Jim Hall, his future long-term associate Bob Cranshaw on bass and Ben Riley on drums. Their first album, *The Bridge*, cut between the end of January and mid-February that year, commemorates the two-year period, or thereabouts, that

Sonny spent out of the public eye – at least in one sense – practising on the Williamsburg Bridge that links Manhattan to Brooklyn.

'I thought there were a lot of extraordinary things about that group,' Sonny reflected, when I asked about the album. 'When I came out, the guys were saying they didn't know what to expect from me, since I'd been away. It seems to have endured and it made quite a mark. Because a lot of the places I've been to, right up to the present [in 2007] people that know my work think that it was an important record and an important group.'

I have always had a fondness for *The Bridge* and its slightly later sequel, *What's New?* (which, as well including plenty of varied Latin rhythms, in recent reissues has a fine version of Sonny's calypso 'Don't Stop the Carnival'). But Sonny was keen to move on in discussing his career, because just over a year later, in July 1963, he got the opportunity to record alongside his idol, Coleman Hawkins, with whom he had recently shared a set at the Newport Jazz Festival. The album *Sonny Meets Hawk!* was produced by George Avakian for RCA, and it deliberately brought old and new school players together, with Paul Bley joining Roy McCurdy in the rhythm section, and bass duties shared between Bob Cranshaw and Henry Grimes. I wondered how Sonny felt about recording with a musician he had admired for so long. 'It was a tremendous thrill to make a record with the man himself, Coleman Hawkins. He was the father of the tenor saxophone, so to speak. And it presented me with a challenge. I never considered myself as being able to compete with Hawkins. It was out of the question. So what I decided to do was try to play completely opposite from the way Coleman sounded, so that it'd be a contrast. I'd heard Coleman Hawkins playing with Ben Webster and Georgie Auld, where they didn't change anything about their playing. But of course, I'm always changing my playing, anyway. So that's what I was after – contrast – instead of trying to sound like a new Coleman Hawkins.'

When the record came out, not everyone who heard it was sympathetic to Sonny's aims. One critic, for example, reviewing 'one of the greatest jazz confrontations in years' wrote: 'Whether it's "Yesterdays", "Summertime", or "Just Friends", the tune is better served by Hawk's taste and undiminished skill.'[24] This echoed some of the reviews of the tenorists' live performance in Newport, where, according to the syndicated critic Russ Wilson, 'The two great artists failed to jell.'[25] Today, with the benefit of hindsight, it's clear that the album was something of a landmark, and in my view one of Sonny's most stimulating 1960s recordings. The current critical consensus is accurately summed up in a *Jazz Times* article that countered the negative views expressed by writers at the time by saying, 'Surely that group wasn't paying attention to Sonny's other records, where he turned his own ideas upside-down even more violently. Nor did they notice that Hawkins responded to the challenge with some of his best, and most far-reaching, late work. Paul Bley moves from one frame of reference to the other with impressive effortlessness, and asserts his own mysterious concept where appropriate.'[26]

Henry Grimes was equally impressed by Paul Bley, with whom he had previously played in some New York loft sessions. 'He seemed to be able to pick up certain notes on the piano and bend them,' he said. 'He's a very fantastic guy, with his own acoustics. At the same time I was just over-awed playing with Coleman Hawkins. There wasn't anything I could do but just grab the axe and start playing! And then Sonny, he really played some "bending sounds" on that record, it really was fantastic.' Maybe the best example of this is on 'Just Friends' where Sonny takes his opening solo (picking up the theme from Hawkins) in his familiar trio setting with just bass and drums 'strolling' behind his increasingly jagged and fragmented melodic lines, before Bley enters and goads him into even more inventive harmonic territory.

A couple of years after the RCA album with Hawkins, Sonny signed with the Impulse! label, and before long he had his first venture into creating a film score. Earlier in the decade there had been a couple of attempts in British cinema to make movies in which the sound of jazz was woven into a story of contemporary urban life. I mentioned Michael Winner's 1963 London-based film *West 11* in Chapter 1, and the previous year Basil Dearden had featured the actor Patrick McGoohan as a jazz drummer in *All Night Long*, which teamed an all-star cast of UK musicians alongside Charles Mingus and Dave Brubeck on the soundtrack.

When director and producer Lewis Gilbert decided to follow a similar route, in a film to star Michael Caine, he sent his son John (who worked with him as an associate producer, and was music director for several other pictures of the period) to Ronnie Scott's club to hear what might be on offer for a potential musical backdrop. In January 1965 Sonny Rollins was playing a long residency there, with the local rhythm section of pianist Stan Tracey, bassist Rick Laird and drummer Ronnie

Stephenson. Tracey had developed a particularly strong musical rapport with Sonny, following all the shifts of key and time signature as his long solos unfolded. John Gilbert was really impressed with what he heard, and decided that Sonny Rollins with this very band would be perfect for the soundtrack. Caine had recently risen to fame playing a heroic soldier in *Zulu*, in 1964, and had just wrapped up his first appearance as the spy Harry Palmer in *The Ipcress File*. Now he was cast as the hedonist womanizer in the title role of *Alfie*. Gilbert wanted a score that could reflect both the happy-go-lucky attitude of writer Bill Naughton's main character and the hollow disappointment that rises up towards the end of the picture when Alfie realizes his carefree ways have not led to happiness, and he muses 'What's it all about?'

When our conversation turned to that film, I asked Sonny how he managed to get so completely into the musical language of a movie soundtrack. 'I grew up looking at films,' he recalled, but he thinks it was also perceptive on the part of John Gilbert, who spoke to him after a night at Scott's, to see his potential. 'We were having a really nice season at Ronnie Scott's that year, and a lot of people were talking about it. The buzz was going round London and throughout the jazz community, so I guess that's how the Gilberts heard about me. He said, "Well, Sonny, your music sounds just like this character Alfie that we have. Would you like to score the movie?" And I said, "Great!" After I saw the film I realized what a terrible guy Alfie was, so I wasn't sure if it was actually a compliment or not! The movie was made in London, with just Stan, Ronnie, and a few other people including Phil Seamen on drums, who were all London musicians, and myself on the soundtrack. It was the first time I did a movie score, but because I had been looking at movies since I was a child, it was something I could do easily.'

According to Stan Tracey, Sonny sketched out the main theme for the movie on 'half a sheet of manuscript paper'. The other cues (as each section of music in a film is called) were worked out, improvised and then written down at the club by Sonny, Stan and the others, before being recorded in mid-1965. 'Little Malcolm' was mainly Tracey's work, and the rest were Sonny's ideas that were developed by all the members of the band, so the end result was a genuine collective effort.

When I talked to Tracey about the film he laughed: 'They used to say they locked Sonny in at Ronnie's after hours to finish the music for the film. He was staying at the Dorchester, and when I think of Ronnie's cellar at the Old Place and the Dorchester ... well you wouldn't want to be locked in that cellar!'[27] The music they recorded can be heard on the DVD of the movie,[28] but was never released on CD, possibly because the full recordings of the cues did not survive after the film was edited.

When producer Bob Thiele at Impulse! wanted to record a soundtrack album of the film, instead of using the British musicians who had created the score with Sonny, he decided to involve the arranger Oliver Nelson, whom he had also signed to the label, for a more ambitious project. His job was to transcribe the cues from the movie and to arrange the music for a band of New York session players. The film was to be released in March 1966, so Nelson and Rollins worked hard to get the music recorded during January, at exactly the same time as Burt Bacharach and Hal David were working flat out to get Cilla Black to record the song for the closing titles, so that everything could be released together.

In the opening sequence of the movie, just bass and tenor saxophone start the soundtrack as the camera pans across the London skyline at night. Rollins plays the jaunty theme intended to depict the roguish hero, but before we see Michael Caine, we see a little dog scuttling across Waterloo Bridge. The south bank of the Thames looks vaguely familiar until we realise that there's no London Eye or any of the bright lights of the new Hungerford pedestrian bridge that arrived with the millennium. This is 1965 London, and the dog is a metaphor for Alfie, taking the back streets behind the Strand until it ends up in an alley full of dustbins. It disturbs a pair of other dubious-looking dogs and then runs into another side road where Alfie's Vauxhall is parked, its windows steamed up as Alfie makes love to 'a married woman', whom he refers to as 'it' in his first of several monologues to the camera.

Oliver Nelson's score compresses that long action into a shorter, crisper preamble, appropriate for a record with no visual cues to keep our attention, and not only does he begin with a drum flourish, he quickly pulls in the accompanying ensemble behind Rollins, somewhat faster than on the screen version. This is a piece of jazz designed solely for listening, not an atmospheric background to a lingering, grainy, night-time scene of London. As well as Sonny, the soloist who contributed most to the Impulse! album is guitarist Kenny Burrell, but there are also fine contributions from pianist Roger Kellaway, and from Walter Booker and Frank Dunlop on bass and drums. Nelson's scoring for three additional saxophones and two trombones creates a memorable atmosphere that is both wistful and occasionally sombre. 'I think I played pretty well with that group,' reflected Sonny, 'and I was impressed with Oliver Nelson. I thought he did a fantastic job with it, and we got a Grammy nomination for that album.'

The final return to the theme on the album brings us full circle, just as the movie itself ends back on Waterloo Bridge with Alfie confronting the same dog that scampered through the opening title sequence. In the film this gives way to the Bacharach/David song 'What's It All About, Alfie?' sung by Cilla Black (or on the American release by Cher). But Oliver Nelson's album version of the score suggests what might have happened if Sonny himself had played over the closing credits, his urgent fragmented solo taking apart the jaunty character of Alfie and ushering in an equally episodic solo by Roger Kellaway, before the full theme returns. This is an older, wiser, sadder musical portrait of the hero.

One collaboration that pushed Sonny's inventiveness into a slightly different direction was his 1970s work with the jazz bagpiper Rufus Harley, immortalized on their 1974 Montreux album *The Cutting Edge*. What I hadn't known until we talked was that as a tenor saxophonist back in his home town of Philadelphia, Rufus was known as 'Little Sonny'. But the interest went both ways. 'I started playing the bagpipes, after I got a set of them when I was in London,' Sonny told me. 'It was one of my first times there, around the time I worked on the movie *Alfie*, and I was playing at Ronnie's original club on Gerrard Street, the Old Place, in the basement. So I was interested in the bagpipes because I'd become enamoured of this guy Bismillah Khan, who played the shehnai, the Indian oboe. And he used to do this circular breathing, so there weren't any breaks in the things he'd play. In the bagpipes I heard that same type of continuous droning sound, similar to the four people or so who played drones on Indian oboes in Khan's group. Because I saw this connection in the bagpipes, I got a set. In any case, playing with Rufus was great because I was really trying to get into that wavelength – the drone – at the time.'

By this time, after a couple of years on Impulse!, Sonny had teamed up once again with his former Riverside producer, Orrin Keepnews, at Milestone, a relationship that began with his *Next Album* and lasted some 25 years, until he launched his own Doxy label in 2006 with the album *Sonny Please*. Our talk meandered through the Milestone years and covered some of his solo appearances, but at the time we met, Sonny was – as he usually was throughout his playing career – looking forward, and eager to talk about his current band that featured both a drummer and percussionist, but had dispensed with a keyboard player. 'I'm keeping guitar now,' he said. 'So that's what we're doing, just the bass and the guitar, plus of course Clifton Anderson on trombone and myself in the front line. He's fantastic. I don't know if I could do what he does, to be able to play under the other player, like myself, who's the main player on the front line and still make it interesting, knowing when to play accompaniment, when to come in, when to stay out of the way – it's a formidable talent, and I don't know how he does it!'

This conversation with Sonny was one of the most fulfilling and rewarding I've had in many years of journalism and broadcasting. He claimed not to listen to his old records, but his recall of the sessions, of the details of his music and his clear love and affection for those who had worked with him along the way was little short of miraculous, and after we met it was wonderful to hear him performing again, several times, in concert, before he finally retired from the stage in 2012.

14 OSCAR PETERSON AND HIS TRIOS

Many elements of bebop piano owe their coming together to the work of Bud Powell and Thelonious Monk. But just as the 1950s saw those saxophonists who had grown up on Charlie Parker's music developing new and different ways of playing, the decade also saw a new generation of pianists appear. Unquestionably the most virtuosic of those, whom I have been lucky enough to hear in person, was Oscar Peterson, a man equally at home accompanying swing titans such as Lester Young or Coleman Hawkins as he was playing for Dizzy Gillespie. The first time I heard him perform live was an unaccompanied solo concert in 1972 at Oxford's New Theatre, while I was an undergraduate. By then he had been working with his trio for the best part of two decades, but in 1970 Norman Granz, who was by then his manager, persuaded him to make a solo album, and the result was *Tracks*, recorded by Hans Georg Brunner-Schwer at MPS. In 1972, at Granz's suggestion, Oscar took the unexpected step of following this up by going on the road to play a series of solo recitals, of which the Oxford event was one. His Amsterdam concert, from just a few days later on 4 November, makes up a substantial portion of the Pablo album *Solo*,[1] and gives a good impression of what one of these marvellous evenings was like.

'I was adamantly against going solo,' he told me later, 'and I wanted to go on touring and recording with the trio. For some reason or another, Duke Ellington got caught up in the conversation, and I'll never forget his advice. As ever, he didn't cut straight to the chase, but he found a higher level of conversation. He said, "Oscar, I think you should do as Norman suggests. Don't you think occasionally people like caviar on its own, without the eggs and the onions?" Duke always found the elegant way to say things, even if it was the long way round to get to the point. And he had such charm!'[2]

This comes from just one of a series of conversations I had with Oscar over the years. In the early 1990s, I was writing liner notes for various artists on the Telarc label, to whom he was signed. After he returned to playing, following his stroke in 1993, I found myself doing this for some of his albums.[3] The process involved frequent exchanges of faxes, and as the decade – and technology – moved on, emails. In due course, round about 2000, he and his co-author, Richard Palmer, approached me to see if I would be interested in publishing Oscar's autobiography, because by then I was the editor responsible for commissioning music books for Continuum in London and New York. The manuscript duly arrived. But as I read it, I became less and less happy, realizing that it would need a huge amount of work to make it publishable.

By the turn of the century, Oscar had become a very public figure, and part of his appeal was that over the years he'd developed into a completely natural performer on television: his wit, charm and affability every bit as significant for that general audience as his playing. But the book seemed to have been written by someone completely different – someone, indeed, who never used a simple word if a complex polysyllabic one was available instead. Reading how his father 'had regularly chastised me by beating me about the posterior' might have been funny as an isolated remark, but it was the prevailing tone of the entire text. So I returned the manuscript with a long letter saying that the book really needed to be rewritten from start to finish, giving some examples of how this might be done, and saying that the warm, communicative person we all knew from our screens needed to be the voice telling the story, not someone who had swallowed a dictionary.

The letter was met with total silence. No acknowledgement, no return letter, no fax, no email.

Then about four months later a brown paper parcel arrived on my doorstep. In it was a completely rewritten version of the book. Yes, there were still some long words, but the prevailing feeling on every page was the sound of Oscar's familiar voice talking to the reader. During the final copy-editing and typesetting of the book, in November 2001, Norman Granz died, and we included a memorial note as a preface to the published edition.[4] I contacted Oscar with my condolences, and in a follow-up phone call, asked why, before sending the revised manuscript, he'd been silent for such a long period. He chuckled, and told me he'd sent a copy of my letter to Granz, who by that stage was already quite seriously ill with cancer, but almost immediately Norman had messaged him: 'If he's got the balls to say that to you, he is the right publisher for your book!' So Oscar had buckled down and with Richard Palmer's help had done the revisions.

The chuckle is something I remember from almost all our conversations. Even during the years when his playing career had been fundamentally changed by his stroke, Oscar found the positive in life. He had always been a camera buff (something he had in common with Milt Hinton and drummer Alvin Queen, who played on his last London concerts) but after the stroke, he became a fanatical convert to digital photography. Remembering the piles of camera equipment I'd once seen in one of his hotel rooms, I asked him if he'd taken the challenge seriously to move away from film. 'Just ask my bank manager,' was the reply. 'I love the immediacy of it. It's so quick and personal. I've never particularly liked having to take rolls of film into the drugstore and then having to wait while they were developed. Even though that process is very quick now, compared to the old days when I was on tour, hoping to be able to stay in the same place long enough to get the prints back before we moved on, I rejoice in not having to go through that! I started because, in a life of travelling, I wanted to remember the places I'd been. And before I knew it, I had a collection. It was a great hobby for me when we'd be on the road for months at a time, in the days before my family could travel with me. It made up for missing home and friends, and of course there was always something to show them of my travels.'

Oscar's travels beyond his native Canada began seriously in 1949, after Norman Granz heard him on the radio in a cab on his way to the airport in Montreal, and persuaded the driver to turn round and take him to the club where the pianist was playing live on air. Not long afterwards, Granz brought Oscar to the United States and called him up from the audience to play on a Jazz at the Philharmonic (JATP) concert at Carnegie Hall in New York. In duo with Ray Brown he played 'Fine and Dandy' and 'I Only Have Eyes for You' and thus began his international career. Yet even before that, from 1945 onwards, his broadcasts and local recordings with his first trio, whom Granz had heard playing at the Alberta Lounge, meant that he was well known among those American jazz musicians who had played in Canada. 'During that period, Montreal was known as the "little Paris" of America,' Oscar recalled. 'A lot of musicians used to come not only to perform, but just to hang out there. And I'd have a chance to play with them. My trio at that time was made up of bass and drums, and everybody from Roy Eldridge to Coleman Hawkins, when they came through town, inevitably would wind up coming to hear us, and at some point or another we would get the chance to play with them.'[5]

One of the first guest musicians to do this was Dizzy Gillespie. 'He came to visit my house, because my mother kept saying, "If you love him so much, why don't you invite him to dinner?" So I said, "Okay, I'll invite him." He came down for dinner in the afternoon as he had to play that night, and he'd told me we had to do this early. He had dinner, and waiting on dessert he excused himself, and went upstairs to the gents' room. And we sat there and we sat there. Twenty minutes went by, then half an hour, and when it got to around forty-five minutes, my mother said, "Where's your guest?" I said I'd go find out, and went upstairs. And there was Dizzy Gillespie, stretched out on my mother's bed, reading the comics! I said, "Birks?" He said, "Oh! Dessert!" and he got up and came back down. And that was his crazy attitude. We went to a club one night. The Club Algiers in Montreal. They had a fountain in the middle of the entrance-way. He walked right through it. He had his suit and everything on, but he just kept going. That was the joy of Dizzy Gillespie!

'When we later worked together on Jazz at the Philharmonic, you never knew what was coming with him. He'd call the wildest tunes sometimes. There's a picture that I've seen in print every once in a while, of me at the piano and he's bending over my shoulder and playing some kind of chord configuration on the keyboard that he was showing me. Actually, he was teaching me the chords to his tune "Con Alma", but Dizzy always had a different set of chords that he wanted you to use, and you had to keep this in mind when you were playing for all these other people – a little light would go on in your head, saying "Don't forget Dizzy's chords!" Actually that was one of the joys of Jazz at the Phil, which was that it was totally spontaneous. I miss him very much. I'll never forget that Montreux concert where he and Roy Eldridge and Clark Terry were on stage. It's an incredible album, I forget that I'm on it, I just listen to what they did, and it's imprinted on my memory.'

It took a year following Oscar's informal JATP debut at Carnegie Hall before he accepted Granz's invitation to join the troupe on a regular basis. In the interim, back in Montreal he continued playing with his trio, but in late 1950 he began touring with the package show. Also booked by Granz, he started working independently in a very minimal setting, just as he had at Carnegie Hall. He recalled, 'My first group was a duo of just Ray Brown and myself. Norman said, "That's a great grouping. That way they'll really get to hear you."'

According to Ray, it wasn't quite so instant. He said, 'It was sort of like a marriage. You meet a lot of girls and then you meet one all of a sudden where something happens and you've been zapped, and you know this is the one. I think this is what happened with us. I played with him in Carnegie Hall, and then I didn't play with him. We made a record, and then, again, I didn't play with him. The record got really famous and he was using other bass players, I think Major Holley was with him most of the time. But the next time we played for Jazz at the Philharmonic, he said "You know, I've been listening to those records, and you and I do something different. We oughta be playing together." I said, "Yeah, I think maybe you're right." So that's how we really started, as a duo! And I remember that our first gig was a club in Washington DC called Louis and Alex.'[6]

Before long, in addition to lengthy seasonal appearances on the road with JATP, Granz was booking them all over the country in their own right. 'I remember,' said Oscar, 'We were opening at a club in L.A. called the Tiffany, and I came in the first night. I forget whatever it was they were paying us at the time, but I came in the door and a man said, "Hi, I'm Chuck Landis, I'm the owner."'

'"Hi," I said, "I'm Oscar Peterson."'

'He said, "Your dressing room is round to the left." So as I walked over to it, just at the same moment as Ray came in through the door, lugging his bass. And the owner said, "Where's the rest of the group?"'

'And Ray said, "He just passed you!"'

'The owner said, "What? I'm paying all that money for just two guys?"'

'And Ray said, "We make a helluva lot of music for that kind of money!"'

'And the amazing thing about that was on opening night, we played only to about eight people, and I was devastated. But the word spread through the colony of studio musicians out there in Hollywood, and by the end of the week the club was jammed. Which was quite rewarding! Later on we added Barney Kessel, because Norman said, "You can make it a trio now, if you want to do that kind of thing. And it'll take some of the load off you." So we added Barney, and the agreement was that he would stay on the group for one year, and then he'd go back to L.A. He then was followed, eventually, by Herb Ellis.'

With Oscar having been voted 'America's No. 1 Keyboard Artist'[7] in the 1951 round-up of the year by *Time* magazine's Canadian edition, that first trio with Barney Kessel garnered quite a lot of press attention, not least in the column inches devoted to their role in Jazz at the Philharmonic where they would 'weave through a dozen of the more beautiful melodies of our time'.[8] The torrent of press releases sent out by Granz's office not only talked of how he had 'discovered' Oscar, but also that 'Peterson has climbed steadily in popularity and is a major Mercury recording star.'[9]

In all our conversations, Oscar always said that being in the company of so many great musicians in JATP was a tremendous training ground, and that he learned on the one hand from observing Hank Jones' skill as an accompanist, and on the other from adapting to the different requirements of all the other soloists, ranging from specific chords to the sense of time they needed to suit their own way of soloing. On JATP concerts, for part of each show, the trio was usually teamed with one or other of the finest drummers in jazz, such as Gene Krupa, Buddy Rich and Louie Bellson, adding playing as part of a conventional rhythm section to their wide spectrum of experience. Yet what many reviewers singled out about the concerts from this period was not the grandstanding and jousting of the horn players, or what one writer called the 'Frankenstein monster' of the drum battles between Krupa and Rich, but the trio's own set. 'Oscar Peterson and his trio with Brown and Kessel,' ran a typical example, 'soothed and pleased the listeners with a half dozen piano solos. His playing is reminiscent of George Shearing's, except that Peterson's was more elaborate and his left hand more forceful. Peterson was the most interesting musician of JATP.'[10] Maybe the most memorable review from the period, by critic Dorothy Campbell, reads: 'Feather-fingered guitarist Barney Kessel, bassist Ray Brown, who is always in there with the best of them, and Canadian-born Oscar Peterson make some of their numbers sound like a softly-accented conversation on a park bench. But the Oscar Peterson Trio could jazz it up too!'[11]

In the majority of reviews of that first trio there's a focus on Oscar's 'phenomenal' piano playing, but over and over again the underlying message is that compared to the rest of the JATP bill, the trio had something special about it. One reviewer in particular contrasts the almost routine playing of some of the best-known musicians on the programme with 'the parade of ingenious and infinite variations, marked by the spontaneity which is the heart of jazz [that] appeared with the Oscar Peterson trio – Oscar, Kessel, and Brown.'[12]

When Herb Ellis joined in place of Kessel, the first so-called 'classic' Peterson trio was born. Herb's mixture of technical skill, invention and – above all – combative spirit fitted exactly with Oscar's philosophy, which he explained to me like this: 'I like to factor the individual personalities of the musicians into what we do, so they come through musically. I'm always after the sense of a productive musical competition. We all go after each other, to keep the spirit alive, and that's the essence of jazz.' Yet for all that, from the outset of this trio, Oscar liked to create a framework for their musical spontaneity. He aimed to 'digest new arrangements before we go out on the road, and then play them into reality'.[13]

As I discovered from Ray Brown, there was a sound reason for putting in this kind of backroom work with the trio, even if they were learning new repertoire as they travelled, compared to the generally informal atmosphere of JATP. 'From my standpoint,' he said, 'I became jammed out with Jazz at the Philharmonic. I did that for years and years and years with all of the most prominent musicians you can think of. So I preferred playing with the trio, or maybe with one horn and rhythm.'[14] Oscar agreed, confirming that this was equally true for him and for those bassists who followed Ray, such as Sam Jones or Niels-Henning Ørsted Pedersen: 'The secret of the bass player in the group is unselfishness. They play for me as I play for them. When they're doing a solo I don't always play pre-determined chords, I take liberties. And if they're listening, they'll pick up on it. And the same goes for me. I think the best way I can describe it is that we open rooms for one another to create in.'[15]

The trio's work both in concert and in the recording studio with 'one horn and rhythm' was prolific. But because it was a regular working band, and its members had developed their musical antennae to such a high degree, it also provided some of the finest small group accompaniment to singers, most notably Ella Fitzgerald. Although her marriage to Ray Brown broke up in 1953, they continued to work together in the years that followed. Playing for her, just as for Dizzy, Oscar seemed to have not only a brilliant memory, but also a sixth sense about the appropriate voicings and harmony that he used. He dates this to the long tours they did with JATP. 'There was a game we used to play when we were travelling,' he recalled. 'It was either about the verse or the bridge, the middle part, of a song. We'd ask her to sing different tunes, and she'd start and then she'd say, "Who knows the bridge?" She'd look around and you had to sing the bridge. Then it really got deep when she'd sing part of the chorus of a tune before saying, "Somebody give me the verse!" (Which she knew, of course). It didn't mean a lot to me in terms of the singing, but the phrasing of a verse means an awful lot. I didn't work with Ella originally, because Hank Jones was her accompanist, but she and I became great friends. That night when I first went to Carnegie Hall in 1949, the first person I saw was Roy Eldridge, so I sat and talked to him, and he introduced me to Ella. And we became friends after that.'

Hank Jones' influence as Ella's accompanist was not just important to Oscar Peterson, but also to another of her long-term accompanists, Tommy Flanagan. 'Hank was an early influence on me,' he reflected.[16] 'I'd heard him while I was coming up in Detroit, and when I got to New York I wanted to sort out some tutoring from him. When I finally contacted Hank he said, "Why, Tommy? I've got all your records!" That blew me away! But over the years we each spent a long time working with Ella, and we tackled the job in different ways, except for one thing – we both worked to create space for her. She demanded space, and when we got that right it was wonderful to hear. Hank was my model as an accompanist, and not just with singers, in all his work. I think this comes from the fact he was a fine solo pianist and he was always *there* in any group he played with. Hank had a nice manner about him, he was quite hard to approach, almost formal, until he was playing, and then – just like his brothers Thad and Elvin – the really communicative Jones side came out.

'That really worked with Ella, because she was one of the few singers who could phrase and improvise like an instrumentalist. And one thing really struck me, and that was her incredible range. Not just her compass, I mean the range of the songs she sang. She took songs from all over – I think sometimes I encouraged her to go overboard on some of the ones I didn't really want to play. Some were real pop tunes that I was almost embarrassed about like "Raindrops Keep Falling on My Head", but she had a knack of hearing them in such a way that she could draw something out of the song. She might change it slightly, or use it to hook onto something else, maybe a quote from another piece, so that she connected to the tune her way. She was very like a horn player when she did that – and yet on a different song, with lyrics that mattered, she could deliver them so well, and so musically.'

Returning to Oscar, among the most enduring recording sessions the Peterson Trio-plus-one made with Ella were two albums with Louis Armstrong. They were certainly highlights for Ray Brown. 'Louis was practically everybody's idol,' he said. 'He was almost like the guy that invented jazz for most of us, and nobody probably did it better than he did. When I met and played with him, he was an old man, but he was still fantastic.' And for Louie Bellson, drafted in to work on the second *Ella and Louis* album with the trio of Oscar, Ray and Herb, he remembered, 'Norman Granz knew that Ella and Louis had a great relationship music-wise and otherwise, and he knew that Ray Brown, and Oscar and Herb Ellis and myself would be the perfect rhythm section for those two. Norman had that uncanny way of producing things. He knew all the players, he knew what kind of music they played, and he wanted us to come on a record date and have fun, and go away happy. And he paid you a lotta money, and that's not so bad!'[17]

One interesting aspect of these sessions is that – as far as one can tell from photographs – in the studio Louie Bellson used exactly the same kit as he did on JATP or big band concerts, yet he got exactly the right intimate sound to support Ella and Louis. I discussed this once with the drummer Billy Cobham, who tended to build his kit specifically for each context in which he was playing. When we spoke I'd seen him in London playing in a trio using just snare, hi-hat, a couple of tom-toms and a pair of ride cymbals, compared to his jazz-rock gigs, where he had one of the largest kits I'd ever seen. Billy said: 'You're right. Louie Bellson – whether it was Oscar Peterson's trio or Duke Ellington's big band – always used the same set-up. I marvelled at that, thinking, "How does he do that?" with the two bass drums and all. I heard it live and it worked, but I thought it was not as personal as if one actually designed a configuration. Which means that you can change the personality of the drum set. It can alter the way you draw the tones from the drums.'[18]

Somehow Bellson's skill was such that he always seemed to sound right for the context.

Certainly Oscar recalled these sessions with affection, but he was quick to point out that in the 1970s, he, Ray and Louie, together with Joe Pass in place of Herb Ellis, had also made a record with Sarah Vaughan.[19] And just like Roy Haynes, his opinion of her consummate musicianship was very high.

'I didn't think it would happen, because of the association with Ella, that I had the chance to do an album with Sarah. That's one of my favourite albums, because it's so diversified in terms of the material choice. We found out just what a musician she was at the record date. We had a thing going in the trio, I don't know if it was chauvinistic or not, that vocalists, and particularly female vocalists, were hard to work with. So, there was a certain amount of apprehension when it came to Sarah, because I knew she played piano. Anyway, I started holding back, trying to be as neat as possible, playing behind her. But she said, "It's going great, sock it to me, I wanna hear it!" Then there was one tune, and when we were sitting in the control room listening to it on playback, she said, "What did you play in the bridge of that?"

'I said "I don't remember exactly what I played."

'She said, "No, but what chord did you play?"

'I forget now exactly the chord, but it was an e minor ninth or something, which I believed was correct. So when we were back in the studio, she said, "Let's run it!" And we played through that bridge – and it turned out I was right. We didn't have any dispute after that. I don't know what she had been hearing at the time, but at first I figured we were going to get into a scuffle over it. I said to myself, "Oh no! Not in the middle of this date." But actually she was an admirer of my playing, I'm proud to say, and she repeated "I don't want you holding back, I want you to run over me, because I enjoy that!" Sarah was really something.'

To complete the trio of great singers, I knew that quite some time before that Sarah Vaughan session, Oscar had also recorded three sessions with Billie Holiday, between March 1952 and April 1954. Had that been a comparable experience to working with Sarah?

'Yes, she was much the same way. When I came in for the date with Billie, she just said, "Go ahead and play for me. Play as if we were in a concert." So I said okay. But actually we did hold back, to a certain degree, because we didn't want to step on any of her vocal lines. That's something I learned from Hank Jones. You have to be so careful. You have to play *for* a vocalist – playing *with* a vocalist isn't enough. You have to play *for* them. You have to feed them certain things that they want to hear.'

The diversion into Oscar's work with singers had taken our conversation away from the biggest change that took place in his trio, which was when, in 1958, Herb Ellis left to be replaced by Ed Thigpen on drums, which was a major shift away from the piano, guitar and bass line-up that he had led along the lines of the earlier groups fronted by Art Tatum or Nat King Cole. Oscar described Thigpen as the 'neatest' drummer he had ever worked with. 'It was a kick,' he continued. 'There was such an interchange of musical personality, that it was quite a thing to change a member of our group. Our arrangements were so tightly knit that whoever the new man was that came in, they needed time to really get the parts together. So Ed was under a handicap until he felt easy. But once he was there, we kept things fresh by changing the library around. If you go through our old LPs, you'll also find the approach changed over time, even with the same group. What made it interesting is that some of the parts were fairly intricate, but each player gave it a different meaning. The drum option is primarily percussive. It changes my lines and I don't play the same way I play without drums. I love the heat a drummer generates, and that always has an impact on me.'

I met Ed in the oddest of circumstances. I was in Paris to cover the Martial Solal piano competition for the BBC in 1998, and after a formal studio conversation, Martial suggested we went on to the Rue Des Lombards, as a number of the finalists could be heard (a day or two before the competition itself) in various of the street's several jazz clubs. I'd just finished a further interview outdoors with Martial and some of the contestants, when a man emerged from the nearby Sunset club, and Martial immediately introduced him as Ed Thigpen. It turned out that Ed would be in London soon afterwards and, after chatting for a while, he agreed to meet me while he was in Britain.

I was interested to have the chance to talk to him, as his father Ben had been the drummer with Andy Kirk's Clouds of Joy. I'd read much about the older Thigpen while working on Andy's memoirs, but I hadn't realized that his reputation helped his son on his way. This was when Ed first came to New York in September 1951 after saxophonist Candy Johnson's band (in which he'd been playing) broke up, because its leader was recruited by Count Basie. Ed had only been in the city

a few days when a fellow musician suggested he went to the Savoy
Ballroom where Cootie Williams was playing, because he needed
a drummer. 'Next day was a Sunday, so after Mass I went to the
matinee, and introduced myself, saying, "I understand you're looking
for a drummer?"

'He said, "What's your name?"

'I told him, and he said, "Are you Ben Thigpen's son?"

'I said, "Yessir!"

'He said, "If you're half as good as him you can probably have
the job. Come up and play!" So I did and I got the job, and went out on
the road with him. It was a sextet, and we travelled all through the South
and then right across the country with some of the first doo-wop groups,
like the Ravens and the Orioles. Those were pre-rock-and-roll days, and
we wound up alongside Dinah Washington on that tour. But then I got
drafted into the army.'[20] Just over three years later, Ed returned from
service in Korea, knowing that servicemen were supposed to be offered
their old job back. So he tracked down the selfsame package show in
Chicago, but when he got there, he didn't rejoin Cootie, instead finding
himself (along with bassist Keter Betts) as a member of Dinah
Washington's backing group. In the years that followed, Ed worked
with many other singers, but his main association was (like Oscar's)
with Ella Fitzgerald, with whom he played for a total of six years. 'I like
singers,' he mused. 'I'm a fan of great artists. My mentor, Jo Jones, used
to say, and my father said this too, "You please the people that you
work for. They're the ones that hire you." But Jo also dropped a line of
wisdom on me, he said, "When you play with different people in the
front line, and you're the accompanist, if you make 'em feel good, you'll
have the best seat in the house, because they'll entertain you all day
long!" Carrying that forth really worked.'

The time with Ella followed the six years or so that Ed spent in
the Oscar Peterson trio alongside Ray Brown. 'I loved them, both of
them,' Ed told me. 'I was already a big fan, and I wanted to please them,
to accompany them, and to be a part of that group. There was a poster
of the band made in Germany, showing our three heads, and the image
captured something. It was really like we were inside of each other. That
was the idea – the orchestra became an instrument, and each of us had
a particular place, but it was shifting all the time. Oscar was the focal
point, because stylistically, and as an arranger, he's incredible. And Ray,
of course, being his soulmate – they'd had the chance to grow so much

together before I got there. My role was to create something, to make sure the form was there, and to bring the percussive aspect to it.

'Seeing the breadth of Oscar's playing, from the classical end of it, through his touch, and his pianistic capabilities, I tried to treat my instrument as a percussion ensemble. The tom-toms became timpani, the cymbals became a whole range of things. Oscar had a way of playing and arranging that made us sound like a big band. It's a very orchestral effect, so you had to think that way. I think one of the things that prepared me for that was working with people like Dr Billy Taylor, and doing his television show *The Subject Is Jazz*,[21] where you were exposed to all these different styles of music, and combinations of orchestra. Being able to play with musicians like Johnny Hodges and Harry Carney, and knowing the sound of these people and how the orchestra sounds, you try to bring that through the drum set, so to speak. And with Oscar we all had that same type of background, and influences, so when he orchestrated for the trio, that's what you were hearing. We could be next to Stan Kenton's band and it wouldn't be any more powerful, or project any more than we would, because of the way we played. It was a great experience.

'I mentioned those arrangements for the trio, and they're like a framework. At point "A" you might have an interlude followed by a shout, and then you have to work out how you're going to get out of it. Everything else in between is spontaneous creativity. That's the improvisation, but I call it a gift really – the being in tune with one another is a spiritual happening, as we all react instantaneously to this event that's going on. Some people would ask me if I felt I had to subvert myself, to be less in some way, having to play in the trio, but I'd say you can only be *more*, if you know what your role is. You grow from it. They'd say, "But you didn't take many solos?"

'I'd say, "Did you hear the piano solo, did you hear the bass solo? That was me. And that's before we got to the drum solo." I learned a great deal, and I liked having the discipline, knowing what your role is, but being free to express your own individuality within that role.'

Ed had a natural eloquence when he talked. My BBC colleagues were amazed that there were none of the 'ums', 'ers', and other conversational tics that normally appear in this kind of studio interview. He spoke in measured, balanced sentences, and he put this down to his years in education, teaching drums. This began in the army, but continued during his work for Billy Taylor. His consummate command of drum styles is one of the delights in those episodes of *The Subject Is Jazz* that survive. A particular highlight is the 'Swing' episode, where Ed's variety of authentic big band drumming, in a group that included Buck Clayton, Doc Severinsen, Jimmy Cleveland, Paul Quinichette and Ben Webster, takes us through charts associated with Jimmie Lunceford, Lionel Hampton and Count Basie. Yet unlike some musicians, Ed was as cogent talking about this music as he was playing it, and all his life – including his last decades in Europe – he shared Billy Taylor's zeal for spreading the word about jazz to new audiences.

Ed Thigpen left the Peterson trio in 1965, and the following year, after working continuously with Oscar for over fourteen years, Ray Brown also left. I wondered if this had created problems for Peterson. 'I've been through a whole mélange of bassists,' he said. 'And it's been great, I've enjoyed all of them. But I realized when George Mraz was in the band that what I needed was more than a bassist who was brilliant at following what I did, but who wasn't pushing me enough. This is not to denigrate George, because he was almost telepathic in picking up what I was doing, but he never had the all-encompassing competitive spirit I look for. Maybe it's just because he is a very nice guy, but he wasn't as abrasive as he needed to be in the band. But there are some who just stick out in my mind, and I'd have to speak particularly of Niels-Henning Ørsted Pedersen, who I think is a phenomenal bassist in his own right. His knowledge of the instrument along with his swinging proficiency and his solo ideas are incredible. His solos are a catalyst for the whole group. That's opposed to Sam Jones, who was very directional in the way he played. Sam didn't play many solos, but he had great time and a deep-rooted sound that we all used to love.'

On most of his last visits to Britain, Oscar brought what he came to call his 'NATO' quartet, with Swedish guitarist Ulf Wakenius, British drummer Martin Drew, and the aforementioned Danish bassist Niels-Henning. But on his 2005 visit, where he played at the Royal Albert Hall and at the Bridgewater Hall in Manchester, there was a sudden change of plan, because Ørsted Pedersen died suddenly in April that year, only eight weeks before the tour began. His place was taken by the Canadian bassist David Young, whose work I already knew from Oscar's 1995 Christmas album. 'It was a huge shock,' Oscar told me, 'when news came though of Niels' death. He was only 58. It affected my whole routine, because he and I would always get together for a few days at my house in Canada before we went on the road. We'd play together, work stuff out before the concerts, that kind of thing ... He was almost one of the family, so it's pretty earth-shattering that he's gone. Indeed my 13-year-old daughter Celine is the one who has taken it hardest, because she just can't believe that uncle Niels isn't coming back to visit us.' For those concerts, too, Alvin Queen, an old friend from Oscar's American years, and as I mentioned, a fellow camera buff, was on drums.

I wrote at the time that 'Peterson's most delicate and assured playing came on his own pieces, such as the haunting "Love Ballade"' with its delicate Chopinesque beginning, its broad dynamic range, and singing piano sound. Hearing this, there was no doubt we were listening to one of the world's greatest jazz pianists ... On "Backyard Blues" the playing was much crisper and the piano's goading bluesy runs and gospelly turnarounds prompted some flying playing from all concerned.'[22] Yet despite some excellent playing from David Young, what I realized was that in the years after Oscar's stroke, Niels-Henning had almost become his left hand. The power and swing that used to come from the piano now came from the bass, and probably no one could replace the mixture of empathy, telepathy and musicality that the 'great Dane' as Oscar called him, provided.

Maybe it's appropriate to end this chapter with Niels' own observations about his role, and the very special place his work with Oscar played in both their lives. 'The instrument I play,' he said, nodding at the case in the corner of the room where we met at the Brecon Jazz Festival, 'tends to be the background for the other people in a group, and I'm not a background person. I like the idea of music as a way of communicating, and, by communicating, also having a conversation with another person on the bandstand. My inner voice always told me that actually I should have been a piano player.' Niels joined Oscar initially in 1971 just for a couple of concerts in Budapest, where George Mraz was unable to play as he was a Czech refugee, and his passport would not allow him entry. The following year NHØP (as he is universally known) became a full-time member of the trio. 'I've played with few people, apart from Oscar, who are that *present* on the bandstand, which means that if you haven't played with someone of his calibre it can catch you by surprise. That's because you get up there and you're used to being asked "What would you like to play? What tempo? What key?" But with him it starts before you go on the bandstand. It's like creating the possibility of magic. It's funny how it hits you. In the beginning it scares you a bit, because you're not used to it, because before you actually hit the bandstand you're already up there mentally. Once you've experienced it, there's nothing quite like it. And to go back to the old "What would you like to play?" routine – actually it's a let-down. Whereas with Oscar you look forward to the fact that it pays to be really present, and if you're not – then you pay for it!'[23]

15 THE DAWN OF FUSION

Although my teenage band played traditional jazz, we reached our final years of school at the very moment that jazz-rock fusion was beginning in Britain. And, by chance, during the 1969 Farnham Festival, we met some of the players who became its pioneers. Every other year, the committee commissioned a set of new works for young musicians to perform. For the most part, these were contemporary classical pieces, written for all ages between primary pupils and school-leavers. In earlier events our West Surrey Youth Orchestra had already given premieres by some of Britain's major classical composers. But on this occasion the sponsors thought they would try a jazz commission. So pianist Michael Garrick, who lived nearby, was asked to write a large liturgical work, along the lines of his 1967 *Jazz Praises*, which had been very well received at St Paul's Cathedral in London.

The result was *A Jazz Mass For Martin Luther King*, later known as *Mr Smith's Apocalypse*, with a libretto by the poet John Smith, for speakers, solo singers and a youth choir, together with Mike's sextet. In the event, the choristers were recruited from the neighbouring Farnborough Grammar School, just over the border in Hampshire. But as we were school musicians with an interest in playing jazz, the members of my little group were given time off from our lessons to attend the rehearsals. And so it was that we met trumpeter Ian Carr, saxophonists Don Rendell and Art Themen, bassist Coleridge Goode and drummer John Marshall, who, together with Mike himself, were pretty much at the cutting edge of 1960s British jazz. Not being in the choir meant that we could sit close to the band as it rehearsed and take note of how the players interacted. We didn't know it at the time, but John Marshall and Ian would be founder members of the jazz-rock band Nucleus the following year.

All the band members were encouraging to us, and a couple of decades later when I was playing in Vile Bodies and, as mentioned in Chapter 7, Don Rendell gigged with us, he remembered that Farnham concert and was really pleased that at least one of the aspiring musicians whom he had met then was still playing. Equally, I bumped into Ian Carr several times over the years and he was continually encouraging not only about my music-making, but also about my writing, eventually entrusting me to become his biographer.

The consequence of spending time with musicians of this calibre was that we went away from the rehearsals and concert wanting to know more about their music. Some of us in my band not only bought all the LPs we could find of the Rendell–Carr quintet, and Mike Garrick's sextet, but we also kept track of the foundation and development of Nucleus. The grooves on our copy of its first album, *Elastic Rock*, were almost worn white on the gramophone in the sixth form common room. From avid reading of *Melody Maker* we knew all about the group's success in winning the 1970 Montreux Jazz Festival band competition, its reward being that Nucleus became one of the pioneers in bringing British jazz-rock to America for the first time.

It took forty-four years to appear, but after some excellent detective work, in 2014 Gearbox records issued a double LP of Nucleus at Montreux, mainly from an extended set backing the American singer Leon Thomas. When I was asked to annotate the album, listening to this music – which until then I had no idea existed – made me realize how extraordinarily ahead of the curve it was for 1970. In setting up Nucleus, Ian Carr wanted to combine the 'rock thing', as he put it, 'with the roots of the music'.[1] The contemporary feel, the raw excitement of jazz-rock, is palpable on this set, but so too is the sense that this band knows how to play the blues, not to mention the ins and outs of many other aspects of contemporary jazz.

If one ever got talking to Ian about the dawn of Nucleus, the music he said most inspired him was that of Miles Davis. But what the Montreux album shows is that there was a much wider range of reference: the freedom of Coltrane's *Ascension* on the opening of 'The Creator Has A Master Plan'; the unorthodox experiments of players such as Derek Bailey in Chris Spedding's scrabbly, scratchy, squeaky incursions on 'Echoes'; the harnessing of blues guitar (as Eric Clapton and John McLaughlin had done with Graham Bond's Organization) on 'Damn Nam'; and the nod towards Herbie Hancock, Ron Carter and Tony Williams in the intro and walking sections of 'One'. Here was a band that took material which Thomas had previously sung and recorded with a broad swathe of his American contemporaries, including Pharoah Sanders, James Spaulding, Lonnie Liston Smith and Roy Haynes, and which retained the spirit of those originals, while giving them a unique and personal identity that was all Nucleus.

When it was formed, the collective experience of Nucleus included everything from orthodox bebop playing to free jazz as well as ventures into rock. Guitarist Chris Spedding had just played on one of the CBS label's new 'Contemporary British Jazz' albums with vibes player and arranger Frank Ricotti. (Chris would go on the following year to record with the pop singer/songwriter Harry Nilsson on the album *Nilsson Schmilsson*, bringing his characteristic scratchy chords and an anarchic ending sequence to the song 'Gotta Get Up'. His later career encompassed everything from the Mike Gibbs orchestra to punk rock, and he has latterly worked frequently with Bryan Ferry.) Drummer John Marshall and keyboard player, saxophonist and oboist Karl Jenkins had both worked with Graham Collier, and on Graham's 1967 album *Deep Dark Blue Centre* their playing ranged from the proto-fusion of 'Crumblin' Cookie' to the free exchanges of the title track. That record also involved some other key figures in fusion: trumpeter Kenny Wheeler, trombonist Mike Gibbs and guitarist Phil Lee. Ian Carr himself had recorded free jazz, along with Nucleus bassist Jeff Clyne, on the *Springboard* album, with altoist Trevor Watts and drummer John Stevens, recorded in 1966 but not released until 1969 by Polydor. Yet Ian had also led a big band that played riffs and modal vamps behind Eric Burdon and the Animals. It was Ian's vivid memories of how this 'big rough band' had connected with an ecstatic crowd at the Richmond Festival in 1965 that finally tipped him in the direction of fusion rather than free jazz.

This potent combination – the visceral excitement of rock combined with some of the experimental mindset of the free jazz scene – seems to have underpinned most British ventures into fusion. For example, the drummer and future leader of the band Colosseum, Jon Hiseman, recalled that his first experiences of playing were very much in the free area. 'I was still at school,' he recalled, 'and I became everybody's dep.

The word went round that there was this young guy available ... I think Ginger Baker had been playing with the pianist Mike Taylor, and he left. So I was recommended alongside bassist Tony Reeves, and we both went in there to where Mike was playing with Dave Tomlin on saxophone. Mike – even if he played a standard – would reduce it. One night Ian Carr encouraged Mike to sit in with him and Don Rendell, at the 100 Club. I was playing drums that night, depping for Trevor Tomkins. Mike came up on the stand. He played nothing for the first two choruses. When it was his turn for a solo he played one note – "dong, dong, dong" – all the way through, and then when his solo was over, he played the same note at odd times during the next solo, and finally played that note again to finish with. Marvellous performance – although maybe there was something of the emperor's new clothes about it. But that was Mike, and you had to understand that he came from a different place.

'Most people in those days who hired a drummer wanted you to sound like someone – Philly Joe Jones, maybe, or "Can you sound like Art Blakey?" Mike never asked. He played the music and you had to find your own way in. In the end, I couldn't hear where his pulse was all the time, so I stopped playing on- and off-beats, I just played pulse. It seemed the logical thing to do, but people heard me playing and thought, "What's he doing?" They heard it as something new, but I was just trying to find my place in the music.'[2]

As well as trying to assimilate Mike Taylor's very abstract musical concepts, Jon also played in a similarly free setting in the trio of pianist Howard Riley and bassist Barry Guy. This gave him a wealth of further experience in creating what he called 'musical conversations' with the others. But the melting pot, and the forum for exchanging ideas, was the New Jazz Orchestra. This grew out of a smaller group formed by saxophonist Clive Burrows, and it became a big band in search of an organizing talent, until the writer and arranger Neil Ardley took it on.

'He was a composer in search of an orchestra,' Jon explained. 'He immediately took it by the scruff of the neck. He began to rearrange what we had and to write completely new compositions of his own. This became the seminal New Jazz Orchestra with so many young players involved who went on to do interesting things in the music business. I was a founder member and I met Barbara Thompson in that band, so it was very important for both our careers. Ian Carr [who played in the Orchestra] was very important for me too, because I learned a lot about the business of being a producer by recording a couple of his albums. He was a friend and colleague throughout his life, and we worked together in the United Jazz and Rock Ensemble for 35 years.'

For a while, the bassist in the New Jazz Orchestra was Jack Bruce. He and Ginger Baker had been working together in the Graham Bond Organization, but Jack had left that group by the time he joined the NJO. As it turns out, Graham Bond's band was also an extremely important catalyst for the generation that developed jazz-rock in Britain. 'Ginger and Jack fought, tooth and nail, throughout their entire relationship,' Jon observed. 'Ginger had ousted Jack from Graham's band, and Graham always maintained that this was a mistake, that he should have stood up and fought for Jack, but he didn't. And then a few months later, Ginger announced that he was leaving Graham to form a new band with Eric Clapton and … Jack Bruce. Graham couldn't work it out, and felt somewhat betrayed.'

When Jack discussed this much later with Barbara Thompson, for a BBC series that I helped to produce, she asked him why he had joined Eric and Ginger, given this tempestuous background. 'We were trying to apply free jazz rules to pop songs,' he said. 'I was trying to use the bass in exactly the same way that a free jazz player would. I was using it as a melodic instrument. But then the drums are also a melodic instrument, so we had three people battling it out to "play the tune".'[3] So just as Ian Carr wanted to explore the conjunction of freedom and rock rhythms, this was the impetus for Cream, and for many of Jack's subsequent ventures.

Meanwhile, a little before this, as Jon Hiseman recalled, Graham Bond had wandered into a New Jazz Orchestra rehearsal, at the 100 Club on a Sunday morning, along with his colleague Dick Heckstall-Smith. Jon said, 'He heard the band, turned to Dick and said, "If ever Ginger leaves us, this is the guy to play drums." So I got a call, but I wasn't professional at the time, and said, "No, no, I can't." It had never occurred to me to turn professional. But Graham went on and on and on. Finally over one long night, he rabbited me to death, and I agreed. He forced his way in by pressing £35 a week into my hand, which I never actually got, but it sounded like a good game at the time. Graham was a heroin addict and it was really my induction into all that. Here I was, a professional musician, and here was this guy going into Watford Gap[4] and wiping the blood off the walls in the toilets. But he managed to get money out of Polygram, and they said, "We'll give you

£250, go do a set of demos that we can listen to." And we went with Eddie Kramer, who subsequently left Olympic and formed Electric Lady Studios in America, and for six hours, from midnight until six in the morning, we played the tracks that eventually came out as part of the *Solid Bond* album.[5] I took the tapes back into Polygram and they had a listen, and the guy threw me out. But if you listen to "I Can't Stand It", Graham is the essence of blues, of soul and of jazz.'

It took four years before Warner Brothers finally issued those tracks, along with three earlier ones featuring Graham with John McLaughlin, Jack Bruce and Ginger Baker. But after making those recordings with the Bond Organization in 1966, Jon left Graham and went on to work successively with Georgie Fame and John Mayall, before founding his own band Colosseum in 1968. Reed player Dick Heckstall-Smith came with him from the Bond Organization and he was also reunited with bassist Tony Reeves (from the Mike Taylor days), and keyboard player Dave Greenslade, who had been with him in a very early band. Jon's idea was 'a mix of jazz and vocals, to rock rhythms. The blues wasn't interesting to me. I wanted to take it much further than that.'

Colosseum's first album from 1969, *Those Who Are About To Die Salute You*, opened with a piece by Graham Bond. 'I always thought that the best track that Graham wrote was that one: "Walking in the Park",' said Jon. 'Because it's got this strange three-bar construction. It's a blues in theory, but it doesn't work that way. I really liked it and our agent decided to put it out as a single.' With Dave Greenslade's vocals, some additional trumpet from Henry Lowther (a member of the New Jazz Orchestra, and soon to be a member of Michael Garrick's sextet) and two saxophones played simultaneously by Dick Heckstall-Smith, this track pointed towards much of what would become the established musical personality of Colosseum.

One thing I discovered from Jon was that – great soloist that he was – Dick's saxophone sound was particularly unusual. He bent notes in a very individual way. Playing two parts at the same time himself, he used this facet of his sound well, yet the instinctive variability of his pitching made him virtually impossible to multitrack in the studio, and quite a liability in a horn section. Consequently, Colosseum – at least in the studio – often used other brass and reed players, such as Henry Lowther or Jon's wife Barbara Thompson, to do any necessary over-dubs. Yet an interesting aspect of the band was that, because it had been organized with its members on salary, they met every day to rehearse, even if there was no gig in the evening, and so they developed their repertoire collectively. The result became a group exercise in aural memory, and when the band re-formed in 1975 (having temporarily broken up in 1971) there were no written arrangements, and the parts had to be re-learned from records. When Heckstall-Smith died shortly before another reunion tour in 2005, Barbara Thompson agreed at almost no notice to take his place, but there were still no parts, and Jon had to arrange for them to be transcribed overnight for her to learn. As the band's *Live '05* album shows, she more than succeeded in making the music her own, particularly on the 'Valentine Suite'. But Colosseum stands – like Nucleus – as an innovative and very individual British fusion band that had a life of over thirty years.

When the first version of the group broke up, Jon temporarily fronted a band called Tempest, which brought together the vocalist Chris Farlowe and the guitarist Allan Holdsworth, who would go on to a distinguished career in the USA, after making his first ever tour there with Tempest. Among the musicians Holdsworth would later work with in the States was the ex-Miles Davis drummer Tony Williams, in his band Lifetime.

Williams had been only 17 when he joined Miles' band in 1963 and became part of a long-lived rhythm section with Herbie Hancock on piano and Ron Carter on bass. It was this second great quintet that took Miles from the modal territory of *Kind of Blue* into many of the areas that were simultaneously being explored on the European side of the Atlantic by the likes of Ian Carr and Jon Hiseman. Particularly towards the end of its life, this edition of the Davis quintet was simultaneously exploring ideas of freedom and of funk rhythms. We know from press accounts of the band's gigs and the two nights recorded at the Plugged Nickel in Chicago at the end of 1965 (after Miles had suffered a long lay-off following hip surgery) that the band's live shows still drew on some of his older repertoire, some of it dating back to his mid-1950s sessions, made for Prestige. Thus we find pieces such as 'If I Were a Bell', 'My Funny Valentine', 'Stella By Starlight' and 'Walkin'' appearing in several set-lists, albeit played with a greater degree of abstraction. Indeed the methods the band used to explore this music underpinned the way the players approached developing the material on the three albums they made in 1966–7 – *Miles Smiles*, *The Sorcerer* and *Nefertiti*. As Ian Carr put it in his biography of Miles, 'the improvisations are explorations of . . . factors posited by the theme, and so the soloist tends to refer back to thematic fragments . . . In fact the soloist was free to play any kind of melodic shapes he wished because the bass and piano players were using their ears to follow wherever his inspiration took him.'[6]

The technique was known as 'time – no changes' because there might be little or no harmonic movement under a solo, as the conventional harmonic sequence was often abandoned. But whilst Carr focuses on the way horn players such as Davis or Shorter might solo, to my mind there's an equally interesting development in the rhythm section, in that over its life the rhythmic intensity of the band changed quite dramatically. I asked Dave Holland, who took over the bass chair from Ron Carter, where he thought this had come from.

'Knowing the relationships that existed in the band before I joined,' he mused, 'I'd say that Tony Williams was the instrumental focus point for its rhythmic development. And if you speak to Herbie, he talks of Tony as being a very important influence on him, in terms of how he approached rhythm. It really changed his idea of how to use the piano rhythmically and how a rhythm section can function. I think when you look at that band with Ron Carter, Herbie Hancock and Tony Williams, plus Wayne Shorter and of course Miles, I think the key thing for me is the synthesis of all those people: Wayne's compositions that gave them a vehicle to do the things that they did; Ron Carter's approach to rhythm and harmony that reworked a lot of the songs from the bass point of view; Herbie's approach to comping and his search for alternatives to the traditional way of using the piano; and Miles' way of bringing all these elements together and making them cohesive. As in any great band it's the sum of the elements becoming more than the individual parts that produced such great music. I sat in London waiting for the new records to come out, put them on the turntable and practised with them, trying to work out what the heck was happening.'[7]

In fact it wasn't just those, like Dave, listening to the band from afar, who needed to keep pace with its extraordinary rate of change. When I spoke to Herbie Hancock about this period, he reflected on what they had done in the studio and what happened on the road, saying, 'Usually you record something before you tour, which is the common way to do it. You write a piece of music, you record it and then you go on tour. During the tour, pieces have the opportunity to kind of marinate, and also you have a live audience. That goes into the equation too, so there's a whole area of discovery that has the chance to develop in a live situation, in a tour that has several concerts. I always looked forward to how the music was going to shape and re-shape. What you hear in the studio and what you hear by the tenth concert might be quite different.'[8]

Aiming to explore this period of development a little further, I suggested to Ron Carter that, during this period, his timing and choice of notes strayed quite a distance from some of the ideas in his subsequent book *Building Jazz Bass Lines*,[9] which would in due course become essential reading for bassists everywhere. But he assured me 'I'm using the same type of concept. They just don't come so close together. If Herbie played a note that lasted four beats, I got the chance to put one of those strange notes in that could take him somewhere else.'[10]

One musician in particular could explain what it felt like to be parachuted into this working quintet. In January 1968 guitarist George Benson joined the band in the studio, to make the track 'Paraphernalia' for the album *Miles In The Sky*. 'I knew the old band,' he recalled. 'The one with Paul Chambers, Wynton Kelly and Jimmy Cobb, and I thought they really were the best jazz recordings being made at the time. Some of the best in history! So I remember when they left Miles' band and he formed the new one, with a name that I knew from a long time ago, Ron Carter. The big surprise was that he'd picked up this kid from Boston, who'd sat in with me a few times when he was fifteen years old, Tony Williams. And the word got out that Miles had hired this kid to play in his band. Nobody believed it at first. I did bump into them in Europe, and as a matter of fact, that's how I ended up with the band. We were all on tour in Europe, and that's when I bumped into Tony, whom I'd only heard when he sat in with me in Boston. Now here he was in the greatest jazz band in the world, with Miles. He was still seventeen or so, and he couldn't buy a beer. I had to get him one at the bar because he was too young to order his own. And it was after that that I ended up getting the call from Miles in New York.

'I'd never played with Miles and I really didn't understand what he wanted me to do. I had good ears in those days, but I'd never played anything that allowed for dissonant harmonies. I'd certainly never played anything that was as freewheeling as what we recorded. But that was the thing that made Miles great. He let cats be all they could be. You could build your own dream within the song. You could make it your own, and I think that's why so many cats excelled and found themselves playing better than they could in any other situation. The cats around you understood what you were trying to do, and gave you the space to do it. I really regret that I didn't join the band, because he did ask me to join him.'[11]

Although George recorded other tracks with Miles that day alongside 'Paraphernalia', it is another track on *Miles In The Sky*, without Benson, that gives the clue to the jazz-rock fusion direction that Miles would eventually take. This was a track called 'Stuff' in which Ron played bass guitar, Herbie switched to electric keyboard, and Tony showed a completely different side of his all-round accomplishment as a great drummer. Yet Miles did not immediately follow this route. He ventured into free jazz for a while with the new rhythm section of Dave Holland, Chick Corea and Jack DeJohnette. By contrast, on leaving Davis, Tony Williams went all out for fusion. Jon Hiseman mentioned Lifetime, the band that Tony formed at the very end of 1968, in connection with guitarist Allan Holdsworth. But Allan was preceded in the first edition of that band by another Yorkshireman, the guitarist John McLaughlin, who – like Hiseman – had worked with Graham Bond.

In 2008 I set off to the South of France to talk to John McLaughlin about his career in music, and I arrived at the small town where he lives a little early. Checking my recording machine, I realized the batteries might not last through a lengthy interview, so I zipped into Monaco to buy some replacements. I got them, clipped them into the machine and set off back towards Nice along the Corniche, the picturesque road cut into the cliffs above the Mediterranean. Just before I arrived back at John's town, a lorry had been parked on my side of the road, facing the wrong way, on the inside of a blind bend. As I pulled out to pass it, a car materialized on the other side of the road, hurtling towards me, travelling well over the speed limit. I had three options – plunge over the left side towards the sea, meet the other vehicle head on, or put my foot down and try to squeeze past the lorry. I decided to try and get past, but just as I cleared the back of the truck, my wing mirror clipped a spur of metal sticking out of the tailgate. The mirror snapped off and the end of the metal gouged an ugly gash in my rear passenger door. It was a hire car, so I pulled up as soon as I could to take some details, only to see the lorry draw away and disappear back towards Monte Carlo. An old villager looked at me sympathetically. 'Pas d'assurance,' he said, helpfully.[12]

I had some sticking plaster in my bag, so after picking up the remains of the mirror from the road, I taped up the worst bits of metal and wire hanging off the door, and made for the little car park at the top of the town, where I'd agreed to meet John. When he got there, I asked if he lived far away. 'Ten minutes' walk or a couple of minutes in the car,' he said.

'Okay, I'll give you a lift,' I replied.

He took one look at my car with the gash in the door and the remains of the mirror taped up with Band-Aid and said, 'No, I think we'll walk.'

Fortunately, on the way down, after I explained what had happened, he could not have been kinder, giving me tea and biscuits to calm me down following the accident and reassuring me that we had plenty of time. The reward was a fine, relaxed conversation that took me back to the very dawn of jazz-rock in Britain. Before working with Graham Bond, John had played with other organists, including Mike Carr (Ian's brother) and Georgie Fame. But then, he said, 'With Graham I got to play with Ginger Baker and Jack Bruce for the first time, and that was a very interesting group. I'd left Georgie Fame's band before he made it big, because I liked the musical provocation that was in Graham's band. Ginger was a great drummer, and Jack equally, a great bass player, and Graham – God bless him – was a wild man on the organ and also playing alto sax. But the music was jazz meets r'n'b, and r'n'b was very much part of jazz to me. It still is today. It's got the blues thing, which you can't take away from jazz.'[13]

Ironically, it was *Extrapolation*, a record that veered towards free jazz, which was John's first recording under his own name, and cemented his fame in Britain. It was produced by the mercurial entrepreneur Giorgio Gomelsky, for his short-lived Marmalade label (distributed by Polydor). Born in Georgia, and a Swiss national, Giorgio initially worked, after coming to Britain, with Chris Barber at the Marquee club, on the band management side. Not only did he then nudge Barber into playing music by Mingus and John Handy, but also, with the help of co-producer and guitarist Steve Hammond, Gomelsky then moved this most traditional of jazz bands into working with such significant fusion figures as Paul Buckmaster and Peter Robinson. Marmalade Records also had a pop hit with Julie Driscoll (later known as the free jazz singer Julie Tippetts) and Brian Auger with 'This Wheel's On Fire'. Before it folded, over a disagreement with

Polydor, the company's range extended from the completely free improvisations of John Stevens and the Spontaneous Music Ensemble to the
raw blues of Sonny Boy Williamson (teamed with such contemporary
jazz figures as Alan Skidmore and Joe Harriott).

For *Extrapolation*, John McLaughlin's quartet included the
baritone saxophonist John Surman (who had made a stellar reputation
working with Mike Westbrook), the drummer Tony Oxley, and bassist
Brian Odges. 'It was the first record,' said McLaughlin, 'on which I was
recording my own music. For me it was like one of my first paintings,
which is basically what recordings are – images in sound. I was very
happy to have had the opportunity to record my music, because I had
been playing since I was in school. By the time I recorded this, I had an
album's worth of music. And to be able to play with John Surman was
great. Normally, Dave Holland would have been on bass, because he
had been in the band, the quartet, when we played live. I think the
timing of the recording helped, because just after it was finished, I went
over to play with Tony Williams and Larry Young in New York in the
Lifetime group. The record actually came out after I'd gone, which
I think really helped it, because the fact that I'd gone was big news:
"Boy from UK goes to play with greats in America!" I loved Tony
Oxley's drumming, by the way. The first time I really got to play with
Tony was in the Gordon Beck quartet with Jeff Clyne, but I was really
delighted to have him on the record.'

What *Extrapolation* and the story behind it represents is
another coming together of musicians from various different areas of
jazz, again demonstrating the fluid exchange of ideas between – as Ian
Carr put it – 'the rock thing and the roots of the music'. So how had John
McLaughlin ended up in Lifetime, exploring jazz-rock on the other side
of the Atlantic?

'I got a call from Dave Holland. Dave and I had been living in
a flat together before he left for the US, and as I said, he'd been in the
Extrapolation band until he left the country and was replaced by Brian
Odges, a great bass player. In any event, Dave got the gig with Miles,
which must have been some time in July 1968. Miles saw Dave play and
asked him to come over and join his band. And we were thrilled –
"Dave's going to go and join Miles!"

'In November '68 Dave called me and said that Tony Williams
wanted to talk to me. And I found out that Tony had listened to a tape
that had been recorded by Jack DeJohnette, who had also been at

Ronnie Scott's that summer with the Bill Evans trio. Jack loved to jam, so Dave and I went down to jam with him at Ronnie Scott's in the afternoon. Unbeknownst to me, Jack recorded this jam session. He went back, and one day Tony, who was considering leaving Miles' group and forming Lifetime, was talking to Jack and said, "I'm looking for a guitar player". And apparently Jack said, "Really? Well, listen to this guy, because I just played with him!" By this time Dave and Tony were playing together with Miles, and so Dave put Tony on the phone, and he said, "I wanna do Lifetime with you." It was a thrill. I had to get some things together, and Ronnie Scott was very kind to me, because he helped me get the special papers I needed to get my visa to go to America. But it was one of the greatest things that could have happened to me to get that call from Tony.

'I didn't even know until the first rehearsal who was in Lifetime except Tony and me. So I walked into the club where Tony was playing with Miles, finishing his last week with the band. This is when I met Miles, later on the same day. We rehearsed in the afternoon, because Tony's drums were set up there, at the Baron Club up in Harlem.[14] In walked Larry Young. I was so thrilled because Larry had made recordings like *Unity*[15] with Woody Shaw, Joe Henderson and Elvin, and he'd also done a recording with Grant Green, the great guitarist, and he was *the* new Hammond organ player. And of course I'd grown up with organ trios, with Mike Carr, Georgie Fame and Graham Bond.'

And it was a key member of the Bond Organization from John McLaughlin's time in the group who, a little later, would become the fourth member of Lifetime, namely Jack Bruce. 'Jack came to New York with one of his bands,' remembered John. 'Cream had broken up by this time, and he was playing at the Fillmore East. I called Tony and said, "You know, Jack's playing in town. Let's go down, and just say hi." They got on very well, and Tony – basically because Lifetime was Tony's band – wanted to try to get a little more commercial success. Which we needed. You need to have a certain amount of sales and audience attendance, just to keep a band together. And Lifetime was notoriously successful musically, but notoriously unsuccessful commercially. I was lucky, because when I wasn't playing with Lifetime, Miles had me playing with him. So I had the best of both worlds. I was very fortunate, in that respect. So Jack came in, and we did a recording called *Turn It Over*.'[16]

From Jack's point of view, joining Lifetime was bringing him together with a drummer he greatly admired, but interestingly not so much for Williams' work with Miles, but for his association with a completely different musician. 'I'd been a huge fan,' he said, 'since Eric Dolphy's album *Out To Lunch*, which was the one which completely revolutionized jazz drumming. We were all very much in love with that, anybody of my generation who played jazz, we'd all say, "Yeah, *Out To Lunch*, that was the turning point." When Tony came to my gig at the Fillmore East and asked me to join Lifetime, I just said, "Yes!" The music we were doing was a completely new direction. The rhythms were very much jazz-rock rhythms, but the harmonies and melodies – I remember there was one completely polytonal one where I was singing in E and playing in C, or maybe the other way round – were very adventurous, and I'd say that probably my time with Tony, McLaughlin, Larry Young and myself was the high spot of the fusion thing. We also had huge volume but with a jazz sensibility, and maybe the band was a bit ahead of the technology.'[17]

Jack recalled that engineers in the studio didn't quite know how to record the band at the volume it normally used. Yet musically – particularly on live gigs – he really liked the results. McLaughlin was sure that Jack brought a missing ingredient to the mix. 'The music did change,' he said, 'once Jack was singing in the band, and he's a great singer. And we carried on for another year. Musically it was very important, especially for me, compared to Miles – well, Miles directed everything, and everybody, but in a wonderful way. And everybody was delighted just to do it. All of those musicians, they loved him ... and I still do today. I miss him. We were just happy to go whichever way Miles wanted to go, and sometimes he didn't even know which way he was going. That's what made it interesting. But with Tony – he was a very schooled musician. He'd studied harmony at Juilliard, and he really encouraged me to write. He liked the way I wrote music. He constantly encouraged me to write for Lifetime, which I did. And it's safe to say that the groundwork for all the music with Mahavishnu was done in Lifetime, because of Tony's encouragement.'

Late in 1969, Lifetime, complete with Jack Bruce, came to Britain and played a gig in Hampstead. Ian Carr, together with some of the musicians who would join him in Nucleus, went along, and, as Ian recalled, 'They were incredibly loud! But we liked what they were doing. Fundamentally they had a very different approach from ours, with some very highly arranged things that featured Larry Young's organ blending with the guitar, as well as intricate passages where Tony doubled the melody on the drums.'[18] Ian was to hear the band again at Newport, at the 1970 edition of the Rhode Island festival, where Lifetime played the closing set on the Saturday, before Nucleus appeared the next afternoon. By this point the two bands were following distinctly different paths into fusion. In Lifetime, the 'intricate passages' that Ian mentioned were an increasingly prominent feature (along with Jack's vocals), and these unison phrases that combined speed and dexterity – as John said – later became part of the bedrock of Mahavishnu. By contrast, the Nucleus set, with Ian blowing forcefully on flugelhorn, as his trumpet had been damaged at the side of the stage, was noted in one review as 'a well integrated and inventive set ... heavily electronic in the jazz rock idiom'.[19] Compared to Lifetime's complexity, Nucleus was more about starting from an almost minimalist position, rather interestingly aligned both with Jon Hiseman's memory of Mike Taylor sitting in with the Rendell-Carr band, and with the Davis quintet's 'time – no changes'.

'What we do in Nucleus,' Ian said, 'is simply to have one note which is a root, and over that root we can play literally anything. That is the kind of freedom we are interested in. Not total freedom where you don't even have a root, but we have that one note and over it we have complete harmonic choice. We are interested in building up tension and in the release of it.'[20]

When Nucleus moved on from Newport to a short residency at New York's Village Gate, even though Miles Davis had already released *In A Silent Way* in 1969, listeners were puzzled. Ian recalled spending time with Karl Jenkins explaining to interested audience members what they were doing, and how their unorthodox time signatures worked, particularly after someone in the crowd shouted out 'What do you call this music?' Nucleus, in terms of British jazz-rock, became an outstandingly successful example, and was eventually signed a few years later to the US Capitol record label. Jon Hiseman's various bands also made inroads into the US market.

In contrast to these achievements, Lifetime was a band that never quite managed the success it deserved, on either side of the Atlantic, not least because the albums it made mainly suffered from poor sound quality. The visceral excitement of the group's live performances somehow dissipated on disc. As a result, McLaughlin left Tony Williams and formed the Mahavishnu Orchestra in 1971. This lasted through two main incarnations until 1974, when Shakti was launched. The hallmark of Mahavishnu was that it took the powerful and aggressive elements of Lifetime and developed them. It drew into jazz the techniques of distortion and high volume that had been pioneered by Jimi Hendrix in the rock world, and as McLaughlin told me, it was 'louder and faster' than any other band on the jazz circuit.

When I spoke to the band's drummer Billy Cobham about that era, he agreed, summarizing the concept they shared. 'In Mahavishnu what we want is intensity – but to be as intense at a very low level of volume as we are at a very high level of volume, without losing control of the speed. We want to be in synch with our ideas, which means first you have to be in synch with yourself, literally meaning that you have to be so strong on your instrument that the ideas you play, you could actually play standing on your head, no problem. You have to learn to co-ordinate these ideas. You have to be able to hear them, before you play them in concert, before you present them as an individual to the table of the group.

'It was living on the edge in Mahavishnu, because there were a lot of things I didn't know. There were many things we were accomplished and successful at, but I didn't understand why. More questions came to me, and I kept questioning, "Who am I? Why? Where am I?" But I think the end result is in the music. I'd come into it from Dreams, which was much milder, more laid-back. We were some spaced out cowboys, I'll tell you that! But we had some very, very intense pieces. Dreams never had the chance to blossom as far as I'm concerned. We had a lot of elements in place, but we weren't ready. We didn't know how to be. It's naïve. But then you listen to Randy and Michael and Abercrombie now, and those guys *really* stand out!

'I think there was a similar feeling of immaturity about Mahavishnu. We let something slip through our fingers because we were too immature to understand what we had. Later, when John went off to start Shakti, I started working with our keyboard player Jan Hammer. I was trying in my own little way to keep it together. So I would pass on and share whatever projects I had that I felt Jan could do. He was a real goldmine, I felt. If I could have used Rick Laird on bass I would have used him too. Jerry Goodman I didn't think I could use very much because I didn't know how to use violin. Becoming a leader was a step I felt desperate that I had to take. I had no alternative, thinking that if this is what life has dealt me, then I will have to deal with this deck of cards, and this hand. I was extremely lucky to have success with my first solo album *Spectrum*. I had no idea. I thought maybe it was something I could take round to Max Gordon at the Village Vanguard or to the people at the Village Gate and try and get a gig. I didn't know it'd sell 50,000 units in the first two weeks!'[21]

The guitarist on *Spectrum* was Tommy Bolin, who was working at the time in the rock band James Gang. Talking about him – and the way rock and jazz musicians were working together at this period – led us on to consider the other guitarists Billy had worked with. We talked about John McLaughlin, John Abercrombie and John Scofield, but Billy reminded me that there was one musician he'd played with in concert and recorded with in the early 1970s (notably on the album *White Rabbit*) whom he held in the highest regard – none other than George Benson. 'George played the guitar as if it was part of his means of conversation,' said Billy. 'He knew the words that were coming. And the guitar just spoke to you though him. The other guys would still be trying to decide – "Is it going to be this approach? Or that one?" But George is like "Bang! This is me, man. This is where I've been, this is where I am going!" He knew what he was doing on that one instrument, the hollow body Gibson L5, in those days. And some of those tempos were *way* up there!'

I mentioned that during the period of Lifetime's formation, Miles had moved on to work with a regular band in which he and Wayne Shorter were joined by Chick Corea on keyboards, Dave Holland on bass and Jack DeJohnette on drums. On a track such as 'Sanctuary' from *Bitches Brew*, its feeling is far freer and more spacious than most of the music recorded by the previous quintet. In my conversation with him, Dave Holland described this as 'extremely intense' music. And Chick Corea painted a word picture for me of this 'whole new era' of music. He said: 'I was absolutely in love with that quintet. And I know that Dave Holland, Jack DeJohnette and Wayne also shared that enthusiasm for those months that we were experimenting with that music. I think Miles, for a while, was enjoying seeing all these sparks happen, as we took these new directions. He just crouched down at the edge of the stage to watch and listen, before he'd come in and set a new direction and try very different things. But I think it was a huge transitional point for Miles. During the time we were out there playing, I think he was searching for a direction. He knew he wanted to change, and the word "change" was on his lips. He was in the process of changing, having had this great quintet that had just finished. We were still playing some of the repertoire, in fact a lot of the repertoire, from that quintet, but we were introducing new things. And he wasn't sure what he was about to get into, so there was this period of really freewheeling that the band was into, that I thought made some great music.'[22]

By contrast *Bitches Brew* also contained some of the hardest-edged funk Miles had ever recorded, such as 'Miles Runs the Voodoo Down'. This aggressive rock-inflected music would underpin the direction of Miles' music for much of the rest of his life. The aggression Miles felt at the time emerged not only in the sound of the band but also in an altercation in the studio with his producer Teo Macero, during the recording of that album, that ended in fisticuffs. Teo stood up to Miles, who had wanted him to sack one of the production secretaries, which the producer refused to do.[23] The scuffle ended in a draw and greater mutual respect between the two men, which was important, because in the years that followed, Teo would take an increasingly significant role in curating Miles' output for commercial release. *Bitches Brew* itself was the album that crystallized the turning point in Miles' work, and the moment from which he gradually began to opt for fusion rather than out-and-out freedom.

This was also a matter of where and how the band played live. Up until shortly before *Bitches' Brew*, the band was still wearing smart Italian suits and playing jazz clubs. But just prior to its release, at the urging of Columbia's president Clive Davis, the band made a shift to playing quite different types of venue – those more associated with rock music. Producer and author Michael Cuscuna summed it up thus: 'Clive had witnessed the strong connection between rock artists and the Youth Culture at the Monterey Pop Festival in 1967. He thought the older artists' careers could be jumpstarted if they were made relevant to the underground rock scene.'[24] So, on 7 March 1970, the quintet, with Airto Moreira added on percussion, took to the stage at Fillmore East in New York, on a triple bill with Neil Young & Crazy Horse, and the Steve Miller Band.

In one of several conversations I've had with Jack DeJohnette over the years, I asked him to describe what happened: 'We were doing the music of *Bitches' Brew*. We'd been in the studio, so this was a continuation of work in progress. It was basically seamless music in suite form, conducted by Miles giving a cue from his horn, playing certain melodies. We used these as signals that we were going to go into another piece, so the sets flowed seamlessly, which was a great way to play. It kept the energy flowing, and kept everybody on their toes.

'Miles took from that era what suited him. Carnaby Street in England was happening then, so some of us began wearing clothes from there. I had an afro and bell-bottom pants, and Miles started wearing a vest with fringes and scarfs, so he took from the scene, and put it into Miles' impeccable style. Dave was wearing a headband and beads and things like that and Chick was also the same. I think Wayne maybe wore a vest, but he was sort of low-key! But also when Chick and Dave joined the band we were all into microbiotics. And Miles caught the wave. He stopped doing drugs, he stopped doing anything, and instead he was working out, and swimming, or going to the gym. And his playing in that period was very strong. It was great playing – high notes – showing he was in really peak form.'[25]

By October 1970, both Chick Corea and Dave Holland had left the band and Miles gradually replaced the members of the quintet with more rock-orientated musicians. Wayne Shorter had left in early 1970 and his successor Steve Grossman was replaced first by Gary Bartz and then in 1972–4 by Dave Liebman.

'You've really got to give Miles credit,' said Dave, when I spoke to him in New York, in the cramped backstage band room at Birdland, 'for turning his back on a twenty-year period in which he was one of the main voices in jazz and a trend-setter several times. By the time I joined he had just completely changed it to a rock beat, electric bass and keyboards. If you just think about the instruments, let alone what he played, they were all completely foreign elements to everything he'd done pre-1967. So that's an extraordinary leap that he made. It's like he came back as another person and completely reinvented himself.

'In the studio we never really knew what was going on. There was never any music, no figures, even. He'd been up for a few days, probably, when we got the call from the road manager to say "Come in". He might start us off with a riff he'd play on the keyboard, or he might sing something to Michael Henderson, the bass player, though he didn't really sing pitches, he just croaked rhythms, "Cha-chk, chk, chk". But somehow he built the stuff from the bottom up, and the tape was always on, so it wasn't like "Take 1 . . . Take 2". You walked in and the red light was on, so everything was on tape. And Teo's job – right through the 70s – was to find a way to put it all together. And in those days of LP, you were looking at 40–45 minutes or so. Miles wasn't thinking in terms of songs and titles. You might just take one little piece of a tune and work on that for an hour, or an hour and a half, and that was a session. Maybe we'd listen back and try it again, and then he'd be gone, out of the door with the cassettes in his hands. It was very loose, on the verge of disorganized, but I wouldn't say chaotic, because everybody was giving it their full attention. It was always slightly like walking on coals – you didn't know whether to take a step or not. And I think that was pretty much the way it was from *In A Silent Way* onwards. He might have an idea, he might have a sketch, but by the time we got to 1973, as I say, he didn't even have those sketches on paper, it was just something he'd find in his head, or make up. And some of those tunes found their way to the gig. Most of them didn't. A few of them we might play a couple of nights and then he'd go with one of them and maybe play it over and over.'[26]

I wondered how other musicians at the time viewed this transition in Miles. One of the most innovative jazz composers and leaders at the dawn of the 1970s, on both sides of the Atlantic, ranging from his early 1960s work with fellow Berklee alumni in the United States to his subsequent bandleading career in Britain, was Zimbabwe-born Mike Gibbs. I got to know Mike while working on the 2005 reissue of his 1972 album *Just Ahead*, and after that we occasionally went along to gigs together, most memorably to what turned out to be the final London appearance by Nucleus at Soho's Pizza Express, not long before Ian Carr started to suffer from Alzheimer's disease. Thinking back to the *Just Ahead* period, I asked Mike just how significant Miles' work had been at the time. 'I think *Bitches Brew* was such a big event in that era,' he said, 'that we were all striving for the new, and felt we were supposed to be moving in that direction. But looking back now, I think underneath, I really hankered for what Miles had done a little earlier, for the Coltrane period, or even before that. I think that was music that can be revisited and which can be refreshed and revived.'[27]

As someone who has focused on composing and band directing since deciding not to continue as a trombonist, Mike has long been interested in refreshing and reviving earlier periods of his music. When we spoke on the occasion of his 80th birthday tour in 2017, he focused on this aspect of his work, starting with a piece that had been on his first album, the eponymous *Michael Gibbs*, recorded in Britain in 1969 with (among others) several members of the New Jazz Orchestra. He said: 'Some of my old tunes keep surfacing. For example, a year or two ago, Bill Frisell did a version of "On The Third Day", and when I heard it, I liked what he had done with it so much that I revived it for a concert.

The band loved playing it and the audience loved hearing it. And then quite recently Philip Catherine rang me – I hadn't been in touch with him for the best part of forty years – to say he wanted to issue a version of my song "Tunnel of Love". He'd actually recorded it back when we were last in touch,[28] but he sent it to me, I listened and liked what I heard, so then I started to revise that. So I'm often prompted to look back at music, then I hear something new in it, and so I decide to tackle it again. It's the little things that I notice, and nowadays I often see how to do them in a slightly different way.'[29]

So whereas Miles Davis was taking a more spontaneous route to creating and working with new repertoire, Mike Gibbs opted for a more conventional composer's path. Yet that first 1969 album and the years leading up to it had shown him exploring some of the same questions about tackling freedom and fusion. Mike had arrived in Boston to study at Berklee in 1958 at the age of 21. He studied with George Russell and Gunther Schuller, and played trombone in the band of trumpeter Herb Pomeroy (whom I mentioned in Chapter 10 in connection with Charlie Parker). He soon became a close colleague of both Gary Burton and Carla Bley. On Gary's highly influential album *Duster* from April 1967 (and featuring none other than Roy Haynes on drums, alongside Gary, guitarist Larry Coryell and bassist Steve Swallow), three of the compositions are by Mike Gibbs and one is by Carla Bley. And on the follow-up *Lofty Fake Anagram*, cut just four months later, with Bob Moses replacing Haynes, there are also contributions from Gibbs and Bley. Alongside straight-ahead pieces such as Burton's 'Good Citizen Swallow', these are both proto-fusion albums, yet with the pull of free form improvisation readily apparent. Hence a piece from the latter record, Swallow's composition 'General Mojo Cuts Up', is primarily a vehicle for free exploration, whereas Gibbs' 'June the 15, 1967' is a tightly structured composition over a rock beat. Sitting somewhere in between is Gibbs' 'Feelings and Things' which has a sophisticated harmonic underpinning, but is played in a loose, open ended way, with a very gentle pulse rather than the foregrounded rhythm of 'June the 15'.

By this period in the mid-1960s, Carla Bley and her then husband Michael Mantler were leading the Jazz Composers' Orchestra, which acted as a rather similar meeting point for musicians and ideas to the New Jazz Orchestra in London. It involved some of the leading lights in the New York avant-garde scene, such as Roswell Rudd and Steve Lacy, but also more established players including Ron Carter, Frank

Wess and Lew Tabackin. In 1967, drawing on some of the personnel from this band, Carla Bley composed her extended work *A Genuine Tong Funeral* for Gary Burton's quartet and additional forces. 'I was interested in integrating my playing into larger compositions,' said Gary. 'As a jazz musician you make a choice. Do you find a certain style and stay with it? It can work terrifically well, but the other type of player, of whom I am one, is a restless spirit. As an improviser you can be a musical traveller, trying out any kind of music that you can understand and quickly joining in. We can all of us work with music from different eras and styles and if you have a wanderlust, it will come out. That's what happened to me with this album.'[30]

In many ways *A Genuine Tong Funeral*, Carla Bley's 'Dark opera without words', is a yoking together of 'music from different eras and styles', and nowhere more so than in the final 'New National Anthem/The Survivors' segment, where the formal brass-band-like opening gives way to freedom and then to anarchy, with Gato Barbieri's tenor saxophone wailing over the Burton Quartet's free playing. But *A Genuine Tong Funeral* was just a curtain raiser for Carla Bley's full-scale jazz opera (or as she called it at the time, 'a chronotransduction') *Escalator Over the Hill*, with words by Paul Haines, which was recorded between 1968 and 1971 and finally released that latter year. It is a sprawling work, but several of the characters who have appeared in this chapter take a turn in the spotlight across its three LPs.

When I asked Carla Bley about it, and the musician who sings and plays the role of 'Jack', she said: 'I first saw Jack Bruce with Cream, in San Francisco at Fillmore West. Later, when I saw him again, I went up to him and said, "I just love your record *Harmony Row*." And he said, "Well I just love ... " and he mentioned some album of mine. So I said to myself, "Boy, this guy likes me, I'm gonna use him!" I thought I'd take advantage of his affection. So I just called him on *Escalator Over the Hill*. The first thing I wrote was "Detective Writer Daughter". Paul Haines was living in India and he sent me a page of words, and the very first words were "Detective writer daughter". I went to the piano where I had been working on a piece, and it fit instantly into the piece I was working on. Then I put the page of words on the piano and the rest of the melody came instantly. So I wrote back to Paul and said, "Let's write an opera". And he said "Okay". And then he sent me everything he wrote for the next couple of months, and that's how *Escalator* was born. And "Detective Writer Daughter" was the first piece that was written."[31]

The final version of this song on the album is a vocal dialogue between Carla and Jack, with some aggressive guitar interludes from John McLaughlin. The original idea was that Jack would do the entire vocal, but there was serious distortion on the vocal recording he sent from London, and Carla used her reference track to replace the unusable segments of the original, hence creating a dialogue almost unwittingly. As this suggests, the process of creating *Escalator Over the Hill* was neither quick nor easy. Yet it stands as a document of fusion in more ways than one, with European musicians such as Bruce, McLaughlin and Italian trumpeter Enrico Rava working alongside American counterparts including Charlie Haden, Don Cherry, Leroy Jenkins and Paul Motian. Much as Miles Davis' music of the time did, it suggested that as the 1970s dawned, anything was possible.

16 A TASTE OF FREEDOM

In July 1997, the Cité de la Musique in Paris played host to three days of concerts curated by and featuring Ornette Coleman. At the time I was co-presenting the late night BBC Radio 3 jazz and free music programme *Impressions* with Brian Morton, and our producer decided that I would be the one to head off to France and talk to Ornette for the programme. I'd also meet the pianist Joachim Kühn, who had just released the duo album *Colors*[1] with Ornette, music from which I would hear on the evening of my trip. The other Parisian events included a performance of Coleman's symphonic work *Skies of America*, and a concert with his regular quartet of the time, including the pianist Geri Allen, bassist Charnett Moffett and Ornette's son, Denardo, playing drums. I had never heard Coleman play live, so this seemed a great opportunity both to witness one of the prime movers in free jazz in action and to start to explore his music in more detail.

By the time I arrived for the second day of the series, Ornette was well settled in the French capital, and was in the mood for a lengthy conversation. This might be because in addition to the music on offer, he had invited the French philosopher Jacques Derrida to do an extended interview with him, which was ongoing during my visit. Indeed not only was Derrida talking at length with Ornette, but he'd been asked to read excerpts from his work on stage between sets. When it was eventually published, their discussion – conducted across the three days in a series of short segments and then joined together – was fascinating, and it appears that Ornette was well-versed in many of the tenets of Continental Philosophy, particularly when he steered the discussion towards the relationship between music and language, or indeed language itself.[2]

When Derrida suggests that as a boy born into an Algerian Jewish family whose original language was not French, he can empathize with Ornette as an African American from the southern States, Ornette turns it on its head. He asks whether the language Derrida is now speaking 'interferes' with his thoughts. Does his 'original' language influence those thoughts? This prompts some reflection from Derrida who says that he cannot know if this is the case. Ornette then goes on to give a lucid explanation of 'Ebonics', the concept that African Americans speak a language distinct from current white American English, and that in the United States Black people have always had a 'langue signifiante' – in other words, a parallel mode of communication both packed with meaning and capable of Signifying. Derrida then goes into more detail of his own separation on account of the laws in wartime Algeria that excluded Jews from certain schools, but Ornette counters by saying that Paris is 'the only city in the world where racism does not exist in one's presence'. Maybe the most bizarre moment is when Derrida asks Ornette what he *does* with words: how for example does he choose titles for his pieces? Coleman says that he recently had to attend the funeral of his niece, and viewing the body in its coffin he noticed that somebody had positioned the woman's spectacles over her face. 'I thought of calling it "She is lying dead, and wears spectacles in her coffin". But then I had an idea and called it "Blind Date".'[3] Apart from appearing not to get the joke, the overall experience seems not to have been a pleasant time for Derrida, who later reported that when it came to reading his work in public before Ornette played, 'His fans were so unhappy they started booing. It was a very unhappy event. It was a very painful experience.'[4]

I knew none of this when I zipped across town to La Villette, after leaving the Eurostar at the Gare du Nord, to meet Ornette for the first time. The BBC had recently adopted minidisc as the standard for recording face-to-face interviews, so when I got to Ornette's hotel suite to begin talking to him, I unpacked the machine and a pair of standard BBC microphones. The publicist had told me I had thirty minutes, so I was determined to use every second of the time that I could. But the moment Ornette saw the machine, his eyes lit up. 'I've heard about these,' he said. 'But I've never seen one. What's the quality like?'

I recorded a few seconds of him talking, and then played it back to him through my headphones. 'This is great!' he said. 'And it's so tiny! Far smaller than my Professional Walkman.' And he gestured across to a table where the familiar Sony cassette machine was set out. For the next twenty minutes, he asked for a guided tour of the new minidisc recorder. He needed to know about the edit function, the track marker, and all the other features. When he saw the sticker on the front that read, 'Record up to 320 minutes of music on one MD', Ornette said, 'I have to have one!'

By this time I was worried that I had less than ten minutes left to do the interview. But to my complete astonishment, Ornette suddenly rang down to the front desk and told them we were not to be disturbed until he had finished talking. For the next hour and a half we discussed many aspects of his life and music, and parts of this later became the basis for a five-part series on his work, further extended when I visited his 125th Street headquarters in New York in 2000, and also met many of his fellow musicians and associates.

'I'm constantly trying to do things that are interesting to do musically as well as philosophically and religiously,' he began. 'I'm interested in the human experience, and music is a part of that. But I think the human experience has no set goal, unless that goal is total peace.'[5] Perhaps 'peace' might not be the first thing that springs to mind when listening to Ornette's double quartet on the *Free Jazz* album,[6] or to the high-energy output of his fusion band Prime Time. But offstage, his calm manner and quiet demeanour suggested a man very much at peace with himself and the world. That may not have been true earlier in his career, but what struck me talking to Ornette, and the fellow musicians who had worked with him in the late 1950s and early 1960s as his music coalesced, was that while the direction of travel was different, the starting point was comparable to that of Miles Davis' quintet with Shorter, Hancock, Carter and Williams. There was generally a constant pulse, but the harmonic basis could be suspended or altered, and melodic fragments became the basis for solos.

This was quite succinctly described for me a couple of years later when I went to hear bassist Charlie Haden in duo with pianist Paul Bley (both members of the pioneering 1950s band with Ornette at the Hillcrest Club in Los Angeles) at the Kaplan Penthouse of the Juilliard School of Music in New York. The music was a completely free improvisation, with Bley throwing ideas at Haden, and Charlie trading back developments on them. Talking to the audience between numbers, Paul Bley said, forcefully, at one point in the proceedings, 'Sheet music is the enemy of the creative improviser.' I was sitting next to the pianist Andrew Hill, whom I knew from working on broadcasts with him in London, so I asked him in a whisper what he thought about that. 'I don't know,' he muttered back. 'I'm more worried that I'm playing here with Bobby Hutcherson next month and seeing this crowd, I'm thinking I need to get myself a new tux.'

I caught up with Charlie Haden after the gig to look back at the first time he encountered Ornette, which had been sitting in at an after-hours jam session at the Haig Club in Los Angeles, during the period Gerry Mulligan's quartet was in residence. 'This man came up with a plastic saxophone, and the whole room lit up for me,' he recalled. 'I'd been hearing a way in which I could play without using chord structures, but staying on a certain part of the tune, or staying in a mode, or even creating an entirely new structure. Whenever I tried it, people would get upset, but here I heard somebody actually doing all that. It really startled me.'[7]

This description tallies very much with Ornette's early records, where the elasticity of structure is apparent. But having also had the chance to look at some of the graphic scores that Ornette and Joachim Kühn were using for their Paris concert, it seems that the melodic line has always been all-important in his work. 'When I was learning how bebop is constructed,' Ornette told me, 'I found that I didn't have to transpose to be with the piano. When I found that I could also find notes on the saxophone that were equal to the chords on the piano without being the chords, then I realized I was no longer restricted to doing sequences. When I realized that, I started trying to understand how it worked, in terms of writing music. I started by improvising, but then I took it into writing. I really found that this idea doesn't allow you to compose in sequences. It allows you to compose in what is called in classical music, "movements". It's just a word for making a melody different than the previous melody. So I use "movement" as a way to describe each new melody. A melody may have structures that express themselves at other levels, not just a single line of music, but I also express a musical philosophy that if I'm playing with someone else and they can do better, they have the right to change it.'[8]

While at one level this seems a good starting point for under-standing free improvisation, or indeed a wider notion of 'free jazz', it intrigued me that Ornette had largely come up through a route that was separate from many of the other jazz innovators of the 1950s and 1960s. The idea that Ornette had acquired his knowledge of music in isolation from many of his generation was a topic I discussed with his colleague Dewey Redman, whom he knew in high school and who played with him again in the 1960s. Redman put it down to the horrendous experience of growing up as an African American in Fort Worth, Texas.

'It was known at that time as a redneck town,' he said. 'It was known as "Cow Town" because Fort Worth had the third largest packing centre in the United States – Chicago, Kansas City and then Fort Worth. It was segregated, you were sitting in the back of the bus, going around to find the cafés you could use, being called the "n" word. And at that time it was thought that if you rubbed the head of a Black man you would get good luck. So sometimes you'd be walking down the street with a suit and a tie on, and some white man would come up, and if you were wearing a hat, he'd take it off and rub your head. And then just move off. That was his privilege to do that. Those kinds of things went on. We didn't live in a ghetto, I was raised in a middle-class family, with hard-working parents. But those attitudes were common throughout the South, and they gave rise to the civil rights movement in the sixties, but I'm talking about the forties when Ornette was playing in high school. He was in a band called the Jam Jivers, the trumpet player was named Warnell Goodley, Charles Moffett was in the band, too, and Prince Lasha. And at that time Ornette played like Louis Jordan. I enjoyed his playing and so did everybody else.'[9]

Popular with the local African American audience, when he left high school, Ornette worked with various rhythm and blues bands including those of Silas Green and Pee Wee Crayton. He discovered bebop while he was on the road playing tenor saxophone in such groups, initially in the Texas area. After touring in Louisiana, where he was the victim of a racially motivated attack and his instrument thrown down the street, he largely studied on his own. Although he travelled West as a member of Crayton's band, this self-tuition continued once he settled in Los Angeles, supporting himself by various quite menial jobs in order to study the saxophone in his spare time. It seems that during this period, when he sat in with r'n'b bands they disliked his self-taught attempts to play bebop, yet when he sat in with beboppers, they didn't get what he was trying to do. Charlie Haden remembered that although he was smitten immediately by the originality of Ornette's playing at the Haig Club, 'almost as soon as he started to play, they asked him to stop!'[10]

After that first meeting, Charlie asked around to find out who Ornette was, and was eventually taken along by a fellow musician to a jam where he was scheduled to play. The music went on all night and at nine on Sunday morning, the musicians stumbled out from the darkness of the club into the daylight. Charlie remembered watching people dressed up to the nines going to church, whilst he squeezed into Ornette's little Studebaker with his bass and headed for Coleman's apartment, where they started to play again. 'He had this little one-roomed place and there was music everywhere, on the floors and the chairs and the bed,' recalled Haden. 'I was kind of scared and nervous, but he reached down and picked up a piece of music, and put it on the music stand. He said, "Let's play this". He continued, "I wrote some chord changes here, when I wrote the melody. But after we've played the melody, I want you to make up your own changes. Just listen." I thought to myself, "I'm being given permission to do what I've wanted to do for so long!" Everything just came together. We played all day and all night. I think we took a break to get a hamburger or something, but then we played all the next day.'[11]

In due course, Ornette began practising regularly each afternoon with cornetist Don Cherry, Charlie Haden, and drummer Billy Higgins. Haden and Higgins were members of the quartet led by Paul Bley, at the Hillcrest Club in L.A. 'Somewhere through the third quarter of the second year I was there,' Bley told me, 'Charlie and Billy suggested that we had some friends of theirs sit in as guests. This was not the norm for this club, because we had a jam session night on Mondays with Les McCann, when people could sit in. But because they'd never asked before, I said, "Of course!" So Ornette and Don came on the bandstand. They'd memorized everything, because they had a repertoire of originals. They started to play and the audience left the club with their drinks in hand. Los Angeles is warm at night and they were out on the sidewalk. So I had my Revox tape recorder, and the bartender, and the band, and nobody else. When they started to play I realized that here was a link I'd been looking for, because prior to this time I'd sent for trumpeter Herbie Spanier to come from Toronto, to play totally free improvisations with me. But those didn't involve steady time, despite the lack of harmony, the lack of standards and chord changes and so forth. So we had skipped a stage so to speak, almost jumping ahead to 1964 and the Albert Ayler universe. But this meeting with Ornette was in 1958–9. When they came on the bandstand and played time, although not necessarily four to the bar, and playing free, it was A to Z, not AABA or the other popular Broadway song forms. It didn't take me more than a second to realize that this was the missing link between playing totally free, without any givens, and playing bebop with steady changes and steady time. And the logic of it hit me. They were already doing it, and the best way to learn how to do something is to play with somebody who already can do it. It's how you learn to play fast. You start playing with someone who plays faster than you, they begin the first tune and, guess what – you're playing faster. You can't practise it, because it's not a physical problem, it's a conceptual mental problem. You have to believe it to see it.

'They hit the bandstand. And after the set I walked out the back with Carla, and I said, "What are we gonna do? We've got the quartet with Dave Pike, but if we hire Ornette and Don, we'll probably lose the gig in a week. And we're coming up to the two-year point." Without missing a beat, Carla said, "You have to fire Dave Pike, and bring in Ornette and Don."[12] I admired her lack of hesitancy! So we hired them, and the next day we had our rehearsal in the afternoon and learned ten new tunes – some of Carla's, some of mine, some of Ornette's. And the day after that we had a rehearsal and learned ten more. In six days we had a repertoire of sixty tunes and in ten days we had 100 tunes.'[13]

The theorist, composer, bandleader and educator George Russell had a very similar reaction to Paul Bley's when he first heard Ornette Coleman. After first encountering him at Lenox, Massachusetts, on the quartet's first trip East, he got to know Coleman well, a year or two after the band (without Bley) moved to New York in late 1959. George remembered his thoughts from that Lenox concert, saying, 'He was the first jazz musician to initiate a break with Broadway. He completely disassociated himself from that. He came up with new forms, indigenous forms, forms that were unique and his own. He also brought along new rhythms. I can't say new melodies, because the term for his type of melody is "pan-tonic", that's my term. Any kind of reference to a key would be repeated in another key immediately. Stravinsky did that too, in *Rite of Spring,* so you can't say Ornette was the first! Charles Ives did the same thing. But Ornette is a "pan-modalist". He plays "do-re-me-fa" in all the keys, quickly.'[14]

A year or two later, sitting in George's study in Boston discussing this further, he also talked about his own music, and began explaining the complexities of his life's theoretical work, *The Lydian Chromatic Concept of Tonal Organization.* But when we came back to the topic of his first impressions of Ornette, he was sure that he was in the presence of a musician as formidable and interesting as two remarkable talents with whom he had already worked: Dizzy Gillespie and Miles Davis. He had met Dizzy through Max Roach, after Max took his place in Benny Carter's band in 1944, in which George had been playing drums. 'I went back to 52nd Street, and Max introduced me to Bird and Dizzy, saying 'This guy can write''. Because when I left Benny Carter I threw everything I had into writing.' The upshot, helped by a period of enforced isolation when George was hospitalized with tuberculosis in 1945–6, was the modal section of 'Cubana Be-Cubana Bop', which Dizzy recorded with his big band in December 1947. This was one of the very first examples on disc of a jazz composition based on modes, written for a trumpeter who George knew would immediately grasp what was then a novel harmonic system. After his release from the sanitarium, he also met Miles.

'I got familiar with a trumpet player, and he and I used to go up to his little apartment and sit down at the piano and trade chords. His name was Miles Davis, and something prompted me to ask him what his main aim was. And he said, "To learn all the changes". So I took that away with me. It didn't seem to make sense, because he played like he already knew all the changes. But then something inside my head said to me, "He's really asking for a new way to relate to chords". Then I got the impulse that every chord had a scale. It was just such a unity. There are degrees of unity to be sure, but it was such an iron-clad unity – the scale and the chord being a chord-scale. So I got the idea that I should search for those scales, which led immediately to the Lydian scale being a unity with its tonic major chord. In observing those thoughts, I realized that ideas are real, they're alive! And so the concept mushroomed very rapidly. When I was able to tell Miles about it, early on, it made an impression, but he didn't get into modes deeply until '58 or '59. He tried a lot of other things before that.'[15]

Having talked of his work with Dizzy and Miles, not to mention a long collaboration with the pianist Bill Evans, George relived the thrill he experienced on his first encounter with the Ornette Coleman Quartet at Lenox. 'That fire that I heard that day, when I heard Ornette, doesn't die and isn't diminished.' He recalled how the band appeared to communicate almost telepathically, with no apparent signals or visible preparation before they started playing, yet the quartet 'would instantly play the same melody'. George later shared in Ornette's discovery of the violin, recording some of his very first attempts to play it, including a kind of hoedown, which – transcribed from the tape – later became the basis for George's symphonic composition *Dialogue with Ornette*.

In the mid-1960s, when George was working in Europe with cornetist Don Cherry, whom he'd heard in the Coleman Quartet that day at Lenox, he had some first-hand experience of Ornette's philosophy of 'if you can do better, you have the right to change it' in action. The Russell sextet (with Jan Garbarek and Terje Rypdal) was playing at the huge concert hall in the Tivoli Gardens in Copenhagen, on the same programme as Karlheinz Stockhausen's *Gruppen* for three symphony orchestras. George recalled somewhere around 200 musicians being shoehorned onto the stage, surrounding his little group. 'Rehearsing for this,' George recalled, 'I had to stop Don once, because – as I told him – "You're not playing the melody I wrote". And he replied, "Don't step on *my* melody!" It was said in a threatening, menacing way. So I said, "Okay", thinking there must be something to that. And there was. I realized that what he was doing was embellishing and putting his imprint on the melody, and colouring it, much to my advantage.'

By the time I met Ornette at La Villette in 1997, Don Cherry was no longer with us, having died in October 1995. But when Ornette returned to New York, he took part in a very similar series of concerts to the Paris events, at the Avery Fisher Hall in New York, except that these also included a reunion with Charlie Haden and Billy Higgins, to re-explore the music of his early quartet. Selected to play the trumpet was Wallace Roney. He was an assiduous student of the instrument, with an approach highly sympathetic to that of Ornette, maybe best summed up not long after that Avery Fisher appearance by the American writer Stanley Crouch: 'What one hears is a manipulation of the simple and the complex as well as a conception to improvising in which forms and approaches can be reordered on the spot, allowing the players to redefine melody, harmony and rhythm with the kind of freedom that makes each performance suspenseful, thrilling and unpredictable.'[16]

I was interested to learn more about this when I met Roney, but he quickly turned the conversation to Coleman's own originality as a trumpet player, Coleman having taken the instrument up alongside the violin in the early 1960s. 'One day Ornette took my horn,' he told me. 'He wanted to try out my instrument, and he started playing some stuff that I'd been hearing and trying to play, and I looked at him and said, "How do you do that?" And he just did it again! He could do it. So I said, "Wait a minute!" And he showed me how to do it. And it freed me up, from that point on. This was simultaneous with me playing with Tony Williams, and Ornette helped open the conception of where I was trying to go in what I was already doing. It was amazing that he could do it on my trumpet! And here I am, a trained trumpet player. I play the instrument every day. But when he showed me this, it opened up a whole new thing for me. It was everything I was hearing, wanted to hear and was trying to hear. It wasn't about what he'd studied on trumpet at this point, it was that his ideas, his conception and his knowledge of music overrode the trumpet, or whatever you might think of as "traditional" trumpet playing. And he systematically knew how to do it. Yes, he's a self-taught trumpeter, but he is a great artist. He learned the trumpet in the most natural way and he was able to apply his system.'[17]

Most examples of Ornette playing trumpet are on his own records, but in March 1967 he made an album as a sideman with Jackie McLean for Blue Note, *Old and New Gospel*, which not only demonstrates his trumpet work, but includes two of his original compositions, 'Old Gospel' and 'Strange As It Seems'. Nat Hentoff's liner note rather accurately describes the result – 'the interweaving of Ornette and Jackie is like two simultaneous monologues taking place in each man's mind, and yet emerging as conventional dialogue'.[18]

The idea to put Ornette together with Jackie seems to have come from Alfred Lion and Frank Wolff at Blue Note. 'My contract with Prestige was up in 1956 or so, after I'd done a bunch of albums for them,' recalled Jackie. 'Alfred and Frank came down to one of my gigs and said, "Come and see us at the office, you don't wanna sign with Prestige, you wanna come on over to us!" So I signed with them. They were good in the studio, and I stayed with the Blue Note label ten years. I really enjoyed recording for those guys, and one of the things that happened was that they brought me into a different circle of musicians – everybody that Alfred and Frank liked. So I ended up with people like Blakey and Dexter Gordon, and Ornette.'[19]

The piece 'Old Gospel' draws on gospel rhythms and has a neat choir-like head arrangement. But Ornette's own solo quickly moves into free territory, backed by Lamont Johnson's piano, mainly holding to a single chord, and Billy Higgins managing both to lay down something of a backbeat rhythm and improvise around it at the same time. Ornette continued to double on trumpet and violin for the rest of his career.

Indeed on one of his visits to Britain, in 2005, he celebrated his 75th birthday and the Cheltenham Jazz Festival's 10th anniversary, with a concert in the town's elegant Georgian town hall. I wrote at the time: 'When the diminutive saxophonist took the stage, in a plum-coloured satin suit and pork-pie hat, with his alto slung round his neck, the crowd erupted into the most affectionate welcome I've ever experienced at the festival. Coleman rewarded them with 90 minutes of passionate, intense music, as dazzling, dense and lyrical as at any stage in his long career. The high point was a searing, melancholic "Lonely Woman", with the two double basses of Greg Cohen and Tony Falanga creating a tapestry of plucked sounds beneath him, aided by the colour-istic drums of his son Denardo. Coleman set the tone for the festival with his doubling of instruments – his stabbing high-note trumpet and curi-ous hoedown violin playing.'[20]

The period during which Ornette Coleman recorded for Blue Note under his own name has two distinct highlights. The trio with the virtuoso bassist David Izenzon and Coleman's schoolmate, the drum-mer Charles Moffett, is one, captured in action at the Golden Circle club in Stockholm. For me, however, the finest of his work for the label is the pair of albums *Love Call* and *New York Is Now*, made in the spring of 1968. This brought Ornette (playing mainly alto saxophone but with occasional trumpet) together with John Coltrane's former rhythm sec-tion of bassist Jimmy Garrison and drummer Elvin Jones. The fourth member of the quartet was another of his old friends from Fort Worth, whose description of the town I included earlier, the tenor saxophonist Dewey Redman.

One of the biggest problems when one is recording location interviews in New York is to find places with little or no traffic noise. In the days before 9/11, the place I liked best for this job was the Marriott hotel that stood between the twin towers of the World Trade Center – the back of which overlooked a raised pedestrian concourse, where the only sound was of footsteps and the occasional bicycle bell. It was there on a bright November morning that I caught up with Dewey Redman, looking out over the city, as it glittered in the sunlight. As he took in the roofline and the sky, he told me it reminded him of the time he had met up again with Ornette, not long before those recordings were made. 'I was driving a taxi in San Francisco,' he laughed, 'trying to earn enough money to come to New York. I was at the airport, and I looked up and saw Ornette. He was coming back from Japan, and he was with David

Izenzon and Moffett. So I pulled out of the line of cabs, drove up to them and shouted, "Hey Ornette!" I had to tell the other drivers he was a friend and I hadn't seen him in a long while. He was about to play in a place in San Francisco called the Both/And. So I took him there and he asked, "You still playing?"

'I said, "Yeah."

'So he said, "Bring your horn down."

'So I took my horn down there and gave a good account of myself. And he said, "Come to New York, man."

'I said, "I'm trying, but I'm driving a taxi and ... "

'Anyway I made the effort and before long I moved to New York. Very soon after I got there, we went into the studio to make *New York Is Now*. I walked into Blue Note and there was Ornette, Jimmy Garrison and Elvin Jones, and I realized I wasn't supposed to be there. I mean – these guys? I was scared – to – death! I was literally shaking. What the hell am I gonna do? These men had experience but I had no experience like that. I'd played in San Francisco, but not with this calibre of musician. These were great artists. So I remember Jimmy Garrison came over, and said, "Hey man, you okay?"

'I said, "Jimmy, Jimmy, what am I gonna do man?" I was still shaking. And Jimmy put his arm round my shoulder, took me over into the corner and said, "Hey, man, cool down. Don't do anything you haven't tried to do before, just play. You play good."

'We had had a couple of rehearsals, but it wasn't 'til we were actually there that I realized I might be in big trouble!'[21]

Listening to Dewey's coruscating solo on 'Round Trip' from that album, covering the whole compass of the tenor, incorporating rapidfire runs, picking up small melodic fragments and transposing them in line with Ornette's thinking, and alternating pure sounds with vocal tone and even bass honks, he clearly had nothing to worry about. He was to remain in Ornette's working band for the next six years, and he was later to keep the legacy of this music alive, in the quartet Old and New Dreams, founded in 1976 with Charlie Haden and Don Cherry and either Ed Blackwell or Paul Motian on drums.

If Ornette Coleman had only worked in the context of his quartet or similar small acoustic groups, he would still have been a major figure in jazz. But he explored several other areas of music, such as 'Third Stream' music with Gunther Schuller and John Lewis, so-called 'free-fusion' in his band Prime Time, and also the mystic Sufi tradition from North Africa of the Master Musicians of Joujouka.

Over the years I had the opportunity to discuss the first of these with Gunther Schuller himself several times, and I realized that just as Paul Bley had seen Ornette as the link between bebop and totally free improvisation, Schuller saw him as a musician who could improvise in an atonal context. Prior to their collaboration on the 1960 work *Abstraction*, Schuller felt that his own attempts to bring contemporary classical music and jazz together had foundered because even such consummate masters of extemporization as John Lewis and Milt Jackson, with whom he had worked, 'were always basically tonal improvisers'.[22] By comparison, he said, 'Ornette was something of a godsend to me, because he understood my language and I understood his language, so we could improvise and compose together.' *Abstraction*[23] is not an easy listen, but it perfectly demonstrates Schuller's point that Ornette's solos dovetailed very effectively with the composed material played by a string ensemble, guitarist Jim Hall and drummer Sammy 'Stix' Evans.

When I worked in New York in the 1980s, I played a few times with a traditional jazz band at the Cajun jazz club at 129 8th Avenue in New York's Chelsea district, and Stix Evans was the drummer. In the breaks, we chatted a lot about jazz, and his experiences, and we both particularly enjoyed one particular session when the legendary Casa Loma Orchestra clarinettist Clarence Hutchenrider came and played a set with us, his limpid tone and creative ideas undiminished by the passing years. But I had no idea at the time that Stix had worked with Ornette, so we never ever talked about it. Equally when I played with the drummer Wes Landers in New Orleans around the same time, I failed to ask him about the three years he had spent playing hard bop with Gene Ammons in Chicago. In both cases I made the false assumption that because both drummers were masterly players of old-style jazz, it was, and always had been, their main interest.

The interplay between two drummers became an interest of Ornette's in the 1970s. His own Third Stream piece *Skies of America* includes a battle between a kit drummer and a timpanist in the movement 'The Artist in America' and his fusion band Prime Time had both Denardo Coleman and drummer Calvin West from its late 1970s incarnation onwards. However, for me the most interesting album by this band is its first, namely *Dancing in Your Head*. On this Prime Time's then (and sole) drummer Shannon Jackson can be hard interacting with the Master Musicians of Joujouka and their pounding percussionists on the track 'Midnight Sunrise'. The band was playing in Tangier in the 1970s when Coleman, who was on an extended visit to North Africa, first heard them, and on 'Midnight Sunrise' his alto was superimposed on their traditional instruments rather as it was over symphonic accompaniment in his and Schuller's Third Stream ventures. 'I don't know if he heard something special in them,' Denardo Coleman reflected when I asked him about that first Moroccan visit. 'Maybe it confirmed something he was already thinking about. This was because they were playing non-Western instruments and playing music that was not entertainment, but for spiritual purposes and healing. These musicians live to play music.'[24]

Thirty-six years later, in 2009, the association with the Master Musicians was still alive, because when Ornette curated London's South Bank 'Meltdown' Festival, he brought the band to the Royal Festival Hall. They were, as I wrote at the time, 'playing what William Burroughs described as "4,000-year-old rock'n'roll" on raucous rhaita oboes and tebel drums. We had to wait until the finale for them to be reunited [with Coleman], in a long rambling piece over which the bassist Al McDowell and Coleman superimposed the 'Lonely Woman' theme, but which nobody had quite worked out how to finish. Coleman's increasingly desperate attempts at an exit strategy were ignored by the Master Musicians, becoming ever more trancelike until, finally, their charismatic leader Bachir Attar half turned to catch Ornette's eye and they subsided into silence. [In the same concert] when Patti Smith joined in with Ornette's quartet to sing Coleman's 'In All Languages', his fundamental point about music as a meeting of cultures had already been made convincingly.'[25]

Burroughs is important in Coleman's work not only as he had been present at the 1973 recording of 'Midnight Sunrise', but also because, in 1991, Ornette contributed to the soundtrack of David Cronenberg's film *Naked Lunch*, based on Burroughs' novel. This soundtrack draws together three strands in Ornette's music – his own small group, the Master Musicians and a symphony orchestra, in this case playing a score written by Howard Shore.

'I re-read the book,' Shore told me, 'and made note of any musical references in the book. But actually there weren't very many. Burroughs talks about cocaine bebop, but there weren't really many strong references to music. So I started thinking more about locale. I was thinking bebop, New York, late '50s (*when* the book was written) and I was thinking Morocco and North Africa (*where* the book was written). I asked myself if there was a connection between those two, and I thought of Ornette, and "Midnight Sunrise", which he recorded outside of Tangier. I also thought of Charlie Parker, and went back and found the Dean Benedetti informal recordings of him, which were really interesting. There's not much on the Benedetti recordings except Parker, so I started looping the recordings and writing to that. The Parker is very fast, those tempos are really quick, and I used that as a kind of guide, not so much the tonality of it, more just the sound. The pieces that I wrote for the score to *Naked Lunch* are orchestral pieces, but most of them are quite slow – tangos and very exotic sounding orchestrations. But I used the Parker almost like one sound, it wasn't so much playing to what I was writing, it was this other sound. I called Ornette, asked him if he was interested in the project, and he was. He was in Copenhagen at the time, but we got together in London, where the recording took place. We did about a week's preliminary work, with the sketches I had written for the score, using the piano, and then started the recording project with the London Philharmonic, which went on for about five days.'[26]

The results in the film itself are dramatic and remarkable enough, but in 2001 at London's Barbican Hall, Ornette's trio with Denardo on drums and Charnett Moffett (Charles' son) on bass, plus Howard Shore and the BBC Concert Orchestra, the music was played live to a projection of the film in which only the dialogue was retained (although subtitled) from the soundtrack. It was part of a two-day celebration of Ornette's music. His trio plus singers (both traditional and operatic) played a long concert on the evening before the projection of the movie.

I've been to plenty of live music events in that London hall, and numerous film screenings in the Barbican complex as well, but there was a buzz about the *Naked Lunch* event that I've never experienced on any other occasion. There were movie buffs, jazz fans and classical music aficionados, all there to support their particular favourite element of the performance, and the foyer was awash with excited, buzzing conversations about this genuinely multi-media show. I wrote afterwards that 'Music, moving image, and the sense of occasion came together to make this an exceptional event.' And I recalled the way that (without the

Master Musicians themselves) Ornette conjured up some of the sound of their music, together with the orchestra, and equally successfully evoked Burroughs' sense of 'cocaine bebop'.[27]

In parts of the original soundtrack for *Naked Lunch*, Ornette's alto can be heard improvising over the written segments. How had Howard Shore reconciled what Gunther Schuller called Ornette's 'atonal language' with his predominantly tonal orchestral writing?

'I think what happened in performance at the original recording,' he said, 'was that he would zero in on certain players in the orchestra, and he treated the orchestra as if it was a jazz group. Because when he plays in his jazz group, everybody's equal and everybody's playing equally. And orchestral players are the antithesis of that. They are all watching the conductor, which was me, in this case, and sticking to the written parts. They're, in effect, following, and he wants to play *with* them as if they're improvising. So the performance as a whole became something created between my performance with them, his reacting to them, and his different reactions to them as members of a group. Sometimes he would do a take and he would play with the viola, sometimes he'd do a take where he played with the bass clarinet, or he'd find that something in the percussion was interesting, so he'd zero in on that, and improvise with what they were doing, even though they were playing written parts.'[28]

Unlike Schuller's work, which was about finding a common musical language between his classical players and Ornette's solos from the outset, Shore's sections of the soundtrack functioned much more like an improvised concerto grosso, with Ornette and his trio as the concertino and the orchestra playing the scored parts of the ripieno. By contrast Ornette's fusion group Prime Time is all about jazz musicians playing equally, but nonetheless creating an environment for Ornette to shine as a soloist. Yet it has some similarities to the work both with Schuller and with Shore, as Denardo Coleman told me: 'He wanted to set it up like an orchestra, except people weren't confined to certain roles. So he has two bass players. Now, normally a bass player takes a particular role, providing support for the rest of the group. But if you have two, somebody can play support while the other plays more of a lead role, and then they can reverse. Eventually Prime Time became lead roles for everybody! That's how he started thinking about it, with everybody playing the lead.'[29]

At its best, Prime Time can be fascinatingly original, but there are also undoubted moments of chaos. Maybe its most distinctive characteristic is the consistently memorable melodic material which most of the band's repertoire uses as a starting point. One musician who has a lot of time for this aspect of Prime Time is guitarist Pat Metheny, who collaborated with Ornette himself. His interest in Coleman's music came up during a long conversation about his life's work that I had with Pat at his studio in midtown Manhattan, and he told me that what he treasured most was Ornette's melodic imagination. 'He is one of *the* generators of hooks, that can rival any pop composer. All of his tunes always have something about them that really sticks out as an identifying characteristic. He's got an unbelievable melodic skill, and as far out as Ornette is perceived by a lot of people, it's always mystified me a little bit, because the essential thing about him is the song form. And there's a tune-like quality that almost all of his improvisations have.'[30]

In December 1985, by which point Ornette had been playing predominantly in Prime Time for the best part of a decade, Metheny brought him back into the acoustic jazz sphere, with their collaboration *Song X*.[31] It put the pair of them together with Charlie Haden and Jack DeJohnette, along with Denardo Coleman playing additional percussion. It followed some gigs earlier that year at the Village Vanguard, where Pat had been playing in a trio with Charlie Haden and Billy Higgins, and Ornette had come down to hear them. He suggested to Pat that they should work together, and a little later Pat called him to make the record, which was his debut for the Geffen label. He told me that experiencing the unique chemistry in the studio between Charlie and Ornette made him feel almost like a fan as much as a fellow player. Jack DeJohnette had also been playing often with Pat and Charlie, so he joined what Pat called his 'regular rhythm section' for a record 'unlike anything either of us had ever done before'. Ornette and Pat worked together for several days prior to the record date, playing for hours, not least, as Pat said, to create a role for his guitar that was that of 'an equal front-line instrument'. He singled out the track 'Endangered Species' as his favourite, and something unlike anything else in either his or Ornette's catalogue of work.

Charlie Haden may not have recorded with Ornette during the Prime Time years before *Song X*, but he assured me that he'd never lost contact with Ornette and on every occasion they were both in New York at the same time, they found space to play with one another. However, by the time of the matched pair of 1996 *Sound Museum* albums, *Three*

Women and *Hidden Man*, Ornette was working regularly with another bassist, Charnett Moffett. The quartet for those records also included Denardo on drums, and – a new departure for his acoustic bands – Geri Allen on piano.

Although there had been a keyboard player, Dave Bryant, in Prime Time, Ornette told me the reason that he had not had a pianist in his acoustic quartet since the Paul Bley days was that most jazz pianists adopted the traditional rhythm section role. That was not what he wanted, but he heard something in Geri Allen's work that he realized was more in keeping with his Harmolodic theory. She got the call to join him in 1994 for a concert in Germany. 'For that particular concert, I didn't rehearse very much at all with him,' she remembered. 'The trio of Ornette, Denardo and Charnett had been playing together for some years, so there was a real cohesiveness already there, and I had to find my way in really quickly, to find a space, and not reduce what was already there. That was my goal. Working in this context I was trying to expand, trying to make something more as opposed to being restrictive ... To be in this atmosphere in the years since has meant that his ideas about the piano have really expanded my way of thinking about music.'[32]

I was interested that Geri had not rehearsed much before that first concert, because I knew that in those subsequent years she had put in a lot of work. Indeed, even though the fourth member of the quartet, Charnett Moffett, had grown up with Coleman's music, his father having played drums with Ornette at several points, and his very name being a fusion of 'Charles' and 'Ornette', he knew it was necessary to put in plenty of backroom time to play at the highest level in this band. 'We spent a lot of time rehearsing, which was very necessary, because Ornette is such a genius at his artistry that you really need to be prepared 100%. He gives you that freedom, but that very freedom is done with a structure, and a concept. It's not just "Get on stage and do whatever you want." You have to express yourself within the context at hand, which requires a lot of practice and chemistry to take place. So we spent time rehearsing and then we went on tour, playing in Europe, mostly, and actually not very much in the United States.'[33]

The separate career and life commitments that Geri Allen had, particularly after she won the Danish Jazzpar Prize in 1996, the same year as the *Sound Museum* albums were recorded, meant that although her connection with Ornette continued, she was never a regular member of his band in the same way as Charnett and Denardo. Nonetheless, she is one of the few musicians for whom Ornette appeared as a sideman, on one of her albums. At the end of 1995 he joined her at the Clinton Studios on 10th Avenue in New York City to record their joint compositions 'Vertical Flowing' and 'The Eyes Have It', on her CD *Eyes . . . In the Back of Your Head*. When I asked her to pick her favourite back catalogue items for a live recording of my *Jazz Library* programme at the Purcell Room during the 2010 London Jazz Festival, she chose one of those tracks, saying, 'Isn't that something? And that sound he has – I think that's really pure. A pure conception. It's like a voice, when you hear him. And when he plays something, you want to answer that question or statement that's being made.'[34] After we played the track, I wondered if she could look back for me on her years working with Ornette. She said, 'I'm really very grateful for that experience of having played with him, and being in his band. It's an honour, I learned so much from watching his abilities. It's a mastership of such completely being true to who you are, mixed with a fearless kind of brilliance. It was a very thrilling experience for me.' Before we left this period of her work to move on to later albums I had one more question: Did she understand his theory of Harmolodics? There was a huge laugh, and then she said, 'I just opened my ears and I prayed!'

In fact it was when Geri was expecting her son Wallace IV that Coleman first asked Joachim Kühn to play with him. Ornette recalled: 'I had a job in Verona, and I had been using Geri Allen along with Charnett and Denardo, but she couldn't travel, and so I called Joachim to play that job with me. He asked me to play with him before that job, and that set the tone for the true interests that we had in common. I had listened to his playing and the one thing that was unique about it was most pianists play the piano in a pop style – in other words, they play chords, and they're always put in the situation where they have to be the support. But Joachim doesn't play like that. He plays in a truly orchestrated concept. And the piano is basically designed to do that – you know if you have a symphony, you can play all the parts? Well he plays the piano individually like that. And that alone made me more comfortable writing the music for us to play, since I had been writing for different musical settings.'

While I was upstairs in Ornette's Paris hotel room, having our long conversation, Joachim Kühn was patiently waiting in the lobby for me to talk to him. He had no idea why I was taking so long, but he was very gracious when I finally arrived. At least I was able to make it up to him the following year at the Bath Festival Jazz Weekend, where before his solo appearance the following day, we not only chatted in a more relaxed way over a few drinks, but went to a couple of concerts together. That year in Bath he played a stunning solo set, but nothing quite like his duo with Ornette at Cité de la Musique, which was a very special event. In our snatched conversation in Paris, during the limited time left before he had to set off for the hall, I realized that if I had been a bit star-struck meeting one of my musical heroes, it was nothing compared to his experience of being invited to play with Ornette – a musician he had admired since childhood. 'When I was fourteen, I first heard his music in East Germany,' he said. 'He played jazz without chord changes and his freedom of expression really meant something to us. I knew I wanted to spend my life with this man's music, but it's taken forty years for us finally to work together.'[35]

And it's Joachim who has the final words in this chapter. We were discussing the whole business of playing jazz, of performing in the moment, when he suddenly turned to me, looked me straight in the eye and said with the utmost seriousness, 'Life itself is an improvisation.'

17 LOOKING BACK AND LOOKING FORWARD

When my broadcasting career took off in earnest in the 1990s, I had less time for playing live jazz, and for much of that decade I only managed to do so occasionally. Leaving full-time publishing to become a freelance commissioning editor of music books, plus working as a newspaper critic and presenting radio shows that, between them, took me to many of the UK's leading concert halls, as well as to overseas festivals, left little time for keeping up the bass to a high standard, and travelling to gigs in far off places. Fortunately, living near Oxford, there was always a local demand for classical bassists, and thankfully, despite not playing much jazz in the 1990s, I was lucky to keep my hand in on the instrument (and practise my sight-reading) by playing with several orchestras, particularly one that was based in Sutton Courtenay, near Abingdon.

Although that village is best known as the last resting place of George Orwell, it has a thriving choral society. At the time, the All Saints Singers were coached by the former operatic soprano April Cantelo, whose stunning talent in turning a relatively small group of amateur village singers into a professional-sounding chorus was little short of miraculous. She also coaxed some of her professional colleagues to join us as soloists. Haydn masses, Bach passions, Telemann oratorios, and much more fell easily within the orbit of this stimulating group. April's work, along with that of the conductor Patrick Salisbury and his orchestra, led to some marvellous concerts, culminating in Patrick's 2008 retirement performance of Mozart's version of Handel's *Messiah*. That turned out also to be my last appearance with the orchestra, because by then I had returned to playing jazz.

At the end of the 1990s, an old colleague of mine, Bill Greenow, who lived successively in Stockholm and Paris, returned to the UK and coaxed me back to play in his band. Bill had always been a very accomplished clarinettist and saxophonist (indeed back in the 1970s and early 1980s he had played on the Freddie Kohlman and Don Ewell London sessions mentioned previously) but during his years in France, he had fallen in love with the soprano saxophone, and the sound of Sidney Bechet. His band Rue Bechet, which he asked me to join, focused on this repertoire. Not only did we play many of the pieces that Bechet had created during his years in France in the 1950s, such as 'A moi d'payer', 'Un coup de cafard' and 'As-tu le cafard?', but with the vocalist Katherine Lanham and the French accordionist Maryse Edon, we also took songs from the Charles Trenet and Georges Brassens chanson repertoire, and interpreted them as Bechet might have done.[1]

As well as our regular pianist Martin Litton (who later joined the Buck Clayton Legacy Band) and guitarist Jez Cook, we were often joined by the drummer Stan Greig and trombonist Bob Hunt. Stan was also a first-rate pianist and composer who had worked with Sandy Brown, Ken Colyer, Humphrey Lyttelton and Acker Bilk, as well as leading his own big band. He was a link back to the early days of the traditional jazz revival in Britain, and never lost his enthusiasm for the music. He told us he loved the chance to play drums again with Bill, as by this time he mostly worked as a pianist. His drumming, inspired by the New Orleans veteran Zutty Singleton, fitted the band perfectly. Bob – who went on to be the arranger and organizing force behind the Big Chris Barber Band – was one of the most accomplished exponents of the Ellingtonian trombone style pioneered by 'Tricky Sam' Nanton. In the two-piece front line with Bill, he produced some scintillating playing. All of us shared Bill's enthusiasm for this band and for exploring lesser-known elements of Bechet's considerable legacy. We also gave an airing to some of Stan's original compositions as well as seldom-played pieces by American musicians with whom Bill had worked, such as the trumpeter Johnny Letman.

A particularly memorable tour with Bill's Rue Bechet band took us to Anduze, in the South of France, known as the 'Gateway to the Cevennes', from where we set out to play a number of concerts in the Languedoc. Playing in rural France was a reminder of what a vital ingredient of French cultural consciousness Bechet's music had been. I remember hearing his records quite frequently on jukeboxes in Paris in the early 1970s, but thirty-five years later, our audiences, made up of people of all ages, still sang along to the tunes and shouted back the traditional audience response in 'Les oignons'. Stan Greig was our pianist on that trip, shortly before his playing career was brought to a sudden halt by Parkinson's disease. He and I shared a small flat in Anduze for the week, and it was a great experience not only to spend time together listening to his myriad stories of the heyday of traditional jazz in Britain, but also to hear his sparkling piano at its very best every night. Stan's boogie-woogie playing was the closest I ever experienced to working with Sammy Price, which maybe goes to show that whether you grow up in Edinburgh or Texas, it's the instinctive feel for the music that matters.

From Bill Greenow's group I went on, with Matthias Sueffert, to found the Buck Clayton Legacy Band, and in just the same way as Bill had explored lesser-known elements of Bechet's work, we were – as I mentioned in Chapter 5 – able to play music that Buck had written, but in many cases not managed to record himself. Once the band was established, we realized that this was a suitable-sized ensemble for investigating various other elements of the swing repertoire. How might Buck and his fellow musicians have tackled a variety of different music from that period? The first chance to find out followed some broadcasts with the young British singer Gwyneth Herbert.

She had made quite a stir on the British jazz scene when, following a well-received debut album, she was signed up first by Universal and then by Blue Note. Eventually she opted to stay with neither of these major labels, so as to pursue her own musical ambitions, rather than surrender control to a large organization. Her work took an extremely original turn in 2012, when she became artist in residence at Aldeburgh in Suffolk, and composed a set of songs exploring connections between music and the sea, designed to involve members of the audience as everything from the women of Alderney to pirates! Yet, while her own work was moving away from her jazz roots, she continued listening to those musical heroines who had originally drawn her into singing. She told me, 'I loved the way Anita O'Day appears in the movie *Jazz on a Summer's Day*, her hands up in the air, shifting tempo so effortlessly. And then I would listen to Peggy Lee and her storytelling, playing with timing, or Nina Simone's ability to condense and compress a story in song.'[2]

Four years before her Aldeburgh *Sea Cabinet* show took shape, I had been looking for someone to discuss some of the great jazz singers for my *Jazz Library* series on BBC Radio 3, in order to suggest their essential records. Following a couple of earlier interviews about her own work, I knew Gwyneth had the knack of speaking cogently on the radio, so from late 2008, she joined me for several editions of the show. We covered, among others, Ella Fitzgerald, Dinah Washington, Nina Simone and Peggy Lee. Talking, over a bottle of Pinot Grigio, after recording the Peggy Lee programme, we found that both of us particularly liked some of Lee's lesser-known songs. Somehow or other, by the time we set off for our respective trains and buses, we had decided to put together a collection of these, and to perform them with the Clayton Legacy Band (which proved to be ideal to recreate backing charts by the likes of Quincy Jones, Jack Marshall and Billy May). In just the same way as Bill Greenow had found new things to explore in Bechet's music, we found equal riches in Peggy Lee's songbook. Along with our loyal public, others liked the show too, including the critic and author Duncan Heining, who seems to have had as good a time at our 2012 London Jazz Festival show as we did, when he described it thus: 'One of the most purely enjoyable affairs of the festival ... It was great fun – a collection of great songs associated with Lee, including a marvellous "Is That All There Is?" delivered with love and joy.'[3]

We did the Peggy Lee programme – which we called 'Life is for Living' – on and off for a couple of years, appearing at several major jazz clubs and at the Gateshead Jazz Festival.[4] On the back of it, we developed a second show, exploring Buck Clayton's musical connections with Billie Holiday. For this, among other examples of her work, Menno Daams and our trombonist Adrian Fry took some of the orchestral arrangements from Holiday's album *Lady in Satin*, and reconfigured them for a small group, similar to those in which Buck and Teddy Wilson had backed her in the late 1930s. After launching this 'Buck and Billie' programme at one of Britain's finest and most supportive jazz clubs, the Watermill, in Dorking, Gwyneth's own burgeoning career made it too difficult for her to commit to further dates with us, so another fine British singer-songwriter, Julia Biel, further developed this concert package with the band.[5]

At the same time, we began exploring some of the arrangements that Buck himself had produced for blues singer Jimmy Rushing, and paired them up with Ernie Wilkins' charts for Big Joe Turner, thereby creating a show exploring the Kansas City Blues shouting tradition. We were fortunate that Michael Roach, an African American blues singer from Washington DC, who lives in Britain, and has delved deeply into the history of the music, joined us to tackle this repertoire with skill and conviction. Michael was featured on several of our festival appearances, including Swansea and Cheltenham, and he also broadcast with us from Dame Cleo Laine's annual Garden Season from the Stables at Wavendon.

'Making a documentary series in 2003 for BBC Radio 4 called *Deep Blue*,' recalled Michael, 'I interviewed Jay McShann back in his house in Kansas City. He was talking about Big Joe Turner, and how, back in the day, he would come into a club and would just spit out lyrics one behind another. He would improvise, going for about a half hour, just singing lyric after lyric, and we aimed to do some of these kinds of songs that Joe Turner was known for. I grew up listening to Big Joe Turner, and also Jimmy Rushing, who was very popular in African American music collectors' circles. You'd go through anybody's record collection and you always saw Jimmy Rushing or Jimmy Witherspoon – the two Jimmys I call them! So I was always very familiar with the sound – but not in the context of me being a participant. So bringing these songs to life was a new experience for me.'[6]

Playing with a regular band but also adding additional musicians, both to expand the musical palette and to delve into almost forgotten areas of jazz history, has been one of the most rewarding aspects of the last few years. In the relentless quest by festivals, record companies and broadcasters to present the very latest music, up-and-coming musicians, or one-off projects, there's the danger that so much rewarding (and as Duncan Heining pointed out, very enjoyable) music might be lost. I have revelled in bringing this repertoire back to life and seeing just how effectively it works with present-day audiences as it did back when it was first created. This also gives a sense of purpose and creative direction to my other work as a jazz historian.

There's a similar buzz about the most recent musical project (at the time of writing) that I've been involved in as a player, which was temporarily put on hold by the Covid-19 pandemic. This has been a return to my New Orleans roots, as discussed in the first chapters of this book. In 2018, I was asked to join a specially assembled quintet at the Davos/Klosters Sounds Good Festival in Switzerland, fronted by the drummer Emile Martyn (the son of Barry Martyn who led the Legends of Jazz back in the 1970s). The band was modelled on the George Lewis Ragtime Band, and it featured the brilliant clarinettist Adrian Cox. All of us had grown up immersed in these sounds, and suddenly here I was, back playing the very music with which I had started out. Before the festival was over, we had agreed that this band was something we wanted to continue, and so the idea grew – once again – to explore a neglected area of the repertoire. We seized on the *Jazz at Vespers* album that Lewis had made at the Holy Trinity Episcopal Church in Oxford, Ohio, on 21 February 1954, and which gathered together gospel songs, spirituals and hymns, which had underpinned the early jazz tradition.

We wondered if it might be possible to play all our concerts in churches, or former churches that were now arts centres or concert halls, where we could work completely acoustically with no amplification. To start with, we were booked into a number of former places of worship, as far afield as Devon and Cornwall.[7] I took on the leadership of the band, and with my 'New Orleans Friends' we began the tour, appropriately enough, sixty-five years after Lewis' original recording, at the church of St John the Evangelist in Oxford, England, which has become one of the city's main concert venues. For this we were joined by my colleague from the Freddie Kohlman days, the pianist Richard Simmons, who still lives up to Freddie's billing as the 'most swinging piano player in London'.

I think we all felt an emotional shiver or two as this wonderful music reverberated around the old church, and never more so than in one of the spirituals, when a group of Ghanaian exchange students suddenly started singing along, their voices adding to the instruments of the band in a thrilling climax of sound. After joining in on further numbers, they told us later that they had learned these songs at their Missionary School in Accra, and had never expected to hear them played in Oxford. We were all touched by a review of the event that said, 'this concert straddled the religious and the secular beautifully and all with great reverence for the man who inspired it'.[8] We were able to bring this programme to the London Jazz Festival in November 2019, where we realized that we could attract a full house to the Pizza Express Jazz Club in Soho playing music that looked back to the very earliest days of jazz and its roots in gospel. It is inspiring that it still touches audiences today as powerfully as it did sixty-five years ago, or more.

Yet at the same time, the last decade has also been one of the most exciting and innovative periods in the development of jazz in its history. One major benefit of being out on the festival circuit with my various bands has been the chance to catch up with a wide spectrum of other musicians and hear their music. Alongside long-established figures, such as Cleo Laine, Debbie Harry (with the Jazz Passengers), Joe Lovano and Mike Stern, this has brought us into green rooms and concert venues with the likes of Tord Gustavsen, Robert Glasper, Gregory Porter, Zoë Rahman, John Scofield, and Yazz Ahmed. Additionally, my ongoing work for the BBC has similarly kept me aware of many other current developments in jazz. Since 2012 I have presented the long-running *Jazz Record Requests* on BBC Radio 3, and every week is an education from listeners about music that they have discovered and want to share with a wider audience.

In 2016, I began a three-and-a-half-year run in charge of Radio 3's weekly concert series *Jazz Now*, as executive producer. On the one hand this offered the opportunity to be at the cutting edge of technology, so a fifteen-month project following the Dutch-based trio Tin Men and the Telephone, who use a smartphone app to dictate the course of their live performances, culminated in a live broadcast from Birmingham Conservatoire with somewhere in the region of 10,000 listeners online, helping to shape the very concert they were hearing on air. It was certainly one of the very first (if not *the* first) live, fully interactive, jazz concerts ever to be broadcast on the BBC. On the other hand, the *Jazz Now* series allowed us to bring music from many parts of the world to the radio audience, and to offer a national platform for new music. As well as many American artists who are seldom heard in the UK, we featured two bands led by the Danish drummer Mikkel Hess, the big band fronted by his fellow Danish percussionist Marilyn Mazur, the experimental Swiss trio Schnellertollermeier, the perpetually inventive French bassist Henri Texier, and Belgian multi-instrumentalist Esinam.

Editorially, such an opportunity is a fine balancing act, but working with a very flexible and open-minded production team, alongside our presenters, Soweto Kinch, Emma Smith and Al Ryan, who constantly suggested fresh sounds or artists to be featured, we could keep one eye on the jazz tradition, and the other firmly fixed on the new. My own passion for and belief about jazz, that it is a living, breathing art-form where a century or more of tradition extends forward into music that is as experimental today as Louis Armstrong and Sidney

Bechet must have seemed in the 1920s, was borne out by that series. We were as wholeheartedly committed to the broadcasts we did with such keepers of the flame as Lee Konitz, Chuck Israels, and Benny Golson, as to the shows by Tomeka Reid, Makiko Hirabayashi, Iro Haarla, Marc Ribot, Tim Berne, Dave Douglas, Ambrose Akinmusire and Vijay Iyer. And we also offered a platform to the generation of young British musicians who are changing the way jazz is heard in the UK, such as trumpeter Sheila Maurice-Grey, the all-female band Nerija, saxophonist Nubya Garcia, the duo Binker and Moses, and pianist Ashley Henry.

If one musician whom we featured more than once on *Jazz Now* epitomizes both what that series aimed to do and my own belief in the continuity of jazz and the positive future for the tradition, it is the African American trumpeter Theo Croker. Having grown up in Florida and studied at Oberlin, he spent several years in Shanghai. There he widened his musical influences and experiences and worked both in jazz and blues club residencies (including the jazz bar of what is now the Fairmont Peace Hotel) and in the house band of a late night television show. He then played and toured alongside the singer Dee Dee Bridgewater, and in 2016 released his fourth studio album *Escape Velocity*, which took him from a relatively low profile to considerable international attention. When we last met, he was in London playing music from his subsequent Grammy-nominated album *Star People Nation*. This record spans a wide spectrum of music, reflecting the breadth of Croker's own career, and encompassing tracks as varied as one featuring the Jamaican reggae artist Chronixx and another with ELEW (pianist Eric Lewis) paying tribute to drummer Elvin Jones.

I wondered if he had been surprised by the success of *Escape Velocity*, and he replied, 'Any time instrumental music does well, it's a bit of luck. But I think the times are changing and younger people are getting more aware of the power of music without words, or the power of the music that supports words. I think people are getting keener to be more involved in all the layers involved in music, instead of just the surface of it.'[9]

He went on to discuss how much he had learned from working with such a seasoned artist as Dee Dee Bridgewater, gaining experience in everything from both the practical and aesthetic aspects of touring, to the business of putting together an album. 'She taught me how to produce a record myself, without needing any kind of external support from somebody, and then how to license it. I think this is something very important in our community, especially the Black community in America, to own our music and own our property. She also taught me how not to be afraid to push all the musical boundaries that I wanted to cross. I don't mean boundaries within the music itself, I mean the genre, or the market. So I learned not to worry about that so much and to put everything I have into the record. It's specially important to remember that jazz, or what they call jazz, has always been experimental music. The tradition has always been pushing forward, breaking boundaries, incorporating other things, or crossing over into other types of popular music. Jazz has always been the foundation of anything popular. So it's never been about withholding a tradition, but it has been about knowing your lineage as a musician, and knowing your history, so you can then say something informed.'

Theo Croker certainly knows his jazz history. Among those who taught him was the trumpeter Donald Byrd. 'He had one of the most beautiful sounds and great bebop chops, but he was also a great bandleader and composer. He was a really good educator. He helped me connect a lot of dots, musically – things I didn't understand harmonically and theoretically. He really played a big role in that for me, and taught me a couple of really effective ways to write music without getting in your own way. He wasn't playing that much when I knew him, but I used to sit in front of him and wonder "How did you play like that?" And so he would teach me things that I would have learned from Dizzy, or tell me things I would have learned from Freddie Hubbard or Lee Morgan, because he knew all these cats, and he was really able to pass a lot of that stuff on.

'The other end of the spectrum for me was Roy Hargrove, who to me was one of the most masterful jazz improvisers. His sound is beautiful, his ballad playing is amazing – he's one of the few people, if not the only one, I've ever heard play two ballads in a row. His vocabulary is huge: funk, r'n'b, bebop. He was one of the few cats who was *really* playing bebop among trumpet players from that generation.[10] He was just so musical, one of a select group of exceptional trumpeters along with Jon Faddis, Wynton Marsalis and Marcus Belgrave. Roy was the prime definition of a true educated jazz man. He knew the lineage, he knew the history, yet he knew what was going on right at the present moment, and he could draw on all of that, whether he was playing "Girl From Ipanema" (which I have heard him do), or an r'n'b cover. It doesn't matter. With him it stayed consistent, the reach and depth of his artistry.'

Hearing the Theo Croker Quartet in London, where the focus was consistently on his own eloquent and full-toned trumpet sound, the lessons from these masterly players are ones he has learned well, but he also features his own original music. He told me that he took a break from composing and producing after *Escape Velocity*, because it had been a draining experience to create the album. So he spent 2017 and 2018 focusing on his own trumpet playing, which gradually became the inspiration for *Star People Nation*. "I wanted my trumpet voice to be the main storyteller – not the main character, but the main storyteller, kind of like the narrator. And as I wrote, I felt that, as an artist, I had to keep moving forward. So every time I arrived at something that sounded even a little like *Escape Velocity*, I had to break away and go in another direction.'

And yet, although on the finished result the trumpet is indeed the storyteller, the composing process was anything but straight-forward, and Theo spent time telling me how he had used samples – for instance, one from a Bobby Hutcherson record, one from his own piano playing – as the basis for tracks that he then built up electronic-ally, little by little, until he was ready to bring the band into the studio to play them live. Having kept the same line-up in place for some years with pianist Michael King, bassist Eric Wheeler and drummer Kassa Overall (as well as saxophonist Irwin Hall, who was not with them in London), he feels that they know each other well enough to be able to play on stage or in the studio with the minimum of preparation.

'I like for the musicians to not really know what's coming. In the studio I want the rawest, most natural live feeling I can get, because too much work on a song can get stale. On the road, the way I avoid any kind of stiffness, or sameness from playing similar repertoire, is I don't tell them the set-list. When we play a show, they don't know what song we're going to play. Sometimes when I start it, they don't know what it is yet, which keeps them on their feet, but I also allow them to bring any type of interpretations to a song. I never want a song to sound the same way. Compositionally, when I write there are some specifics – the bass-line, the melody – but this means that when we play, it's all familiar enough, no matter what we do with it. You can't change somebody's penmanship, but the guys that have been working with me have been playing with me for so long – five or six years – that we can go places without talking about it. It just creates this organic thing. Them not knowing too much about the music means I say to myself, "OK, fine, I'll just play how I feel today," and a lot of times, that's what I'm looking for.'

With his band playing live in London, that sense of spontaneity, simultaneously fresh, yet keeping the music on the album in view, was exactly what Theo achieved. His approach – not revealing a set-list, just starting a tune, and knowing the musicians are sufficiently familiar with the music to fall naturally into place – took me back to some of my first experiences with Ken Colyer (not counting my very first schoolboy gig) getting on for fifty years ago. Listening to recordings of Ken's band on successive nights, it's clear we repeated very little, and when we did tackle the same number on two back-to-back concerts, the treatment was often quite different. It was just the way Ken himself had experienced things in New Orleans, the very year I was born.

It's no real surprise that Theo Croker is more than aware of the richness of the jazz tradition, as he is the grandson of another great trumpeter, Doc Cheatham. Doc talked proudly of him, when Theo was still a small boy, while we worked together on his autobiography, and I'm sure he would be more than pleased today to see that Theo has become the living embodiment of jazz as 'The Sound of Surprise'. For me, it is Theo and players like him who show that jazz is not just in safe hands but in hands that are also prepared to be risky and creative. They are ready to try new ideas, yet without ever losing sight of over a century of tradition, the very same tradition that my personal voyage through these pages has sought to explore.

When I started out in jazz, I was already in the midst of an exceptional classical music education. And I was lucky enough to hear some exceptional musicians in local concerts – including Paul Tortelier, Marisa Robles, Jaqueline du Pré, the Vienna Octet, John Williams, Julian Bream, Fou Ts'ong, John Ogdon and Jack Brymer, not to mention attending the annual seasons by Denys Darlow's Tilford Bach Society, for whom my father was a club official. As a child, I was moved to tears by Alexander Young, the evangelist in their *St John Passion*. Rogers Covey-Crump, later a key member of the Hilliard Ensemble, similarly inspired me, as he began his career in equally important roles, and alongside the wonderful double bass virtuoso Francis Baines, a young Barry Guy showed us a masterclass in continuo playing.

Yet despite all this extraordinary classical virtuosity on the doorstep, I felt that nothing could compare with the emotional thrill of the first occasions I heard live jazz. I knew, from that time on, that this was the music in which I wanted to immerse myself as both a player and listener. I also had a quite mistaken perception as a teenager that classical players were not so much fun as jazz musicians. In the 1990s, when I revived my classical playing, that idea evaporated. On one level, very little matches the grandeur and thrill of playing together in Bach's *St Matthew Passion* in an Oxford college chapel, or performing Handel oratorios in Dorchester Abbey alongside the celebrated cellist Dougie Cummings playing continuo. The players I worked with were every bit as much fun and as engaged as anyone I had met playing jazz.

Yet at 21, I nevertheless parked my classical career and plunged wholeheartedly into the jazz world. Many years later, having devoted most of my life to trying to find out as much as possible about this music, I remain as enthused as ever. Whether it's Andy Sheppard holding concert audiences rapt with Espen Eriksen's *Perfectly Unhappy* compositions in concerts on both sides of the English Channel, Norma Winstone sparkling alongside young Royal Academy singers such as Ella Hohnen-Ford and Alma Naidu, or the late Tomasz Stańko raising the hairs on the back of my neck at his final London appearance, the variety, riches and depth of jazz continue to draw me in. As this book shows, almost every time I have knocked on a door to try and find out more, it has been opened, and I have been welcomed in. My curiosity as a historian was aroused early on by trying to discover the stories that had not been told. Despite the twenty-four jazz autobiographies that I have published or co-edited, countless magazine and radio interviews with musicians from all walks of jazz, or the adrenaline rush of meetings on the bandstand, there's still plenty to be discovered about the music's past; but equally, much to be done to help chart its future. And it will be a privilege, as it always has been, to be a part of that process.

ACKNOWLEDGEMENTS

Firstly I'd like to thank all those who have read and commented on sections of this book as it was in preparation, in particular Alan Barnes, Halina Boniszewska, Anna Celenza, Michael Pointon, Brian Priestley, Sonny Rollins, Ray Smith and Catherine Tackley. Their generous feedback has been most helpful and several chapters have benefitted from their detailed questions and observations.

Since 1989 I have been fortunate enough to make programmes for BBC Radio and I am grateful to all my colleagues there for the opportunity to meet and interview so many figures in the world of jazz. I'm thankful, too, that over the years the following producers put up with me supplementing the questions I was asking for broadcast with more enquiries of my own, namely Felix Carey, Terry Carter, Derek Drescher, Anna Harrison, Sam Hickling, Oliver Jones, and Dave Tate. I should like to thank 7Digital Creative, and my colleague Kerry Luter, for permission to reproduce extensive quotations from interviews broadcast in the *Jazz Library* series for BBC Radio 3, and Oliver Jones for similar help with BBC World Service *Jazzmatazz* material. Thanks are also due to the Controller of Radio 3, Alan Davey, and his colleagues Yvette Pusey and Simon Brown, for allowing me to use excerpts from other programmes, commissioned for the network by his predecessor Roger Wright, and broadcast during 2000 as episodes in the series *The Kid From Red Bank* and *The Shape of Jazz to Come*.

Equally I have been privileged to write for *Jazzwise* magazine almost since its inception, and I am grateful to the Editor-in-Chief, Jon Newey, and the Editor, Mike Flynn, for permission to reproduce interviews done for their excellent publication. When I first started writing seriously about jazz in the 1970s, Terry Dash, the editor of *Footnote*, was kind enough to be the first to commission me to write for him, which was a tremendous start.

I have been very lucky to have had several friends and mentors along the way who introduced me to people, recordings and documents that helped me to learn more. Most of these are mentioned in the text, but I was extremely fortunate in the 1980s to have been the publisher of the *New Grove Dictionary of American Music* and the *New Grove Dictionary of Jazz*, and to work with a group of enthusiastic and knowledgeable scholars who helped me to understand more about the way music had developed in America. From that formidable community of researchers and editors, three colleagues in particular should be singled out: Stanley Sadie, the editor of the *Grove* family of dictionaries, whose own quest for knowledge and prodigious memory made him a role model in many respects, as well as a walking Filofax of academic contacts; H. Wiley Hitchcock, the co-editor of 'Amerigrove' as we called it, brought a calm and balanced historical approach to my understanding of music in the United States; and Barry Kernfeld, the editor of the jazz dictionary, prompted me to explore many areas of the music that had hitherto been hiding behind mysteriously closed doors.

Twenty years of reviewing concerts and festivals, and doing in-depth interviews for *The Times*, all over the world, also meant that I heard many musicians and encountered areas of the music that I might never otherwise have explored, and the editorial team there were greatly supportive, particularly Richard Morrison, Debra Craine, Alex O'Connell and Neil Fisher, not to mention my fellow jazz reviewers Chris Parker, John Bungey and Clive Davis.

Professor Tim Jones and his colleagues at the Royal Academy of Music have unfailingly supported my research efforts over the last decade, and I owe him and the Academy a huge debt of gratitude.

Playing live music has been a vital part of my jazz experience and I should mention just some of the musicians who have made this possible. From the early days, Ken Colyer and Mike Casimir were very supportive. I have barely mentioned Sammy Rimington in the text, but playing in his band on and off for several years in the UK and Europe was a privilege as well as a great opportunity to work alongside many fine New Orleans players. Dick Cook and Ray Smith led the London Ragtime Orchestra with distinction and it was tremendous to be a part of that from the outset. Bill Greenow coaxed me back to playing jazz after a hiatus in the 1990s, and finally Matthias Seuffert has co-led the Buck Clayton Legacy Band with me from its inception and helped realize Buck's hopes that his music would continue to be played and remembered.

A book such as this depends on the words of many of those with whom I have spoken or corresponded about jazz. Without them there would be no book. So my profound thanks to all those who have spent time discussing the music with me over many years: Geri Allen, George Avakian, Chris Barber, Blue Lu Barker, Danny Barker, Louie Bellson, Tony Bennett, Carla Bley, Paul Bley, Eddie Bo, Colin Bowden, Carmen Bradford, Jewel Brown, Ray Brown, Clora Bryant, Gary Burton, Ian Carr, Ron Carter, Al Casey, Topsy Chapman, Doc Cheatham, John Chilton, Buck Clayton, Billy Cobham, Bill Coleman, Denardo Coleman, Ornette Coleman, Ken Colyer, Chick Corea, Theo Croker, Jack DeJohnette, Harry Dial, Harry Sweets Edison, Teddy Edwards, Tommy Flanagan, Michael Gibbs, Al Grey, Henry Grimes, Charlie Haden, Herbie Hancock, Roy Haynes, Percy Heath, Gwyneth Herbert, Milt Hinton, Jon Hiseman, Dave Holland, Franz Jackson, Milt Jackson, Freddie Kohlman, Joachim Kühn, Pete LaRoca, Stan Levey, Father Al Lewis, John Lewis, Dave Liebman, Abbey Lincoln, Lawrence Lucie, Teo Macero, John McLaughlin, Jackie McLean, George Melly, Butch Miles, Grover Mitchell, Charnett Moffett, Sonny Morris, Niels-Henning Ørsted Pedersen, Truck Parham, Oscar Peterson, Cousin Joe Pleasant, Bennie Powell, Mac Rebennack, Dewey Redman, Sammy Rimington, Sonny Rollins, Wallace Roney, George Russell, Maria Schneider, Gunther Schuller, Billy Scott-Coomber, Arvell Shaw, Howard Shore, Jabbo Smith, Evelyn McGhee Stone, Jesse Stone, Buddy Tate, Dr Billy Taylor, Clark Terry, Ed Thigpen, Butch Thompson, Sir Charles Thompson, Stan Tracey, Mal Waldron, Benny Waters, Joe Wilder, Michael Winner, Jimmy Woode and Chester Zardis.

Finally, there would be no book were it not for my commissioning editor Kate Brett, at Cambridge, who not only proposed the idea, but, together with her colleague Alex Wright, encouraged me to get on and write it. I'd also like to thank my copy-editor Janice Baiton for her close reading of the text and penetrating questions, which have improved the end result immeasurably.

Picture Credits

I would like to acknowledge prints and artwork supplied by Alan John Ainsworth, Danny Barker, Dave Bennett, Liz Biddle, Doc Cheatham, Tim Dickeson, Derek Drescher, Laure Fabry, Tim Knox, Renée Long, Roy Porter, Caroline Richmond, Toby Silver and Tom Tierney at Sony Columbia, John Watson and Jimmy Woode. In the plate section that follows Chapter 9, the credits for those pictures that are not drawn from my own collection are: Plate 1 Courtesy Renée Long/Upbeat Records; Plate 3 Courtesy Caroline Richmond; Plate 4 Courtesy Caroline Richmond; Plate 5 Courtesy Remy Steinegger; Plate 9 Courtesy Dave Bennett; Plate 10 Photo: Don Hunstein © Sony Music Entertainment; Plate 11 Courtesy Derek Drescher; Plate 13 Photo: Don Hunstein © Sony Music Entertainment; Plate 14 Courtesy Danny Barker; Plate 15 Courtesy Derek Drescher; Plate 16 Courtesy John Watson/Jazzcamera. co.uk; Plate 17 Courtesy Derek Drescher; Plate 18 Courtesy Tim Knox/ timknoxphotography.com; Plate 19 Courtesy Tim Dickeson/timdicke-son.com; Plate 20 Courtesy John Watson/Jazzcamera.co.uk; Plate 21 Courtesy John Watson/Jazzcamera.co.uk; Plate 22 Courtesy Tim Dickeson/timdickeson.com; Plate 23 Courtesy Tim Dickeson/timdick-eson.com.

NOTES

Preface

1. Alyn Shipton, 'New Jazz Histories', *Jazz Research Journal*, vol. 3, no. 2 (2009), p. 133.
2. Mineke Schipper, *Imagining Insiders: Africa and the Question of Belonging* (London: Cassell, 1999), pp. 70–1.

Chapter 1 Getting Started

1. Interview with Sonny Morris, 17 Aug. 1998.
2. Interview with Morris. John R. T. Davies, later to be Britain's leading restorer of 78 rpm jazz records, played the trombone (although he was also an accomplished saxophonist) and Julian played bass. Sunshine was the band's regular clarinettist, but he told trumpeter John Keen that he actually followed Cy Laurie and then Ray Bush into the band. Bill Colyer played washboard initially, and then Ron Bowden became the band's drummer.
3. Interview with Chris Barber, 17 Aug. 1998.
4. Interview with Michael Winner, 27 Sept. 2004.
5. Interview with Colin Bowden, 18 Aug. 1998.
6. Rosina Scudder appears on the album *Ken Colyer's Jazzmen Live* (Upbeat URCD 257).
7. The programme we made was part of the series *Heir Hunters*, about people who had died intestate, in which the TV company tried to locate any legal heirs. The Scudder episode was broadcast on 6 March 2017.
8. Interview with Colin Bowden, 18 Aug. 1998.
9. Ken Colyer's All Stars, *Recently Discovered Late Period Colyer* (Upbeat URCD 271) and Ken Colyer, *Rare Footage from the Vaults* (Upbeat URDVD 267).
10. Richard Cook, *Richard Cook's Jazz Encyclopedia* (London: Penguin, 2005), p. 131.
11. Interview with Morris. Decca paid a standard fee for an LP, but Colyer seems to have bolstered this to allow for a greater number of musicians than usual, as well as covering the cost of the refreshments.

12. It had also participated in 1958, when the march took the reverse direction from London to Aldermaston, but in subsequent years the organizers realized that many more people would join as it entered London.
13. George McKay, *Circular Breathing: The Cultural Politics of Jazz in Britain* (Durham, NC: Duke University Press, 2005), p. 54.
14. Interview with Morris.
15. Reissued on *Bunk's Brass Band and 1945 Sessions* (American Music CD 6).
16. Alyn Shipton, 'George Melly', *Isis* (4 May 1973), p. 18.
17. George Melly, *Mellymobile* (London: Robson Books, 1982), p. 13.
18. John Chilton, *Hot Jazz, Warm Feet* (London: Northway, 2007), p. 126.
19. This is related in Tom Sancton, *Song For My Fathers: A New Orleans Story in Black and White* (New York: Other Press, 2006).

Chapter 2 New Orleans 1976

1. Alyn Shipton, 'New Orleans Jazz and Heritage Festival 1976', *Footnote*, vii/5 (June/July 1976), p. 25.
2. Mingus playing 'Themes From a Movie' on piano in that concert on 18 April 1976 was issued on *10th Anniversary New Orleans Jazz and Heritage Festival* (Flying Fish FF099, released 1979).
3. Interview with Butch Thompson for BBC World Service, 26 June 1998.
4. Sadly Robinson was to die just over a couple of weeks later on 4 May 1976.
5. GHB BCD 533, recorded in 1980 and released in 2014.
6. A night from that residency is preserved on the LP Freddie Kohlman, *All of Me* (Camelia TF1).
7. As on the album George Lewis, *Concert!* (Blue Note 1208) recorded on 28 May 1954.
8. Alyn Shipton, 'New Orleans Bass Playing', *Footnote*, viii/1 (Oct./Nov. 1976).
9. Author's conversation with Al Lewis, Apr. 1976. Narvin was the son of the pioneer jazz bassist Henry Kimball.
10. Author's conversation with Zardis, Ascona, Switzerland, July 1989.
11. This band was recorded during its visit on *Kid Thomas in England* (Lulu White's Black Label, DTS 046).
12. This band can be heard on *Louis Nelson All Stars* (GHB CD231) recorded in 1987 in Japan.
13. *Remembering Pat Halcox* (Lake LACD 338, released 2015).

Chapter 3 Before Katrina

1. While Johnny's other 24/7 bars on Bourbon Street shut down permanently in 2020, the original one at 733 St Peter Street continues to be run and owned by the White family, although it was temporarily closed by the Covid-19 pandemic.
2. The resulting record only has one proper example of this, the song 'Big Bass Drum', which can be heard on Chris Barber, *Take Me Back to New Orleans* (Black Lion 760163).
3. Sequence confirmed by email 4 Dec. 2020 from Colin Strickland, producer of the *Sammy Rimington on Washington Avenue* album featuring Chester.
4. Dr John, *N'awlinz: Dis Dat or D'Udda* (Parlophone 7243 5 78603 2 1).
5. Alyn Shipton, 'Dr John: Route to the Roots', *Jazzwise* 77 (July 2004), pp. 24ff.

6. Dave Williams, *I Ate Up the Apple Tree* (New Orleans Records 7204, recorded 1974).
7. Shipton, 'Dr John', pp. 24ff.
8. Ibid.
9. Eddie Bo's double-sided single 'Hook and Sling' was released on Scram Records 117 in 1969.
10. Interview with Eddie Bo for BBC World Service, Ascona, Switzerland, 28 June 1998.
11. The area of synaesthesia and music is worthy of further research. As a starting point, I gave a preliminary paper at the Oxford Centre For the Creative Brain conference on 2 Nov. 2017, on 'Ellington and Synaesthesia', revised and expanded for the joint Birmingham City University/Duke Ellington Society UK conference on 26 May 2018.
12. Interview with Bo.
13. Lillian Boutté and Dr John, *The Jazz Book* (Blues Beacon BLU10202, released 1994).
14. Dr John, *Goin' Back to New Orleans* (Warner Bros, 926940-2, 1992).
15. Jack V. Buerkle and Danny Barker, *Bourbon Street Black: The New Orleans Black Jazzman* (New York: Oxford University Press, 1963).
16. Al Kennedy, *Big Chief Harrison and the Mardi Gras Indians* (Gretna, LA: Pelican, 2010).
17. Donald Harrison Jr, *Indian Blues* (Candid 79814). There is a full transcription of the lyrics in Alan Lomax, *Mister Jelly Roll* (New York: Duell, Sloan and Pearce, 1949), pp. 17–18.
18. Conversation with Danny Barker, New Orleans, Mar. 1987, part of which appears in the new edition of Danny Barker, *A Life in Jazz* (New Orleans: NOHC, 2016).
19. Kennedy, *Big Chief Harrison and the Mardi Gras Indians*, p. 31.
20. Ibid., p. 37.
21. Traditional lyrics. These tracks of Indian songs are most recently reissued on Baby Dodds, *Jazz à la Creole* (GHB BCD 50), which also includes Barker's record session with Albert Nicholas of Creole French songs in New Orleans patois.
22. Harrison, *Indian Blues*.
23. Michael P. Smith, *Mardi Gras Indians* (Gretna, LA: Pelican, 1994).
24. Jelly Roll Morton, *Library of Congress Recordings*, Rounder 11661–1888-2 CD 8; pdf transcription of Morton. This is slightly at odds with Alan Lomax's edited version in *Mister Jelly Roll* that describes the 'second' line 'out in front of everybody'.
25. Lomax, *Mister Jelly Roll*, p. 15.
26. Smith, *Mardi Gras Indians*. I discussed Mardi Gras Indians further in a paper for the Open University Music Department 'Hidden Histories' conference, given 11 January 2016.

Chapter 4 Two Women of New Orleans

1. Interview with Blue Lu Barker, 7 Mar. 1997. The Decca recordings are on the CD *1938–39* (Classics 704). The 1946 Apollo sessions are on *Don't You Feel My Leg – Apollo's Lady Blues Singers* (Delmark DE 683). Her 1948–9 Capitol recordings were collected on the vinyl LP *Here's A Little Girl* (Capitol 1566301, 1986).
2. 'Around here' was the Gentilly area of New Orleans, not far from where she and Danny later lived on Sere St
3. She first told me this story in the 1980s. See Alyn Shipton, 'Blue Lu Barker', *Footnote*, vol. 17, no. 5 (June/July 1986), p. 18.

4. 'Don't You Make Me High' was the title on the label of Decca 7506 by Blue Lu Barker with Danny Barker's Fly Cats.
5. In some sources Henry Allen is listed as trumpeter on the first Blue Lu session, as I originally believed, but she was adamant in the 1997 interview that it was Carter.
6. Sylvia's age confirmed in the report of her wedding to René Brunner: 'N.Y. Jazz Musicians' Daughter', *Jet* v/22, 8 Apr. 1954.
7. Blue Lu might be confusing two periods of the trio here as Herbie Nichols himself recalled working with her and Danny in 1946 on one of the Apollo recordings, according to his biographer. Mark Miller, *Herbie Nichols: A Jazzist's Life* (Toronto: Mercury, 2009), p. 56.
8. Interview with Topsy Chapman for BBC World Service, May 2002.

Chapter 5 Finding Fats

1. A good example of its music is *Buck Clayton Swings the Village* (Nagel Heyer CD 5004).
2. Part of a concert from Vienne in France can be seen and heard here: www .youtube.com/watch?v=nudSi8RRWuo.
3. Exemplified on the album *Buck Clayton All Stars, Basel 1961* (TCB 02072), vol. 7 in the Swiss Radio Days series.
4. The Buck Clayton Legacy Band's work is exemplified by the album *Claytonia* (BCLB001) recorded by BBC Radio in Mar. 2011.
5. Alain Charbonnier, 'The Buck Clayton Legacy Band en concert exceptionnel à Limoges', *Bulletin du HCF*, no. 686 (Jan. 2020), p. 29.
6. Buck Clayton and Nancy Miller Elliott, *Buck Clayton's Jazz World* (London: Macmillan, 1986), p. 13.
7. Interview with Al Casey, Apr. 2002. Al slightly mis-remembered, as their actual name was Southern Suns and the show was *Moon River* on which Fats played on Cincinnati's WLW station, listed for example in the *Indianapolis Times*, 9 Nov. 1932, p. 7. The show went out at 11 pm, after *Fats Waller's Rhythm Club* on the same station, on which the Southern Suns also appeared. An edited version of some segments of this interview appears in the second edition of my Waller biography.
8. I originally thought this meant high school but by this time Al, aged 18, was studying music in college and uses 'school' in the American sense.
9. There is more detail on the very band that Harry played with in the autobiography of the group's trombonist: Clyde E. B. Bernhardt, *I Remember: Eighty Years of Black Entertainment, Big Bands and the Blues*, 2nd ed. (Philadelphia: University of Pennsylvania Press, 2015).
10. A full account of his career is in his autobiography: Harry Dial, *All This Jazz About Jazz* (Chigwell: Storyville, 1984). My interview was intended to supplement that book's information about Waller. The Armstrong session was 26 April 1933.
11. Eli Oberstein (1901–60), who established the Bluebird division of Victor, was the producer of Waller's first sessions and his successor, Ken McComber, continued to feature Dial the same way.
12. The session in question was actually on a Wednesday – 7 November 1934.
13. The Ubangi, at 7th Avenue and 131st Street in Harlem, had previously been known as Connie's Inn, and Waller had worked there himself as a teenager.
14. Joe Thomas eventually did join Waller's big band some five years later, by which time Dial was no longer the band's drummer.

15. This was the same November 1934 date on which Coleman joined the group, but from then on, apart from a handful of recordings and tours when he was otherwise engaged, Sedric was still in the band for what turned out to be its final week at the Regal Theatre in Chicago in January 1943 according to Laurie Wright, *Fats in Fact* (Chigwell: Storyville, 1992).

16. On this Autrey and trombonist Floyd O'Brien play a swing riff under Mezzrow's clarinet solo that sounds arranged, but the pattern had actually been signalled to them by Fats in the previous chorus! It's also worth noting that for this session only, the Rhythm was a racially integrated band.

17. Since the trumpet and tenor were B flat instruments, they played the written piano part at sight and Fats and the rhythm section transposed down a tone.

18. Interview with Thompson, 1 Mar. 2003.

19. Thompson plays both clarinet and piano, but was the clarinettist with the Hall Brothers Jazz Band of Minneapolis.

20. Interview with Thompson.

21. All this session is available on the *Complete Recordings of Fats Waller, Vol. 3, 1934–1936, Rhythm and Romance* (JSP Records, JSP 496).

22. The composer of the piece, James P. Johnson, had made a piano roll of the song in August 1917.

23. Interview with Milt Hinton, 23 Mar. 1993.

24. According to Laurie Wright, the band did play briefly in Oakland after leaving L.A., and then one job in Denver. Gigs in Kansas City, St Louis and Indianapolis were cancelled after the promoter of the Kansas gig pulled out. Wright, *Fats in Fact*.

25. Interview with Franz Jackson for BBC World Service, 30 June 1998.

26. An attempt to capture this big band routine on record is 'I Got Rhythm' (HMV HE2902) from 4 Dec. 1935, but despite members of the band shouting to Hank 'Show him how to swing!' Duncan is under-recorded compared to Waller.

Chapter 6 Swing Era Legends

1. Alyn Shipton, *Fats Waller: The Cheerful Little Earful*, 2nd ed. (London: Continuum, 2002). Originally published in shorter form by Universe Books, New York, 1988.

2. Frankie Newton and his Uptown Serenaders, with James P., Mezz, Pete Brown, Cozy Cole, John Kirby and Al were actually recorded in January 1939, so Panassié's discs would only have helped Al in terms of Waller's 1939 visit to Europe.

3. The Esquire All Star Jam Session at the Metropolitan Opera House on 18 January 1944, and the subsequent 1945 touring Esquire Jam Session.

4. His name was Nathan Gangursky. While working in the studio band in Los Angeles (as well as continuing his symphonic career) he recorded with Mel Tormé, Judy Garland and Frank Sinatra. He also recorded briefly with Artie Shaw.

5. Interview with Truck Parham, 30 June 1998.

6. Interview with Jimmy Woode, 2 Nov. 1992.

7. Len Lyons, 'Lyons Den', syndicated to *Cedar Rapids Gazette*, 6 Nov. 1946.

8. *Syracuse Herald Journal*, 29 Nov. 1946.

9. *Daily Princetonian*, 18 Dec. 1946.

10. Interview with Al Casey, 31 Oct. 1996.

11. Adolphus 'Doc' Cheatham, *I Guess I'll Get the Papers and Go Home*, ed. Alyn Shipton (London: Cassell, 1996) p. 55.

12. Interview with Mal Waldron for BBC World Service, 1995.

13. Al Moses, 'Footlight Flickers (ANP)', *Blackfoot Bingham County News*, 16 Dec. 1939, p. 2.

14. Ibid.
15. Harold Jovien, 'Radio Raves (APN)', *Indianapolis Reporter*, 18 Nov. 1939.
16. 'Teddy Wilson organizes small combine', *Indianapolis Reporter*, 11 May 1940.
17. Cheatham, *I Guess I'll Get the Papers and Go Home*, p. 52.
18. Issued back-to-back on Columbia 35354, recorded 11 Dec 1939.
19. Cheatham, *I Guess I'll Get the Papers and Go Home*. p. 52.
20. *Swing That Music*, broadcast on successive Mondays in 1993.
21. Cheatham, *I Guess I'll Get the Papers and Go Home*, p. 3.
22. 12 July 1947.
23. Eddie Determeyer in his biography of Lunceford, *Rhythm Is Our Business* (Ann Arbor: University of Michigan Press, 2010) suggests it was a nearby restaurant, but with me Parham was adamant it was the Bungalow Ballroom itself.
24. Wendell Green, 'Joe Thompson (*sic*) slated to head the band', *L. A. Sentinel*, 24 July 1947. Green meant 'Joe Thomas' but this is how the story appeared.
25. Howard Reich, 'Danny Barker's restored '86 memoir recalls early days of jazz', *Chicago Tribune*, 14 Feb. 2017.
26. Unedited interview with Danny Barker for *A Life in Jazz*, 2nd ed. (New Orleans: HNOC, 2016).
27. Karl Gert zur Heide, *Deep South Piano: The Story of Little Brother Montgomery* (London: Studio Vista, 1970), pp. 36–7; Joe Darensbourg, *Telling It Like It Is*, ed. Peter Vacher (London: Macmillan, 1987), p. 21; Austin M. Sonnier Jr, *Willie Geary 'Bunk' Johnson* (New York: Crescendo, 1977), p. 8.

Chapter 7 Louis Armstrong

1. Alyn Shipton, 'Not So Much An Artist', *Isis*, no. 1649 (25 Feb. 1973), p. 24.
2. Buck Clayton and Nancy Miller Elliott, *Buck Clayton's Jazz World* (London: Macmillan, 1986), p. 46.
3. Ibid.
4. Adolphus 'Doc' Cheatham, *I Guess I'll Get the Papers and Go Home*, ed. Alyn Shipton (London: Cassell, 1996), p. 16.
5. Interview with Doc Cheatham, Nov. 1993.
6. Danny Barker, *A Life in Jazz*, ed. Alyn Shipton, 2nd ed. (New Orleans: HNOC, 2016), p. 176.
7. Interview with Lawrence Lucie for BBC Radio 3 *Jazz Library*, Apr. 2002.
8. Published by Jazz Media, Copenhagen, 1999. I had approached Bill about publishing it at Macmillan but ultimately, although a co-publishing deal was set up with a US university press, Bill passed the book to Knudsen as he had recently taken away the rights to his American Music label from Storyville by licensing the sessions to the Dan record label in Japan, and felt this was a 'compensation' to Knudsen.
9. At the 2010 London Jazz Festival, Keith Nichols and I presented a programme at the Royal Academy of Music to celebrate the 120th anniversary of Morton's birth for BBC Radio 3. Our recreation of part of the Bluebird session (following some of Morton's earlier works) using the band parts can be heard at 52.14 here: www.bbc.co.uk/programmes/b00yrhf7/clips.
10. This can be heard on the CD of the soundtrack, paired with music from Ann Miller's other film of the time *Reveille with Beverly* (Hollywood Soundstage 4007).
11. *Albert Nicholas and Herb Hall, with the Trevor Richards New Orleans Trio*, GHB BCD-64.

12. Interview with Arvell Shaw for BBC Radio 3 *Jazz Library*, recorded Oct. 2001.
13. Clayton and Elliott, *Buck Clayton's Jazz World*.
14. The Armstrong All Stars with Jewel played the Royal Festival Hall on 28 April 1962.
15. Jewel was slightly incorrect here: Velma died on 10 Feb. 1961, and Jewel joined in June of that year.
16. Interview with Jewel Brown for BBC World Service, June 1998.
17. Barney Bigard, *With Louis and the Duke*, ed. Barry Martyn (London: Macmillan, 1986).
18. Ricky Riccardi, *What a Wonderful World: The Magic of Louis Armstrong's Later Years* (New York: Pantheon, 2011), p. 196.

Chapter 8 Count Basie

1. Candid 79050, recorded at Birdland, New York City, 27/28 Apr. 1990.
2. Interview with Buddy Tate, 22 Feb. 1993.
3. 'Routings', *Baltimore Afro-American*, 14 May 1927. Its original run is referenced in the same paper on 24 July 1926, and on 25 May 1929 the paper reported 'Coming to Broadway next month, George and Connie Immerman's "Tan Town Topics" from Connie's Inn'. It noted: 'music by Waller and Brooks, lyrics by Razaf and choreography by Leonard Harper'.
4. John Dollard, 'The Dozens, Dialectic of Insult', *American Imago*, vol. 1, no. 1 (Nov. 1939), pp. 3–25.
5. Interview with Clark Terry for BBC Radio 3 *Jazz Library*, originally recorded 8 Oct. 2000.
6. George Shearing (with Alyn Shipton), *Lullaby of Birdland – The Autobiography of George Shearing* (New York: Continuum, 2004), p. 99.
7. Interview with Al Grey for BBC Radio 3 *Jazz Library*, originally recorded 29 Oct. 1999.
8. Interview with Bennie Powell for BBC Radio 3 *Jazz Library*, originally recorded Feb. 1993.
9. Chris Sheridan, *Count Basie – A Bio-Discography* (Westport, CT: Greenwood Press, 1986), p. 14.
10. Interview with Jesse Stone, 9 Mar. 1997.
11. Interview with Evelyn McGhee Stone, 9 Mar. 1997.
12. Interview with Sweets Edison for BBC Radio 3 *Jazz Library*, originally recorded Nov. 1992.
13. Clark was far too diplomatic to go into details but the 'illness' was severe heroin addiction. See Frederick J. Spencer, *Jazz and Death, Medical Profiles of Jazz Greats* (Jackson: University Press of Mississippi, 2002), p. 15.
14. Interview with Grover Mitchell, 21 Sept. 1999.
15. Interview with Butch Miles, 21 Sept. 1999.
16. Interview with Louie Bellson for BBC Radio 3 *Jazz Library*, originally recorded 13 July 1999.
17. Interview with Joe Wilder, 24 Mar. 1997.
18. Interview with Tony Bennett for BBC Radio 3, broadcast 22 Jan. 2000.
19. Interview with Carmen Bradford, 21 Sept. 1999.
20. Interview with Grover Mitchell, 21 Sept. 1999.
21. *A Classy Pair* was recorded on 15 Feb. 1979; *Ella and Basie – A Perfect Match* was 12 July 1979, and, apart from one number 'Basella' with Basie on piano, features Paul Smith, Keter Betts and Mickey Roker as the rhythm section (with the ever-present Freddie Green).

22. Interview with Miles.
23. Interview with Tommy Flanagan, 4 Jan. 2000.
24. *Hot and Cool, Tony Bennett Sings Ellington* (Columbia C63668) 1999.

Chapter 9 Duke Ellington

1. Interview with Bennie Powell for BBC Radio 3 *Jazz Library*, originally recorded Feb. 1993.
2. Interview with Clark Terry for BBC Radio 3 *Jazz Library*, originally recorded 8 Oct. 2000.
3. These dates are more accurate than those in Klaus Stratemann, *Duke Ellington Day by Day and Film by Film* (Copenhagen: Jazz Media, 1992), p. 354. He suggests Woode replaced Wendell Marshall in New York in January, but that was when Raglin (who had previously replaced Jimmie Blanton) rejoined. Stratemann also dates the Storyville appearance after Carnegie Hall on 16 March, but *Newport Daily News* (25 Feb. 1955, p. 7) confirms that the band went straight from the Newport Navy Base on 24 Feb. to Wein's club. The *Duke Where and When* website suggests Woode played on a 17 February broadcast from Canada, but Jimmy's account disproves that.
4. Interview with Jimmy Woode for BBC Radio 3 *Jazz Library*, originally recorded Nov. 1992.
5. Quoted in Katherine Williams, 'Duke Ellington's Newport Up!', in Roger Fagge and Nicolas Pillai (eds.), *New Jazz Conceptions: History, Theory, Practice* (Milton, Oxon: Taylor and Francis, 2017), p. 116.
6. George Avakian, liner notes to *Ellington at Newport* (Columbia CL 934).
7. Ibid.
8. The 7 February 1956 sessions for Bethlehem called *Historically Speaking* and *Duke Ellington Presents* are excellent examples from the pre-Newport era, with the rhythm section excelling on 'Stompy Jones' and 'Midriff' on the former and interacting with Gonsalves on 'Cottontail' on the latter.
9. Definitely not 'Philly Joe Jones' as Katherine Williams erroneously suggests in the essay previously cited.
10. *Sex, Drugs and Four Minutes of Silence*, BBC Radio 4, 26 Apr. 2001.
11. *Piano Moods*, CL 6139, released in 1950, was the 10-inch LP, also issued simultaneously as Columbia B230, a box of four 45 rpm discs. But George is incorrect about the playing times, which – at this point in Garner's career – did not exceed 3 minutes and 48 seconds per track. The 45s were singles not EPs, and the same recordings also appeared on 78. But by 1953, the durations were generally closer to those George remembered.
12. The Columbia Legacy edition of the W C Handy record (88697720092–05) was issued in 2011, and also includes an interview with Handy.
13. Interview done for Radio 3 *Jazz Library* broadcast on 19 Mar. 2011, the week of George's 92nd birthday.
14. Michael Ross, 'Duke Ellington', in Dave DiMartino, *Music in the 20th Century* (New York: Routledge, 2016), p. 195.
15. Interview with Louie Bellson, broadcast on *Jazz Library*, BBC Radio 3, 21 Mar. 2009, as part of a tribute to Louie, who died on 14 February that year.
16. Recorded for Columbia, 10 May 1951.
17. Jack Lewis, LP liner notes to Duke Ellington, *Seattle Concert* (RCA Victor, LJM 1002, 1954).
18. Gunther Schuller, *The Swing Era* (New York: Oxford University Press, 1989), p. 156.
19. Williams, 'Duke Ellington's Newport Up!', p. 112.

20. Eddie Lambert, *Duke Ellington: A Listener's Guide* (Lanham, MD: Scarecrow Press, 1999), p. 181.
21. George Avakian, liner notes to Duke Ellington, *Ellington Uptown* (Columbia ML 4639, 1951).
22. Jack Sohmer, 'Ellington at Newport (Complete)', *Jazz Times*, 1 Oct. 1999.
23. *Mitchell Daily Republic*, South Dakota, 21 Sept. 1953, p. 2.
24. *Cedar Rapids Gazette*, 12 Oct. 1954.
25. *Indianapolis Recorder*, 6 Nov. 1954 (both reviews included in that paper).
26. *Ithaca Cornell Daily Sun*, 14 Jan. 1955, p. 8.
27. *Newport Daily News*, 25 Feb. 1955, p. 7.
28. *Moline Daily Despatch*, 14 Feb. 1956.
29. *Newport Daily News*, 11 May 1956.
30. *Berkshire Eagle*, 12 July 1956, p. 12.
31. *Fairfield County Fair*, 26 July 1956, p. 9.
32. Thomas Owens, 'Rudy Van Gelder', in Barry Kernfeld (ed.), *The New Grove Dictionary of Jazz*, 2nd ed. (London: Macmillan, 2002), vol. 2, p. 826.
33. Interview with Rudy Van Gelder, 18 May 1997.
34. John Fass Morton, *Backstory in Blue* (Newark: Rutgers University Press, 2008), p. 105.
35. Interview with Avakian, 24 Feb. 1999.
36. *Ellington at Newport 1956 (Complete)*, 1999, C2K 64932.
37. Morton, *Backstory in Blue*.
38. Thanks to BBC Radio 3's Marvin Ware and Robin Cherry for useful information.
39. Interview with Avakian, Mar. 2011.
40. The Buck Clayton Legacy Band at Schützenhaus, Thalwil, 25 Nov. 2017, played Adrian Fry's arrangement for nine instruments of the *Newport Suite*.

Chapter 10 Dizzy and Bird

1. Interview with Billy Taylor for BBC World Service, 31 Oct. 1996.
2. Interview with Sir Charles Thompson for BBC World Service, 9 May 2001.
3. Berg's was the club where Dizzy Gillespie and Charlie Parker are generally assumed to have brought bebop to the West Coast, although Coleman Hawkins with Howard McGhee and Sir Charles, and then local drummer Roy Porter's bebop band with McGhee and Teddy Edwards, were playing the style there first.
4. The earliest sessions by Sir Charles and Illinois were indeed in Los Angeles in 1945, but this tune was actually cut in New York, by Illinois Jacquet and his All Stars (with Sir Charles) on 21 May 1947.
5. The 'Takin' Off' session for Apollo was on 4 Sept. 1945.
6. Interview with Jimmy Woode, Nov. 1992. In fact in our chat Jimmy conflated two different appearances with Parker in Boston. He broadcast with Parker, Thompson, Clarke and trumpeter Herb Pomeroy in September 1953 from George Wein's Storyville Club, but the three-week stay at the Hi-Hat was in December, with Rollins Griffith, piano, and Marquis Foster, drums. The New England dates Jimmy mentioned seem to have been after the Hi-Hat and before Bird hooked up with Stan Kenton in late February 1954.
7. Ken Vail, *Dizzy Gillespie: The Bebop Years* (Cambridge: Vail Publishing, 2000), p. 35 and Ken Vail, *Bird's Diary* (Cambridge: Vail Publishing, 1996), p. 15. While researching my Gillespie biography I worked together with Ken on trying to establish as accurate a chronology for this period as possible.
8. Interview with Ray Brown, 11 Apr. 1996.

9. Alyn Shipton, liner notes to *Oscar, Ray and Milt: The Very Tall Band* (Telarc 83443, 1998), p. 3.
10. During that year, Dizzy and Bird were in the Billy Eckstine Orchestra, which Parker left on 24 August 1944.
11. Interview with Stan Levey for BBC World Service, 9 May 2001.
12. 'Poon Tang' and 'Blues Before Dawn' (Black and White 1206, recorded 29 Dec. 1944).
13. *Downbeat*, 1 Nov. 1945. Hank Jones was in Bailey's trio so it is highly possible that it was during this residency that Ray Brown met Dizzy for the first time, prior to the 21 October rehearsal.
14. *Bird* (1988), a Charlie Parker bio-pic, was directed and produced by Clint Eastwood, and written by Joel Oliansky.
15. Berg's was at 1356 North Vine Street.
16. Larry Frankley and George Epstein, 'On the discs', *Stanford Daily*, 1 Feb. 1946, p. 2.
17. Interview with Brown.
18. Aline Mosby, '"Bebop" music is banned by KMPC as too naughty', *Dunkirk Evening Observer*, 14 Mar. 1946, p. 2.
19. Ibid.
20. Interview with Clora Bryant for BBC World Service, 10 Mar. 2001.
21. Interview with Teddy Edwards for BBC World Service, 10 Mar. 2001.
22. Interview with Clora Bryant.
23. Roy Porter (with David Keller), *There and Back* (Oxford: Bayou Press, 1991), p. 55.
24. Interview from the Radio 3 *Jazz Library* tribute to Jackson, broadcast 22 Apr. 2012.

Chapter 11 The Modern Jazz Quartet

1. Alyn Shipton, *Groovin' High: The Life of Dizzy Gillespie* (New York: Oxford University Press, 1999).
2. Interview with Ray Brown, 1996.
3. *New York Amsterdam News*, 19 Apr. 1947, p. 21.
4. Interview with Percy Heath broadcast in the Heath Brothers edition of *Jazz Library*, BBC Radio 3, 11 Apr. 2009.
5. Interview with Jackson recorded in Aug. 1997, broadcast on BBC Radio 3 *Jazz Library*, 22 Apr. 2012.
6. The control alters the speed of the vanes that turn under the keys of bars of the vibes, creating the characteristic 'throb'.
7. Interview with John Lewis, broadcast in his memory on BBC Radio 3 *Jazz Library*, 17 Jan. 2009.

Chapter 12 The 'Swing Drummer'

1. Interview with Ray Brown, 11 Apr. 1996.
2. Interview with Roy Haynes for BBC World Service, 4 May 1999. Percy Brice (born in 1923) died in November 2020, while this book was being written.
3. Interview with Brown.
4. Interview with Roy Haynes for BBC World Service, Sept. 2001 at Tanglewood.

Chapter 13 Jackie McLean and Sonny Rollins

1. My suspicion is that Jackie was already 16 when he met Bud as 'Buzzy' was recorded on 8 May, only a few days before his 16th birthday on 17 May.

2. Interview with Jackie McLean, 22 Nov. 1999.

3. Alan Groves and Alyn Shipton, *The Glass Enclosure: The Life of Bud Powell* (Oxford: Bayou Press, 1993).

4. Originally just four tracks were issued in 1949 on 78 – 'You Go To My Head' and 'Ornithology' on BN 1566 and 'Bouncing with Bud' and 'Wail' on BN 1567. First collected in 1952 on 10-inch LP *The Amazing Bud Powell, Volume 1* (Blue Note BLP5003).

5. Interview with Sonny Rollins for BBC Radio 3 *Jazz Library*, 16 Sept. 2007.

6. Sonny is referring to the 23 August 1946 session for Savoy, with a typically cross-stylistic personnel, including bassist Al Hall and drummer Wallace Bishop. The follow-up session (which produced 'Good Kick') had Kenny Clarke on drums.

7. Sonny had gone to Chicago after quitting heroin and gradually returned to music.

8. Interview with Tommy Flanagan, July 1994.

9. This can be heard on www.youtube.com/watch?v=ClVD0F_JRw8.

10. Sonny Rollins, liner notes to *Freedom Suite* (Riverside RLP 12–258, recorded 1958).

11. Pettiford was only eight years older than Rollins, but it still made a significant difference.

12. Alyn Shipton, 'Sonny Rollins at the Barbican', *The Times*, 27 Nov. 2007.

13. On the album *Wholly Earth* (Verve/Gitanes 559 538–2, 1998).

14. Interview with Abbey Lincoln for BBC World Service, 1998.

15. Nat Hentoff, liner notes to *We Insist!* (Candid 79015, 19610).

16. Ibid.

17. Interview with Lincoln.

18. Abbey Lincoln was born Anna Marie Wooldridge, in 1930.

19. Baby Dodds, *Talking and Drum Solos* (Folkways FJ2290, released 1951 as a 10-inch LP).

20. Interview with Pete La Roca for BBC World Service, 15 May 1997.

21. *Sonny Rollins Trio Live in Europe 1959, Complete Recordings* (Essential Jazz Classics 55693, released 2016).

22. Interview with Henry Grimes for BBC Radio 3 *Jazz Library*, Cheltenham Jazz Festival, 2 Apr. 2009.

23. Kenny played as a guest with the trio at Aix-en-Provence on 11 March 1959.

24. 'Record Roundup', *Tucson Daily Citizen*, 7 Dec. 1963, p. 19.

25. Russ Wilson, 'Mixing Musicians Can Be Productive', *Oakland Tribune*, 11 Aug. 1963.

26. Duck Baker, 'Sonny Meets Hawk', *Jazz Times*, 25 Apr. 2019.

27. Interview with Stan Tracey for BBC Radio 3 *Jazz Library*, at Gateshead International Jazz Festival, 27 Mar. 2010.

28. *Alfie* (DVD; Paramount PHE 8084).

Chapter 14 Oscar Peterson and His Trios

1. Oscar Peterson, *Solo* (Pablo 2310975–2, released in 2002); the other half of the album, from earlier in that 1972 tour, was recorded in Baalbek.

2. Alyn Shipton, 'The Importance of Being Oscar', *Jazzwise*, no. 88 (July 2005), p. 38.

3. Examples include *An Oscar Peterson Christmas* (Telarc 83372, 1995), *Oscar Peterson Meets Roy Hargrove and Ralph Moore* (Telarc 83399, 1996), and *Summer Night in Munich* (Telarc 83450, 1999).

4. Oscar Peterson, *A Jazz Odyssey: The Life of Oscar Peterson* (London: Continuum, 2002).

5. Interview with Oscar Peterson for BBC Radio 3 *Jazz Library*, broadcast 8 Feb. 2008.

6. Interview with Ray Brown, 11 Apr. 1996.
7. 'Column Chronicle of Show Business, 1951', *Baltimore Afro American*, 1 Jan. 1952, p. 8.
8. 'Oscar Peterson Trio on Jazz Program', *Madison Wisconsin State Journal*, 5 Oct. 1952, p. 41.
9. 'Granz's Jazz at Philharmonic Here Sunday', *Long Beach Press Telegram*, 5 Nov. 1952.
10. Sterling Sorensen, 'Wild frenetic music brings din, tremors, no place for "Squares"', *Madison Capital Times*, 10 Oct. 1952, p. 17.
11. Dorothy Campbell, 'Krupa, Rich feud with sticks as drummers lead jazzers', *Austin Daily Texan*, 30 Oct. 1952, p. 7.
12. Bill Doudna, 'Spotlight Jazz Concert', *Madison Wisconsin State Journal*, 10 Oct. 1952, p. 31.
13. Shipton, 'The Importance of Being Oscar', p. 38.
14. Ray Brown interview, 11 Apr. 1996.
15. Shipton, 'The Importance of Being Oscar', p. 38.
16. Interview with Tommy Flanagan, July 1994.
17. Interview with Louie Bellson, broadcast on *Jazz Library*, BBC Radio 3, 21 Mar. 2009.
18. Interview with Billy Cobham for BBC World Service, 2002.
19. Sarah Vaughan and Oscar Peterson, *How Long Has This Been Going On?* (Pablo 2310–821, 1978).
20. Ed Thigpen interview for BBC Radio 3 *Jazz Library*, broadcast 13 Mar. 2010.
21. This was a thirteen-part NBC series that aired across forty-two US regional TV stations on Wednesday evenings in 1958.
22. Alyn Shipton, 'Oscar Peterson', *The Times*, 5 July 2005.
23. Interview with Niels-Henning Ørsted Pedersen, broadcast on BBC Radio 3 *Jazz Library*, 13 Aug. 2011. Originally recorded at Brecon Jazz festival in 1999.

Chapter 15 The Dawn of Fusion

1. Interview with Ian Carr for National Sound Archive, 20 June 2000.
2. Interview with Jon Hiseman for BBC Radio 3 *Jazz Library*, 4 June 2011.
3. Jack Bruce interviewed by Barbara Thompson for *Jazz Rock in Britain* Episode 2, BBC Radio 3, broadcast on 5 Aug. 2000.
4. Watford Gap services are 75 miles north of London on the M1 motorway. In the 1960s and 1970s the southbound-side café was the main meeting place for London-based rock and jazz bands on the road, travelling back to London at night, as one could get a hot meal in the small hours of the morning. I met the Humphrey Lyttelton Band there on more than one occasion in the late 1970s when I was travelling back after gigs in the Midlands with Ken Colyer.
5. Graham Bond Organization, *Solid Bond* (Warner Bros, WS 3001).
6. Ian Carr, *Miles Davis – The Definitive Biography* (London: HarperCollins, 1999), pp. 205–6.
7. Interview with Dave Holland, Nov. 1997 for BBC World Service, broadcast Sept. 2001.
8. Interview with Herbie Hancock for BBC World Service, Sept. 2001.
9. Ron Carter, *Building Jazz Bass Lines* (New York: Hal Leonard, 1998).
10. Interview with Ron Carter for BBC World Service, 2002.
11. Interview with George Benson for BBC World Service, broadcast Sept. 2001.
12. 'No insurance.'

13. Interview with John McLaughlin for BBC Radio 3 *Jazz Library*, broadcast in two parts on 1 and 8 Nov. 2008.
14. The Baron Lounge was at 132nd Street and Lenox Avenue.
15. Larry Young, *Unity* (Blue Note 84221, recorded 10 Nov. 1965).
16. The Tony Williams Lifetime, *Turn It Over* (Polydor 24 4021, recorded May 1969).
17. Jack Bruce interviewed by Barbara Thompson for *Jazz Rock in Britain* Episode 3, BBC Radio 3, broadcast on 19 Aug. 2000.
18. Alyn Shipton, *Out of the Long Dark: The Life of Ian Carr* (London: Equinox, 2006), p. 93.
19. Martha Sanders Gilmore, 'Newport 1970', *Jazz Journal*, vol. xxiii, no. 9 (Sept. 1970), p. 12.
20. Shipton, *Out of the Long Dark*, p. 94.
21. Interview with Billy Cobham, 2002.
22. Interview with Chick Corea for BBC World Service, broadcast Sept. 2001.
23. Interview with Teo Macero for BBC World Service, broadcast Sept. 2001.
24. Michael Cuscuna, 'Miles at the Fillmore', liner notes to *Miles Davis 1970: The Bootleg Series Vol. 3* (Columbia 88765433812, 2014).
25. Interview with Jack DeJohnette for BBC World Service, broadcast Sept. 2001.
26. Interview with Dave Liebman for BBC World Service, broadcast Sept. 2001.
27. Interview with Mike Gibbs for *Jazzwise*, Sept. 2017.
28. Philip Catherine, *Solo Bremen 1979 and 1982* (Warner 0190295857097, 2017).
29. Interview with Mike Gibbs.
30. Interview with Gary Burton in the liner notes for the UK reissue of *A Genuine Tong Funeral* (BGO 723, 2006).
31. Interview with Carla Bley for BBC Radio 3 *Jazz Library*, 19 Sept. 2009.

Chapter 16 A Taste of Freedom

1. Ornette Coleman and Joachim Kühn, *Colors* (Verve 314 537 789, 1997).
2. 'Quand Ornette Coleman improvisait avec Jacques Derrida', the original interview, can be read at: www.lesinrocks.com/actu/ornettecoleman-et-jacques-derrida-la-langue-de-lautre-94053-20-08-1997/.
3. Ibid. Translated by the author.
4. Derrida quoted in Joel Stein, 'Life with the father of deconstruction', *Time*, 18 Nov. 2002.
5. Interview with Ornette Coleman, July 1997.
6. *Free Jazz: A Collective Improvisation by the Ornette Coleman Double Quartet* (Atlantic SD 1364, recorded 21 Dec. 1960).
7. Interview with Charlie Haden, 20 Feb. 2000.
8. Interview with Ornette Coleman, July 1997.
9. Interview with Dewey Redman, 22 Feb. 2000.
10. Interview with Charlie Haden, 20 Feb. 2000.
11. Ibid.
12. Dave Pike was a vibraphone player who recorded with Bley in 1958. He signed with Riverside after leaving the band, recording *It's Time for Dave Pike* in 1961.
13. Interview with Paul Bley, 21 Feb. 2000.
14. Interview with George Russell, 19 Feb. 2000.
15. Interview with George Russell, Mar. 2002.
16. Stanley Crouch, 'Don't Ask the Critics. Ask Wallace Roney's Peers', *New York Times*, 24 Sept. 2000.
17. Interview with Wallace Roney, 20 Feb. 2000.

18. Nat Hentoff, liner notes to *Old and New Gospel* (Blue Note BST 84262, recorded 1967).
19. Interview with Jackie McLean, 22 Nov. 1999.
20. Alyn Shipton, 'Cheltenham Festival', *The Times*, 3 May 2005.
21. Interview with Dewey Redman, 22 Feb. 2000.
22. Interview with Gunther Schuller, 10 Mar. 2000.
23. Included on the album *John Lewis Presents Contemporary Music: Jazz Abstractions* (Atlantic 1365, recorded 19 Dec. 1960).
24. Interview with Denardo Coleman, 20 Feb. 2000.
25. Alyn Shipton, 'Ornette Coleman/Charlie Haden at the Royal Festival Hall', *The Times*, 22 June 2009.
26. Interview with Howard Shore, February 2000.
27. Alyn Shipton, 'Ornette Coleman at the Barbican Hall, London', *Jazzwise*, vol. 42 (May 2001).
28. Interview with Shore.
29. Interview with Denardo Coleman, 20 Feb. 2000.
30. Interview with Pat Metheny for BBC Radio 3 *Jazz Library*, broadcast 29 June 2007.
31. Pat Metheny/Ornette Coleman, *Song X* (Geffen 24096, recorded 12–14 Dec. 1985).
32. Interview with Geri Allen, 20 Feb. 2000.
33. Interview with Charnett Moffett, 20 Feb. 2000.
34. Interview with Geri Allen for BBC Radio 3 *Jazz Library*, 27 Nov. 2010.
35. Alyn Shipton, 'Coleman teamed with a partner of notes', *The Times*, 4 July 1997.

Chapter 17 Looking Back and Looking Forward

1. This music can be heard on the rare, limited edition CD, *Bill Greenow's Chansons at New College School, Oxford* (Mistral CD02, 2000).
2. Interview with Gwyneth Herbert, 29 Mar. 2021.
3. Review at: www.allaboutjazz.com/london-jazz-festival-november-9–18–2012-by-duncan-heining.php.
4. An example of the Peggy Lee tribute with Gwyneth Herbert is at: www.youtube.com/watch?v=ZoQpPiEVry8&list=RDMM&start_radio=1.
5. One of the *Lady in Satin* rearrangements can be heard at: www.youtube.com/watch?v=SVEkKdvgfnY.
6. Michael Roach interviewed by Kevin Le Gendre for BBC Radio 3 *Jazz Line-Up*, Wavendon Garden Season, 8 June 2013.
7. Part of our concert at the former church in Calstock on the Devon/Cornwall border can be seen at: www.youtube.com/watch?v=D-8M5xxpNpE and at: www.youtube.com/watch?v=B-80A6WlYqQ.
8. Amelia Gabaldoni, 'Sincerity and Down Home Charm', *Daily Information* (Oxford), 24 May 2019.
9. Interview with Theo Croker, 13 Oct. 2018.
10. Roy Hargrove (1969–2018) made his first bebop recordings in 1988 with saxophonist Bobby Watson. Theo Croker was 3 years old at the time.

SELECT BIBLIOGRAPHY

Barker, Danny, *A Life in Jazz*, ed. Alyn Shipton (New Orleans: NOHC, 2016)

Bernhardt, Clyde E. B., *I Remember: Eighty Years of Black Entertainment, Big Bands and the Blues*, 2nd ed. (Philadelphia: University of Pennsylvania Press, 2015)

Bigard, Barney, *With Louis and the Duke*, ed. Barry Martyn (London: Macmillan, 1986)

Buerkle, Jack V. and Barker, Danny, *Bourbon Street Black: The New Orleans Black Jazzman* (New York: Oxford University Press, 1963)

Carr, Ian, *Miles Davis: The Definitive Biography* (London: HarperCollins, 1999)

Carter, Ron, *Building Jazz Bass Lines* (New York: Hal Leonard, 1998)

Cheatham, Adolphus 'Doc', *I Guess I'll Get the Papers and Go Home*, ed. Alyn Shipton (London: Cassell, 1996)

Chilton, John, *Hot Jazz, Warm Feet* (London: Northway, 2007)

Clayton, Buck and Elliott, Nancy Miller, *Buck Clayton's Jazz World* (London: Macmillan, 1986)

Cook, Richard, *Richard Cook's Jazz Encyclopedia* (London: Penguin, 2005)

Dial, Harry, *All This Jazz About Jazz* (Chigwell: Storyville Publications, 1984)

DiMartino, Dave, *Music in the 20th Century* (New York: Routledge, 2016)

Fagge, Roger and Pillai, Nicolas (eds.), *New Jazz Conceptions: History, Theory, Practice* (Milton, Oxon: Taylor and Francis, 2017)

Groves, Alan and Shipton, Alyn, *The Glass Enclosure: The Life of Bud Powell* (Oxford: Bayou Press, 1993)

Kennedy, Al, *Big Chief Harrison and the Mardi Gras Indians* (Gretna, LA: Pelican, 2010)

Kernfeld, Barry (ed.), *The New Grove Dictionary of Jazz*, 2nd ed. (London: Macmillan, 2002)

Lambert, Eddie, *Duke Ellington: A Listener's Guide* (Lanham, MD: Scarecrow Press, 1999)

McKay, George, *Circular Breathing: The Cultural Politics of Jazz in Britain* (Durham, NC: Duke University Press, 2005)

Melly, George, *Mellymobile* (London: Robson Books, 1982)

Miller, Mark, *Herbie Nichols: A Jazzist's Life* (Toronto: Mercury, 2009)

Morton, Jelly Roll (with Alan Lomax), *Mister Jelly Roll* (New York: Duell, Sloan and Pearce, 1949)

Morton, John Fass, *Backstory in Blue* (Newark: Rutgers University Press, 2008)

Peterson, Oscar, *A Jazz Odyssey: The Life of Oscar Peterson* (London: Continuum, 2002)

Sancton, Tom, *Song For My Fathers: A New Orleans Story in Black and White* (New York: Other Press, 2006)

Schipper, Mineke, *Imagining Insiders: Africa and the Question of Belonging* (London: Cassell, 1999)

Schuller, Gunther, *The Swing Era* (New York: Oxford University Press, 1989)

Shearing, George (with Alyn Shipton), *Lullaby of Birdland: The Autobiography of George Shearing* (New York: Continuum, 2004)

Sheridan, Chris, *Count Basie: A Bio-Discography* (Westport, CT: Greenwood Press, 1986)

Shipton, Alyn, *Fats Waller: The Cheerful Little Earful*, 2nd ed. (London: Continuum, 2002)

  Groovin' High: The Life of Dizzy Gillespie (New York: Oxford University Press, 1999)

  A New History of Jazz, 2nd ed. (London: Continuum, 2007)

  Out of the Long Dark: The Life of Ian Carr (London: Equinox, 2006)

Smith, Michael P., *Mardi Gras Indians* (Gretna, LA: Pelican, 1994)

Spencer, Frederick J., *Jazz and Death: Medical Profiles of Jazz Greats* (Jackson: University Press of Mississippi, 2002)

Stratemann, Klaus, *Duke Ellington: Day by Day and Film by Film* (Copenhagen: Jazz Media, 1992)

Vail, Ken, *Bird's Diary* (Cambridge: Vail Publishing, 1996)

  Dizzy Gillespie: The Bebop Years (Cambridge: Vail Publishing, 2000)

Wright, Laurie, *Fats in Fact* (Chigwell: Storyville, 1992)

INDEX